Living Poetically

Literature & Philosophy

A. J. Cascardi, General Editor

This series publishes books in a wide range of subjects in philosophy and literature, including studies of the social and historical issues that relate these two fields. Drawing on the resources of the Anglo-American and Continental traditions, the series is open to philosophically informed scholarship covering the entire range of contemporary critical thought.

Already published:

J. M. Bernstein, *The Fate of Art: Aesthetic Alienation from Kant to Derrida and Adorno* (1992)

Peter Bürger, *The Decline of Modernism* (1992)

Robert Steiner, *Toward a Grammar of Abstraction: Modernity, Wittgenstein, and the Paintings of Jackson Pollock* (1992)

Mary E. Finn, *Writing the Incommensurable: Kierkegaard, Rossetti, and Hopkins* (1992)

David Jacobson, *Emerson's Pragmatic Vision: The Dance of the Eye* (1993)

Reed Way Dasenbrock, ed., *Literary Theory After Davidson* (1993)

Gray Kochhar-Lindgren, *Narcissus Transformed: The Textual Subject in Psychoanalysis and Literature* (1993)

David P. Haney, *William Wordsworth and the Hermeneutics of Incarnation* (1993)

Christie McDonald and Gary Wihl, eds., *Transformations: The Languages of Culture and Personhood After Theory* (1994)

Living Poetically

KIERKEGAARD'S EXISTENTIAL AESTHETICS

Sylvia Walsh

The Pennsylvania State University Press
University Park, Pennsylvania

Library of Congress Cataloging-in-Publication Data

Walsh, Sylvia, 1937–
Living poetically : Kierkegaard's existential aesthetics / Sylvia Walsh.
p. cm.
Includes bibliographical references and index.
ISBN 0-271-01328-1 (alk. paper)
1. Kierkegaard, Søren, 1813–1855—Aesthetics. 2. Aesthetics—Religious aspects—Christianity. I. Title.
B4378.A4W35 1994
111′.85—dc20 93-38703
CIP

Printed in the United States of America

Published by The Pennsylvania State University Press,
University Park, PA 16802-1003

It is the policy of The Pennsylvania State University Press to use acid-free paper for the first printing of all clothbound books. Publications on uncoated stock satisfy the minimum requirements of American National Standard for Information Sciences—Permanence of Paper for Printed Library Materials, ANSI Z39.48–1984.

Contents

Acknowledgments

I am grateful to a number of institutions, foundations, professional societies, conferences, journals, and individuals for support of this project in both direct and indirect ways. Initial support for research on the topic of this book was provided by Clark College Mellon Foundation Humanities Summer Research and Travel grants in 1980, 1981, and 1982. Subsequently a Mellon Foundation Research Grant from the United Negro College Fund was awarded for the academic year 1983–84. During the summer of 1985 I received additional support from the National Endowment for the Humanities as director of a summer seminar for college teachers on Kierkegaard. Library privileges and interlibrary loan services were provided by the Søren Kierkegaard Library of Copenhagen University in Denmark, the Howard and Edna Hong Kierkegaard Library of St. Olaf College, Emory University, and Stetson University. Photography services were provided by Chris Carlson and the Public Relations Office of Stetson University.

Opportunities to present some of the results of my research were provided by the Society for Philosophy of Religion in 1984; the Society of Christian Philosophers in 1986; the Conference on Kierkegaard and Contemporary Philosophy at St. Olaf College in 1985; the Southeastern Regional Meeting of the American Academy of Religion in 1978 and 1988; the Clark College Faculty Exchange in 1987; the World Congress of Philosophy in Brighton, England, in 1988; a Kierkegaard conference at the University of San Diego in 1989; the Kierkegaard Seminar at the Annual Meeting of the American Academy of Religion in 1989; the Søren

Kierkegaard Society at the Central Division Meeting of the American Philosophical Society in 1990; and an international conference, "Kierkegaard, the Christian in Love with Aesthetics," held at Durham University, St. Chad's College, Great Britain, under the auspices of the National Committee on Religion and Literature in 1990.

Permission from the copyright holders to use materials from the following articles of mine is gratefully acknowledged: "Don Juan and the Representation of Spiritual Sensuousness," *Journal of the American Academy of Religion,* 47, no. 4 (1979): 627–44; "Kierkegaard's Inverse Dialectic," *Kierkegaardiana* 11 (1980): 34–54; "On 'Feminine' and 'Masculine' Despair," *International Kierkegaard Commentary,* ed. Robert L. Perkins (Macon, Ga.: Mercer University Press, 1987), 121–34; "The Subjective Thinker as Artist," *History of European Ideas* 12, no. 1 (1990): 19–29, reprinted with kind permission from Pergamon Press Ltd., Headington Hill Hall, Oxford OX3 OBW, UK; "Living Poetically: Kierkegaard and German Romanticism," *History of European Ideas* 20, nos. 1–3 (in press), reprinted with kind permission from Elsevier Science Ltd., The Boulevard, Langford Lane, Kidlington, England; "The Philosophical Affirmation of Gender Difference: Kierkegaard Versus Postmodern Neo-Feminism," *Journal of Psychology and Christianity* 7, no. 4 (1988): 18–26, reprinted by permission of Christian Association for Psychological Studies (CAPS); and "Kierkegaard and Postmodernism," *International Journal for Philosophy of Religion* 29, no. 2 (1991): 113–22, reprinted by permission of Kluwer Academic Publishers.

Permission to quote from the following texts is also gratefully acknowledged: Søren Kierkegaard, *The Point of View for My Work as An Author* (New York: Harper & Row, 1962), by permission from HarperCollins Publishers, Inc.; Søren Kierkegaard, *Crisis in the Life of an Actress* (London: Collins, 1967), by permission from the translator, Stephen Crites; Søren Kierkegaard, *Early Polemical Writings* (Princeton: Princeton University Press, 1990), by permission of the translator, Julia Watkin; Søren Kierkegaard, *Christian Discourses,* tr. Walter Lowrie (London: Oxford University Press, 1940), by permission of Oxford University Press; G. W. F. Hegel, *Aesthetics: Lectures on Fine Art,* 2 vols., tr. T. M. Knox (Oxford: Clarendon, 1975), by permission of Oxford University Press; Friedrich Schiller, *On the Aesthetic Education of Man in a Series of Letters,* ed. and trans. Elizabeth M. Wilkinson and L. A. Willoughby (Oxford: Clarendon, 1967), by permission of Oxford University Press; *German Aesthetic and Literary Criticism: Winckelmann, Lessing, Hamann, Schiller, Goethe,* ed. H. B. Nisbet (Cambridge: Cambridge University Press, 1985), reprinted with the permission of Cambridge University

Press; and *Søren Kierkegaard's Journals and Papers,* 7 vols. (Bloomington: Indiana University Press, 1967–78), by permission from Indiana University Press. The portrait of Kierkegaard (after the original by Niels Christian Kierkegaard, c. 1843) on the cover is reproduced by permission of the artist, Sixtus Scholtens, of Boxmeer, the Netherlands.

I am indebted to all the individuals who responded to the research presented at the conferences and seminars mentioned above, especially to the group of twelve college teachers who participated in the NEH Summer Seminar for College Teachers in 1985 on the topic "Kierkegaard on Sexuality, Love, and Self-Identity." I am also much indebted to Julia Watkin, former assistant director of the Søren Kierkegaard Department of Research at Copenhagen University, and now a teacher at the University of Tasmania in Australia, for reading and criticizing a chapter of my work in progress and for sharing the results of her research with me. Dialogues with the following persons, among others, have also been helpful to me in my study: Grethe Kjær of Copenhagen; Vanina Sechi of Italy and Toronto; Wanda Warren Berry of Colgate University; Céline Léon of Grove City College; Miyako Matsuki of the University of Wisconsin–Madison; Lillian Ashcraft-Eason of Bowling Green State University; Ralph Ellis of Clark College (now Clark Atlanta University); C. Stephen Evans of St. Olaf College; Abrahim Khan of Trinity College, University of Toronto; Stephen Dunning of the University of Pennsylvania; David Gouwens of Texas Christian University; Andrew Burgess of the University of New Mexico; David Goicoechea of Brock University; George Connell of Concordia College; and George Pattison, dean of King's College Chapel, Cambridge University, England.

I also want to acknowledge and give thanks to several of my former teachers: Clyde A. Holbrook, now deceased, who first introduced me to Kierkegaard at Oberlin College; Paul L. Holmer, whose lectures and seminar on Kierkegaard at Yale Divinity School inspired a long-term commitment on my part to the study of Kierkegaard; and Jack Boozer, now deceased, my dissertation adviser at Emory University, who excelled in asking tough questions about Kierkegaard's thought that I struggled to answer to his and my satisfaction. I am indebted as well to my students, who over the years have stimulated my thought. Especially memorable is Kevin Dean Houston, recently deceased, who in his short life made a difference to all who knew him.

Special thanks go to my father, now deceased, and to my mother and other family members who supported my academic ambitions over the years; to my recently acquired family of in-laws, whose love and acceptance have provided a warm environment for the completion of this book; to my son Erik, who good-naturedly accepted the loss of many hours of attention and care while I was working on it; and last but certainly not least, to my husband, Robert L. Perkins, whose love, support, and helpful criticisms have been vital to its completion.

Sigla

AC *Kierkegaard's Attack upon "Christendom."* Translated by Walter Lowrie. Princeton: Princeton University Press, 1944. (*Bladartikler* 1–21, *Fædrelandet,* 1854–55; *Dette skal siges; saa være det da sagt,* 1855; *Øieblikket* 1–10, 1855; *Hvad Christus dømmer om officiel Christendom,* 1855.)

AN *Armed Neutrality* and *An Open Letter.* Edited and translated by Howard V. Hong and Edna H. Hong. Bloomington: Indiana University Press, 1968. (*Den bevæbnede Neutralitet,* written 1848–49, published 1965; "Foranledigt ved en Yttring af Dr. Rudelbach mig betræffende," *Fædrelandet,* no. 26, January 31, 1851.)

CA *The Concept of Anxiety.* Edited and translated by Reidar Thomte in collaboration with Albert B. Anderson. Princeton: Princeton University Press, 1980. (*Begrebet Angest,* by Vigilius Haufniensis, edited by S. Kierkegaard, 1844.)

CD *Christian Discourses* and *The Lilies of the Field and the Birds of the Air* and *Three Discourses at the Communion on Fridays.* Translated by Walter Lowrie. London: Oxford University Press, 1940. (*Christelige Taler,* 1848; *Lilien paa Marken og Fuglen under Himlen,* 1849; *Tre Taler ved Altergangen om Fredagen,* 1849.)

CI *The Concept of Irony with Continual Reference to Socrates,* together with "Notes on Schelling's Berlin Lectures." Edited and translated by Howard V. Hong and Edna H. Hong. Princeton: Princeton University Press, 1989. (*Om Begrebet Ironi,* 1841.)

CLA *The Crisis [and a Crisis] in the Life of an Actress.* Translated by Stephen Crites. New York: Harper & Row, 1967. (*Krisen og en Krise i en Skuespillerindes Liv,* by Inter et Inter. *Fædrelandet,* nos. 188–91, July 24–27, 1848.)

CUP *Concluding Unscientific Postscript.* 2 vols. Edited and translated by Howard V. Hong and Edna H. Hong. Princeton: Princeton University Press, 1992. (*Afsluttende uvidenskabelig Efterskrift,* by Johannes Climacus, edited by S. Kierkegaard, 1846.)

EO *Either/Or.* 2 vols. Edited and translated by Howard V. Hong and Edna H. Hong. Princeton: Princeton University Press, 1987. (*Enten/Eller* I–II, edited by Victor Eremita, 1843.)

EPW *Early Polemical Writings.* Edited and translated by Julia Watkin. Princeton: Princeton University Press, 1990. (*Af en endnu Levendes Papirer,* 1838, and early writings from before the "authorship.")

FSE *For Self-Examination* (published with *Judge for Yourself!*). Edited and translated by Howard V. Hong and Edna H. Hong. Princeton: Princeton University Press, 1990. (*Til Selvprøvelse,* 1851; *Dømmer Selv!* 1852.)

FT *Fear and Trembling* (published with *Repetition*). Edited and translated by Howard V. Hong and Edna H. Hong. Princeton: Princeton University Press, 1983. (*Frygt og Bæven,* by Johannes de Silentio, 1843; *Gjentagelsen,* by Constantin Constantius, 1843.)

JFY *Judge for Yourself!* See FSE.

JP *Søren Kierkegaard's Journals and Papers.* 7 vols. Edited and translated by Howard V. Hong and Edna H. Hong, assisted by Gregor Malantschuk. Bloomington: Indiana University Press, vol. 1, 1967; vol. 2, 1970; vols. 3 and 4, 1975; vols. 5–7, 1978. (From *Papirer* I–XIII; and *Breve og Akstykker vedrørende Søren Kierkegaard,* 2 vols., edited by Niels Thulstrup [Copenhagen: Munksgaard], 1953–54.)

OAR *On Authority and Revelation: The Book on Adler, or a Cycle of Ethico-Religious Essays.* Translated and edited by Walter Lowrie. Princeton: Princeton University Press, 1955. (*Bogen om Adler,* written and twice rewritten, 1846–47; unpublished except for one section, "Om Forskjellen mellem et Genie og en Apostel" ["On the Difference Between a Genius and an Apostle"], *Tvende Ethisk-Religieuse Smaa-Afhandlinger,* by H. H., 1849.)

P *Prefaces: Light Reading for Certain Classes as the Occasion May Require.* Translated by William McDonald. Tallahassee: Florida State University Press, 1989. (*Forord: Morskabslæsning for Enkelte Stænder efter Tid og Leilighed,* by Nicolaus Notabene, 1844.)

PAP *Søren Kierkegaards Papirer.* 2d enlarged ed. 16 vols. Edited by Niels Thulstrup, with index vols. 14–16 by N. J. Cappelørn. Copenhagen: Gyldendal, 1968–78.

PC *Practice in Christianity.* Translated by Howard V. Hong and Edna H. Hong. Princeton: Princeton University Press, 1991. (*Indøvelse i Christendom,* by Anti-Climacus, edited by S. Kierkegaard, 1850.)

PF *Philosophical Fragments* and *Johannes Climacus.* Edited and translated by Howard V. Hong and Edna H. Hong. Princeton: Princeton University Press, 1985. (*Philosophiske Smuler,* by Johannes Climacus, edited by S. Kierkegaard, 1844; "Johannes Climacus eller *de omnibus dubitandum est,*" written 1842–43, unpublished, *Papirer* IV C I.)

PV *The Point of View for My Work as an Author: A Report to History and Related Writings,* including "'The Individual': Two 'Notes' Concerning My Work as an Author" and "My Activity as a Writer." Translated by Walter Lowrie. London: Oxford University Press, 1939. Reprint edited by Benjamin Nelson. New York: Harper & Row, 1962. (*Synspunktet for min Forfatter-Virksomhed,* posthumously published 1859; *Om min Forfatter-Virksomhed,* 1851.)

R *Repetition.* See FT.

SLW *Stages on Life's Way.* Edited and translated by Howard V. Hong and Edna H. Hong. Princeton: Princeton University Press,

1988. (*Stadier paa Livets Vej,* edited by Hilarius Bogbinder, 1845.)

SUD *The Sickness unto Death.* Edited and translated by Howard V. Hong and Edna H. Hong. Princeton: Princeton University Press, 1980. (*Sygdommen til Døden,* by Anti-Climacus, edited by S. Kierkegaard, 1849.)

SV *Søren Kierkegaards Samlede Værker.* 1st ed. 14 vols. Edited by A. B. Drachmann, J. L. Heiberg, and H. O. Lange. Copenhagen. Gyldendalske Boghandels Forlag, 1901–6.

TA *Two Ages: The Age of Revolution and the Present Age: A Literary Review.* Edited and translated by Howard V. Hong and Edna H. Hong. Princeton: Princeton University Press, 1978. (*En literair Anmeldelse: To Tidsaldre,* 1846.)

WL *Works of Love.* Translated by Howard V. Hong and Edna H. Hong. New York: Harper & Row, 1962. (*Kjerlighedens Gjerninger,* 1847.)

Prologue: A Touch of the Poet

Kierkegaard was a religious and philosophical thinker who possessed a touch of the poet. The poetic character of his writings is readily apparent in their lyrical style and imaginative construction using a variety of literary genres and techniques. But the poetic temper in Kierkegaard ran deeper than a flair for words, and deeper than a genius for employing artistic forms and figures. A poet, above all, must have pathos or intense passion; as one of Kierkegaard's pseudonyms succinctly puts it, "Without pathos, no poet" (SLW, 404). Underlying the poetic features of Kierkegaard's writings is a poetic passion founded upon an understanding of the poetic as a mode for depicting and relating ourselves to ethical and religious ideals. It is primarily in this sense that Kierkegaard should be regarded as a poet, and it is with this aspect of his aesthetics that the present study is chiefly concerned.

Engaging in a close textual analysis of major works in all periods of Kierkegaard's authorship, from his earliest aesthetic writings to the later, more specifically religious ones, this study traces the development of the concept of the poetic in Kierkegaard's writings as that concept is worked out in contrast to the aesthetics of early German romanticism and Hegelian idealism. In the process of tracking and analyzing this development, I hope to elucidate what it means, in Kierkegaard's view, to be an authentic poet, or poetic writer, and to clarify Kierkegaard's own role as a Christian poet and writer as he understands it. The primary objective of the study, however, is to show that throughout his authorship Kierkegaard maintains a fundamentally positive understanding of the poetic as an essential ingredient in, and in certain works even identical to, ethical and religious forms of life, especially as these are exemplified in a Christian mode of "living poetically," which in his view is a possibility and a requirement for everyone, not just the poet or creative artist.

"Living poetically" is an intriguing phrase that Kierkegaard first uses in his early writings to characterize what he regards as an attempt by the German romantic poets to construct their personal lives in the same manner as they create works of art.[1] Through the exercise of a boundless artistic freedom, he claims, they seek to construct their self-identities through experimentation and play with an infinity of possibilities concocted by the imagination and tried out in a variety of roles and personal experiences with others. Kierkegaard finds this romantic mode of living poetically to be ironic, or negative and nonserious, in its attitude toward actuality, and destructive, rather than constructive, or upbuilding, in its consequences for the development of human personality and personal relations to others. He thus rejects it in favor of an alternative understanding of living poetically construed in an ethical and religious framework. Unlike its romantic counterpart, this mode of living poetically is one that affirms both possibility and actuality, a sense of our historical situatedness and finite limitations as well as freedom, and the construction of human personality through a process of self-development, rather than self-creation, in relation to the infinite or divine.

Although Kierkegaard's characterization and critique of the romantic mode of living poetically is examined in some detail in this study, it is the formulation and subsequent development of his alternative vision of the poetic and living poetically in an ethical-religious manner that I am particularly interested in illuminating in his authorship, since it reveals the role of the poetic to be much more integral and positively valued in his writings than is frequently thought. Like Plato, Kierkegaard is often regarded as a poet who would do away with the poet and poetry.[2] This

1. It should be stressed at the outset of this study that I am primarily interested in elucidating *Kierkegaard's* understanding of early German romanticism, not any other. References to more-recent interpretations of German romanticism will be included in the Epilogue, where I attempt to draw some parallels between postmodernism, especially postmodern French feminism, and German romanticism as Kierkegaard sees it.

2. Comparing himself to Plato in a late journal entry of 1850, Kierkegaard views himself as being "one position ahead" of Plato by virtue of the fact that he is a poet who, "in the boundless turbulence of the religious," points out "the turn, the swing, which has to be made" to the

perception is generated by the presence of a strongly critical attitude toward poetry in some of his writings, and it is reinforced by Kierkegaard's own explanation of his authorship and the personal task of becoming a Christian as involving a movement away from the poetic and aesthetic and toward the religious (PV, 74–75). To be sure, there is a sense in which such a move is appropriate in Kierkegaard's thought inasmuch as a progression from the aesthetic to the ethical and religious stages of existence is envisioned in his writings and the individual's task in this movement is to actualize the ethical-religious ideals, not merely to sustain an imaginary or conceptual relation to them. But this negative stance should be seen as constituting only one aspect, not the total viewpoint of Kierkegaard and the authorship on the poetic. Running counter to it, and present even in those works that are most critical of poetry and the aesthetic mode of life, is a positive perspective of the poetic in which the distinction between the aesthetic-poetic and the ethical-religious is significantly relativized by the identification of the ethical-religious with the truly poetic, on the one hand, and by the inclusion of poetic and aesthetic factors in the ethical-religious, on the other. In this perspective faith itself is understood poetically as a "work of art" that is fundamentally aesthetic, and the poetic in the forms of imagination and possibility is regarded as an essential capacity for the projection and portrayal of ethical-religious ideals. Moreover, aesthetic metaphors, such as the figures of the artist and the dancer, are used to characterize the subjective thinker and the knight of faith, who in the process of striving give concrete expression to the poetic in the historical realization of ethical-religious ideals through the cultivation of ethical inwardness and action, making it appropriate to speak of existing itself as an art.

As I see it, this perspective in Kierkegaard's writings is particularly relevant for our time in that it offers an ethical-religious conception of the poetic in which the aesthetic, ethical, and religious dimensions of human life are envisioned as integrated rather than autonomous and antithetical to one another. Too often in the contemporary world we find ourselves and others living fragmented, multidimensional lives without any clear sense of how these may be understood and brought together in a unified fashion so as to achieve a coherent sense of self-identity and

---

higher ethical life (JP, 3:3328). For an interpretation of Plato as offering a defense of poetry in response to his own famous attack on it in the *Republic,* book x, and elsewhere, see Julius A. Elias, *Plato's Defence of Poetry* (Albany: State University of New York Press, 1984).

wholeness of being. In particular, we lack an understanding of how the poetic and aesthetic dimensions of life are crucial to and may be integrated with an ethical or religious orientation. Conversely, there is also a lack of understanding of how the ethical and religious dimensions of our lives imply or may be understood in terms of poetic and aesthetic categories. Although the importance of Kierkegaard's thought is usually considered to lie in a conceptual clarification of the distinctions between these dimensions, or stages, in human life, I see it as resting ultimately in the way in which he envisions an integration of them. A major aim of my study, therefore, is to reclaim Kierkegaard as a poetic thinker and writer from those who interpret him as an ironic practitioner of an aestheticism devoid of and detached from the ethical-religious as well as from those who view him as rejecting the poetic and aesthetic on ethical or religious grounds.[3]

A corollary but no less important aim of my study is to show that Kierkegaard's concept of the poetic is developed in the context of what may be described as an "existential aesthetics."[4] Aesthetics, as traditionally defined, is the science, or theory, of beauty and its artistic representa-

3. For a recent study stressing the negative implications of Kierkegaard's understanding of the aesthetic and poetic, see George Pattison, *Kierkegaard: The Aesthetic and the Religious* (London: Macmillan, 1992). For interpretations of Kierkegaard as an aesthetic ironist, see Sylviane Agacinski, *Aparté: Conceptions and Deaths of Søren Kierkegaard,* tr. Kevin Newmark (Tallahassee: Florida State University Press, 1988); Louis Mackey, *Points of View: Readings of Kierkegaard* (Tallahassee: Florida State University Press, 1986); Gene Fendt, *Works of Love? Reflections on "Works of Love"* (Potomac, Md.: Scripta Humanistica, n.d.); John Vignaux Smyth, *A Question of Eros: Irony in Sterne, Kierkegaard, and Barthes* (Tallahassee: Florida State University Press, 1986); and Joakim Garff, "The Eyes of Argus: The Point of View and Points of View with Respect to Kierkegaard's 'Activity as an Author,' " *Kierkegaardiana* 15 (1991): 29–54. In line with my study, but more limited in focus than mine, are two recent studies that emphasize the positive role of imagination in Kierkegaard's thought: David Gouwens, *Kierkegaard's Dialectic of the Imagination* (New York: Peter Lang, 1989), and M. Jamie Ferreira, *Transforming Vision: Imagination and Will in Kierkegaardian Faith* (Oxford: Clarendon Press, 1991).

4. Jørgen Schultz, in "Om 'Poesi' og 'Virkelighed' hos Kierkegaard," *Kierkegaardiana* 6 (1966), 7–29, also uses the phrase *eksistens-aesthetik* (existential aesthetics) to characterize *eksistensens uudtømmelige meddelelseskunst* (the inexhaustible art of communication of existence) in Kierkegaard's thought that emerges in the development from a philosophical-abstract aesthetics in *Either/Or* I to a philosophical-concrete aesthetics in volume 2. Schultz surmises that Kierkegaard does not use the term "aesthetics" to designate this existential art of communication, because that word already has a fixed meaning in the authorship as a kind of dreaming that is opposite to actuality. Whereas Schultz applies the term "existential aesthetics" only to the existential art of communication that appears after *Either/Or,* I use it in a more comprehensive sense to characterize the existential thrust of Kierkegaard's aesthetics from the very beginning of his authorship, including *Either/Or,* especially volume 2.

tion in the fine arts.[5] Although numerous examples of traditional forms of aesthetic criticism can be found in Kierkegaard's writings, these are employed, I contend, in service to an underlying existential aesthetics that may be distinguished from the traditional understanding of aesthetics in several respects. First of all, like traditional aesthetics, it is an "aesthetics" in the sense of involving a concept of beauty and artistic representation, but it is "existential" and therefore nontraditional in that it emphasizes the representation of the aesthetic ideal in human life rather than in external or material works of art. In Kierkegaard's thought the term "existential" always connotes the concrete or historical actualization of those factors that are essential to the formation of human personality or the qualitative life of the individual (JP, 1:1054, 1059, 1060, 1062, 1063). These factors are to be realized in the individual's own being and personal relations, not merely in the form of a conceptual, or ideal, actuality envisioned by the imagination and represented in external products of art. For Kierkegaard, therefore, it is the human self in its historical or concrete beauty, rather than an abstract beauty, that constitutes the aesthetic ideal; and the goal of his aesthetics is to reduplicate that ideal in human life, not merely to produce a semblance of it in material works of art.

This emphasis upon a personal, rather than material, form of artistic representation of the aesthetic ideal, however, does not mean that Kierkegaard was opposed to the exercise of the creative imagination in the production of traditional forms of art or to the appreciation of material products of art for their own sake. His own authorship, which in both individual works and as a whole may be regarded as products of art, or poetry, provides ample testimony to the continuing importance of the art of writing in his own life. But Kierkegaard was not disinterestedly related to his authorship, nor did he wish his readers to be. On the contrary, his existential aesthetics calls for the cultivation of an ethical-religious inter-

5. The subject matter, or philosophical interest, to which this term is applied received perhaps its earliest sustained formulation in the dialogues of Plato, who developed a theory of artistic representation, or *mimēsis,* for apprehending the Form of Beauty. In the *Symposium,* for example, the priestess Diotima reveals to Socrates that the object of love (*erōs*) as well as artistic creativity (*poiēsis*) is "reproduction and birth in beauty," which is the source and goal of wisdom and virtue (205C, 206E). Gazing upon the "great sea of beauty," the lover of wisdom catches sight of the highest goal in the vision and knowledge of absolute beauty and thereby gives birth to true virtue, not merely the semblance of virtue, in the presence of and unity with this divine Form (210D, 210E, 211E, 212A). Continuing in the tradition of Plato, many philosophers after him have identified the concept of the beautiful, together with the theory and criticism of the fine arts that represent or give expression to it, as the basic content of aesthetics.

est or subjectivity on the part of every individual, including the poet or artist. In this, a second distinguishing feature of Kierkegaard's existential aesthetics may be identified: the primacy of subjectivity over the disinterested objectivity of traditional aesthetics and other forms of cognitive inquiry with regard to essential truth, or that which defines a truly human life.[6] In Kierkegaard's estimation even material works of art have, or should have, an existential relation to the life of the artist as well as an existential significance for those who view, read, or hear them. Thus even traditional forms of art, that is, artistic products in the various literary, plastic, and musical arts, can and should conform with and contribute to an existential aesthetics that has as its object the edification, or upbuilding and fulfillment, of the human subject.

A third distinguishing feature of Kierkegaard's existential aesthetics may be noted in its interpretation of aesthetic categories as existential categories. Throughout Kierkegaard's writings, aesthetic categories such as the lyric and the epic, irony, humor, comedy, and tragedy are viewed as existential determinants, not merely as intellectual categories for clas-

6. The notion of the disinterestedness of aesthetic judgments is a cardinal point in Immanuel Kant's *Critique of Judgment,* tr. J. H. Bernard (New York: Hafner, 1951), 39. This work is considered by many to mark the beginning of modern aesthetics, but the notion of disinterestedness may also be found in other eighteenth-century aestheticians, such as Francis Hutcheson and the Earl of Shaftesbury. See Peter le Huray and James Day, eds., *Music and Aesthetics in the Eighteenth and Early Nineteenth Centuries* (Cambridge: Cambridge University Press, 1988), 1–2, 23. This criterion was taken over in the nineteenth century by Hegel in his speculative aesthetics (see G.W.F. Hegel, *Aesthetics: Lectures on Fine Art,* 2 vols., tr. T. M. Knox [Oxford: Clarendon 1975], 1:4, 36, 58). See also George Connell, *To Be One Thing: Personal Unity in Kierkegaard's Thought* (Macon, Ga.: Mercer University Press, 1985), 20–22, 35–36, who criticizes Stephen Crites's interpretation of Kierkegaard's aesthetics as requiring disinterestedness. Connell's critique is based on the analysis of Merete Jørgensen in *Kierkegaard som Kritiker* (Copenhagen: Gyldendal, 1978), in which two kinds of aesthetics or aesthetic criticism in Kierkegaard's writings are identified: an "aesthetic critique" and an "ethical critique." According to Jørgensen, the first corresponds to the objective, or disinterested, criticism found in the pseudonymous writings, while the second is to be found, for the most part, in those writings bearing Kierkegaard's own name as author. Although there is some validity in Jørgensen's distinction between these two kinds of aesthetics in Kierkegaard's writings, the strict association of the first form with the pseudonymous writings and of the second with the nonpseudonymous ones is not upheld by the literature, for there are pseudonymous works, such as volume 2 of *Either/Or* (which oddly enough is totally ignored by Jørgensen), that develop the ethical critique, or what I prefer to call an existential aesthetics, and there are works published under Kierkegaard's own name, such as *Two Ages,* that engage in traditional forms of aesthetic criticism. Furthermore, even where the first form of aesthetics is practiced in the literature, I find an underlying existential aesthetics at work in the use of irony and indirect communication to the reader. Finally, in my view, Kierkegaard's ethical critique, or existential aesthetics, extends beyond the several pieces of literary criticism penned in his own name to include the later religious writings as well.

sifying material products of art according to the artistic genres to which they belong. Moreover, these aesthetic categories are regarded as essential to the personal development and fulfillment of the individual. Irony and humor in particular play an important role both in the movement to and within the ethical and religious spheres of human existence, and the comic and the tragic give expression to the discrepancy or contradiction between the inner and the outer, the finite and the infinite, the temporal and the eternal, in human existence.

A fourth distinguishing feature of Kierkegaard's existential aesthetics may be seen in the emphasis placed upon individual striving toward wholeness in his writings—a goal also envisioned in traditional aesthetics but regarded there as being attained in a different way, that is, through the creation of material products of art external to the individual rather than in and through a life of personal striving. Influenced by the neoclassical aesthetics of Winckelmann, Schiller, and Goethe, who articulated an aesthetic vision of wholeness in response to the alienated and fragmentary character of the modern ego, Kierkegaard emphasizes from the beginning to the end of his authorship individual striving, or self-cultivation (*Bildung*), toward the realization of a whole and complete personality, or selfhood, as the goal of human life.[7] Such a personal-

7. On neoclassical aesthetics, see H. B. Nisbet, ed., *German Aesthetic and Literary Criticism: Winckelmann, Lessing, Hamann, Schiller, Goethe* (Cambridge: Cambridge University Press, 1985)—for example, the editor's introduction and the essay on Winckelmann by Goethe, who writes: "Man may achieve much through the purposeful application of isolated faculties, and he may achieve the extraordinary by combining several of his capacities; but he can accomplish the unique, the totally unexpected, only when all his resources are uniformly united within him. The latter was the happy lot of the ancients, especially of the Greeks in their best period; fate has assigned the two former possibilities to us moderns. When the healthy nature of man functions as a totality, when he feels himself in the world as in a vast, beautiful, worthy, and valued whole, when a harmonious sense of well-being affords him pure and free delight—then the universe, if it were capable of sensation, would exult at having reached its goal, and marvel at the culmination of its own development and being" (237). See also Friedrich Schiller, *On the Aesthetic Education of Man in a Series of Letters,* ed. and tr. Elizabeth M. Wilkinson and L. A. Willoughby (Oxford: Clarendon, 1967), where he voices the modern theme of fragmentation that prevents or disrupts the achievement of harmony: "Everlastingly chained to a single little fragment of the Whole, man himself develops into nothing but a fragment; everlastingly in his ear the monotonous sound of the wheel that he turns, he never develops the harmony of his being, and instead of putting the stamp of humanity upon his own nature, he becomes nothing more than the imprint of his occupation or of his specialized knowledge" (35). Schiller thinks art provides a cure for this fragmentation inasmuch as it enables human beings to harmonize the sensuous and formal drives within them through the exercise of a third drive, the play drive (*Spieltrieb*), first identified by Kant, which acts as a relaxing and limiting force upon the other two so as to produce an aesthetic freedom that is the ground of personality and arises "only when man is a complete being, when both his fundamental drives are fully developed" (73, 79–93, 97, 139–43).

ity, in his view, should be integrated in all its dimensions and embody the universally human, or that which every human being essentially is and should become.

But Kierkegaard also regards existential striving as unending, since the individual is related to infinite ideals that are never fully realized in existence but only approximated in this life. In this, his existential aesthetics would appear to resemble the aesthetics of early German romanticism, which also emphasizes infinite striving. But as Kierkegaard sees it, romantic striving is really a finite standpoint that ironically negates existence, whereas the infinite striving of which he speaks constitutes the very essence of life. As one of his pseudonyms, Johannes Climacus, expresses it, "Finitely understood . . . the perpetually continued striving toward a goal without attaining it means rejection, but, infinitely understood, striving is life itself and is essentially the life of that which is composed of the infinite and the finite" (JP, 5:5796).

In contrast to romantic irony, Kierkegaard's existential aesthetics may be described as *anironic,* a term coined by Alan Wilde to designate the modernist vision of "integration and connection, harmony and coherence," in opposition to the fragmentation of modern and postmodern life.[8] As Wilde conceives it, "anironic" does not refer to "anti-irony" but to a vision of wholeness and singleness that complements irony and provides a way of coping with the disparity of life by creating an alternative to it. This term seems admirably suited, therefore, to characterize Kierkegaard's existential aesthetics inasmuch as irony continues to function in his thought as an aesthetic and existential category for expressing aesthetic distance and existential contradiction in the process of striving for wholeness of being. Although romanticism also professed a belief in organic unity and thought it could be achieved through imagination and intuition, in Kierkegaard's view the romantic ironists celebrated and perpetuated both in their lives and in their art the very fragmentation they proposed through poetry to overcome.

Kierkegaard's existential aesthetics may also be seen as partially based upon, yet significantly different from, Hegelian aesthetics.[9] Comparisons between Kierkegaard's aesthetics and the aesthetics of Hegel and J. L. Heiberg, the leading Danish Hegelian aesthetician of Kierkegaard's time, are drawn in greater detail later in this study, but the most obvious

8. Alan Wilde, *Horizons of Assent: Modernism, Postmodernism, and the Ironic Imagination* (Philadelphia: University of Pennsylvania Press, 1987), 30.

9. Thus Stephen Crites, in the introduction to his translation of Kierkegaard's *Crisis in the Life of an Actress,* goes too far in claiming that Kierkegaard is "an unabashed Hegelian in his aesthetics" (CLA, 20).

difference to be noted here is that Hegelian aesthetics is a form of traditional aesthetics and thus is concerned with the artistic representation of the idea of beauty in the fine arts, whereas Kierkegaard's aesthetics is primarily concerned with the artistic representation, or reduplication, of the existential ideal of the self in human life. For Hegel, too, there is an integral connection between the human self and art (as well as between the human self and *Sittlichkeit,* religion, and philosophy), since the production of art is a human activity that in his view gives concrete expression to spirit, or that which essentially defines what it means to be human, or a self. In works of art the human subject duplicates or becomes an object for itself (*für sich*), that is, represents itself to itself as spirit or self-conscious being. Thus, for Hegel, art may be understood as a form of "self-production in external things," or an "external realization" of the human subject that makes explicit what is within or implicit and that gives outward reality to this explicit self.[10] Furthermore, for Hegel, art has world-historical significance, not merely a personal or subjective meaning, inasmuch as it is the embodiment of absolute spirit, or the divine, in sensuous and imaginative form. Kierkegaard, by contrast, views the production of external works of art as accidental, not essential, to the realization of the human subject, which has the task first and foremost of producing itself inwardly and qualitatively in the context of personal relations with others and the divine. Moreover, he does not identify the human spirit with the divine; rather, he encourages us to think of ourselves as products, or works of art, crafted through a process of self-development constituted by and carried out in cooperation with the divine.

Kierkegaard's existential aesthetics thus is informed by a religious—or, more specifically, a Christian—perspective that views the divine as distinct from the human yet envisions God as providing the germinal potentiality and enabling power as well as the infinite measure, or standard, for human selfhood through the incarnation of the deity in time. This perspective further explains, by the presupposition of original sin, the failure to realize the self, inasmuch as the self continually requires divine assistance in the form of grace and striving toward imitation of Christ to overcome sin. In the deepest sense, therefore, Kierkegaard's existential aesthetics may be understood as an ethical-religious, or Christian, aesthetics that grounds the poetic in a relation to the divine. In this, his existential aesthetics may again be distinguished from Hegelian aesthetics in that it views the poetic as integral to, and in certain works even

10. *Aesthetics,* 1:1, 31–32.

identical with, the religious, rather than superseded in religion and philosophy by a higher grasp of truth as claimed in Hegelian thought.

THE PROBLEM OF PSEUDONYMITY

Having identified the existential aesthetics in Kierkegaard's writings as "Kierkegaard's existential aesthetics," I must address the vexing question whether this existential aesthetics can in any and every respect be said to reflect Kierkegaard's own point of view. When a writer is as prolific and complex as Kierkegaard, the viewpoint of the author usually cannot be identified with the ideas of a single work or period but instead undergoes a process of change, development, and refinement over the course of the authorship. In the case of Kierkegaard, who frequently wrote under pseudonyms whose viewpoints he disassociated from his own, this is especially true. To discern the viewpoints of the author and his pseudonyms on a particular subject, therefore, requires a dynamic approach to his writings, looking upon them as a progressive unfolding of thought and staying alert to differences and modifications as well as similarities and continuities between Kierkegaard and the pseudonyms as well as between the pseudonyms themselves. Otherwise, one may end up with a shortsighted interpretation that does not do justice to the total perspective of the authorship.

It is this total perspective, rather than Kierkegaard's own viewpoint as distinct from that of the pseudonyms, that I am presenting as "Kierkegaard's existential aesthetics." Inasmuch as Kierkegaard is responsible for the whole authorship, including the writings of the pseudonyms as well as those published under his own name, all of the ideas presented and developed in the authorship belong to him "in a legal and in a literary sense," as he puts it, and have a role in the totality of the authorship (CUP, 1:627). But this does not mean that all of them express his own viewpoints. On the contrary, in "A First and Last Explanation," appended to *Concluding Unscientific Postscript,* Kierkegaard expressly states that "in the pseudonymous books there is not a single word by me" (CUP, 1:626). This statement may be taken at face value to mean that the ideas presented in the pseudonymous writings are to be attributed to the pseudonymous authors rather than to himself. But it may also be understood as an attempt to distance himself from these works for the purpose of indirect communication, that is, to encourage an existential engagement and appropriation of the ideas presented in these texts independently of the "legal" author's (as opposed to the pseudonymous author's) point of view.[11] Kierkegaard's own point of view may well concur, at least in part, with those of his pseudonymous authors. At least there is no reason to conclude that just because Kierkegaard does not claim the positions of the pseudonymous authors as his own, he totally disagrees with them. On the contrary, in my opinion there is much in the pseudonymous writings that does reflect Kierkegaard's own viewpoint at one time or another and that, in many instances, he continues to hold. Nevertheless, I think we must heed the distinction between Kierkegaard and his pseudonyms, which he insists upon, and not attribute to him everything they say. In my analysis of the pseudonymous works in this book I respect this distinction by referring to the pseudonymous authors, rather than to Kierkegaard, in discussing the works ascribed to them.

To determine to what extent, if any, the views expressed by the pseudonyms concur with Kierkegaard's own viewpoints, we may be aided by consulting the materials written and/or published under Kierkegaard's own name. These include (1) several direct explanations of the nature and purpose of the authorship, (2) a number of religious writings and devotional discourses as well as several pieces of aesthetic criticism, and (3) the voluminous unpublished journals spanning his university years to the last year of his life. In my view, these materials may be regarded, on the whole, as reflecting Kierkegaard's own viewpoints, although one needs to recognize that his own ideas undergo a process of change and development, just as those of the pseudonymous writings do. In taking this position, I am expressly rejecting the hermeneutic of suspicion employed by

11. On the problem of the pseudonyms and Kierkegaard's relation to his pseudonymous writings, see M. Holmes Hartshorne, *Kierkegaard, Godly Deceiver: The Nature and Meaning of His Pseudonymous Writings* (New York: Columbia University Press, 1990), who insists on a firm distinction between Kierkegaard and the pseudonyms and regards all the pseudonymous writings as having been made pervasively ironic and deceptive in order to lead the reader to the discovery of the Christian truth to which Kierkegaard himself was dedicated from the beginning of his authorship. For a critique of this work, see Michael Strawser's review in the *Søren Kierkegaard Newsletter* 26 (November 1992): 10–14. For a more skeptical view of the religious intention of the authorship, see Henning Fenger, *Kierkegaard, the Myths and Their Origins: Studies in the Kierkegaardian Papers and Letters,* tr. George C. Schoolfield (New Haven: Yale University Press, 1980), 21–23, 26–31. While I am sympathetic to Hartshorne's interpretation of Kierkegaard's mission as a religious author (not simply on the basis of Kierkegaard's own self-interpretation but because a Christian orientation is evident as early as his dissertation on the concept of irony), my own viewpoint is closer to that of C. Stephen Evans, *Kierkegaard's "Fragments" and "Postscript": The Religious Philosophy of Johannes Climacus* (Atlantic Highlands, N.J.: Humanities Press, 1983), who not only distinguishes between Kierkegaard and the pseudonyms but also finds some agreement between them.

some recent interpreters of Kierkegaard who regard him as a "falsifier of history" and consummate ironist whose direct as well as indirect communications are not to be trusted.[12] This hermeneutic takes its point of departure primarily from the analysis of two texts by Kierkegaard, *The Point of View for My Work as an Author* and *The Concept of Irony.* Concerning the first of these, which presented Kierkegaard's own interpretation of his authorship as understood by him in 1848, there has long been disagreement among Kierkegaard scholars over its reliability. With the 1980 English translation of Henning Fenger's *Kierkegaard-Myter og Kierkegaard-Kilder* (1976), this debate has become even more prominent as Fenger's highly speculative "fictional theory" of interpretation—formulated primarily with regard to some letters in the early journals of Kierkegaard but applied to *The Point of View* and other writings as well—has been appropriated by some postmodernist interpreters of Kierkegaard seeking to undermine his own interpretations of the authorship in order to legitimize a multiplicity of hermeneutic perspectives, especially those which detect the craftiness of a dishonest, deceptive, disingenuous ironist at work in his writings.

Preferring to believe the character assassination of Kierkegaard as a person who "often made untrue statements, persuading himself that he spoke the truth"—a claim put forth by Israel Levin, one of Kierkegaard's contemporaries who is described by Fenger as being, among other things, "a complainer, boozer, and misogynist" (character traits that bring his own trustworthiness into question)—Fenger places no source value in *The Point of View,* particularly its claim that the authorship is religious from start to finish.[13] This line of attack has been followed up more recently by Joakim Garff, who characterizes *The Point of View* as "fictive documentation," or "documenta(fic)tion," charging Kierkegaard

12. On Kierkegaard as a falsifier of history, see Fenger, *Kierkegaard, the Myths and Their Origins,* chap. 1.

13. Ibid., 15, 27. Like much of his argument in this book, Fenger's reasons for rejecting this claim are rather flimsy. First, he castigates Kierkegaard for omitting any mention of his early political activity, his attack on Andersen, his theological examination, the dissertation, and the story of his engagement—all of which are, in Fenger's view, "pieces which do not easily fit into the puzzle," although he does not explain how or why (28). But none of these negates Kierkegaard's thesis, which applies to the authorship beginning with *Either/Or.* Second, Fenger charges Kierkegaard with inconsistency because he waited three months to publish the edifying discouses after *Either/Or,* but surely the delay of only three months in publishing the accompanying edifying discourses is not enough to invalidate Kierkegaard's claim. Third, Fenger criticizes Kierkegaard for failing to mention *A Literary Review,* a piece of aesthetic criticism written in the period of the specifically religious writings. But Kierkegaard does refer to it in a note, and the production of this work in no way invalidates the essentially religious character of the authorship in that period.

with being a "virtuoso of deception" in the production of a "pious fraud" perpetrated upon the reader as well as upon himself.[14] In like manner, but directing their shots at *The Concept of Irony* instead, other postmodernist interpreters have questioned the earnestness, or seriousness, of Kierkegaard in this work (and others) with respect to his seeming agreement with Hegel concerning the need for a mastery of irony in the personal life.[15] Such an interpretation, however, would make Kierkegaard himself an artful practitioner of the very Socratic and romantic irony he seeks to counter in this work. Of course, it is theoretically possible that Kierkegaard is a thoroughgoing ironist in this work as well as in his other writings, just as it is possible to entertain the thought, as Sylviane Agacinski does, that Hegel may also have been an ironist who feigned hatred of irony and whose entire philosophy may have been writen "as a diversion in order to pull a fast one on us."[16] It is impossible to disprove such suspicions, but there is little or nothing to support them either, whereas there is much in the lives and writings of both

14. Garff, "The Eyes of Argus," 40, 41, 52. Unlike Fenger's treatment of *The Point of View,* Garff's account is based on a close critical assessment in which he accuses Kierkegaard of injecting and arranging documentary evidence and personal protestations in order to make himself appear to be a religious author, just as Kierkegaard earlier engaged in deceptive practices to create the appearance of himself as an aesthete in order to conceal the religious intent of the pseudonymous authorship. Even if Kierkegaard was a religious author, Garff claims, he was self-deceived in thinking he had given a religious accounting of himself and the authorship, while in fact it was an aesthetic writing about the religious in which Kierkegaard aestheticized himself and his relationship with God. Although no one, including Kierkegaard, is immune to some self-deception, few have tried as much or as successfully as he to become transparent, or clear, to themselves, and he merits credit for that. But even if he is self-deceived, *The Point of View* still expresses his own view of the authorship. As for the charge that it is designed to deceive the reader into thinking he is a religious author, Garff's argument rests on about as much flimsy evidence as Fenger's, since it is mere conjecture on his part that Kierkegaard includes historical data to make the reader think he is giving a reliable historical account. For a similar "narrative" interpretation of *The Point of View,* see Christopher Norris, *The Deconstructive Turn: Essays in the Rhetoric of Philosophy* (London: Methuen, 1983), 85–106.

15. Agacinski, *Aparté,* 65–68, 74–77; Mackey, *Points of View,* 1–22; Smyth, *A Question of Eros,* 101–259. See also my critical review-essay focusing in part on Agacinski and Smyth, "Kierkegaard and Postmodernism," *International Journal for Philosophy of Religion* 29, no. 2 (1991): 113–22. If Kierkegaard is being ironic toward Hegel in *The Concept of Irony,* I would suggest that the irony is to be found in the way development of genuine earnestness in the personal life in his view subverts Hegel's claim of a philosophic mastery of irony by making such mastery a moment in the Hegelian system. As I show in Chapter 2, in Kierkegaard's view mastered irony becomes a moment in the development of the personal life and therein acquires its validity. On Kierkegaard's ironic critique of the Hegelian system in *The Concept of Irony,* see also Sanne Elisa Grunnet, *Ironi og Subjektivitet: En studie over S. Kierkegaards disputats "Om Begrebet Ironi"* (Copenhagen: C. A. Reitzels Forlag, 1987).

16. Agacinski, *Aparté,* 72.

Kierkegaard and Hegel to vouch for trust in the genuineness of the views they profess.

To be sure, Kierkegaard frequently employed irony in his writings, and given the use of pseudonyms to detach himself from the positions represented, it is not always easy to discern when he is being ironic toward the contents of those positions even if, as Stephen Dunning has pointed out, "irony always tips its hand, as it certainly must if it is to be understood as irony."[17] But the fact that Kierkegaard uses irony does not justify a total interpretation of him as an ironist, especially in those works issued under his own name. Can one read *Works of Love,* for example, and really believe that Kierkegaard is playing the role of ironist in that deeply reflected collection of Christian discourses?[18] If he is an ironist in his direct communications, I would suggest that he is more likely to be one in the sense of the "existential ironist" in *Concluding Unscientific Postscript* who, as an ethicist for whom irony is an incognito to protect the disclosure of his or her personal inwardness in the external realm (see Chapter 8), is contrasted to the total, abstract ironist. The problem with Kierkegaard's authorship is not that it is ironically irreligious but rather, as Kierkegaard himself points out, that "it is too religious, or that the author's existence is too religious," so that even in his direct communications he has felt his own weakness and inability to express his God-relation fully in a public or direct manner (PV, 64–92).

If, however, one is inclined to trust Kierkegaard's direct communications, as I for the most part am willing to do, and to regard irony as an aesthetic device, or "controlled element," in his writings, employed for the purpose of indirect communication and to protect the privacy of his own religious inwardness, then one may use the viewpoints to which he explicitly subscribes as a guidepost for comparing the views of the pseudonymous authors to his own viewpoints. Where there is a consistency or congruence of viewpoints between them, I think one can safely claim that the pseudonym in a particular instance reflects or perhaps represents an earlier or later stage in the development of Kierkegaard's own viewpoint on a particular subject. Even here one must be careful, however, for given the fact that a process of development takes place in the authorship, a relativizing and modification of viewpoints may occur.

17. Stephen N. Dunning, *Kierkegaard's Dialectic of Inwardness* (Princeton: Princeton University Press, 1985), 5.

18. Apparently at least one Kierkegaard interpreter thinks so, since Gene Fendt suggests as much in *Works of Love? Reflections on "Works of Love."* For a critique of Fendt's book, see my review in *Søren Kierkegaard Newsletter* 22 (1990): 9–10.

What obtains at an ethical level may not hold at the religious stage; and while Kierkegaard may well agree with a pseudonym about the importance of inwardness in an ethical context, for example, he may already be beyond or later transcend that particular understanding of the concept in his own intellectual understanding and personal development.

While I find considerable continuity between the pseudonyms and Kierkegaard on the concept of the poetic, I certainly do not want to claim that they are in total agreement or share the same level of understanding of the existential aesthetics being developed in the authorship. As for Kierkegaard's own interpretations of the authorship, I am guided more by what appears in his texts than by his own claims about them, although I do find these consistent for the most part. For example, I think that Kierkegaard's claim that he was a religious author from the start is borne out in the early literature even before *Either/Or,* which he regarded as the starting point of the authorship, inasmuch as a religious perspective is already apparent in *The Concept of Irony.* What I do not find borne out in the literature, however, is a total or clear-cut movement away from the poetic and aesthetic such as Kierkegaard suggests in *The Point of View.* Rather, it is a particular understanding and use of the poetic and aesthetic that is rejected, not the poetic and aesthetic as such, and these factors are continually reinterpreted in an ethical-religious manner as essential elements in that sphere.

Having put forth these observations and reservations concerning the discernment and reliability of Kierkegaard's point of view in distinction to and/or in continuity with the views of the pseudonymous authors, I nevertheless think that the enterprise of trying to distinguish between Kierkegaard and his pseudonyms is not nearly so important as discerning the movements of thought within the authorship. It is this movement that I am primarily concerned to show with respect to the development of the concept of the poetic and an existential aesthetics in his writings, and it is to an overview of that development that I now turn.

DEVELOPMENT OF THE CONCEPT OF THE POETIC

The development of the concept of the poetic in the context of an existential aesthetics in Kierkegaard's writings may be seen as progressing through three phases that are fundamentally conceptual but correspond on the whole to a historical classification of his authorship in terms of early, middle, and late periods of writing.[19] The first phase is prefigured in *From the Papers of One Still Living* (1838), which sets forth certain aesthetic criteria for becoming an authentic poetic writer of novels, and emerges more explicitly in his academic thesis, *The Concept of Irony* (1841). In this work the truly poetic is identified with the religious, aesthetically defined as a form of self-enjoyment in one's inner infinity, and the notion of "living poetically" in a Christian manner is sketched in contrast to a romantic mode of living poetically. The contrast between these two modes of living poetically is further drawn in *Either/Or* (1843), in which the reader is given an opportunity to experiment with a romantic mode of living poetically in volume 1, against which an alternative ethical-religious pattern for living poetically is again advanced in volume 2. The notion of living poetically thus serves as the basic idea upon which a fundamentally positive view of the poetic in an ethical-religious and existential context is initially sketched and developed in the early literature in contrast to German romanticism. This perspective receives extensive development in volume 2 of *Either/Or*, where "the highest in aesthetics" is viewed as being realized in a personal, rather than artistic, representation of the aesthetic ideal, and an ethical-religious aesthetics of love, marriage, work, talent, and friendship is elaborated in the context of an ethical view of the self and its relation to others. Other pseudonymous writings of the period—namely, *Repetition* (1843), *Fear and Trembling* (1843), *Philosophical Fragments* (1844), and *The Concept of Anxiety* (1844)—contribute to the continued development of a positive existential perspective of the poetic in a religious context. In *Repetition* the figure of the poet plays an important transitional role in the movement to the religious stage of life; in *Fear and Trembling* faith itself, paradoxically understood as aesthetic in its

19. Although Kierkegaard's authorship is frequently divided into two periods—the first consisting of those writings that appeared before *Concluding Unscientific Postscript*, which Kierkegaard labeled his "aesthetic" writings, and the second composed of the specifically religious writings after that point—the practice of classifying the authorship in terms of three periods is not uncommon. I do not see that any particular scheme of division is required, as long as the rationale for employing a particular form of classification is made clear. In the present instance, I employ a tripartite scheme because the development of Kierkegaard's view of the poetic conceptually follows and suggests such a division. Because I start with Kierkegaard's very first book, *From the Papers of One Still Living*, and also examine his doctoral dissertation, *The Concept of Irony*—two works that Kierkegaard did not include in the "authorship" proper, which in his view began with *Either/Or*—the first period is more extended than it would normally be if one simply began with *Either/Or*. For an examination of Kierkegaard's aesthetics, however, it is important to include these two early works.

expression of a religious form of individualism, immediacy, and secrecy, is characterized as a "work of art." Employing "divine poetry" in the form of a love story symbolizing the Incarnation, *Philosophical Fragments* presents faith as the product of divine craftsmanship rather than human artistry, and *The Concept of Anxiety* teaches us how to dance in step with the religious by becoming educated in faith through anxiety, or possibility.

In the second phase, already apparent in the earlier writings but predominant in the cluster of works that appeared between 1845 and 1848—especially *Stages on Life's Way* (1845), *Concluding Unscientific Postscript* (1846), *Works of Love* (1847), and *The Point of View for My Work as an Author* (1848)—Kierkegaard focuses on the dangers and limitations of poetry or the creative imagination and urges a movement away from a poetic relation to actuality and toward an ethical-religious one. In contrast to the positive ethical-religious conception of the poetic advanced in Kierkegaard's early works, these writings reflect a decidedly negative stance toward poetry, but not a total rejection of it, inasmuch as a positive existential perspective of the poetic continues to operate in these and other writings of the period. In the writings of the ethicist Judge William in *Stages on Life's Way,* for example, the truly poetic comes to expression in marriage and the new immediacy of the religious; and in several pieces of literary criticism of this period—*The Crisis and a Crisis in the Life of an Actress* (1848), *Two Ages* (1846), and a section from *The Book on Adler* (1846)—authentic expressions of poetry are recognized in drama, novel writing, and other forms of writing by those who qualify, in Kierkegaard's opinion, as true or essential authors. It is in *Concluding Unscientific Postscript,* however, that the strongest continuing affirmation of the poetic in an existential context may be seen in the characterization of the subjective thinker as an artist and in the interpretation of the aesthetic categories of irony, humor, the comic, and the tragic as existential determinants essential to the art of existing.

While recognizing that poetry can become a substitute for actuality and thus antithetical to existential striving, Kierkegaard, in the third and final phase, comprising journals and a number of specifically religious writings from 1849 to 1852, nevertheless views imagination and possibility as necessary for poetically presenting and striving toward a spiritual form of existence through imitation of Christ. It is during this phase that Kierkegaard most often characterizes himself as a poet in his journals and refers to his whole authorship, not merely the early aesthetic writings, as a form of "poet-communication."[20] It is in this phase, too, that he most clearly comes to an understanding of himself as a religious, or Christian, poet in distinction to the usual poet and finds a legitimate place for the poetic in the portrayal of religious ideals. Kierkegaard thus begins with, then partially but not entirely departs from, and finally returns to a positive concept of the poetic as integrally connected with the portrayal and actualization of ethical-religious ideals in human life.

TERMINOLOGICAL CONSIDERATIONS

A few words of explanation are in order concerning the term "the poetic" and related terminology. In Kierkegaard's writings this term and its synonym "poetry" are generally used in a very broad sense to encompass all forms and expressions of the creative or artistic imagination. Thus these terms are not limited to their usual association with the genre of verse or even to the classical division of *poiēsis* (making) into verse, song, and dance, as classified in Aristotle's *Poetics* (chap. 1). Unlike English, Danish has two words for poetry: *Poesie* and *Digtning*. These terms are frequently used as synonyms for one another, but they may also be distinguished. Whereas *Poesie* is usually restricted to the art of writing a poem, *Digtning* may also refer to creative writing or composition in general. In Kierkegaard's writings the latter term and its synonym *det digterisk* ("the poetic") are also used in an existential context to refer to the capacity of human beings to relate themselves to possibility in the form of ideas and ideals via imagination and concrete ethical action.[21]

20. The notion that Kierkegaard thought of himself as a poet only in the earlier pseudonymous writings he labeled "aesthetic" is certainly contrary to Kierkegaard's characterization of himself and his task in the later journals and literature, but it is one that frequently appears in Kierkegaard scholarship. See, for example, Knud Hansen, *Søren Kierkegaard: Ideens Digter* (Copenhagen: Gyldendalske Boghandel, 1954), where it is suggested in the preface that up until the time of the Corsair affair Kierkegaard considered himself a poet whose task was to describe in poetic form the possibilities for a life in hidden inwardness, whereas after that event he thought of himself as an extraordinary individual whose task was to express the idea in existence and eventually through martyrdom. But this view of Kierkegaard is certainly not upheld in the later journals, as I show in Chapter 8.

21. The distinction between an "idea" and an "ideal" is spelled out in Kant's *Critique of Reason,* tr. Norman Kemp Smith (London: Macmillan, 1956), 485, and in *The Critique of Judgment.* In the latter work Kant states the difference thus: "*Idea* properly means a rational concept, and *ideal* the representation of an individual being, regarded as adequate to the idea" (69). Hegel makes a further distinction between the *Idea as such* (absolute truth itself) and the *Idea as the beauty of art,* which he defines as "the Idea with the nearer qualification of being

Thus these terms are not limited in meaning to the poetic enterprise of creative writing and its products but refer more fundamentally to a dimension of human existence that Kierkegaard regards as essential to the development and attainment of a whole and integrated human life.

Another term frequently used in Kierkegaard's writings and closely related to the other two is the word "art" (*Kunst*). Like poetry, art may refer generally to any product of the human imagination in distinction to a work of nature, and in Danish the plural form of this word is used to refer collectively to the various media of poetic expression called the fine arts (*Kunster*). But "art" may also be understood more fundamentally in the Greek sense of *technē* as the natural possession or acquisition and cultivation of skill or dexterity in the performance of a task. It is this sense of the term that Kierkegaard most frequently exploits in the development of an existential aesthetics in his thought, although for him the art of existing is a skill that must be acquired and cultivated via a relation to the infinite, rather than performed simply on the basis of natural talents and capacities in life.

This distinction between natural and acquired capacities leads to the introduction of another term, "the aesthetic," and to a further distinction between "the aesthetic" and "aesthetics" in Kierkegaard's thought. Etymologically these terms are derived from the Greek word for sense perception (*aisthēsis*).[22] In the writings of Kierkegaard "the aesthetic" is a major term signifying that condition and stage in human life where every human being begins and in which some remain, living in an immediate or reflective manner on the basis of natural inclinations and capacities in an effort to gain satisfaction and enjoyment through the senses.

---

both essentially individual reality and also an individual configuration of reality destined essentially to embody and reveal the Idea" (*Aesthetics,* 1:73). The Idea as individual or concrete reality "shaped in accordance with the Concept of the Idea" constitutes the Ideal for Hegel (74). Kant and Hegel thus essentially agree on their understanding of this distinction, and Kierkegaard appears to accept their view on the matter.

22. The term "aesthetics" was first introduced in 1735 by Alexander Gottlieb Baumgarten to designate a theory of poetic discourse he called "sensate discourse," or "discourse whose various parts are directed toward the apprehension of sensate representations" (*Reflections on Poetry,* tr. and ed. Karl Aschenbrenner and William B. Holther [Berkeley and Los Angeles: University of California Press, 1964], 38–39, 78). Being a rationalist, Baumgarten regarded sensate representations as ideas received through the senses, or the "lower part" of the cognitive faculty. Thus they do not belong to the category of "things known" (by logic or reason) but to "things perceived," which are the object of the science of perception, or aesthetics (78). In conformity with its original spelling, I use the term "aesthetics" rather than "esthetics" except when quoting from the new Princeton edition of Kierkegaard's works, which uses the latter spelling of the term.

One way sensuous enjoyment may be had is through poetry and art. Since these forms have historically been understood as sensuous representations or expressions of the idea of beauty as perceived or experienced through the senses, there is a close connection between the aesthetic and the poetic, and consequently between the aesthetic and aesthetics as the science of poetic representation. Frequently, therefore, the terms "aesthetic" and "poetic" are used interchangeably, although a distinction between them may also be drawn. In itself, the aesthetic refers to those elements that are constitutive of the immediate, sensate life, whereas the poetic connotes sensate representation of an idea or ideal in works of art and in human life. In the chapters that follow, I am concerned, on the one hand, to point out aesthetic and/or poetic elements in the ethical and religious dimensions of Kierkegaard's writings and, on the other hand, to show that the aesthetic and poetic have a spiritual as well as sensuous dimension and connotation in his thought.

TOWARD AN APPRECIATION OF KIERKEGAARD AS A POET AND AESTHETICIAN

Unlike Kant, Hegel, and others among his predecessors and contemporaries, Kierkegaard did not work out a systematic aesthetics in either traditional or existential form. Perhaps for this reason his aesthetics has received little or no attention in the standard histories of aesthetics in English and Danish.[23] This neglect is remarkable considering the highly literary character of Kierkegaard's authorship and the emphasis placed on the aesthetic and poetic in his thought. But it may be explained in part by the fact that Kierkegaard scholarship in general has not placed

23. For studies in the history of aesthetics, either written in or translated into English, see Monroe C. Beardsley, *Aesthetics from Classical Greece to the Present: A Short History* (New York: Macmillan, 1966); Bernard Bosanquet, *A History of Aesthetic* (London: Allen & Unwin, 1949); Katharine Everett Gilbert and Helmut Kuhn, *A History of Esthetics* (New York: Macmillan, 1939); Wladyslaw Tatarkiewicz, *History of Aesthetics,* 2 vols. (The Hague: Mouton, 1970); and Monroe C. Beardsley, "Aesthetics, History of," in *The Encyclopedia of Philosophy,* ed. Paul Edwards (New York: Macmillan, 1967), 1:18–35. Evidence that interest in Kierkegaard as an aesthetician has increased in recent studies may be seen in Terry Eagleton, *The Ideology of the Aesthetic* (Oxford: Basil Blackwell, 1990), which includes a chapter on Kierkegaard. On Danish literary history, see P. M. Mitchell, *A History of Danish Literature* (Copenhagen: Gyldendal, 1957), 135–49, where Kierkegaard is briefly treated in a chapter on Heiberg and his school; and Gustav Albeck, Oluf Friis, and Peter P. Rohde, *Dansk Litteratur Historie,* vol. 2, *Fra Oehlenschläger til Kierkegaard* (Copenhagen: Politikens Forlag, 1971), 609–38.

much emphasis on Kierkegaard's aesthetics, in spite of the fact that there has long been an international cadre of scholars concerned with aesthetic, literary, or poetic aspects of his thought. I regard my own work in this area as an amplification of the work these scholars have initiated, although there are of course various points of disagreement between us.[24] There are many facets of Kierkegaard's aesthetics that have not been noted or adequately analyzed, not least of which is its fundamentally existential character. In my view, this existential character is what is most distinctive about Kierkegaard's aesthetics, and my concern with this feature of his aesthetics is chiefly what distinguishes my scholarship from that of others, who have focused primarily on traditional forms of aesthetic criticism in his thought. Although Kierkegaard has numerous aesthetic insights to offer in the various pieces of traditional aesthetic criticism included in his writings, it is the existential thrust of his aesthetics that potentially constitutes, I believe, his most significant contribution to aesthetics, especially the formulation of a religious, or Christian, aesthetics.[25] In an age that suffers increasingly from a loss of poetic pathos and imagination, on the one hand, yet threatens to collapse into the practice of an ironic and hollow form of aestheticism, on the other, Kierkegaard's aesthetics provides an important alternative to traditional aesthetics, especially romantic and Hegelian aesthetics, in its concern first and foremost with the edification and fulfillment of the human personality, not merely with artistic creativity and representation in traditional forms of art.[26] Thus a reconsideration of his authorship in

24. In addition to those already cited, recent studies focusing on some aspect of Kierkegaard's aesthetics include David Cain, "Reckoning with Kierkegaard: Christian Faith and Dramatic Literature" (Ph.D. diss., Princeton University, 1975); Rune Engebretsen, "Kierkegaard and Poet-Existence with Special Reference to Germany and Rilke" (Ph.D. diss., Stanford University, 1980); Louis Mackey, *Kierkegaard: A Kind of Poet* (Philadelphia: University of Pennsylvania Press, 1971); Richard Summers, "A Study of Kierkegaard's Philosophical Development up to *Om Begrebet Ironi*" (Ph.D. diss., University of London, 1980); George Pattison, "Kierkegaard's Theory and Critique of Art: Its Theological Significance" (Ph.D. diss., University of Durham, Great Britain, 1983); and Nelly Viallaneix, *Écoute Kierkegaard: Essai sur la communication de la parole*, 2 vols. (Paris: Éditions du Cerf, 1979).

25. On the possibility of a Christian aesthetics, see Nicholas Wolterstorff, *Art in Action: Toward a Christian Aesthetic* (Grand Rapids, Mich: Eerdmans, 1980); Frank Burch Brown, *Religious Aesthetics: A Theological Study of Making and Meaning* (Princeton: Princeton University Press, 1989); and George Pattison, *Art, Modernity, and Faith: Towards a Theology of Art* (New York: St. Martin's Press, 1991).

26. For a perceptive analysis of the crisis of the imagination in the present age, see Richard Kearney, *The Wake of Imagination* (Minneapolis: University of Minnesota Press, 1988). On the movement toward aestheticism, understood as "the attempt to expand the aesthetic to embrace the whole of reality" so as to regard " 'art,' or 'language,' 'discourse,' or 'text' as constituting the primary realm of human experience" (2), see Alan Megill, *Prophets of Extremity:*

terms of the existential aesthetics developed in it will lead, I hope, to a greater appreciation of him as a poet and aesthetician as well as religious thinker and philosopher.

Finally, it is hoped that by acquiring a deeper understanding of the poetic as envisioned in Kierkegaard's existential aesthetics, we may all—whether poets or not—be aided in appropriating the poetic in our own lives for the sake of striving toward that wholeness of being projected in his writings. The fragmentary character of modern life to which his existential aesthetics is addressed is still with us and in many ways constitutes an even greater problem with which we must grapple both as individuals and as a society in the present age. In a concluding epilogue to my study, therefore, I bring Kierkegaard's thought into dialogue with postmodern deconstructionist views, particularly those of some postmodern French feminists, concerning the crisis of self-identity that presents itself in the present age. In contrast to those who interpret Kierkegaard himself as a proto-postmodern thinker, I see postmodern French feminism and postmodernism more generally as advocating a romantic mode of living poetically and therefore, from a Kierkegaardian point of view, an inauthentic form of living poetically. Finding Kierkegaard more compatible with a feminist position that emphasizes both commonalities and differences between the self and others, men and women, I conclude with a discussion of how Kierkegaard's views on self-identity, gender differences, and the concept of the other may contribute to the working out of an authentic mode of living poetically in the context of the particular problems and issues that characterize the present age.

Nietzsche, Heidegger, Foucault, Derrida (Berkeley and Los Angeles: University of California Press, 1985). Although Megill regards these thinkers as therapeutic and edifying in that they encourage the development of a capacity for self-transcendence, or *ekstasis,* from a Kierkegaardian point of view this merely continues the poetic movement away from the self in the creation of external products instead of directing the self inwardly to the production of itself as a work of art.

1

The Making of a Poetic Writer

What does it take to be a poet, or poetic writer? Is it merely the writing of verse or the creation of some other kind of artistic product? Does it consist in having a special temperament, an eye for beauty, an imaginative mind, a sense of vision? Is there a necessary fund of experience and a particular way of viewing the world that are prerequisite to being an authentic poet? The question of what, if any, aesthetic criteria are to be applied to the creative artist is a vexing one that literary critics and philosophers of aesthetics in every age must ponder. As a student of aesthetics and budding author during his university years, Kierkegaard was also much concerned with the nature and requirements of poetic creativity. Aspiring to establish himself in the elite literary circle of J. L. Heiberg, the leading Danish aesthetician of the time, he published in 1838 a literary review of a novel by a contemporary writer, Hans Christian Andersen, whose qualifications as a novelist are severely questioned in the review. Issued under the odd title, *From the Papers of One Still Living,* this was the first piece by Kierkegaard to be published except for some short polemical essays that appeared in periodicals between 1834 and 1836.[1] Although Kierkegaard ironically

1. On the title of Kierkegaard's first book, see Frithiof Brandt, *Syv Kierkegaard-Studier* (Copenhagen: Munksgaard, 1962), 58–66; H. P. Rohde, in *Gaadefulde Stadier paa Kierkegaards Vej* (Copenhagen: Rosenkilde & Bagger, 1974), 39–51; and Julia Watkin's note on the title in EPW, 247. For a reprint and discussion of Kierkegaard's newspaper articles in Danish, see Teddy Petersen, *Kierkegaards polemiske debut: Artikler 1834–36 i historisk Sammenhæng* (Odense: Odense Universitetsforlag, 1977). See also the historical introduction and English translations of these articles in EPW.

discounts the significance of this review, suggesting in a postscript to the preface that it would not matter if the reader happened to skip over the review along with the preface, he introduces in this work certain aesthetic criteria for becoming an authentic poetic writer of novels (*Romandigter*), criteria that are fundamental to the existential aesthetics that emerges in the first phase of his authorship and that continue to be espoused in his writings. It is thus important to begin with a brief consideration of this work and the literary-historical background from which Kierkegaard's fundamental aesthetic criteria are derived.

Kierkegaard's assessment of Hans Christian Andersen's qualifications as a novelist in *From the Papers of One Still Living* is based primarily on a critique of Andersen's third novel, *Only a Fiddler.* Older and more established as a writer than Kierkegaard, Andersen at this point in his career had received far more acclaim as a novelist than as a writer of verse, fairy tales, and plays. His first novel, *The Improvisator* (1835), was an instant success, although Kierkegaard quips in an early journal entry that he can "find nothing in it" (JP, 5:5211). Like Kierkegaard, Andersen sought membership in the select Heibergian camp, but after an initial measure of acceptance, he met with disfavor apparently because Heiberg and his wife, Johanna Luise Heiberg, the most celebrated Danish actress of the time, did not think much of his ability as a dramatist.[2] Andersen responded to their rejection of him by satirizing and caricaturing Heiberg and his followers in some of his tales. One of these caricatures, a conceited parrot in "The Galoshes of Fortune," may have been intended as an unflattering portrait of Kierkegaard. Since Andersen's story appeared about three and a half months before Kierkegaard's critical review of *Only a Fiddler,* Frithiof Brandt has suggested that Kierkegaard attacked Andersen in reaction to this satirical characterization of himself.[3] But while Kierkegaard makes some strong charges with respect to Andersen's personality, he denies having overstepped the limits of aesthetic jurisdiction and competency in doing so, even without appealing to the fact that, as he puts it, "I as good as do not know Andersen

2. Henning Fenger and Frederick J. Marker, *The Heibergs* (New York: Twayne, 1971), 18. On Andersen as a dramatist, see F. J. Marker, *Hans Christian Andersen and the Romantic Theatre* (Toronto: University of Toronto Press, 1971).

3. Frithiof Brandt, *Den Unge Søren Kierkegaard* (Copenhagen: Levin & Munksgaard Forlag, 1929), 115–59. Motives of a less personal nature have been suggested by other scholars. For example, Georg Brandes, in *Samlede Skrifter* (Copenhagen: Gyldendalske Boghandels Forlag, 1899), 2:272–73, thinks it was Kierkegaard's objection to Andersen's view of poetic genius that provoked the attack; and Søren Gorm Hansen, in *H. C. Andersen og Søren Kierkegaard i Dannelseskulturen* (Copenhagen: Medusa, 1976), 136, believes it was occasioned by Andersen's view of actuality.

personally" (EPW, 83). And in the conclusion he even claims, though perhaps with a touch of irony, that his remarks have been written with "sympathetic ink" (EPW, 102). Two years later, when Andersen once again subjected Kierkegaard to caricature by having a character in one of his plays repeat lines from Kierkegaard's review, Kierkegaard wrote a response objecting to Andersen's portrayal of him this time as a "prating Hegelian" (EPW, 218–22; cf. xxvi–xxvii), but he refrained from publishing it and thus prolonging the public dispute between them.

Whether or not a personal vendetta against Andersen is intended in *From the Papers of One Still Living,* he is viewed there in a wider perspective as the paradigm of a whole cycle of phenomena in the contemporary philosophical, literary, and political spheres of Denmark that are also targets for criticism in this work. The beginning of the nineteenth century had brought the flourishing of the romantic movement in Germany, and with it the rise of the novel, or *Roman,* from which the movement takes its name.[4] German romantic philosophy was introduced to Denmark in 1802 by Henrik Steffens, whose lectures inspired the young Danish poet Adam Oehlenschläger and opened the door to the development of the novel and of a new genre—the novella, or short novel—in Danish literature.[5] With the waning of Danish romanticism around 1820, however, there arose a new generation of writers—including, among others, J. L. Heiberg, Poul Møller, Henrik Hertz, and Madame Gyllembourg (Heiberg's mother)—who in that decade established themselves as a school of poetic realism emphasizing "local color" and "everyday life."[6] Although a number of historical and epistolary novels were produced during the 1820s in Denmark, Henning Fenger maintains that the real breakthrough in the development of Danish prose writing came in the 1830s, most notably with the novels of Hans Christian Andersen.[7] Andersen's novels represented a new wave of romanti-

4. René Wellek, *A History of Modern Criticism: 1750–1950: The Romantic Age* (New Haven: Yale University Press, 1955), 13. See also Hans Eichner, ed., *"Romantic" and Its Cognates: The European History of a Word* (Toronto: University of Toronto Press, 1972).

5. On the theory of the novella and its development as a historical genre, see E. K. Bennett, *A History of the German "Novelle,"* 2d ed., rev. H. M. Waidson (Cambridge: Cambridge University Press, 1961), and Martin Swales, *The German "Novelle"* (Princeton: Princeton University Press, 1977).

6. Albeck et al., *Dansk Litteratur Historie,* 247–58, 377–426. On poetic realism in German novellas, see also Bennett, *A History of the German "Novelle,"* 124–92, and Walter Silz, *Realism and Reality: Studies in the German Novelle of Poetic Realism* (Chapel Hill: University of North Carolina Press, 1954).

7. Fenger, *Kierkegaard, the Myths and Their Origins,* 81–131; see also Oluf Friis and Uffe Andreasen, *Dansk Litteratur Historie,* vol. 3, *Fra Poul Møller til Søren Kierkegaard* (Copenha-

cism in contrast to the poetic realism of the earlier prose literature. Fenger theorizes that Kierkegaard, following the realist tradition, was engaged at this time in the writing of materials in the form of fictional letters for an epistolary novel to be modeled on F. C. Sibbern's *Gabrielis Breve.* Although it is true that Kierkegaard was contemplating writing a novel or novella and was looking for ideas to develop in novelistic form at this time, there is little evidence to substantiate Fenger's theory of fictional letters.[8] But Kierkegaard's own novelistic aspirations undoubtedly provided an incentive to competition with Andersen as well as other young novelists of the period. More important, they help to explain his choice of the novel as the literary genre upon which to focus and formulate his aesthetic views in opposition to the second phase of romanticism emerging at that time.

As these literary developments were occurring in Denmark, giving the period the distinction of being called the Golden Age of Danish literature, events in the social-political sector were taking quite a different course.[9] After suffering economic bankruptcy in 1813, the year of Kierkegaard's birth, the state continued to experience economic depression under a conservative government by absolute monarchy. Calls for constitutional rule, voting rights, and other social reforms met with opposition and repression from the government. Gradually, however, continuing social pressure and the rise of capitalism in the first half of the nineteenth century brought political and economic change to the land. During his university years, Kierkegaard's position vis-à-vis most of these

---

gen: Politikens Forlag, 1976), where 1835, the year Andersen's first novel was published, is called "the great novel year" (330).

8. On Kierkegaard's plans to write a novel or novella, see JP, 5:5279, 5281, 5290, 5314. For Fenger's theory of fictional letters, which was first put forth by Emmanuel Hirsch, who is not duly credited by Fenger, see *Kierkegaard, the Myths and Their Origins,* 89–131. Fenger's version of the theory is based on conjecture and often assumes what it sets out to prove or substantiate. Moreover, Fenger finds the figures mentioned in many of these letters to be too transparent to Kierkegaard's contemporaries for them to be published as an epistolary novella—an observation that ironically testifies to the historical accuracy rather than the fictive quality of these letters.

9. For discussions of the economic and political situation in Denmark during this period, see Bruce H. Kirmmse, *Kierkegaard in Golden Age Denmark* (Bloomington: Indiana University Press, 1990); Michael Plekon, "Towards Apocalypse: Kierkegaard's *Two Ages* in Golden Age Denmark," in *International Kierkegaard Commentary: Two Ages,* ed. Robert L. Perkins (Macon, Ga.: Mercer University Press, 1984), 19–52, with references to more extensive studies; and John Elrod, *Kierkegaard and Christendom* (Princeton: Princeton University Press, 1981), 3–11.

changes favored maintenance of the status quo, although he was not as conservative as some have thought.[10]

"FORGET THE ACTUAL"

In *From the Papers of One Still Living* Kierkegaard counters what he perceives to be the main trend of the time in the philosophical, literary, and political spheres, namely, the adoption of a negative attitude toward actuality. The tendency of the "whole newer development," he claims, is to forget the past—all the "struggles and hardships the world has endured in order to become what it is"—in order to make a fresh start in the present (EPW, 61). In this, the present age seeks to establish itself as the real beginning of world history by making itself a "positive era" in contrast to previous existence, which is looked upon as a regrettably long period of serfdom (EPW, 61). This aspiration appears in its most respectable and relatively true form, Kierkegaard thinks, in Hegel's great philosophical attempt to "begin with nothing," that is, without any presuppositions.[11] Hegel's attempt impresses Kierkegaard for the moral strength, intellectual energy, and virtuosity with which it was con-

10. Kierkegaard is often accused of lacking a social-political dimension in his thought, emphasizing only the individual and ethical-religious concerns. But such a claim is far from the truth, since the very first writings of Kierkegaard to be published were on the subjects of female emancipation, which he was against, and the role of the public press in initiating political reforms (see EPW, 3–52). In an unpublished paper, "Kierkegaard's First Brush with the Press," Robert L. Perkins has shown that Kierkegaard was critical of the repressive policies of the government in regard to censorship of the press and that he did not defend, at this stage at least, absolute monarchy against the new political movements.

11. See *Hegel's Science of Logic,* tr. A. V. Miller (London: Allen & Unwin, 1969), where Hegel says "the beginning must be an *absolute,* or what is synonymous here, an *abstract* beginning; and so it *may not presuppose anything,* must not be mediated by anything nor have a ground; rather, it is to be itself the ground of the entire science" (70). Niels Thulstrup, in *Kierkegaard's Relation to Hegel,* tr. George L. Stengren (Princeton: Princeton University Press, 1980), maintains that Kierkegaard was incorrect in interpreting Hegel's philosophy as "beginning with nothing," since for Hegel logic begins with pure being. To Thulstrup this error is an indication that Kierkegaard had not yet read Hegel's works. Thulstrup admits, however, that "in Hegel pure 'being' turns out to be identical with pure 'nothing,' but it is not immediately understood that way" (168). On Kierkegaard's knowledge of and attitude toward Hegel in his early years, see also Fenger, *Kierkegaard, the Myths and Their Origins,* who contests Thulstrup's claim that Kierkegaard was opposed to Hegel very early in his academic career (132–49). Fenger's interpretation appears to be closer to the truth, although there are significant differences between Kierkegaard and Hegel at this early stage.

ceived and carried out in the philosophical system Hegel constructed. But the "entire recent literature" is so preoccupied with writing prefaces and introductions to the new era, Kierkegaard charges, that "it has forgotten that the beginning from nothing of which Hegel speaks was mastered by himself in the system and was by no means a failure to appreciate the great richness actuality has" (EPW, 62).

From this statement it is apparent that it is not so much Hegel himself as followers of his who are the main targets of Kierkegaard's criticism of recent developments in the philosophical sphere. Indeed, at this stage in his philosophical understanding, Kierkegaard shows considerably more appreciation of Hegel than of those who espouse his views. In a footnote to the text, for example, he satirizes those Hegelians who read the master's *Logic* so as to posit the category of "actual secretaries" in thought without there being any corresponding secretaries in actuality (EPW, 62). The principal Hegelians Kierkegaard most likely has in mind are J. L. Heiberg, one of the foremost exponents of Hegelianism in Denmark at that time, who gave an introductory lecture on Hegel's logic in 1834, and H. L. Martensen, whose popular lectures on Hegel in 1837 created what J. H. Schjørring has described as a "Hegelian delirium" among university students and the cultural bourgeoisie.[12] This phenomenon and its instigator are subjected to satirical attack and caricature in a rough draft of a farce sketched by Kierkegaard in 1838 or 1839 under the projected title "The Battle Between the Old and the New Soap-Cellars" but never finished (EPW, 103–24).[13]

Kierkegaard's criticism of the current *literary* attitude toward actuality also echoes one that poetic realists of the period had made against the earlier romantic poets for the alienation from actuality expressed in their attempts to escape the world through poetry.[14] In fact, Kierke-

12. J. H. Schjørring, "Martensen," in *Bibliotheca Kierkegaardiana,* vol. 10, *Kierkegaard's Teachers,* ed. Niels Thulstrup and Marie Mikulová Thulstrup (Copenhagen: C. A. Reitzels Forlag, 1982), 177–207. On Heiberg's lecture, which was subsequently published and then reviewed by Martensen, see Thulstrup, *Kierkegaard's Relation to Hegel,* 92. It is not clear whether Kierkegaard heard or read Heiberg's lecture, but he was acquainted with Martensen's review of it (see JP, 5:5200). On Heiberg and Martensen, see also Kirmmse, *Kierkegaard in Golden Age Denmark,* 136–97; Pattison, *Kierkegaard: The Aesthetic and the Religious,* 9–26; and Robert L. Horn, "Positivity and Dialectic: A Study of the Theological Method of Hans Lassen Martensen" (Th.D. diss., Union Theological Seminary, 1969).

13. For a brief summary and discussion of this play, see the historical introduction in EPW, xxxii–xxxvi. For contrasting interpretations of the play, cf. Thulstrup, *Kierkegaard's Relation to Hegel,* 180–200, and Fenger, *Kierkegaard, the Myths and Their Origins,* 141–42.

14. See Sven Møller Kristensen, *Digteren og Samfundet i Danmark i det 19. Aarhundrede* (Copenhagen: Athenaeum, 1942), 106–14.

gaard's critique of the attempt to "begin with nothing" may be aimed more at the new wave of romanticism than against Hegelianism. In *The Concept of Irony,* where romanticism is subjected to severe criticism, he associates the idea that "only now was actuality supposed to begin" specifically with romanticism and again refers to Hegel as the one who "put a stop to all this continual chatter that now world history was going to begin" (CI, 278). Moreover, the practice of writing prefaces, which is criticized in *From the Papers of One Still Living,* was a technique frequently employed by romantic poets to prepare the reader for responding imaginatively to their writings.[15]

As exceptions to the negative tendencies of the more recent prose literature, Kierkegaard cites a cycle of realist novellas by Madame Gyllembourg that reflect a positive orientation toward actuality. In particular, the first of these, *A Story of Everyday Life,* receives strong appreciation from him for its truly edifying positivity in expressing joy and confidence in the world and in people. Although Kierkegaard admits that her stories can also be said to "begin with nothing" in the sense that they focus on the affairs of immediate, everyday life, in his estimation they reflect what is true in the trend insofar as they present a negative attitude toward the "odious practice" of rejecting the past, a practice that had become established in the genre of prose literature (EPW, 64). Other writings that also receive favorable mention from him are the novellas of Bernhard and Blicher, the latter being described as a "voice in the wilderness" who transforms the novel into "a friendly place of refuge for the imagination exiled in life" (EPW, 69).[16]

In the *political* sphere, Kierkegaard detects an even more deplorable form of the age's delusion with regard to actuality than is found in philosophy and literature. Here the problem is evident in a misunderstanding of historical evolution centered in the notion that "the world always becomes wiser." Implied in this notion is the idea that the present is better than the past, but Kierkegaard notes, with parodic consequences: "We on our forefathers' shoulders stand, We seem so tall—and

15. On this practice, see Kathleen Wheeler, ed. *German Aesthetic and Literary Criticism: The Romantic Ironists and Goethe* (Cambridge: Cambridge University Press, 1984), 9. A few years later, in 1844, Kierkegaard adopted the practice of writing prefaces himself in a little pseudonymous book entitled *Prefaces,* designed to wage a satirical attack on the pretensions of Hegelian philosophy in its claim to a "systematic totality of knowledge" within the confines of a book and on Hegel's notion of a philosophical preface as a kind of "master narrative" revealing the truth of the text before the reader has gone through the dialectical movements of thought and existence requisite to the attainment of that truth (P, 3–4, 11).

16. On Kierkegaard's relation to Blicher, see Fenger, *Kierkegaard, the Myths and Their Origins,* 123–31.

are so small." Kierkegaard attributes this attitude of superiority either to a "youthful arrogance too confident of powers untried in life" or to a "lack of patience to adapt oneself to the conditions of life" (EPW, 63). In either case, he contends, the watchword is "forget the actual," which amounts to an attack upon the given actuality evident in the negative element of distrust with which they seek to begin anew (EPW, 64).

One child of this period who manifests, in Kierkegaard's estimation, its tendency toward a negative view of actuality is Hans Christian Andersen. One can detect in him, Kierkegaard thinks, "a certain gloom and bitterness against the world" that is not only characteristic of his personal life but also autobiographically projected into his novels (EPW, 73). The same "joyless battle" Andersen wages in life against the forces of fate and evil choking the good in the world is taken up again in his writings (EPW, 75). His novels thus provide a good example whereby Kierkegaard can examine a fundamental issue in aesthetics concerning the relation between the life and literary productivity of the poetic writer. To what extent and in what way should a writer's own attitudes and experiences shape or be reflected in his or her poetic works? Kierkegaard sees the life and work of a poetic writer as being integrally connected, but not in the way they are conflated in Andersen's novels. In his aesthetic judgment, Andersen lacks certain fundamental qualifications that are necessary to be a novelist. As a result he stands in a wrong relation both to his artistic productivity and to himself.

There are essentially two aesthetic requirements Kierkegaard thinks Andersen lacks as a *Romandigter,* or poetic writer of novels: a life-development (*Livs-Udvikling*) and a life-view (*Livs-Anskuelse*).[17] Both

17. Kierkegaard scholarship has tended to overlook or neglect the first of these criteria, focusing primarily on the second. See Connell, *To Be One Thing,* 23–33; Gouwens, *Kierkegaard's Dialectic of the Imagination,* 70–71; Pattison, *Kierkegaard: The Aesthetic and the Religious,* 126–32; Gregor Malantschuk, *Kierkegaard's Thought,* ed. and tr. Howard V. Hong and Edna H. Hong (Princeton: Princeton University Press, 1971), 183–86; and Vincent McCarthy, *The Phenomenology of Moods in Kierkegaard* (The Hague: Martinus Nijhoff, 1978), 140–46. Søren Gorm Hansen, in *H. C. Andersen og Søren Kierkegaard i Dannelseskulturen,* finds special significance in the fact that Kierkegaard calls Andersen a *Romandigter* (poetic novelist) rather than a *Romanforfatter* (writer of novels), which is the more commonly used term for a prose writer or novelist. As Hansen distinguishes them, a *digter* is essentially a poet who seeks to poetize actuality, whereas a *forfatter* is a prose writer who seeks to draw poetry down into actuality (188). Merete Jørgensen, in *Kierkegaard som Kritiker,* adopts and further develops this distinction, characterizing a *digter* as naïve, immediate, aesthetic, unreflective, lacking life-development, polemical toward actuality, and given to fantasy, whereas a *forfatter* is self-conscious, reflective, experienced, and oriented in and toward actuality and possesses a life-view (131–32). Although Andersen is correctly described by both of these scholars as falling into the first category, at least as he is characterized by Kierkegaard, the sharp distinction

of these categories were previously employed as artistic criteria by Poul Martin Møller, who emphasized them in a review of Madame Gyllembourg's novel *The Extremes* (1836) and in his treatise on immortality (1837).[18] The notion of a life-development, however, is rooted in German neoclassicism, which emphasized self-cultivation (*Bildung*) and the achievement of wholeness of the individual personality as the goal of life and art. This idea was given theoretical formulation in Schiller's *Aesthetic Education of Man* (1793) and artistic expression in *Bildungsromane,* or novels of individual development, most notably those of Goethe, who was considered the model poet by the young Kierkegaard and his older contemporaries—for example, F. C. Sibbern, Kierkegaard's teacher of aesthetics and psychology, who was a novelist in his own right and shared the neoclassical view of existence as a process of development toward a unified whole.[19]

The necessity of having a life-view that informs a work of art was also a primary tenet of the poetic realism school to which Sibbern and Møller belonged. As George Pattison has pointed out, "the terms *Weltanschauung* and *Lebensanschauung* had been in common usage in Ger-

---

they draw between the two types of writers is not upheld in *From the Papers of One Still Living.* For here Kierkegaard uses the term *Romandigter* not only with respect to Andersen but also to refer to an authentic writer of novels, for whom both a life-development and a life-view are prerequisites. See, for example, EPW, 81 (SV, 13:72), where Kierkegaard speaks of "the necessity of a life-view for a poetic writer of novels and novellas [*en Livs-Anskuelses Nødvendighed for Roman-og Novelle-Digteren*]." In this work, therefore, *Romandigter* is used as a synonym to *Romanforfatter* rather than in contrast to it, and the term *digtning* (poetry) is understood in the broader sense of *poiēsis,* or poetry, as including all genres of the creative imagination, not merely the writing of verse and lyrical prose. According to Eric A. Blackall, *The Novels of the German Romantics* (Ithaca, N.Y.: Cornell University Press, 1983), 16, the novel was regarded as a poetic form by the German romantics. Kierkegaard apparently thinks of it in the same manner.

18. Friis and Andreasen, *Dansk Litteratur Historie,* 408; Uffe Andreasen, *Poul Møller og Romantismen* (Copenhagen: Gyldendal, 1973), 70–76. W. Glyn Jones, "Søren Kierkegaard and Poul Martin Møller," *Modern Language Review* 60 (1965): 73–82, reports that Møller criticized the lack of a life-view in Danish literature as early as 1835. On Møller, see also Pattison, *Kierkegaard: The Aesthetic and the Religious,* 28–34.

19. On the German *Bildungsroman* tradition, see Martin Swales, *The German Bildungsroman from Wieland to Hesse* (Princeton: Princeton University Press, 1978). On Goethe and Schiller, see also Valdemar Vedel, *Studier over Guldalderen i dansk Digtning,* 2d ed. (Copenhagen: Gyldendal, 1967 [original, 1948]), 65. On Sibbern, see Robert Widenmann, "Sibbern," in *Bibliotheca Kierkegaardiana,* vol. 10, *Kierkegaard's Teachers,* 70–88. On the importance of Sibbern for Kierkegaard, see also Connell, *To Be One Thing,* 11–18, and Summers, "A Study of Kierkegaard's Philosophical Development up to *Om Begrebet Ironi,*" 96–97. The Danish equivalent of the *Bildungsroman* is the *dannelses-* or *udviklingsroman* (see Jørgensen, *Kierkegaard som Kritiker,* 117), an example of which is Sibbern's *Gabrielis Breve.*

man literature and philosophy for a generation or more," but the idea of a world-view or life-view came to acquire special significance for Møller, who saw it as providing a "religious comprehension of being within the horizon of a transcendent unity."[20] The notion of a world-view was also prominent in Hegelian thought, but there it signified a philosophical, rather than religious, comprehension of being and was synonymous with "the system," or a total comprehension and explanation of being through reason. Although Kierkegaard sometimes uses the term "world-view" as a synonym of "life-view," he generally employs the latter term, which has for him a more personal and less systematic connotation than is found in Hegelian philosophy.

In adopting the notions of life-development and life-view as aesthetic criteria, Kierkegaard fuses them with certain aesthetic ideas drawn from J. L. Heiberg, whose aesthetics his own shows an affinity with yet also differs from in some important respects.[21] In *From the Papers of One Still Living* Kierkegaard thus formulates in his own distinctive manner an aesthetic theory of what it takes to be an authentic poet in the form of a *Romandigter,* or poetic writer of novels. To see how these aesthetic criteria are conceptualized and specifically applied to Andersen as a paradigm of the philosophical, literary, and political developments of the time, let us examine them more closely.

THE LIFE-DEVELOPMENT OF A POETIC WRITER

To be an authentic *Romandigter,* or poetic novelist, Kierkegaard claims, one must first undergo a strong life-development so as to become a personality. This life-development is further characterized by him in aesthetic terms as an "epic development," or "epic stage," in life (EPW, 70–71, 76). As Kierkegaard understands it, the epic involves action and heroic striving toward a single goal in life—something he thinks the present political

20. George Pattison, "Nihilism and the Novel: Kierkegaard's Literary Reviews," *British Journal of Aesthetics* 26, no. 2 (1986): 161–71.

21. Richard Summers, in "A Study of Kierkegaard's Philosophical Development up to *Om Begrebet Ironi,*" argues that in spite of Kierkegaard's acceptance of Heiberg's aesthetic ideals, the essentially Christian perspective advocated by Kierkegaard in *From the Papers of One Still Living* is incompatible with Heibergian Hegelianism, and that Kierkegaard wanted "to appear a good Heibergian while in fact owing allegiance elsewhere" (176). I do not find this work to be as clearly oriented in a Christian perspective as Summers does, and even Kierkegaard's aesthetic views are not entirely identical to those of Heiberg, as is pointed out later on in this chapter.

environment, being a "period of fermentation" (*Gjaerings-Periode*) rather than a "period of action" (*Gjernings-Periode*), has not fostered in Andersen, whose personal life and writings are situated in the lyrical stage rather than an epical one (EPW, 71). As a genre and stage of life, the epic, in Kierkegaard's view, follows upon the lyrical, which is concentrated in the expression of poetic mood. In adopting this understanding of these genres, Kierkegaard follows the schema proposed by J. L. Heiberg, who appropriates much of Hegel's aesthetics into his aesthetic theory. In this instance, however, Heiberg reverses the order of these genres in Hegel's *Aesthetics,* where the stages of aesthetic development are viewed historically as moving from the epic to the lyric to a synthesis of these in the dramatic.[22] According to Hegel, the epic corresponds to the immediate, objective, positive stage of world history; the lyric to the reflective, subjective, negative moment; and the dramatic to a synthesis of these in the progressive manifestation of spirit. By contrast, Heiberg proposes a lyric-epic-dramatic schema in which the lyrical is expressive of immediacy, the epic of reflection. In a journal entry dating from 1836, Kierkegaard acknowledges the correctness of Heiberg's transferal of Hegelianism to aesthetics with regard to the notion of a lyric-epic-dramatic triad, although he expresses some doubt as to its meaningfulness on a greater scale, since in his view the classical, the romantic, and the synthesis of these in absolute beauty all contain lyrical, epic, and dramatic forms (JP, 2:1565). Then, as if having some second thoughts on his endorsement of Heiberg's schema, he raises the further question, "To what extent, for that matter, is it right to begin with the lyrical; the history of poetry seems to indicate a beginning with the epic" (JP, 2:1565). Apparently Kierkegaard at this time had not yet read Hegel's *Aesthetics,* since he seems unaware that Heiberg's triad differs from Hegel's; but in questioning Heiberg's formulation, he comes close to adopting Hegel's view. By the time of his literary review of Andersen, however, his skepticism and vacillation on the matter had been resolved in favor of Heiberg's formula.[23]

Since, in Kierkegaard's opinion, Andersen has not progressed beyond

22. For Hegel's views on the epic and the lyric, see *Aesthetics* 2:1040–93. For a discussion of Heiberg's aesthetic system in relation to Hegel's, see Paul Rubow, *Dansk Litteraer Kritik i det 19. ärhundrede indtil 1870* (Copenhagen: Munksgaard, 1970), 88–118. See also Pattison, *Kierkegaard: The Aesthetic and the Religious,* 9–18.

23. Kierkegaard seems to have been influenced most directly by Heiberg on the question of the priority of the lyric over the epic, but according to Nisbet in *German Aesthetic and Literary Criticism,* both Johann Gottfried Herder and Johann Georg Hamann also believed the lyric to be prior to the epic in the historical development of poetic forms (16). Kierkegaard was a great fan of Hamann, but there is no indication that he knew or was influenced by Hamann on this issue.

a lyrical stage of elegiac moodiness in which he is continually turned in upon his own person, he may be characterized as only "a possibility of a personality" rather than an actual or real personality (EPW, 70). This explains why, as Kierkegaard sees it, none of Andersen's novels has an epic character.[24] Not having undergone an epic development, or life-development, in his own person, he omits it in his novels as well. Such a phenomenon may seem rather odd, Kierkegaard admits, inasmuch as the period is otherwise rich in epic material. But the form of epic literature characteristic of the period, he claims, is one in which "each one has his epic and his epic poet in himself" (EPW, 70). By this Kierkegaard may mean that the poet's own life-development forms the content of his or her poetic productivity, as in romantic confessions and autobiographical novels.[25] Or perhaps he means that the poet's epic development takes place only imaginatively in and through epical poetizing. In either case, as Kierkegaard sees it, the self-projection of the modern epic poet in his or her writing is similar to that of Andersen except that the latter lacks the epic quality in both his life and his writings. Nevertheless, Kierkegaard finds Andersen's lyrical "self-absorption" (*Selvfortabelse*) more pleasing than the "self-infatuation" (*Selvforgabelse*) of the modern

24. In associating the novel with the epic, Kierkegaard reflects the close historical connection that has existed between these two genres, with the novel growing out of the epic tradition. He differs, however, from the German romantic school of Friedrich and August Schlegel, who distinguish between the epic and the novel, associating the epic with impersonal, objective poetry in the classical epic tradition, and the novel with the subjective, ironic, and fantastic in the form of an "arabesque," or all-embracing genre. Friedrich Schlegel was against realistic novels, especially those of the eighteenth-century English variety, whereas Kierkegaard stands squarely in the Danish poetic realism school with its emphasis upon orienting the novel toward an appreciation of the given historical actuality. Like the Schlegels, Goethe also distinguished between the novel and the epic, associating the novel with sentiment and passive agency on the part of the hero, whose fortune is decided by chance happenings, and the epic with character development and action in an accepted moral and religious order. But Goethe was against the mixing of genres that was characteristic of the romantic movement. For Goethe's views on the novel and epic, see Eric A. Blackall, *Goethe and the Novel* (Ithaca, N.Y.: Cornell University Press, 1976), chap. 5, e.g., 78–81; and p. 275. On the development of the epic, see Paul Merchant, *The Epic* (London: Methuen, 1971). On the Schlegels, see Wellek, *A History of Modern Criticism,* 13, 19, 20, 51. On the novel in German romanticism, see also Blackall, *The Novels of the German Romantics.* Interestingly, Marshall Brown, in *The Shape of German Romanticism* (Ithaca, N.Y.: Cornell University Press, 1979), points out that Goethe was the one who was responsible for making the term "arabesque" fashionable, through an essay of 1789 entitled "Von Arabesken" (90). For a discussion of the influence of Goethe's essay on F. Schlegel, see Karl Konrad Polheim, *Die Arabeske: Ansichten und Ideen ans Friedrich Schlegels Poetik* (Munich: Schöningh, 1966).

25. That Kierkegaard has in mind here romanticism's tendency to write autobiographical novels is suggested by the editors of the third Danish edition of his works, *Søren Kierkegaards Samlede Værker,* ed. A. B. Drachmann, J. L. Heiberg, and H. O. Lange (Copenhagen: Gyldendal, 1962–64), 1:337. See also EPW, n. 69, where the English translator, Julia Watkin, concurs.

political-epic literature. A proper epic development, he insists, must not be understood as "a literary paying of compliments" to oneself or as "a languishing staring at some chance individuality." Rather, it is constituted by a "deep and earnest embracing" and admiration of, as well as life-strengthening rest in, one's given actuality, regardless of how one loses oneself in it or gives expression to it (EPW, 71).

For Kierkegaard, then, an epic development, or life-development, consists in forming a positive relation to actuality through striving toward a single goal in life, even if that is never given expression in a literary work or some other artistic product. Without such a development an individual is not properly qualified to be a novelist, for otherwise the work becomes nothing more than an egotistical projection of the writer's own moods and life experiences. By failing to separate himself from his writings, thereby creating an aesthetic distance in relation to them, Andersen in particular is guilty of infusing his novels with his own unreflected life experiences. His poetic productions thus merely narrate in their details the misfortunes, bitterness, and discontent with the actual world that characterize his own life. At the same time, by so closely identifying with the characters of his novels, his own personality becomes lost or evaporated in his poetic productions. Kierkegaard thus concludes that Andersen does not stand in a proper relation to his poetic productivity or to himself but belongs instead to that class of novelists who offer "an unpoetic surplus of their own merely phenomenological personality" in their works (EPW, 82).

Kierkegaard's charge against Andersen echoes one that Heiberg had made earlier against Adam Oehlenschläger, namely, that he is an unreflective, lyric poet who lacks a sense of irony or aesthetic detachment in relation to his poetic works.[26] But whereas Heiberg criticizes Oehlenschläger as a dramatist, Kierkegaard concentrates on Andersen as a novelist. There are other differences between Kierkegaard and Heiberg as well. Being primarily interested in the drama, Heiberg did not develop much of a concept of the epic (in spite of the fact that his mother, Madame Gyllembourg, was one of the most celebrated novelists of the time) and was dependent upon Jean Paul for his view of the genre.[27] For Kierkegaard, however, the epic is a crucial category in his understanding of the novel as well as of the life-development of the novelist or poetic writer. In Heiberg's formal, speculative aesthetics, which requires objectivity or

26. On Heiberg's critique of Oehlenschläger, see Fenger and Marker, *The Heibergs,* 124–32, and Pattison, *Kierkegaard: The Aesthetic and the Religious,* 17–18.

27. Rubow, *Dansk Litteraer Kritik i det 19. ärhundrede indtil 1870,* 108. See also Friis and Andreasen, *Dansk Litteratur Historie,* 227.

irony on the part of the poet, the life and art of the poet are seen as having no essential connection.[28] In Kierkegaard's view, by contrast, the categories of the lyric and the epic are understood not only as stages of development in the evolution of genre forms in aesthetic theory but also as stages of development in the poet's personal life, which are reflected in transmuted form in the creative products of the poet. In fact, these categories correspond closely to what Kierkegaard later designates the aesthetic and ethical stages of life. Like the lyrical, the aesthetic stage, as characterized in Kierkegaard's pseudonymous masterpiece, *Either/Or,* is associated in its most elemental form with the life of immediacy, centered unreflectively in the gratification of one's natural drives, moods, and desires. Like the epic, the ethical stage of life is reflective, active, and teleological, having the choice and development of the self in the context of the social environment as its goal. Since *From the Papers of One Still Living* is primarily concerned with Andersen as a poetic writer of novels, a genre closely associated with the epic, Kierkegaard does not explore in this work what Hegel and Heiberg in agreement propose as a third category synthesizing the lyric and the epic (or vice versa) in the dramatic. Thus an aesthetic parallel for what Kierkegaard later designates as the religious stage of existence is missing from the work.[29]

In describing human development in terms of aesthetic categories, Kierkegaard also differs from Heibergian and Hegelian aesthetics in applying these categories to the personal existence of the individual rather than to a world-historical evolution of Absolute Spirit, as they do. Furthermore, Kierkegaard apparently sees no necessity of movement from the lyrical stage to the epic, since Andersen, in his view, has not undergone such a transition and might remain a lyrical writer. But Kierkegaard does regard the lyrical stage as a precondition of the epic, and were Andersen to embark upon a life-development, the epic would be the next stage he must go through.

THE LIFE-VIEW OF A POETIC WRITER

The second essential element Kierkegaard finds lacking in Andersen as a novelist is a life-view by which to understand and transcend his individ-

28. Vedel, *Studier over Guldalderen i dansk Digtning,* 153, 179–84, 212.

29. For a dramatic parallel, see EO, 2:137, where Judge William envisions the ethical individual, oriented concentrically in the religious, as feeling himself "present as a character in a drama the deity is writing."

ual experiences in life. Weighed down by a joyless struggle against what he views as the forces of fate and evil choking the good in the world, Andersen projects into his poetry his own battle against actuality. He thus promulgates the idea that life is not a "process of development" (*Udviklings-Proces*) but a "process of downfall" (*Undergangs-Proces*) of the great and distinguished (EPW, 79). But such a negative standpoint does not qualify, in Kierkegaard's judgment, as a life-view. For a life-view, he contends, is constituted by more than a collection of abstract, neutrally held propositions about experience, and by more than experience itself, which is always fragmentary in character; a life-view involves a "transubstantiation," or inward transformation, of experience so as to gain "an unshakable certainty in oneself," regardless of whether the life-view is oriented in a worldly manner within a purely human context or more deeply within a religious one (EPW, 76). A life-view thus provides a comprehensive center of orientation that enables one to take a firm, positive stance toward life, with a sense of self-confidence in meeting the challenges of life rather than being overcome by them.

Having such a life-view, Kierkegaard maintains, is a *conditio sine qua non* for being a novelist, although admittedly as a comprehensive standpoint it can only be approximated in time. But that does not mean one must wait until the hour of one's death to acquire a life-view. Noting the nulling consequence to which this would lead, Kierkegaard suggests instead that "for the one who does not allow his life to fizzle out too much but seeks as far as possible to lead its single expressions back to himself again, there must necessarily come a moment in which a strange light spreads over life without one's therefore even remotely needing to have understood all possible particulars, to the progressive understanding of which, however, one now has the key" (EPW, 77–78). Paraphrasing the German right-wing Hegelian Carl Daub, Kierkegaard describes this moment as one when "life is understood backwards through the idea," a notion that later reappears in *Philosophical Fragments* (EPW, 78; PF, 80).

Kierkegaard's description of how one acquires a life-view is strikingly similar to J. L. Heiberg's account of how he became converted to Hegelianism, suggesting that Kierkegaard is using Heiberg as a model for how a life-view is acquired, even though he does not subscribe to the particular (Hegelian) life-view Heiberg espouses. In his *Autobiographical Fragments* Heiberg states that he was "seized by a momentary inner vision which, like a flash of lightning, illuminated at once the entire region for me and evoked in me a hitherto concealed central idea. From this instant the entire System in its broad outline became clear to me, and I was fully convinced that I had comprehended its innermost core, no matter how many details there were which I had not yet assimilated."[30] Heiberg goes on in this account to remark about the peace and sense of security this moment brought to him. Although Heiberg's autobiographical work was not published until 1839, a year after *From the Papers of One Still Living,* Kierkegaard would have had occasion to be familiar with Heiberg's account of this experience through personal contacts with him. Whatever its explanation, the similarity between the two descriptions is too close to be accidental. At a later time, when a full-scale attack on Hegelian philosophy is launched in *Concluding Unscientific Postscript,* Kierkegaard subjects this same account of Heiberg's conversion to parody, making Heiberg appear to be a fool (CUP, 1:184–85). But at this stage of his career he is still considerably influenced by Heiberg's aesthetics.

Kierkegaard further clarifies his concept of a life-view over against other standpoints by distinguishing it from the notion of a single, or "fixed," idea (EPW, 79). In his view, the fact that a single fixed idea constantly occurs in a novel does not constitute a life-view. Rather, a life-view is determined by the *content* of the idea, that is, by whether it fosters a certain confidence in life. If the idea is composed of what amounts to a "loss-theory" (*Fortabelens-Theorie*), in which life is envisioned as ending in a final shipwreck for the novel's hero, it does not qualify as a life-view (EPW, 80). Such a loss-theory may result, Kierkegaard suggests, either from "an abortive activity" in working long and unsuccessfully against the world or from an "original passivity" in reflecting one's own suffering in one's view of the world (EPW, 80–81). Manifesting a stereotyped view of gender associations, Kierkegaard labels the first a "broken manliness," the second a "consistent womanliness" (EPW, 81). The second is typical of Andersen's novel, Kierkegaard thinks, in that Andersen does not depict any actual development that might lead to an abortive end but instead leaps from the showing of original great strengths and talents to their losses in his hero. As examples of this passivity, Kierkegaard cites Andersen's metaphorical descriptions of a genius as "an egg that needs warmth for the fertilization of good fortune" and as a pearl in the sea that must wait for the diver to bring it up to the light (EPW, 81n). The notion that genius develops only if it has luck, not on its own, is one that Kierkegaard emphatically rejects and brands as

30. Quoted and translated in Fenger and Marker, *The Heibergs,* 73. See also CUP, 2:224 n. 239, for a partial translation of the passage by the Hongs. For the Danish text, see *Johan Ludvig Heibergs Prosaiske Skrifter* (Copenhagen: C. A. Reitzels Forlag, 1861–62), 11:500.

"superstition" in its ascribing to a single chance occurrence a significance for the whole of life (EPW, 87). In contrast to a loss-theory—whether active or passive, masculine or feminine—which portrays the downfall of a genius or hero, Kierkegaard sees a life-view as the operation of providence or a guiding light that provides an immanent sense of unity and purpose to the novel, enabling it to have its center of gravity (*Tyngdepunktet*) in itself; otherwise, he claims, the work becomes arbitrary and doctrinaire, propounding a theory insufficiently substantiated by experience, or else aimless and subjective, merely portraying accidentals of the author's own life (EPW, 81).[31]

THE MAKING OF AN AUTHENTIC POETIC WRITER

From Kierkegaard's point of view, then, in order for a novelist's life and productivity to stand in a proper relation to each other, the writer needs first and foremost to gain a competent personality by undergoing an epic development, or life-development; it is only such a "transfigured personality," Kierkegaard contends, "who ought to and is able to produce." The fact that so many novels contain "a residue, as it were, of the author's finite character" attests to the difficulty of winning such a personality (EPW, 82). Second, there must be present in the novel a life-view in the form of "an immortal spirit that survives the whole," so that the death of the hero in a novel does not signify the fate of the author as well (EPW, 83). A writer who possesses such an overarching standpoint "is the only one qualified to produce the writing in which a whole development takes place," Kierkegaard claims, for otherwise the perspective of a single age (childhood, youth, adulthood, or old age) becomes the yardstick, and every age is not given its due (EPW, 85).

In the interplay of these two factors—the poet's own life-development and the positive, overarching life-view resulting from it—the poetic production itself, Kierkegaard claims, may be seen as a "second power" that reproduces in a freer fashion that which has already been "poetically experienced" to the "first power" by the author (EPW, 83). A genuine poetic work does not simply reproduce the life experiences of its author, as in the case of Andersen, "whose novels stand in so physical a relation to himself that their genesis is to be regarded more as an

31. On the importance of personal and artistic unity in Kierkegaard's thought, see Connell, *To Be One Thing*.

amputation than as a production from himself," Kierkegaard charges (EPW, 84). Rather, authentic writers of novels must gather through their life-development the necessary fund of experience and understanding that will enable them to form a life-view by which to transcend the vicissitudes of life they have encountered and to transmute that which is cast poetically so as not to identify with the poetic characters or perspective of a particular work. An integral relation between a novelist's life and his or her poetic productivity is needed, then, in order to be an authentic poetic writer and to produce genuine poetry in the form of novels. But it is one that is considerably more complex than Kierkegaard finds in Andersen's life and novels, involving a dialectic of transmuted personal experience and ironic detachment in the creation of a work of art, not merely the wholesale projection of one's personal experiences into a work and identification with its characters and viewpoints.

In *From the Papers of One Still Living* the configurations of Kierkegaard's concept of an authentic poet in the form of a *Romandigter,* or poetic writer of novels, thus begins to take shape. This viewpoint is later amplified in another literary review translated as *Two Ages* (1846), where he advocates silence, or the bracketing of one's own personality, as a condition for expressing ideality, which involves an "equilibrium of opposites," or the ability to experience and reproduce poetically the possibility of one thing as well as its opposite (TA, 98–99). "The more a person has ideality and ideas in silence, the more he will be able even in his daily associations to reproduce his daily life and that of others in such a way that he seems to be speaking only at a distance even about specific matters," Kierkegaard claims (TA, 99). These works thus provide an important clue to how Kierkegaard should be understood, or at least wishes to be understood, as a poetic writer in relation to his own poetic productions.[32] The use of pseudonyms and literary figures to create a sense of aesthetic distance in some of his works does not mean that his own life experiences and viewpoints are not reflected in them, but neither does it mean that the experiences and viewpoints of the pseudonyms and/or literary figures can simply be identified as his own.

32. Biographical approaches to the interpretation of Kierkegaard's authorship such as that of Josiah Thompson, *The Lonely Labyrinth: Kierkegaard's Pseudonymous Works* (Carbondale: Southern Illinois University Press, 1967), and Naomi Lebowitz, *Kierkegaard: A Life of Allegory* (Baton Rouge: Louisiana State University Press, 1985), tend to project Kierkegaard's life into his writings in ways that are inappropriate to his aesthetic theory. On this problem, see the discussion by the Hongs in the historical introduction to FT/R. See also Mark C. Taylor, *Kierkegaard's Pseudonymous Authorship* (Princeton: Princeton University Press, 1975), 27–30, and my review of Lebowitz's book in *International Journal for Philosophy of Religion* 26, no. 1 (1989): 57–58.

What Kierkegaard mainly achieves in this first work is to establish a connection between existential and aesthetic, or poetic, categories and to show how these are properly interrelated and correlated in the life and work of a poetic writer of novels. Although the aesthetic criteria set forth in this work are applied only to novelists, they have a broader application in Kierkegaard's existential aesthetics. As he proceeds to explore the relation between the poetic and the personal life further in his early writings, it becomes clear that in his view every individual, not just the creative writer, needs to undergo a life-development and to acquire a life-view so as to "live poetically" in an authentic manner.

2

Living Poetically

"Well deserving, yet poetically / Man dwells on this earth." These lines from the poem "In Lovely Blue" by the German romantic poet Friedrich Hölderlin (1770–1843) envisage the human mode of existing as fundamentally poetic.[1] We do not know to what extent, if any, Kierkegaard was familiar with Hölderlin's poetry, as it is not mentioned in any of his writings, but Hölderlin's verse beautifully illustrates what Kierkegaard saw as a central theme in romantic poetry. The great demand of romanticism, as Kierkegaard understood it, was that one should "live poetically" (CI, 297). What the romantic poets meant by this comes under close scrutiny and strong criticism by Kierkegaard in his academic dissertation, *The Concept of Irony* (1841). In this work Kierkegaard agrees with the romantic call for a poetic life, but he conceives the nature and conditions of such a life quite differently from the romantics. Woven into the fabric of his critique of romanticism in the dissertation, therefore, is the outline of an alternative design for living poetically. This design provides a background, as it were, against which the romantic pattern of living poetically is highlighted and aesthetically appraised. So interwoven is the presentation of these two patterns in *The Concept of Irony* that Kierkegaard's own design for living poetically is easily over-

1. Friedrich Hölderlin, *Hymns and Fragments,* tr. Richard Sieburth (Princeton: Princeton University Press, 1984), 249. For an interpretative analysis of Hölderlin's poem, see Martin Heidegger, *Poetry, Language, Thought,* tr. Albert Hofstadter (New York: Harper & Row, 1971), 213–29, who uses it as a basis for formulating his own view of poetry and authentic human existence.

looked behind the prominence given to the analysis of romanticism in the work.[2] When this design is brought to the foreground and allowed to stand out in its own right, however, it becomes apparent that Kierkegaard has sketched in his dissertation the basic pattern for a poetic mode of living that incorporates and integrates ethical-religious dimensions with the aesthetic in a unified process of becoming. Moreover, the ethical-religious, or Christian, life (ethical, religious, and Christian forms of existence are relatively undifferentiated in this early work) itself is defined and understood in aesthetic terms.

The basic elements of this alternative design are prefigured in *From the Papers of One Still Living,* whose aesthetic criteria are taken over and applied within a more developed—though still lightly contoured—aesthetic framework in *The Concept of Irony.* Subsequently, in *Either/Or,* the lines of this pattern are etched in greater detail and concretely illustrated in volume 2 of that work, in contrast to the romantic mode of living poetically, which is again presented and more extensively characterized in volume 1. The notion of living poetically thus constitutes a major theme in Kierkegaard's early writings and serves as the basic idea upon which his own view of the poetic is initially shaped and developed.

2. Although Kierkegaard's critique of romanticism in *The Concept of Irony* has been widely recognized and studied, his formulation, in this work, of an aesthetic-ethical-religious alternative to a romantic mode of living poetically has not been generally noted or emphasized. More sensitive than most to the close connection between the aesthetic and religious dimensions of Kierkegaard's thought, Richard Summers, in "A Study of Kierkegaard's Philosophical Development up to *Om Begrebet Ironi,*" suggests that Kierkegaard incorporates the romantic ideal of living poetically into a religious view of life, which enables him to express a Christian conception of humanity in terms of romantic aesthetics (220). On the contrary, I show that Kierkegaard clearly rejects the romantic conception of living poetically in favor of a Christian aesthetics that is fundamentally different from that of the romantics. David Gouwens, in *Kierkegaard's Dialectic of the Imagination,* also interprets *The Concept of Irony* as presenting religion as an alternative to romanticism, but he does not discern the way in which the religious itself is construed in this work in aesthetic terms and is seen as constituting an authentic mode of living poetically (see 72–73). In line with the present study, Rune Engebretsen, in "Kierkegaard and Poet-Existence with Special Reference to Germany and Rilke," perceives that Kierkegaard sets forth a concept of living poetically in contrast to romantic aesthetics, but he does not elaborate this insight beyond a brief comparison with Judge William in *Either/Or,* nor does he discern the religious context within which it is understood (135–36). Likewise, Merete Jørgensen, in *Kierkegaard som Kritiker,* makes reference to the notion of living poetically as forming part of Kierkegaard's "ethical criticism," but she does not treat the concept in any systematic fashion in her discussion of *The Concept of Irony* or her discussion of his ethical criticism in general (see 103, 143–50). Although George Pattison, in "Kierkegaard's Theory and Critique of Art," offers the most extensive treatment of Kierkegaard's philosophy of art to date, he too misses the religious context within which Kierkegaard's aesthetics is developed in contrast to romanticism, and interprets Kierkegaard's view of art in a Hegelian fashion as one in which the poetic is transcended by the religious (see 130–31, 135, 186).

To understand this phase of his aesthetics, therefore, we need to inspect not only the romantic pattern of living poetically that he rejects but also the alternative ethical-religious pattern that he advocates for fashioning an authentic poetic form of life.

ROMANTICISM AND POETRY

In formulating his critique of romanticism in *The Concept of Irony,* Kierkegaard builds upon the understanding of romanticism and poetry he had acquired during his university years and upon his analysis of Socratic irony he had undertaken in the first part of the dissertation. Like a number of his contemporaries, the young Kierkegaard initially went through a romantic phase. In several early journal entries he shows an inclination toward romanticism over classicism and even regards Christianity as having a romantic character.[3] Under the influence of the antiromantic realist school of literature, however, he soon developed a critical posture toward romanticism and by the time of his dissertation had clearly distinguished his own position from it. The journals of these years indicate that Kierkegaard was particularly interested in gaining a clear conception of the romantic. From his reading of Christian Molbech's lectures on modern Danish poetry, he learns that the fundamental condition for the romantic lies in an infinite, unhampered freedom of the imagination, the use of intuition in grasping the ideal, a fullness and depth of feeling, and the orientation of reflection toward the ideal (JP, 5:5135). In passages copied from Molbech, Kierkegaard notes that the romantic is associated with "the eternal yearning, the wistful, the infinite and unfulfilled bliss in feeling, the presentient and supraterrestial in imagination," and with "the mystical and the profound in thought, which silmultaneously seeks to be identified with feeling and imagination." As Molbech sees it, the romantic forms a bridge between the world of phenomena and the eternal, infinite, divine, or supernatural reality, which can never be fully drawn into the world or bound by the arts or any other finite form. Molbech thus accepts Jean Paul's aesthetic definition of the romantic as "the beautiful without boundaries or the beautiful

3. See especially JP, 1:422, 699, 852; 3:2304, 3805, 3809, 3811, 3818; 5:5131. For other treatments of Kierkegaard's early journal entries on romanticism, see Malantschuk, *Kierkegaard's Thought,* 48–58; Gouwens, *Kierkegaard's Dialectic of the Imagination,* 47–53; and Pattison, *Kierkegaard: The Aesthetic and the Religious,* 43–56.

infinite," as well as his description of romantic poetry as "the poetry of presentiment" (JP, 5:5135).

Appropriating these characterizations of the romantic, Kierkegaard in his journals concludes that the romantic cannot be "captured in a definition." In agreement with Jean Paul he thinks that "the romantic lies essentially in flowing over all boundaries" (JP, 3:3796). He thus resorts to various similes to describe it: like the great African desert or the Jutland heath, the romantic lacks a relative standard by which things can be measured (JP, 3:3797); like an allegory, it is "a continual grasping after something which eludes one" and in its more sentimental form is "a longing gazing into an eternity" (JP, 3:3816, 3802); like a seesaw, it is dialectical, an "infinite wrestling" or "constant pendulum movement" between positions that lack any continuance by themselves (JP, 1:755; 2:1565, 1688). Kierkegaard thus associates the romantic with dreaming, possibility, and restlessness (JP, 3:3798, 3801, 3806). The emphasis of the Middle Ages upon wandering about, typified by the figure of the Wandering Jew, exemplifies, he thinks, this restless quality of the romantic (JP, 2:1183; 3:3814). Although multiplicity is also associated with romanticism, Kierkegaard maintains that romanticism does not consist in variety or multiplicity but is that which *evokes* variety through a perpetually unsatisfied need (JP, 3:3803, 3819; 4:4063, 4398). Unlike classicism, which has no ideal, or else one that is wholly attainable in actuality, romanticism has an infinite idea or ideal to strive for; in that consists the romantic quality of Christianity, which in Kierkegaard's view presents an ideal "so great that all others disappear alongside it" (JP, 1:422, 852). Classicism, by contrast, is mythological inasmuch as it reflects a "human weakness which can never grasp a concept in all its infinite evanescence but always must stake it off by using boundaries" (JP, 3:3815). For all its striving, however, Kierkegaard concludes that romanticism finally resolves itself into classicism, for romantic striving is self-consuming and cannot be rendered eternal; even if it could, its eternity would consist of nothing more than an abstract, "infinite aggregate of moments" (JP, 3:3815, 3805).

In his early journals Kierkegaard also begins to formulate a conception of poetry, which he associates at this stage with the representation of an idea or ideal as a possibility. As he sees it, the content of poetry may be distinguished from that which is actual as well as that which is represented imaginatively under the categories of actuality, that is, mythology:

> Mythology is the compacting (suppressed being) of the idea of eternity (the eternal idea) in the categories of time and space—

> in time, for example, Chiliasm, or the doctrine of a kingdom of heaven which begins in time; in space, for example, an idea construed as being a finite personality. Just as the poetic is the subjunctive but does not claim to be more (poetic actuality), mythology, on the other hand, is a hypothetical statement in the indicative—and lies in the very middle of the conflict between them, because the ideal, losing its gravity, is compacted in earthly form. (JP, 3:2799)

Elucidating the linguistic designations used above, Kierkegaard explains in another passage that "the indicative thinks something as actuality (the identity of thinking and actuality)" whereas "the subjunctive thinks something as thinkable" (JP, 3:2310).

In associating the poetic with the subjunctive, or possibility, Kierkegaard contrues poetry in terms of romantic poetry, which he specifically associates with possibility and the representation of ideality. Fundamentally, however, he is following here the tradition of Aristotle, who in his *Poetics* says that "the poet's function is to describe, not the thing that has happened, but a kind of thing that might happen, i.e., what is possible as being probable or necessary" (chap. 9, 1451a, 36–38). Aristotle distinguishes the poet from the historian, not on the basis of what literary form—that is, verse or prose—each one typically employs, but by the fact that the latter describes actuality, what has been, rather than possibility, what might be, as the former does (chap. 9, 1451b, 1–5). In Aristotle's opinion, poetry is "more philosophic and of graver import than history" because its statements are universal, that is, they refer to types of persons and probable or necessary utterances and actions, rather than to the deeds or statements of a specific individual (chap. 9, 1451b, 5–11).

The relation of poetry to actuality is an issue Kierkegaard also reflects upon in his early journals. Noting an observation in Apollonius of Tyana's *Life of Philostratus* concerning Aristotle's view of poetry, he writes, " 'All poetry is imitation' (Aristotle)—'better or worse than we are.' Hence poetry points beyond itself to actuality and to the metaphysical ideality" (JP, 1:144). Poetry thus may direct itself toward actuality as well as toward the ideal, but in doing so it inevitably enacts a change of the actuality being represented: "All poetry is a glorification (i.e., transfiguration [*Forklarelse*]) of life by way of its clarification [*Forklarelse*] (in that it is explained, illuminated, developed, etc.). It is truly remarkable that language has this double ambiguity [*Tvetydethed*]" (JP, 1:136; cf. 2:1629). Through a play on the double meaning of the Danish word

Forklarelse, Kierkegaard is seeking here to make the point that in attempting to explain or illumine life, poetry transfigures it, that is, makes it more glorious or more perfect than it really is. Thus poetry, it seems, cannot give a true picture of actuality but always construes it under the conditions of ideality. Maintaining that this is so not only in poetry but also with respect to language generally, Kierkegaard declares, "I cannot express reality in language, because I use ideality to characterize it, which is a contradiction, an untruth" (JP, 3:2320).

In the early journals, then, Kierkegaard perceives a broad chasm between the finite world and the infinite, the actual and the ideal, as well as between actuality and poetic representations of it. In line with Molbech, he views poetry as a bridge between the finite and the infinite, maintaining that "the poetic is the divine woof of the purely human existence; it is the cord through which the divine holds fast to existence." Exploiting this image further, Kierkegaard describes poets as "living telegraph wires between God and men" (JP, 1:1027). Romantic poetry in particular strives nobly but unsuccessfully, he thinks, to bridge the gap between the finite and the infinite by breaking through the boundaries between them. By its ideal character, however, poetry creates another gap between itself and actuality. This leads Kierkegaard to pose the following question: "To what extent are poetry and art reconcilable with life—something is true in esthetics—something else in ethics?" (JP, 1:808). Philosophically he is posing here the question of a double truth, one at the level of ideality (poetic actuality), another in actuality, and asking whether these can be brought to agree with one another in life. Is there a form of poetry that can give a true representation of actuality? Or to put it another way, is there a form of life that can give actual expression to the poetic ideal? Must we conclude that a qualitatively different dialectic obtains in ethics than in aesthetics, making them incompatible expressions of human life? By the time the passage quoted above was written (1842–43), Kierkegaard had already effectively answered the question posed in it. For he had already worked out in his writings the rudiments of an aesthetics (or, if you will, an ethics) that reconciles poetry and life through the notion of living poetically in an ethical-religious—or, more specifically, a Christian—mode of life.[4] In that, as we shall see, he moves beyond both the Aristotelian and romantic conceptions of poetry, which

4. In a note to the text of the older English version of *The Concept of Irony* (London: Collins, 1966), the translator, Lee Capel, suggests that in this work "Kierkegaard is attempting to translate his aesthetic into an ethic" (421 n. 19). Perhaps a more accurate description, however, is to say that he is attempting to construct an ethical-religious, or Christian, aesthetics as suggested in note 2 above.

in his view do not offer a true reconciliation of the poetic ideal with actuality.

SOCRATIC AND ROMANTIC IRONY

Kierkegaard's chief dissatisfaction with romanticism has to do with the way that movement relates itself to actuality. In *From the Papers of One Still Living* this same dissatisfaction is expressed with respect to the whole of the newer developments of his time, of which romanticism is a part. When Kierkegaard returns to the subject of romanticism in *The Concept of Irony,* his characterization and critique of it are framed around this same issue. The problem, as he sees it, does not lie so much in the inability of romantic poetry to represent actuality accurately (for that, in his view, is a limitation of poetry in general) as in the stance it takes *toward* actuality. According to Kierkegaard, the romantic poet is essentially an ironist who maintains a negative standpoint toward existence. Following Hegel's interpretation of modern irony, Kierkegaard defines irony as the expression of an "infinite, absolute negativity" (CI, 26, 254, 261, 271). Romantic irony has its basis in the irony of Socrates, in whom the concept of irony had its inception. Like the witch who devours everything in sight, even her own stomach, Socrates' irony, he claims, had a purely negative result, nullifying "life, development—in short, history in its most universal and widest sense" (CI, 56, 60). Through irony Socrates was able to emancipate himself as an individual from the state, or established order (*det Bestaaende*), of his time. The introduction of irony thus marked the beginning of subjectivity, or consciousness of oneself as an individual in distinction from family and state.

Although Kierkegaard goes to great lengths in his dissertation to show that Socrates lacked any positive content in his thought, he does admit that in this respect Socrates was positive. Even so, he argues, Socrates' subjectivity was, as a mere beginning, still negative and egoistically turned in on itself, lacking the richness and fullness of a subjectivity that incorporates objectivity and a positive relation to the eternal (CI, 169, 211). Socrates was aware of the idea of the eternal only negatively, that is, as a limit to the finite realm. As Kierkegaard puts it, "He knew that it was, but he did not know what it was" (CI, 169). The positivity of the eternal was dimly intimated by his negation of the temporal, but it remained undefined and elusive, never receiving determinate form or becoming concrete in his own existence (CI, 170).

Socrates' ironic position was most graphically portrayed, Kierkegaard thinks, by the Greek dramatist Aristophanes, who in his play *Clouds* situates Socrates in the "Thoughtery" in a suspended basket, hovering, as it were, "like the coffin of Mohammed between two magnets": heaven (ideality) and empirical actuality (CI, 48, 152). Having freed himself from the latter through irony, Socrates only glimpsed the former in the form of possibility.

Kierkegaard points out that there are actually two kinds of irony and, corresponding to them, two kinds of dialectic in the Platonic dialogues of Socrates (CI, 87, 121). The first is the negative, emancipating irony of Socrates described above. This form is found primarily in the early dialogues. The second is a speculative, abstract standpoint that he thinks belongs to Plato rather than to Socrates. Whereas the first standpoint is that of an ego that continually swallows the world and goes beyond actuality by negating the validity of experience, the other seeks to assimilate the world and construct actuality on the basis of certain positive yet abstract ideas that lie beyond the world (CI, 124). In Plato, therefore, the ideality that Socrates was unable to grasp is given a more positive, albeit still abstract, determination in speculative thought. Already in the early dialogues that ideality is dreamingly produced by the imagination, in the form of myth, as an unconscious poetic reaction on Plato's part to Socrates' "hungry dialectic." The mythical element in the Socratic dialogues thus belongs to Plato rather than to Socrates, Kierkegaard thinks, though there is a certain correspondence between the mythical and Socratic dialectic: "If one may characterize the dialectic corresponding to the mythical as longing and desire, as a glance which gazes upon the idea so as to desire it, then the mythical is the fruitful embrace of the idea" (CI, 103; cf. 121). Although the mythical is poetically produced by the imagination of Plato and in that sense is poetical, it is not a free creation of his but comes rather from "a presentiment of something higher" that "overwhelms" him (CI, 98). But since myth is not a conscious product of the imagination and represents ideality "in the indicative," that is, as an actuality rather than as an ideality or possibility, it is in another sense nonpoetical. Kierkegaard repeats here the distinction drawn earlier in his journals between myth and poetry, namely, that "the poetic is a hypothetical statement in the subjunctive mood; the mythical is a hypothetical statement in the indicative mood" (CI, 101). In contrast to the mythical, which represents the ideal under the conditions of actuality unconsciously, the poetic is fully conscious that it is dealing with ideality and is not concerned with anything other than an ideal actuality. When the mythical is taken up into consciousness, as it is in Plato's later dialogues, it is transformed into an image or reflection of the idea and is no longer identified with the idea itself. Both consciously and unconsciously, then, Plato fills the void left by Socrates' negativity, but in doing so he makes irony into an instrument in service of the idea, no longer an end in itself.

Irony in the form of infinite, absolute negativity reappears in romantic irony, which in Kierkegaard's view is even more thoroughgoing in its rejection of historical actuality than is Socratic irony. Whereas Socrates negated only the given actuality or established order of his time, not actuality as such, Kierkegaard interprets the romantic ironists as finding the whole of existence to be inadequate, meaningless, and boring. Thus they seek to free themselves from the historical and to set in its place a self-created actuality springing from the imagination. Influenced by Fichte's theory of the self-constituting ego, they acknowledge nothing higher than themselves and assume absolute power, Kierkegaard claims, "to bind and to unbind," to let stand and to destroy (CI, 276). Free from cares and responsibilities, making no commitments, and admitting no claims upon themselves, they abandon themselves to reckless play (CI, 279).

It is in this manner that the romantic ironists may be said to be "living poetically." Essentially, Kierkegaard charges, they attempt to create themselves by imaginatively playing or experimenting with various poetic possibilities in life. Only when one is radically free in this manner can one be said to live poetically from a romantic point of view. For only when one is able to create oneself, to become whatever one wills—even, if one so wills, to become nothing at all—does one possess the poetic license necessary to make one's life, like one's poetic productions, a work of art. Life for the romantic ironist thus takes the form of a drama in which the poet plays a variety of roles. Like a child reciting "rich man, poor man, beggar man," the romantic poet runs through a multiplicity of possibilities, poetically trying out and living through in an experimental fashion whatever poetic personage he or she chooses to be. "For the ironist, everything is possible," Kierkegaard observes (CI, 282). But because the romantic ironists flit from possibility to possibility, living, in his opnion, in a "totally hypothetical and subjunctive way," their lives lose continuity and lapse under the sway of moods and feelings that are themselves subject to sudden and drastic change (CI, 284). While being actors, they are at the same time spectators who stand aloof from the world and cloak their feelings ironically in opposite form—

grief in jest, joy in lament (CI, 285). In an attempt to produce their environment as well as themselves, they suspend the ethical mores of society and thus come into collision with it (CI, 283–84).

Of the foremost representatives of romantic irony, Kierkegaard focuses on three in early nineteenth-century Germany: Friedrich Schlegel, Ludwig Tieck, and K.W.F. Solger. In their aesthetic productions, if not also in their lives, Kierkegaard thinks these men portray the romantic attitude toward actuality and its ideal of living poetically. In a direct attack against actuality, Schlegel's celebrated novel *Lucinde* seeks quite consciously and arbitrarily, Kierkegaard charges, to destroy the established ethic and to negate spirituality in favor of a "naked sensuality" that revels in the enjoyment of the flesh (CI, 289, 291). Julius, the main character of the novel, lives in a confused state of mind in which "fantasy alone" prevails, Kierkegaard claims (CI, 292n). In a passage of the novel that supports Kierkegaard's contention that the romantic poets seek to live as well as to produce poetically, Schlegel writes of Julius, "Just as his artistic ability developed and he was able to achieve with ease what he had been unable to accomplish with all his powers of exertion and hard work before, *so too his life now came to be a work of art for him,* imperceptibly, without his knowing how it happened. A light entered his soul: he saw and surveyed all the parts of his life and the structure of the whole clearly and truly because he stood at its center" (emphasis added).[5] Of Julius's wife Lucinde, Schlegel writes that she "had a decided bent for the romantic" and "belonged to that part of mankind that doesn't inhabit the ordinary world but rather a world that it conceives and creates for itself." Describing her in more detail, he continues, "Only whatever she loved and respected in her heart had any true reality for her; everything else was spurious: and she knew what was valuable. Also she had renounced all ties and social rules daringly and decisively and lived a completely free and independent life."[6] In Lisette, a woman who initiates Julius into the nocturnal mysteries of love, Schlegel sets forth as poetic the enjoyment of a life of indolence; indeed, Kierkegaard claims

5. *Friedrich Schlegel's Lucinde and the Fragments,* tr. Peter Firchow (Minneapolis: University of Minnesota Press, 1971), 102. It is interesting that the second sentence quoted here from *Lucinde* bears a close resemblance to Kierkegaard's description, in *From the Papers of One Still Living,* of how one acquires a life-view as well as to Heiberg's account of his conversion to Hegelianism (see Chapter 1). Thus it could be that Schlegel's novel is the original inspiration of their accounts, though each, of course, understands the meaning of enlightenment differently from Schlegel, who makes the self-centered artist, rather than the speculative idea (Heiberg) or a personal life-view (Kierkegaard), the interpretative standpoint for understanding existence.

6. Ibid., 98. Cf. CI, 290–91.

that "it is this collapsing into an esthetic stupefaction that actually comes out in the whole of *Lucinde* as a sign of what it is to live poetically" (CI, 294–96). As evidence for this claim, he points to a section of the novel called "An Idyll of Idleness," which celebrates passivity, in the form of pure vegetation, as the "highest, most perfect life."[7] Schlegel's view of the poetic life as set forth in *Lucinde* is thus one that Kierkegaard brands with the scathing epithets "obscene," "immoral," "irreligious," and finally even "unpoetical" (the ultimate insult to a romantic poet) because it is irreligious (CI, 286, 296, 297).[8] In Kierkegaard's view, the truly poetic is not antithetical to the religious but, quite the contrary, receives authentic expression in it.

In the satirical dramas and lyrical poetry of Tieck, Kierkegaard finds that existence becomes merely a game for a poetic arbitrariness and abandonment that is so indifferent toward actuality that it neither rejects anything nor retains anything (CI, 302). In the poetic world that the characters of his works inhabit, all sorts of unheard of and improbable things happen: "Animals talk like human beings, human beings talk like asses, chairs and tables become conscious of their meaning in existence, human beings find existence meaningless. Nothing becomes everything, and everything becomes nothing; everything is possible, even the impossible; everything is probable, even the improbable" (CI, 318). Kierkegaard recognizes as beneficial the attempt by Tieck and the whole romantic movement to rejuvenate the social situation then current, which had become "fossilized" and "philistine" in its customs and conventions. In his view, however, this resulted in the substitution of a somnambulant, dreamlike childishness that does not grasp actuality or give it any truer expression but instead takes flight into an ideal actuality or fantasy world of the romantic poets' own construction (CI, 303–4). In line with his earlier description of romanticism as dialectical, Kierkegaard thus charges that the poetry of Tieck and his romantic cohorts vacillates between the opposite poles of the philistine given actuality, which it caricatures, and an ideal actuality, which is not truly poetic, because it does not represent the true ideal but merely the eccentric and bizarre or that which is "interesting" (CI, 305–6).[9] Ever

7. Ibid., 66. See also CI, 295–96.

8. It should be noted, however, that Schlegel considered *Lucinde* to be religious inasmuch as it sets forth a religion of love combining the sensuous and the spiritual. On this point, see the introduction to the translation by Peter Firchow, 3–39.

9. On the category of the interesting as a principle of romantic aesthetics, see Friedrich Schlegel, *Über das Studium der Griechischen Poesie, 1795–97,* ed. Ernst Behler (Paderborn: Ferdinand Schöningh, 1982). See also the discussion of this category in Robert L. Perkins,

in search of a more interesting poetic mood to exploit, Tieck's contentless lyricism thus vanishes like music into nothingness (CI, 306).

Employing a contemplative form of irony, Solger's aesthetic essays give poetic-philosophic expression to this romantic vision of the ultimate nothingness of all things. Describing Solger as "the metaphysical knight of the negative," Kierkegaard qualifies his characterization by pointing out that Solger "does not come into collision with actuality in the sense that the other ironists do, since his irony did not in any way take the shape of opposition to actuality" (CI, 309). Nevertheless, for Solger, the finite is viewed as the *Nichtige,* or that which must be destroyed, and the positive ideal that is envisioned for the future always turns out to be a new negation, in the manner of Hegel's notion of a "double negation," which presumably renders the finite infinite and the infinite finite (CI, 310). Through negation, therefore, Solger seeks to bring about an absolute identity of the finite and the infinite and to do away with the boundary between them (CI, 311). Kierkegaard maintains, however, that Solger is unable to render the infinite concrete in such a manner as to give validity to the finite. For in Solger's aesthetics every actuality is but an approximation of an ideal or higher actuality that is envisaged in art and poetry "only in the infinite approximation of intimation" (CI, 319). Thus true actuality is never manifested in these art forms but is constantly in the process of becoming.

As Kierkegaard sees them, therefore, the romantic poets are engaged in an ideal striving that has no ideal, for "every ideal is instantly nothing but an allegory hiding a higher ideal within itself, and so on into infinity" (CI, 306). Thus there is no final goal or repose, no poetic unity or totality, in the romantic poet's life and work. Inasmuch as poetry, romantically conceived, constitutes a victory over the world by opening up the possibility of a higher and more perfect actuality for the individual, Kierkegaard admits that it offers "a kind of reconciliation" with actuality, but not a true one, because it fails to reconcile us to the actuality in which we live (CI, 297). Instead, the imperfect actuality is negated and transfigured into an ideal actuality created by the imagination. In the end, therefore, the actuality the poet would posit is no actuality at all but merely a dream in which the poet, reminiscent of Socrates, vacillates

"Abraham's Silence Aesthetically Considered," in *Kierkegaard on Art and Communication,* ed. George Pattison (New York: St. Martin's Press, 1992), 100–113. Perkins rightly points out that romantic art emphasizes "the personal, the characteristic, the individuating rather than the universal," which leads to an association of the interesting with the eccentric and bizarre (108).

between actuality and ideality, negating the one and ever newly envisioning the other.

In fundamental outline and content, the characterization and critique of romanticism in *The Concept of Irony* appears to be based directly on Hegel's remarks about irony in the introduction to his *Aesthetics.*[10] Although no indebtedness to Hegel as the source of his account is expressly stated by Kierkegaard, it is clear that he had read Hegel's treatments of both Socratic and romantic irony, and he even criticizes Hegel on various points. In his comments on romantic irony, Hegel, like Kierkegaard, locates the roots of romantic irony in Fichte's philosophy, and the same three figures—Schlegel, Tieck, and Solger—are briefly discussed by him. Even though Kierkegaard's analysis of these figures is quite limited, especially in comparison with the extensive treatment of Socrates in the dissertation, it is considerably more developed than Hegel's. Kierkegaard's analysis concurs with Hegel's description of the ironic creative artist as "disengaged," "free from everything," "not bound," and "just as able to destroy . . . as to create" anything. It also reflects Hegel's view of the negativity of romantic irony as declaring "the vanity of everything factual, moral, and of intrinsic worth."[11] Most important, Kierkegaard's account parallels Hegel's in describing romantic irony as requiring the poet to live poetically, or artistically. In discussing the connection of Fichte's philosophy to irony, Hegel makes the following statement about romantic irony:

> The ego is a *living,* active individual, and its life consists in making its individuality real in its own eyes and in those of others, in expressing itself, and bringing itself into appearance. For every man, by living, tries to realize himself. Now in relation to beauty and art, this acquires the meaning of living as an artist and forming one's life *artistically* [*Kunstlerisch*]. But on this principle, I live as an artist when all my action and my expression in general, in connection with any content whatever, remains for me a mere show and assumes a shape which is wholly in my power. In that case I am not really in *earnest* either with this content or, generally, with its expression and actualization. For genuine earnestness enters only by means of a substantial interest, something of intrinsic worth like truth, ethical life, etc.,—by means of a content which counts as such for me as essential, so that I only

10. Hegel, *Aesthetics,* 1:64–69.

11. Ibid., 66.

> become essential myself in my own eyes in so far as I have immersed myself in such a content and have brought myself into conformity with it in all my knowing and acting. When the *ego* that sets up and dissolves everything out of its own caprice is the artist, to whom no content of consciousness appears as absolute and independently real but only as a self-made and destructible show, such earnestness can find no place, since validity is ascribed only to the formalism of the *ego.*[12]

Hegel goes on to point out that irony "has not stopped at giving artistic form to the personal life and particular individuality of the ironical artist; apart from the artistic work presented in his own actions, etc., the artist was supposed to produce external works of art also as the product of his imagination."[13] As Hegel sees it, then, romantic irony requires both poetic living and poetic productivity on the part of the artist.

These passages quoted from Hegel illustrate the influence Hegel seems to have had on Kierkegaard in regard to his critique of the romantic notion of living poetically. But more than that, the first passage, with its emphasis upon showing "earnestness," or seriousness, toward the content of life, seems also to have provided the germinal idea for the alternative mode of living poetically that Kierkegaard sketches in *The Concept of Irony.*[14] To see how Kierkegaard develops and gives positive content to Hegel's notion, let us look finally at Kierkegaard's own design for living poetically in an authentic fashion.

LIVING POETICALLY IN A RELIGIOUS MANNER

Over against what is perceived as reckless playfulness and caprice on the part of the romantic ironists in relation to historical actuality and the content of their personal lives, Kierkegaard advocates in *The Concept of*

12. Ibid., 65.

13. Ibid., 67.

14. Sylviane Agacinski, in *Aparté,* suggests that as a written document published apart from its original context and situation as a dissertation, *The Concept of Irony* may be read as an ironic work that lacks earnestness and thus is ironic in its seeming agreement with Hegel's call for earnestness with respect to the content of the personal life (see 65–68, 74–77). But as pointed out in my discussion of postmodern hermeneutics in the Prologue, this would make Kierkegaard an advocate of the very romantic irony he seeks to criticize in this work, thus undermining the point and coherence of the work.

Irony a religious mode of living poetically based upon the exercise of "artistic earnestness" and a regard for the basic human worth and originally given nature of the individual as affirmed in Christianity (CI, 280). Presupposing an ultimate purpose, or *telos,* for personal existence in contrast to the aimless striving of romanticism, he contends that the absolute purpose of personality is to become for itself (*für sich*) what it is in itself (*an sich*) and, in and through the realization of that purpose, to enjoy itself in life (CI, 281).[15] There is, then, a given content or particular character that defines personality and that constitutes the goal for human becoming in life. As Kierkegaard sees it, human existence is not merely a process of becoming or simply a matter of becoming whatever we happen by chance or will to become, as in the case of the romantic ironists; rather, it is a process of becoming something in particular—namely, ourselves, that which we are originally defined as being and are intended to become.

Within this perspective the task of the individual, as Kierkegaard sees it, is not "to compose oneself poetically" (*at digte sig selv*), as the romantic poets did, but rather "to be poetically composed" (*at lade sig digte*) through a cultivation of what is unique and originally given in oneself (CI, 280). Identifying the latter as a Christian mode of living poetically, Kierkegaard asserts that "the Christian lets himself be poetically composed, and in this respect a simple Christian lives far more poetically than many a brilliant intellectual" (CI, 280–81). From a Christian standpoint we are not totally free, as the romanticists think, to make ourselves into anything we wish. Instead we must become, as it were, "accomplices" of God, lending assistance in a synergistic fashion to perfecting the "seeds," or potentialities, implanted in us by the Creator (CI, 280, 313 and accompanying note).[16] These God-given traits constitute the limit within which poetic freedom and artistic productivity are to be exercised in relation to the personal life.

For Kierkegaard, then, living poetically is a matter not of self-creation but of self-development in accordance with one's given nature. In line

15. The terms "in itself" (*an sich*) and "for itself" (*für sich*) are taken over from Hegel, who associates the former with potentiality, or possibility, and the latter with actuality, or the concrete realization of potentiality through a process of development. For a good introductory explanation of these categories, see *Hegel's Introduction to the Lectures on the History of Philosophy,* trans. T. M. Knox and A. V. Miller (Oxford: Clarendon Press, 1985), 71–86.

16. Kierkegaard's synergism has also been noted by Louis Pojman in *The Logic of Subjectivity* (University: University of Alabama Press, 1984), 11, where he quotes a supporting passage from Kierkegaard's early journals (JP, 1:29). It is interesting that Hegel also uses the metaphor of the "seed" in describing the process of self-development in existence. See *Hegel's Introduction to the Lectures on the History of Philosophy,* 72–73, 77–79.

with his earlier emphasis, in *From the Papers of One Still Living,* on the importance of undergoing a life-development in order to become an authentic poet, he further stresses in the dissertation that this development must be carried out in accordance with the poet's given nature and within the context of a specific historical setting to which the poet must accommodate him- or herself (CI, 283). We are not merely products of our environment, Kierkegaard contends, but neither are we completely independent of it, as the romantic ironists think. Expressing strong appreciation for Hegel's conception of history, which transcends the past in thought but does not reject it, Kierkegaard maintains that the past is subject to being outlived and displaced by a truer actuality, but it will not be "overlooked or ignored" (CI, 277). In a play on words to indicate the dual manner in which a subject is related to historical actuality, Kierkegaard states that actuality must be regarded "partly as a gift (*en Gave*) that refuses to be rejected, partly as a task (*en Opgave*) that wants to be fulfilled" (CI, 276). Every moment thus has a relative validity in shaping the life of an individual.

Kierkegaard asserts that a true reconciliation with actuality, in contrast with the rejection and transfiguration of actuality by romantic poetry, first comes about through a "transubstantiation" of the given actuality by the religious (CI, 297). The use of the term "transubstantiation" is significant here inasmuch as it suggests, from its traditional religious connotation, an inward change that takes place in the substance of an actuality that outwardly remains the same. This term is also used in *From the Papers of One Still Living* to describe the qualification of experience brought about by the acquisition of a life-view (EPW, 76). In *The Concept of Irony* the transubstantiation that the religious effects in the actuality of an individual is characterized as one that renders it "inwardly infinite" (CI, 297). By this, Kierkegaard means that the religious relates one to the infinite or ideal as a potentiality within one's given actuality. Romantic poetry, by contrast, relates one to an "external infinity" beyond or outside oneself. But the true ideal, Kierkegaard claims, is not in any way beyond; rather, "it is behind us insofar as it is the propelling force; it is ahead insofar as it is the inspiring goal, but at the same time it is within us, and this is its truth" (CI, 305). In his view, only inward infinity is truly infinite and truly poetic (CI, 289). As such it constitutes the absolute condition for living poetically. Kierkegaard agrees with the romantics that to live poetically is to live infinitely in poetic enjoyment, but only when one has one's enjoyment in oneself rather than outside oneself is that enjoyment truly infinite. For in enjoying that which is outside oneself, even if it were the whole world, one still lacks the enjoyment of oneself. "To enjoy oneself," Kierkegaard proclaims, "is the only true infinity" (CI, 297). He carefully adds parenthetically, however, that he is speaking here of self-enjoyment in a religious sense, not in a Stoic or egotistical sense. As an example of what he has in mind, Kierkegaard contrasts indulging in revenge like a pagan god, which provides merely an egotistical and external self-enjoyment, to the inward mastering of anger by the simplest human being. Only the latter, he claims, experiences true self-enjoyment, possesses inward infinity, and really lives poetically. The highest enjoyment and true happiness in life comes when one no longer merely dreams but possesses oneself in infinite clarity or absolute transparency. That is what it means truly to live poetically: "Living poetically is not the same thing as being in the dark about oneself, as sweating oneself out in loathsome sultriness, but it means becoming clear and transparent to oneself, not in finite and egotistical self-satisfaction but in one's absolute and eternal validity" (CI, 298).

In Kierkegaard's view, living poetically in such a manner is a possibility only for the religious individual, who possesses an inward infinity by virtue of his or her relation to the eternal as a potentiality within (CI, 298). But the poet—indeed, every individual—also has a responsibility to live poetically in this way. Reiterating a key point made earlier in *From the Papers of One Still Living,* Kierkegaard contends in the conclusion to *The Concept of Irony* that the poet in particular must have gained clarity of insight so as to obtain a total view of the world (*Totalt-Anskuelse*), or life-view, which enables the poet to transcend the point of view of a particular poetic production (CI, 325). The poetic production thus stands in an internal, rather than external, relation to the poet inasmuch as it is seen as constituting an element in the poet's own personal development. In this way the poet-life of the poet is made to correspond with the actuality of the poet, and irony itself is mastered, becoming in the manner of Platonic irony "a serving spirit," rather than the existential standpoint, of the poet (CI, 325).[17]

As examples of poets who have succeeded in mastering irony in their poetry, Kierkegaard cites J. L. Heiberg, Shakespeare, and especially

17. The new Hong translation of *The Concept of Irony* renders the Danish *behersket Moment* as "controlled element" rather than "mastered moment," as it was translated in the older Capel version, although in some instances the Hongs continue to speak of irony as being mastered. While the new Hong rendition is technically correct, it lacks the alliteration and flair of the established translation as well as the intended allusion to Hegelian dialectic. On this issue, see especially Stephen Dunning, *Kierkegaard's Dialectic of Inwardness,* 27–30, and nn. 1 and 23 to the chapter on *The Concept of Irony.*

Goethe, who, ironically, was lauded as a model poet by the romanticists as well.[18] For Heiberg and Goethe, Kierkegaard claims, phenomenon and essence, actuality and possibility, are identical inasmuch as in their poetic works irony is reduced to an element, or serving spirit, within the whole (CI, 325). In his life as well as in his poetic vision Goethe in particular is seen as having achieved the reconciliation with actuality that Kierkegaard envisions for the authentic poet.[19] Essentially this reconciliation is understood as one in which the poet is positively oriented and integrated in the age to which he or she belongs (CI, 326).

Just as it is requisite for the poet to live poetically in an authentic manner, Kierkegaard also maintains that "what holds for the poet-existence holds also in some measure for every single individual's life" (CI, 326). In his view, therefore, every human being has an "inalienable claim" upon living poetically, and anyone who truly desires to do so can lead a poetic life (CI, 298–99, 326).[20] For it is not the fashioning of a work of art as such but a particular way of orienting ourselves to life that constitutes the essential condition for living poetically. Like the authentic poet, we must relate ourselves positively to actuality and strive to actualize ourselves within our given historical environment. In this way the content of life acquires validity and significance for us as we strive for the clarity and fullness of that higher actuality that is the self.

Irony likewise acquires its true validity and proper significance in the life of the individual who truly lives poetically. "No genuinely human life is possible without irony," Kierkegaard claims, yet we become rightly oriented in actuality only when irony is mastered as a standpoint toward existence. Once that happens irony can function properly in its threefold role as a disciplinarian, guide, and surgeon in the dialectic of life. As a disciplinarian, it acts in opposition to romantic irony inasmuch as it now "limits, finitizes, and circumscribes and thereby yields truth, actuality, content" to the personal life, Kierkegaard claims. In addition, it "disci-

18. See Wheeler, ed., *German Aesthetic and Literary Criticism: The Romantic Ironists and Goethe,* 6–7, and Schlegel's review, "On Goethe's *Meister,*" 59–73, in that work.

19. Kierkegaard's journals indicate, however, that he later became disillusioned with Goethe, accusing him of being a "cold egotistical rationalist," lacking integrity, and representative of the modern lack of character (JP, 2:1461, 1462). For a detailed study of Kierkegaard's relation to Goethe, see Carl Roos, *Kierkegaard og Goethe* (Copenhagen: G.E.C. Gads Forlag, 1955).

20. In making this claim Kierkegaard goes against not only the elitism of the romantic poets, who regarded themselves as a privileged class of genuises, but also that of Heiberg, who divides humanity into two groups, an "upper house" of representative individuals comprising artists, poets, teachers of religion, and philosophers, and a "lower house" composed of the cultured and uncultured masses. For a presentation of Heiberg's views in this regard, see Kirmmse, *Kierkegaard in Golden Age Denmark,* 140–45.

plines and punishes and thereby yields balance and consistency" (CI, 326). As a guide, irony is not itself the truth, Kierkegaard contends, but it serves as the negative way to the truth by destroying every claim to truth that is not translated into and appropriated by the personal life (CI, 327). As a surgeon, it prunes like "so many wild shoots" that which must be repudiated in the personal life so that it can acquire "health and truth" (CI, 328).[21] Kierkegaard does not spell out the indirectly positive role of irony in any detail in this characterization of it as a ministering spirit, but his comments are enough to show that, in his view, irony remains an integral element in the life and craft of the poet as well as in the life of every individual who aspires to live poetically.

When Kierkegaard's alternative pattern of living poetically is brought to the foreground and allowed to stand out in its own right, as has been done here, it becomes apparent that he has drawn the contours of an existential aesthetics that integrates the aesthetic and the ethical-religious, or Christian, in such a way as to unite and virtually identify them with one another. The truly poetic is seen as constituted by the religious in that it relates one to an ideal within oneself rather than to one outside or beyond the self. Moreover, the religious itself is defined in aesthetic terms as a form of self-enjoyment in which one becomes transparent to oneself in one's highest potentiality. Living poetically is understood as striving to become oneself through a process of self-development in cooperation with the divine. Transubstantiation, a religious concept, is substituted for transfiguration as the appropriate term for describing the change wrought by the truly poetic, or religious, upon the actuality of an individual. It should also be noted that faith too is defined in this poetic context as involving striving and victory in the realization of itself. For just as true actuality becomes what it already is (in contrast to merely becoming in romanticism), Kierkegaard likewise claims that "faith becomes what it is. Faith is not an eternal struggle, but it is a victory that is struggling. Consequently, in faith that higher actuality of the spirit is not only becoming but is present,

21. On the role of irony as essential to a healthy life, see Ronald L. Hall, *Word and Spirit: A Kierkegaardian Critique of the Modern Age* (Bloomington: Indiana University Press, 1993), 121–30. On Hall's reading, Kierkegaard regards Socratic irony as well as mastered irony as contributing to a healthy life, in contrast to romantic irony, where it appears, according to Hegel's analysis, as a sickness. While Kierkegaard admits in his dissertation that "history has judged Socrates to be world-historically justified" in his ironic negation of the substantial actuality of the Greek world (CI, 271), Socrates surely does not embody a healthy subjectivity such as Kierkegaard envisions in mastered irony, which Hall virtually admits in recognizing that Socrates realizes only a negative freedom in irony.

although it is also becoming" (CI, 319). Philosophically, the category of actuality is of central importance for the young Kierkegaard, and the thrust of his aesthetics in this phase is to insist that we must properly relate ourselves and our poetic ideals to it. This does not mean, however, that he denies or denigrates the importance of change and possibility; rather, his point is that imagination must not cut itself loose from actuality but should serve as a medium through which a transformation and development of our given actuality within a religious orientation can take place. Ultimately, he envisages, like Goethe and Heiberg, an identity in which "actuality is possibility" (CI, 325), wherein we have acquired in our personal lives the poetic ideality to which we stand personally as well as artistically related through a combination of imagination, controlled irony, and existential striving.

3

Patterns for Living Poetically

Kierkegaard's *Either/Or,* published in 1843, is a rich and variegated work that can be likened to a kaleidoscope. Through mirrors that reflect fragments of colored glass, different patterns appear as this tubelike instrument is rotated, so that what one sees through it is constantly changing in shape and color. Mimicking a penchant of the romanticists and others of the time for the use of the fragment or aphoristic form to indicate the incomplete and imperfect nature of life and literature in striving for an unattainable infinity, *Either/Or* is subtitled "A Fragment of Life" and is made up of a mixture of literary genres—aphorisms, essays, diaries, letters, and a sermon—that corresponds to what Friedrich Schlegel has dubbed an "arabesque" novel.[1] One of its essays is titled "A Venture in Fragmentary

1. On the use of fragments by the German romantics, see Wheeler, *German Aesthetic and Literary Criticism,* viii and the introduction. See also the fragments of the great German forerunner of romanticism, J. G. Hamann, who wrote in a letter to his friend J. G. Lindner, "I have no aptitude for truths, principles, system; but for crumbs, fragments, fancies, sudden inspirations" (translated in Ronald Gregor Smith, *J. G. Hamann: A Study in Christian Existence with Selections from His Writings* [London: Collins, 1960], 22). In his collection of "Fragments" in 1758, Hamann states, "Here on earth we live on fragments. Our thoughts are fragments. Our knowledge itself is patchwork" (ibid., 160).

Schlegel's theory of the arabesque novel may be found, in "fragmentary form," in his *Dialogue on Poetry and Literary Aphorisms,* tr. Ernst Behler and Roman Struc (University Park: Pennsylvania State University Press, 1968), in his "Letter About the Novel," 94–105. There he associates the arabesque with the fantastic or imaginary and defines the romantic as presenting "a sentimental theme in a fantastic form" (98). The practice of mixing genres that is characteris-

Endeavor," and the "Diapsalmata," or refrains, with which the work begins take the form of aphorisms in the manner of Schlegel's *Lyceum* and *Athenaeum* fragments and those of Kierkegaard's intellectual mentor Poul Møller.[2] Moreover, members of the society to which three of the essays are addressed—the *Symparanekromenoi,* or Fellowship of the Dead—are described as "aphorisms in life," persons who "live aphoristically" in a segregated state without community with others (EO, 1:220).

Within this fragmentary structure of the work, two basic patterns of life are brought to view and reflected in the variety of changes in form that they can take. As in *The Concept of Irony,* these two designs constitute alternative patterns for "living poetically." Instead of being interwoven as they are in the earlier work, however, here they appear separately in the two volumes of the work. The pattern presented in the first volume of *Either/Or* illustrates a romantic mode of poet-existence; the other pattern, set forth in volume 2, depicts an ethical mode of living poetically in congruence with what was earlier identified in *The Concept of Irony* as a Christian mode of living poetically. *Either/Or* thus can be regarded as a "repetition" of *The Concept of Irony* in the sense that it takes up again an important theme of that work and, by etching in greater detail the alternative patterns outlined there for leading a poetic

tic of romantic works of art goes back, Schlegel claims, to Cervantes (102). For secondary discussions, see John D. Mullen, "The German Romantic Background of Kierkegaard's Psychology," *Southern Journal of Philosophy* 16 (1978): 649–60, and F. J. Billeskov Jansen, *Danmarks Digtekunst: Romantik og Romantisme,* 2d ed. (Copenhagen: Munksgaard, 1964), 301–5, where *Either/Or* is classified as a novel. Aage Henriksen, in *Kierkegaards Romaner* (Copenhagen: Gyldendal, 1954), identifies and treats only the "Diary of the Seducer" as a novel. Following the interpretation of Carl Roos, in *Kierkegaard og Goethe,* Louis Mackey, in *Kierkegaard: A Kind of Poet,* sees *Either/Or* as modeled on Goethe's *Wilhelm Meister.* Thus it may be classified as a *Bildungsroman,* or novel of self-cultivation, although, in Mackey's view, volume 1 of *Either/Or* constitutes a parody of the *Bildungsroman* inasmuch as it lacks *Bildung* (274). Although I think Mackey is correct in his classification, another analogue to Kierkegaard's novel may be found in Schlegel's *Lucinde,* which is an arabesque novel composed of a mixture of genres like *Either/Or,* only the latter is an example of the arabesque much superior to Schlegel's. The reflective seducer whose diary is included in *Either/Or* also appears to be modeled after the hero of *Lucinde,* only he is far more calculating and intellectually sensuous than Julius, Schlegel's romantic hero. In a note written on the front flyleaf of a copy of *Either/Or* I, Kierkegaard suggests that *Either/Or* is not a random collection of loose papers from his desk but "has a plan from the first word to the last" (JP, 5:5627). Understood as taking the form of a *Bildungsroman* in the fragmentary style of an arabesque novel, the work's hidden plan and structure may become more apparent, and in its incompleteness may be seen to conform to the fragmentary character of the genre it represents.

2. For Schlegel's aphorisms, see *Dialogue on Poetry and Literary Aphorisms.* In addition, see W. Glyn Jones, "Søren Kierkegaard and Poul Martin Møller," where it is suggested that Kierkegaard was also influenced by Møller's practice of writing aphorisms.

life, carries forward the notion of living poetically. But whereas the earlier work is published under Kierkegaard's own name and is highly critical of romanticism, the two volumes of *Either/Or* are issued through the auspices of a pseudonymous editor named Victor Eremita, who makes no judgment on the preferability of one pattern over the other. The title of the work, however, implies that a choice between them should be made. To aid us in making this decision, the editor, by permitting us to read a collection of papers he supposedly found in a secret compartment of an old secretary he had acquired, enables us get a "feel" for what it is like to live poetically in each mode. According to Eremita, these papers belong to two anonymous authors, one an aesthete about whom nothing is known except that he is a young man, the other a judge named William, whose surname is not given. Eremita designates these authors "A" and "B" respectively. Without altering their papers in any way except to provide translations of Greek quotations used by A and titles for the papers of B, which consist of two very long essays written in epistolary style and apparently addressed to A, the editor allows each author to speak for himself. The papers of A, therefore, constitute volume 1 of the work, while those of B make up volume 2. Peering through the kaleidoscope of these papers, in this chapter I look at the romantic pattern for living poetically, and in the next chapter, the ethical alternative mode of living poetically in the existential aesthetics of Judge William.

Through the papers of A we get a privileged view of the aesthete's own attempt to live poetically in a romantic fashion. But more than that, in a very real sense we can engage in the enterprise of living poetically along with him, for in the romantic mode of living poetically, as characterized in *The Concept of Irony,* aesthetic enjoyment is gained essentially by experimenting with different possibilities. One can do that in an immediate manner by maximizing one's life experiences, sampling a variety of lifestyles, jobs, partners, friends, abodes, material goods, cultural events, sports, and so forth. Or one can do it in an imaginative and reflective fashion by recapturing a kind of immediacy of experience through art and aesthetic criticism.[3] If one is a poet or artist, one can experiment creatively by producing a work of art for one's own enjoyment and perhaps for that of others. If one is a critic, one can entertain new possibilities by reflectively analyzing the creative products of oth-

3. For illuminating discussions of A's attempt to recapture immediacy aesthetically, see Mackey, *Kierkegaard: A Kind of Poet,* chap. 1, and Connell, *To Be One Thing,* in which the relation of A (reflectivity) to Don Juan (immediacy) and his vicarious enjoyment of Don Juan's activities are emphasized (59).

ers and, insofar as one produces a work of aesthetic criticism, also engage in the creative process. If one is a spectator of art, as most of us are, one can enrich one's experience by imaginatively entering into the creative products of the artist or the reflective analysis of the critic. That is, one can project oneself into the situations, moods, and figures presented or discussed in them and thereby identify with the poetic products of others. Sometimes that which is being artistically presented is not so much a new possibility as the reproduction of a life experience of the artist, perhaps a particularly memorable one that the artist seeks to recapture and imaginatively experience again through recollection. Similarly, if one is a spectator, one may find in a work of art a reproduction, as it were, of one's own life experiences, so that one can see oneself reflected in it and in this way relate to and enjoy oneself aesthetically at a distance. In relation to the papers of the aesthete in *Either/Or,* we play the role of spectators, while the aesthete himself is both an artist and a critic; but we can engage his papers poetically essentially in the same manner as he.

Artistically, the kaleidoscope of papers through which we enter into aesthetic experimentation with the aesthete consists of a collage of literary forms, styles, moods, ideas, and poetic figures. Through aphorisms, several aesthetic essays, and a diary (which A attributes to yet another author), we are made privy to a wide variety of existential possibilities. In this respect, the simile of a kaleidoscope fits the papers of A more truly than those of B, for they present an array of variations in pattern, illustrating the infinite range of identities open to the romantic lifestyle, whereas the papers of B are interested in refining a single identity, the given self of the individual. Within this pattern too an infinity of possibility presents itself, but in a manner quite different from the romantic.[4]

Although, according to Kierkegaard, everything is possible for the romanticist, the possibilities A places before us reflect the range and types of interests and attitudes characteristic of the romantic personality. These run a gamut from attempts to recover a lost immediacy to a preoccupation with subjects having to do with the negativities of life—

4. Judge William, in distinguishing the ethical individual from the aesthetic individual, explicitly rejects comparison of the ethical individual to the image of a kaleidoscope, or what he calls a "magic picture," which he associates with the aesthete's tendency to become distracted by the juggling of possibilities (EO, 2:258 and n. 95). But insofar as the ethical lifestyle also includes possibility via a relation to the eternal, or God, it too undergoes change and development in the process of becoming a self, so that, having the universal as its telos, its pattern has a true infinity against which to measure itself and is constantly in the making, never finished, in time. For further discussion of this issue, see the next chapter.

suffering, grief, boredom, indolence, meaninglessness, anxiety, melancholy, and despair. In the manner of a practice that A associates with the Middle Ages, these states are explored through representative figures—sometimes a projection of A himself, frequently through characters drawn from classical literature, and in a couple of instances via characters of A's own imaginative creation.

In the process of presenting and critically interpreting these figures, a good deal of aesthetic theory is also set forth in the volume. Since the papers purportedly belong to an anonymous or pseudonymous author who is, moreover, an avowed aesthete, we cannot unequivocally identify these views as Kierkegaard's. Nevertheless, some of them do substantially reflect his own views, as can be corroborated by the presence of the same or similar ideas in his journals and in other works published under his own name. In particular, the writing of the first volume of *Either/Or* gave Kierkegaard an opportunity to articulate some of the aesthetic ideas he had formed from his earlier preoccupation with the literary figures Don Juan, Ahasverus, and Faust during his university years. These figures, he suggests in an early journal entry, should be interpreted respectively in the lyrical, epic, and dramatic modes, with Faust being regarded as embodying the other two in a more mediate third stage (JP, 1:1179; cf. 1180). Accordingly, three of the aesthetic essays of volume 1 in *Either/Or* are devoted wholly or in part to an interpretation of these figures in their appropriate modes. Of the three, the essay on Don Juan is richest in aesthetic theory and substantially reflects Kierkegaard's own aesthetic views on the musical-erotic. For the most part, however, we must be guarded in associating the aesthetic views of volume 1 with those of Kierkegaard, since they generally reflect a romantic aesthetics corresponding to the romantic mode of living poetically he wishes indirectly to criticize in this work.

THE UNHAPPY POET

Turning to the collage of representative figures that appear in the kaleidoscope of A's papers, we begin in the lyrical mode, in accordance with the Heibergian-Kierkegaardian theory of aesthetic development set forth in *From the Papers of One Still Living.* But we do not begin immediately with the lyrical figure of Don Juan. The essay on Don Juan is preceded by a series of aphorisms, or refrains, described in *Concluding Unscientific Postscript* as "purely poetical outpourings"—unreflected, unrestrained, emotional or lyrical expressions of suffering such as might persist in a poet-existence (CUP, 1:226). Indeed, the speaker of the opening refrain—who is presumably A himself—intimates that he is a poet. The poet is characterized here as "an unhappy person who conceals profound anguish in his heart but whose lips are so formed that as sighs and cries pass over them they sound like beautiful music" (EO, 1:19). This is the sad fate of the romantic poet: that in exercising his talent for poetic expression his words betray him, become ironic, and cause him to be misunderstood. Unable to communicate the torments of his soul to others, he thus addresses his poetic effusions *ad se ipsum,* "to himself" (EO, 1:17). Finding life meaningless and empty, the poet laments to himself, "Life for me has become a bitter drink, and yet it must be taken in drops, slowly, counting" (EO, 1:26). Feeling the insignificance of being only one thread among many and thus not the master of his life, he defiantly protests, "Well, then, even though I cannot spin, I can still cut the thread" (EO, 1:31). But indolence and indifference toward life have overtaken him to the point where he declares, "I don't feel like doing anything. I don't feel like riding—the motion is too powerful; I don't feel like walking—it is too tiring; I don't feel like lying down, for either I would have to stay down, and I don't feel like doing that, or I would have to get up again, and I don't feel like doing that, either. *Summa Summarum:* I don't feel like doing anything" (EO, 1:20). Whatever action one engages in, the aesthete philosophizes, one will regret it (EO, 1:38). Love to him is but the content of a dream; pleasure is disappointing; joy culminates in death (EO, 1:20, 41–42). Nevertheless, like a pregnant woman, he is driven by impatient desires, sometimes the most trivial of things, for which he would give more than his birthright (EO, 1:26). The only faithful and intimate confidant the poet has is his own depression; sorrow is his only love, the echo of sorrow his only friend (EO, 1:20, 33). Stalemated in life like a chess piece in checkmate, he cannot be moved: "Time stands still, and so do I. All the plans I project fly straight back at me; when I want to spit, I spit in my own face" (EO, 1:26). Just as the Fenris wolf of folklore was bound by a chain made from strange ingredients, so he too is bound "by a chain formed of gloomy fancies, of alarming dreams, of troubled thoughts, of fearful presentiments, of inexplicable anxieties" (EO, 1:34).

By his own description, the author of these lyrical effusions shows himself to be a thoroughgoing romantic ironist in his moods and attitudes toward life. He thus constitutes a representative figure through whom we may experiment poetically in a romantic fashion with a romantic personality. The transfigured character of his poetry enables us to listen to his cries and moans without being disturbed by them. We can get a feel for his melancholy and sorrow without actually making them our own. We can entertain the possibility of life being as he pictures it without really embracing his views. And if we do not like the poetic figure we see, we can rotate the kaleidoscope and entertain another. That is the privilege and advantage of the romantic mode of living poetically. To rush on too quickly, however, may belie a hidden disquietude not unlike the despairing poet's, an unwillingness on our part to admit a resemblance to him, a reluctance to face torments deep within our own souls. The aphorisms depicting his life may reflect our own more than we care to admit. On the other hand, to dally too long with his words of sorrow, to become too absorbed in his cries of woe, may mean that we are using them as a way of echoing and nursing our own. For the despairing poet—a soul subject to contradictory moods and radical swings of the pendulum in the way he relates to life—solace is found in the poetry of music, in an escape from reality via a momentary return to a lost immediacy.

> Where the rays of the sun do not reach, the tones still manage to come. My apartment is dark and gloomy; a high wall practically keeps out the light of day. It must be in the next courtyard, very likely a wandering musician. What instrument is it? A reed pipe? . . . What do I hear—the minuet from *Don Giovanni.* Carry me away, then, you rich, strong tones, to the ring of girls, to the delight of the dance.—The pharmacist pounds his mortar, the maid scrubs her kettle, the groom curries the horse and knocks the currycomb on the cobblestones. These tones are only for me; only to me do they beckon. Oh, thank you, whoever you are! Thank you! My soul is so rich, so hearty, so intoxicated with joy! (EO, 1:41–42)

From the doldrums of an unhappy poet-existence, therefore, let us be carried away with him—still in a lyrical mode, but now encountered more reflectively through aesthetic criticism—to the operatic stage where we meet a figure whose life is "effervescing like champagne" in its lust for enjoyment (EO, 1:134).

DON JUAN

Don Juan, the mythical great lover of women whose seductions number a thousand and three in Spain alone, is a perennial figure in Western drama, music, and literature with whom many men and perhaps even some women can identify more pleasantly and vivaciously than with the unhappy poet.[5] His popularity and persistence as an artistic subject indicate that he is a symbol for something very common in human life—something perhaps lost or repressed that we seek poetically, if not actually, to regain. What does he represent? Why does he remain so attractive to us, men and women alike?

As the aesthete presents him to us in his essay "The Immediate Erotic Stages or the Musical Erotic," Don Juan is a product of the popular world-consciousness of the Middle Ages, a period noted for the personification of single aspects of life in representative figures.[6] Springing from the unconscious medieval psyche, Don Juan represents the sensuous-erotic, or sensuousness—the elemental passion, or primitive life force, within us in erotic form. He is the embodiment of our primal, insatiable desire for enjoyment through an immediate gratification of the senses, especially sexual desire. As such, Don Juan represents the basic characteristic of our aesthetic or immediately given drives and inclinations in life. He thus portrays, at its most immediate level, what Kierkegaard identifies as the aesthetic stage of human existence or that stage in which we live primarily on the basis of satisfying our natural desires and inclinations. No wonder, then, that we can so easily identify with him and are so irresistibly attracted to him. For Don Juan is a projection of that which is most elemental in ourselves, whether that is denied expression, moderately allowed, or indulged.[7] For some of us, he represents the stage in which our lives are

5. For an overview of representative treatments of the Don Juan figure in Western drama and literature, see my article "Don Juan and the Representation of Spiritual Sensuousness," *Journal of the American Academy of Religion* 47, no. 4 (1979): 627–44, published under the name Sylvia Walsh Utterback. This article serves in part as the basis for my analysis of the Don Juan figure in the present study. Although Don Juan is a male figure, he is interpreted by A as representing an aesthetic element common to both males and females, but that interpretation becomes problematic, if not inconsistent, inasmuch he associates Don Juan specifically with male desire and seduction.

6. As A seems aware (EO, 1:87), the actual origin of the Don Juan idea is obscure, although elements of the tradition appear in ancient as well as early medieval folklore (see Armand E. Singer, *A Bibliography of the Don Juan Theme* [Morgantown: West Virginia University Bulletin, 1954], 16–20). One might be tempted to regard the Don Juan figure as "archetypal," as some literary critics do (see especially Leo M. Lowther, "Don Juan and Comparative Literary Criticism: Four Approaches" (Ph.D. diss., University of Utah, 1971), were it not for the fact that, in its Jungian sense at least, this term refers to a universal image, whereas the Don Juan figure is almost exclusively a Western phenomenon (the only notable non-Western version of the theme being the tenth-century Japanese classic novel, *The Tale of Genji*) and within Western culture essentially a product of the Christian era, as A rightly points out.

7. For interpretations exploring in greater depth the psychological meaning of the Don Juan figure in *Either/Or,* see Kresten Nordentoft, *Kierkegaard's Psychology,* tr. Bruce H.

still oriented; for others, he embodies a lost immediacy that we can, at least for a moment, poetically recover through him.

But Don Juan is not simply the representative of our sensuous nature. He is, more specifically, the embodiment of the sensuous-erotic determined as a *demonic principle* in opposition to spirit.[8] Being an aspect of our given nature, the sensuousness he represents is not as such immoral or sinful.[9] However, with the coming of Christianity into the world, the romantic aesthete maintains, sensuousness came to be excluded in favor of a spiritual form of existence that renounces worldliness and wants no involvement in it (EO, 1:61, 89–90). Rejected by spirit, sensuousness began to assert itself in its raw, pristine form as an independent power in aesthetic indifference to the spiritual. In this sense, the aesthete observes, one can say that sensuousness was first posited by Christianity, even though it existed previously (EO, 1:61–62). For in the moment that Christianity came into existence, sensuousness began to exist in a different sense as a demonic principle in opposition to spirit, no longer harmoniously assimilated in the psyche as it had been in the Greek consciousness (EO, 1:62). Being the representative of sensuousness in this demonic form, Don Juan thus represents, on a spiritless level, the rebel in us, the desire within us to gratify our natural inclinations without constraints, without regard for others, in total freedom and total enjoyment of life. In his kingdom, where "everything is only one giddy round of pleasure," we hear "only the elemental voice of passion, the play of desires, the wild noise of intoxication" (EO, 1:90).

Kirmmse (Pittsburgh, Pa.: Duquesne University Press, 1978), and Niels Barfoed, *Don Juan: En studie i dansk litteratur* (Copenhagen: Gyldendal, 1978). Both give a Freudian interpretation of the figure, but Nordentoft associates him with the id, whereas Barfoed interprets him as an Oedipus figure.

8. On the demonic nature of Don Juan, see Hans Jørgen Svendsen, "Dæmon og menneske: Don Juan og Æstetiker A. i Søren Kierkegaards Enten-Eller," in *Indfaldsvinkler: 16 Fortolkninger af nordisk Digtning tilegnet Oluf Friis* (Copenhagen: Gyldendal, 1964), 40–57.

9. In a note to their translation of *Either/Or,* vol. 1 (Princeton: Princeton University Press, 1959), David F. Swenson and Lillian Marvin Swenson point out that the Danish word for sensuous, *sandselig,* is ambiguous in that it can mean either "sensuous" or "sensual," the former carrying no sense of moral censure, while the latter does. The appropriate meaning and translation therefore must be determined by the context in which the term appears. Although the Swensons rather consistently translate it as "sensuous" in the essay on the musical-erotic, the new Hong translation initially renders the adjective as "sensual" and the noun form as "sensuality" (EO, 161–62) but then generally uses the terms "sensuous" and "sensuousness." For the Hongs, "sensual" is synonymous with "carnal" and means to be "unduly indulgent to the appetites," whereas "sensuous" is a more neutral term pertaining to sense experience (see EO, 1616–17 n. 13).

How can we reexperience or identify with Don Juan in the expression of this demonic sensuousness, this unrestrained immediacy, that the tradition now denies to us? Through a lyrical description and analysis of the figure, the romantic aesthete can give us some sense of the vitality, the immediacy, that Don Juan represents. But it is A's thesis (and Kierkegaard's as well) that the sensuous-erotic in its immediacy, and especially in all its demonic force, can be represented artistically only in music (EO, 1:56, 64; JP, 1:1179; JP, 4:4397). Taking a classical view of aesthetics as requiring a correspondence between content and form in a work of art, A argues that abstract ideas require an abstract medium of expression, concrete ideas a concrete medium (EO, 1:55–56). The abstractness or concreteness of a medium is determined by its relation to history. Thus a medium that is entirely abstract has no relation to historical events, whereas a concrete medium or idea is "permeated by the historical" in that it receives its content from history, as in epic poetry (EO, 1:55). Being constitutive of immediacy prior to any historical modification, sensuousness is the most abstract idea that can be thought. Being an inward determinant, it cannot be depicted in sculpture. Eluding apprehension in precise outline, it cannot be depicted in painting (EO, 1:56). Existing in a succession of moments, it has a kind of epic character; but moving always in immediacy, not yet having advanced to words, it cannot be expressed in poetry (EO, 1:57). This is not to say, however, that these media do not or cannot contain the sensuous. The aesthete grants that sculpture and painting, for example, have their existence in the sensuous but give it static expression in spatial form (EO, 1:67). Similarly, language can describe sensuousness and incorporate it as an instrument of expression but destroys its immediacy by bringing it under the power of reflection (EO, 1:67, 70).

In the aesthete's opinion, music is an ideal medium for the representation of sensuousness because, unlike language, it is able to express the immediate *in its immediacy,* that is, prior to reflection (EO, 1:70). Music is also ideal for expressing the *negation* of sensuousness, since it is constantly vanishing (EO, 1:68). Existing in a succession of moments, music, like language, takes place in time and addresses itself to the ear; but unlike the products of language, it exists only in immediacy, only in the moment of performance. As an abstract medium, music is appropriate for expressing the general and indeterminate, whereas language, as a concrete medium, is suited for that which is posited or made determinate through historical action. Like Hegel and his idealist followers, the aesthete regards language as the proper medium for the expression of spirit, although he acknowledges, as they do, that spirit can be expressed in music (EO, 1:71).[10] Nevertheless, he maintains that music is essentially a sensuous medium and has the sensuous as its absolute subject. For this reason, he suggests, "music has always been the object of suspicious attention on the part of religious fervor"; generally speaking, "the more rigorous the religiousness, the more music is given up and words are emphasized" (EO, 1:71). Although music should not be regarded as the work of the devil, it is "demonic," being a medium for the expression of that which lies outside the realm of spirit (EO, 1:65, 73; cf. JP, 1:133).

In the aesthete's critical estimation, Don Juan received classic expression as the representative of demonic sensuousness in Mozart's opera *Don Giovanni.* In this work a perfect union of content (idea) and form (medium) is realized: an abstract subject with an abstract medium; immediate, demonic sensuousness with an immediate, sensuous, demonic medium. It is to Mozart's opera, therefore, that we must go for a truly immediate experience of Don Juan as the representative of demonic sensuousness in all its force and immediacy. In Mozart's opera, the aesthete tells us, Don Juan expresses the sensuous-erotic in the form of desire, not as an individual who desires but as a demonic principle or independent power concentrated in a figure who is representative of the idea of desire (EO, 1:83).[11] Being the embodiment of sensuous desire,

10. According to Hegel's *Aesthetics,* all art is "produced for apprehension by man's senses and therefore is more or less derived from the sensuous sphere" (32). But, "though sensuous, it is essentially at the same time for *spiritual* apprehension" (35). He goes on to state that "the sensuous aspect of art is *spiritualized,* since the spirit appears in art as made *sensuous*" (39). In its romantic phase, art finally transcends its sensuous form and addresses itself wholly to the inner spirit. Music, though still sensuous, stands at the center of the romantic arts, forming "the point of transition between the abstract spatial sensuousness of painting and the abstract spirituality of poetry" (88).

11. The aesthete views the expression of desire, or the sensuous-erotic, as developing in three stages, each of which may be seen as artistically represented by figures in Mozart's operas. The first stage is portrayed by the page in *The Marriage of Figaro;* the second by Papagano in *The Magic Flute;* and the third is epitomized by the opera *Don Giovanni,* the whole of which "is essentially the expression of the idea" of desire, though that idea is represented more specifically in the opera by the figure of Don Juan (EO, 1:84). According to A, the first stage consists in a state of dreaming or intoxication in erotic love, in which there is still a substantial unity between desire and the desired and only a presentiment of a deeper desire separated from its object. The second stage is one in which desire actively seeks to discover its object in the multiplicity of particularity, but without actually having an object or desiring it. The third stage is characterized by desire of the particular absolutely in a unity of the two previous stages: the one and multiplicity, or the particular and the universal (EO, 1:75–85). For an excellent discussion of the stages of development of desire in the aesthete's essay on the musical-erotic, see Dunning, *Kierkegaard's Dialectic of Inwardness,* 32–38. Dunning detects a Hegelian structure manifested in this and other stages of development of the aesthetic, ethical, and religious spheres in Kierkegaard's works.

Don Juan deceives and seduces women in this opera, but he is not a seducer in a strict sense, for that requires a level of consciousness and cunning in seduction that the lyrical figure lacks. Ever prepared and always triumphant, Don Juan acts with a passion, energy, and exuberance that is completely spontaneous and immediate. But his love for a woman is faithless and momentary, for as soon as he has had one woman, he desires another. It is not a particular woman but all women—or, more precisely, the ideal of "total femininity" (*hele Qvindelighed*) in every woman—that he desires and seeks indiscriminately (EO, 1:95, 100; SV, 1:80).[12] Thus it is not the extraordinary woman but the ordinary woman who constitutes the object of his desire, since every woman is ordinary by virtue of the fact that she is a woman (EO, 1:97). Restless and constantly on the move, Don Juan leads a life that is an endless cycle of repetition of the same thing, but each time with a different woman, with the consequence that his existence is a sum of moments without coherence and continuity. So forceful is his vitality that only spirit—a higher, reincarnated form of life symbolized in the opera by the ghost of the commandant whom Don Juan had killed—is able to triumph over this wild and effervescent aesthetic expression of life. In the aesthete's judgment, this conflict between demonic sensuousness and spirit constitutes the deeper significance of the opera, although it is only intimated through the appearance of the figure of the commandant at the beginning and end of the work (EO, 1:112–13, 124, 126–27). The body of the opera centers on Don Juan, giving consummate expression to the fury of the demonic in this struggle.

The fact that Don Juan is a male figure and that the preceding stages of the immediate-erotic are likewise represented by male figures poses the interesting question whether the immediate-erotic qualified as desire is gender specific and, more particularly, whether the seductiveness of demonic desire is limited to males. In his analysis of the stages of desire, the romantic aesthete specifically identifies desire with the male and the

12. It is interesting that the aesthete, viewing Mozart's Don Giovanni in this manner, does not give the figure a typically romantic interpretation as one who is perpetually and futilely seeking the ideal woman. For that, one must look to the literary works of E.T.A. Hoffmann and Byron, or to Richard Strauss's orchestral tone poem based on verses by Nikolaus Lenau. In Strauss's work, for example, the failure of Don Juan to find the ideal woman results in disillusionment and extinction of desire in the hero at the end. Thus this work is more consistent with the ironic stance of the romantic poet than Mozart's *Don Giovanni.* Although Lenau's poem was written in 1844—a year after the publication of *Either/Or*—Kierkegaard does not refer to it in any of his later works or journals. However, he was aware of Lenau, since he mentions Lenau's treatment of Faust and Martensen's study of Lenau's *Faust* in the journals of 1837 (JP, 5:5226).

desired with the female, and in all three stages the object of desire is femininity (EO, 1:77–78, 100). But if the sensuous-erotic is to be understood as a universal characteristic of human existence in its elemental originality, desire and the seductive character of desire would have to be a feature of women as well as men. Either the romantic aesthete has committed the male chauvinist fallacy of identifying humanity solely with males, or else he clearly intends to identify demonic desire and seduction as primarily a male phenomenon—a point of view that runs contrary to the stereotyped view of woman as a seductress, based on the biblical story of Adam and Eve, but one that is consistent with A's philosophy of male dominance espoused elsewhere in the text.

This ambiguity leads to a consideration of why the romantic aesthete is so infatuated with Mozart's opera and the figure of Don Juan in the first place. Highly reflective by nature or training, A seeks to lose himself in fantasy and to expand his own erotic moods by rediscovering them artistically in the music of Mozart. Finding Mozart's music tempting and irresistible as a stimulus and medium for fantasizing in this manner, he asks:

> Where is the young man who has not had a moment in his life when he would have given half his kingdom to be a Don Juan, or perhaps all of it, when he would have given half his lifetime for one year of being Don Juan, or perhaps his whole life? But that was as far as it went. The more profound natures, who were moved by the idea, found everything, even the softest breeze, expressed in Mozart's music; in its grandiose passion, they found a full-toned expression for what stirred in their own inner beings, they perceived how every mood strained toward that music just as the brook hurries on in order to lose itself in the infinitude of the sea. (EO, 1:104)

The point A is making here is not that men should be inspired by the Mozartian Don Juan to act out their male fantasy life by becoming Don Juans themselves. This is made clear as he goes on to say:

> The bunglers, who think themselves a Don Juan because they have pinched a peasant girl's cheek, put their arms around a waitress, or made a young girl blush, of course understand neither the idea nor Mozart, or how to produce a Don Juan themselves, except as a ludicrous freak, a family idol, who perhaps to the misty, sentimental eyes of some cousins would seem to be a true Don Juan, the epitome of all charm. (EO, 1:104)

It is not the indulgence in an *actual sensuousness* in comic imitation of Don Juan—who, as a mythic figure larger than life and as the symbol of a power rather than an individual, is not to be taken as a role model for virile males—but rather a *poetic sensuousness* that A and all the "more profound natures" moved by the idea seek to enjoy in and through the figure of Don Juan. As a romantic ironist A has essentially rejected actuality and taken flight into the realm of fantasy as a way of recovering a lost immediacy or eroticism that can never be regained in actuality but that may be momentarily, that is, illusively, recaptured and enjoyed in an infinity of erotic moods stimulated by music and the imagination.

Having argued that Mozart captures for us the true essence and significance of Don Juan in his musical presentation of the figure, A proceeds to criticize literary adaptations of Don Juan because he thinks they interpret the figure basically according to ethical categories instead of aesthetic ones (EO, 1:64, 98–99, 103–15). That is, they make Don Juan an individual rather than an idea or ideality, reflective rather than innocent and spontaneous, immoral rather than premoral or amoral, sensual rather than sensuous, a seducer rather than a seductive force of nature. Literary interpretations thus obfuscate the true significance of the figure. For what is essentially at issue is not an individual's moral turpitude or sinful disobedience of religious norms but the fundamental conflict between flesh and spirit that arose with the introduction of Christianity into the world. In this sense Don Juan gives expression to what Kierkegaard regards in *The Concept of Irony* as a romantic tendency, exemplified in Schlegel's *Lucinde,* to oppose and negate spirituality through an enjoyment of the flesh; only in romanticism this opposition operates at a far more imaginative and reflective level than that of the immediate, musical Don Juan. Thus the true romantic counterpart of Don Juan is to be found in the reflective seducer, another figure encountered later on, in "The Diary of the Seducer" at the end of *Either/Or* I. For a preliminary experiment with this type of figure, however, let us move on to the other two figures in the trilogy of romantic prototypes with whom the aesthete identifies.

FAUST AND AHASVERUS

The figure of Faust appears only faintly and indirectly in *Either/Or,* so that we cannot relate to him very well through what the aesthete has to say about him. This figure, one with which Kierkegaard was much absorbed in his university years, undoubtedly receives such scant treatment here because H. L. Martensen, Kierkegaard's tutor for a short time, had already published an essay on Faust interpreting the figure along the same lines as Kierkegaard, much to the latter's chagrin (JP, 5:5225). In *Either/Or* Kierkegaard thus focuses his energies on Don Juan and, to a lesser extent, on Ahasverus the Wandering Jew. Insofar as Faust is portrayed here, he appears only briefly in the essay on Don Juan and in another essay portraying Margarete, the maid whom Faust seduces. Faust is a prototype of the reflective seducer mentioned above and therefore a reproduction of Don Juan at a higher level (EO, 1:205). Like Don Juan, he is a demonic figure, but, the aesthete claims, "a superior one" because "sensuousness does not acquire importance for him until he has lost a whole previous world," the consciousness of which always remains present to him (EO, 1:206). Consequently, he desires the same thing as Don Juan, but in a different manner. For it is not so much enjoyment as a momentary diversion of mind that he seeks in the sensuous, to assuage a doubting soul that cannot find rest in anything. He is thus the representative of doubt and falls under the category of the intellectual, of reflection, rather than that of immediacy, as does the lyrical Don Juan. Whereas Don Juan seduces many, Faust seduces only one, and with a method that makes him a sort of seducer quite different from Don Juan. For whereas Don Juan deceives innocently out of the irresistible force of sensuous desire, Faust uses the power of speech, the lie, to deceive and seduce. In his seduction of Margarete he seeks "not only the pleasure of the sensuous but the immediacy of the spirit," that is, a renewal and strengthening of his sick soul by sucking out, like a vampire, the immediate life of an innocent young woman (EO, 1:206). Through Faust, then, we get a preliminary glance at what it would be like to be a demonic seducer on a reflective, spiritually qualified level. We also get a sense of the deeper agony of doubt and lack of spirit that motivates that seduction, and a taste of the romantic restlessness that grips him in the search for a lost immediacy to provide momentary solace from doubt.

In his unrest Faust embodies in himself Don Juan and the third figure with whom Kierkegaard was particularly interested in his youth, Ahasverus the Wandering Jew. In *Either/Or* this figure is presented as the unhappiest of all persons because he could not die; consequently he is doomed to endless wandering about the earth in search of a grave of rest and peace. Ordinarily we associate unhappiness with the misfortune of having to die, but if life itself is experienced as a sea of wretchedness from which we long to escape, then it is the greatest of misfortunes not to be able to die. That is the case for Ahasverus and for the members of the *Symparanekromenoi,* "a community of the unhappy" to whom the aesthete's discourse on the unhappiest person is addressed (EO, 1:221). Every unhappy person is eligible for membership in this society, and the unhappiest person is a representative for that class composed of the unhappiest of all. Recalling Hegel's phenomenological description of the "unhappy consciousness" as divided and alienated from itself, the aesthete characterizes the unhappy personality as one who "has his ideal, the substance of his life, the plenitude of his consciousness, his essential nature, outside himself" (EO, 1:222).[13] Such an individual is always absent, never present to himself; but whereas, for Hegel, consciousness is seen as coming upon its "grave" in this condition, the aesthete sees it as forever seeking and unable to find repose in the grave.[14]

Unhappy individuals become absent to themselves, the aesthete claims, in either of two ways: by living in the past in recollection or by living in the future through hope. But they live in the past or future in such a way as to hope for something they know cannot be realized or so as to recall a past that had no decisive reality for them, with the consequence that neither activity has any real meaning for them (EO, 1:223–24). While the aesthete finds the disappointment of recollection to be more painful than that of hope and thus more characteristic of the unhappiest individuals, the unhappiest of all, he claims, are those who combine recollection and hope in such a way as to experience even greater disappointment because what is hoped for properly belongs to recollection as something they should already have experienced and what is recollected in the realm of thought is properly the substance of hope for future realization. Thus they find themselves alone in the world, unable to die, because they have never really lived, and unable to live, because they are already dead (EO, 1:225–26).

This is the situation that the aesthete and his associates in the *Symparanekromenoi,* literally translated as "a fellowship of the dead," find themselves in. Normally "solitary birds" or "aphorisms" who live segregated lives, they convene once a year to hold an "open competition" for the title of the unhappiest person, an honor for which they vie as fellow contestants as well as serve as judges. The aesthete parades before them and us, like a kaleidoscope within a kaleidoscope, a series of possible candidates for the title: the Greek goddess Niobe, who was turned into a stone image that wept continually; Antigone, the last of the

13. On the unhappy consciousness, see G.W.F. Hegel, *Phenomenology of Spirit,* tr. A. V. Miller (Oxford: Clarendon, 1977), 119–38.

14. Ibid., 132.

family of Oedipus, whose grief she bore; the biblical patriarch Job, who lost everything; the prodigal son's father, who went in vain to search for his son; the martyr, his name now forgotten, whose soul and spirit were broken and paralyzed by his failure to save the world as he set out to do; a young girl whose lover has been unfaithful to her. But none of these quite measures up to the high standards of the *Symparanekromenoi,* who bow down in reverence before the empty grave of that great unknown one who is the unhappiest yet the happiest because only a gift of fate, not anything he does himself, can confer that title upon him (EO, 1:230). In a final paradoxical twist that reveals the full extent of the ironic and cynical mentality of the aesthete and his cohorts, A asks rhetorically, "Who indeed is the happiest but the unhappiest and who the unhappiest but the happiest, and what is life but madness, and faith but foolishness, and hope but a staving off of the evil day, and love but vinegar in the wound" (EO, 1:230).

FOUR BRIDES OF SORROW

The memory of unhappy love, recalled in reflective sorrow, forms the basis for a presentation of several female figures in the remaining addresses of A before the *Symparanekromenoi.* To highlight a difference he sees between modern and ancient tragedy, our literary critic imaginatively creates in one of these addresses a modern Antigone who stands in contrast to the Greek heroine by virtue of the reflective consciousness she possesses in relation to her situation. Relying heavily on Aristotle's theory of tragedy, he views ancient tragedy as characterized by an "epic substantiality" in which the suffering and destruction of the tragic figure comes in part from the individual's own deeds but also as a result of his or her immediate relation to the state, family, and destiny. The action of the play is therefore "just as much event as action," which gives it its epic character. Furthermore, in ancient tragedy, the aesthete claims, "the individuals do not act in order to present characters; rather these are included for the sake of action" (EO, 1:143). The subjective mood appropriate to Greek tragedy is sorrow, which is deepened by the ambiguity of guilt in the plays. Modern tragedy, by contrast, focuses on the character and situation of the tragic figure, who is fully reflective, entirely responsible, and unambiguously guilty. In the aesthete's judgment, this has the dual effect of increasing the pain of the individual but also of nullifying the tragic character of the play, which requires an element of innocence as well as guilt on the part of the protagonist to be truly tragic (EO, 1:144).[15]

Being a woman, the aesthete's modern Antigone possesses enough substantiality or immediate identity with family and state to distinguish her from the typical modern hero, but also enough reflection to transform her sorrow into pain. Her reflectivity is not great enough, however, to reflect herself out of her pain, so that, unlike the Greek Antigone, whose guilt and suffering are externally evident, she nurses in solitude a secret inward pain she cannot reveal, out of concern for her father. For in the aesthete's reconstruction of the classical Antigone's story, only Antigone knows (how she knows, he evades by saying it is not a matter of dramatic interest) that she is the daughter of an incestuous marriage between Oedipus and his mother Jocasta. Out of anxiety she becomes preoccupied at an early age with sorrow, to which she is drawn yet ambivalently fears.

It is in this anxiety of Antigone that the aesthete finds a basis for "a definition of the tragic in modern times" (EO, 1:154). Anxiety is essentially different from Greek sorrow, he claims, in that it is determined by reflection, through which it separates itself from its object. It is therefore a wholly subjective category, whereas Greek sorrow is not. Anxiety also involves reflection on the past and the future, whereas Greek sorrow lies in the present. In attaching itself to sorrow, anxiety may suddenly posit the whole sorrow in the present moment, the aesthete admits, but in such a way that the present instantly vanishes. "In this sense," he states, "anxiety is a genuine tragic category"—a claim he supports somewhat cryptically by applying Sophocles' gloss on the classical *Antigone:* "Whom a god would destroy he first makes mad" (EO, 1:155). Presumably that means anxiety has the tragic effect of continually recalling sorrow in such fullness that one is first driven mad and then destroyed by it. Indeed, the modern Antigone's life is described by the aesthete as essentially over. Although she still lives in the world, she does not belong to it. Her real life is enclosed in a shroud of secrecy and dedicated to sorrow over her father's destiny and her own. She is in love with a man

15. That A has Hegel's view of modern tragedy in mind as the object of criticism on this point has been pointed out by Clyde C. Holler, III, in "Kierkegaard's Concept of Tragedy in the Context of His Pseudonymous Works" (Ph.D. diss., Boston University, 1981), 76–95. Although A and Hegel stand fairly close to one another in their views of the difference between ancient tragedy and modern tragedy, Holler shows that they part company on the issue of tragic guilt. For Hegel, the modern tragic hero is ethically guilty and fully deserves punishment, whereas, for A, "tragedy demands ambiguous guilt, of the sort resulting from the substantial situation of the individual in Greek society" (83).

but dares not confide her secret to him. Therein lies the tragic collision and artistic interest of her life. Her lover must wrest from her the secret that keeps her from marrying him, but only in the moment of death is she free to do so.

The aesthete offers his modern Antigone as a paradigm for the creation of a genuinely modern tragedy in contrast to modern tragedies that effectively nullify the tragic. Like them, it would emphasize the reflective but focus on a subjective element such as anxiety, which saves the tragic figure from isolation by preserving a measure of substantial identity with family and state, as well as ambiguity of guilt in the individual. It is, in fact, the problem of isolation that motivates A's aesthetic endeavor and makes his attempt to recover the tragic so appealing to the *Symparanekromenoi* whom he addresses. For both he and they are representative of a growing isolation and disintegration that is characteristic, he claims, of the age in which they live and that has led to the formation of associations such as theirs in an unsuccessful attempt to counteract it (EO, 1:141). "Our age has lost all the substantial categories of family, state, kindred," A claims (EO, 1:149). Thus what he and his cohorts seek in the rebirth of tragedy is the recovery of a lost substantiality in the renewal and rebirth of their own dead lives.

> If . . . we were to imagine a rebirth of ancient tragedy, then every individual would have to contemplate his own rebirth, not only in the spiritual sense but in the finite sense of the womb of family and kindred. . . . If the individual is isolated, then either he is absolutely the creator of his own fate, and then there is nothing tragic anymore, but only evil, for it is not even tragic that the individual was infatuated with or wrapped up in himself—it is his own doing; or the individuals are merely modifications of the eternal substance of life, and so once again the tragic is lost. (EO, 1:159, 160)

In conjuring up his modern Antigone, A offers, in true fragmentary style, only a "glimpse of the idea" of the truly tragic and engages in the art of writing "posthumous papers," that is, an unfinished characterization of the poetic personality he seeks to poetize so as to evoke a sense of past enjoyment in the artistic product left behind (EO, 1:152). In line with his artistic principles, her outline is left "indistinct" and her form "nebulous" so that, he explains to members of the *Symparanekromenoi,* "each and every one of you can *forleibe sig* [fall in love] with her and be able to love her in your own way" (EO, 1:153). Like them, he points out, "she, too, does not belong to the world in which she lives," and her real life is hidden; like them, "she, too, although alive, is in another sense dead" (EO, 1:157). Thus they—and perhaps we—can easily identify with her, as A himself does ("her thoughts are my thoughts"), even as he projects her as an other whose deep secret has been elicited from her by his cunning ingenuity (EO, 1:153).

The aesthete uses a female character to illustrate the truly tragic because, in his view, woman has more substantiality than man and lacks the infinite reflection by which to reflect herself out of the hereditary guilt she has incurred (EO, 1:153–54). She more clearly portrays, therefore, both the ancient and the modern elements in genuine modern tragedy, that is, both the substantiality of ancient tragedy and the restlessness of the modern spirit. As initially conceived by A, then, she is an epic character in the manner of ancient tragedy, which possesses an epical quality in its emphasis upon substantial determinants (EO, 1:143, 162). But A proposes to go beyond this and make her a *dramatic* character in a modern tragedy in which the *monologue* will play a leading role (EO, 1:162). Thus, while dramatic interest may be stirred by the tragic internal collision of Antigone's love for her betrothed with the secret she cannot reveal to him or anyone, she still does not provide the escape from isolation and the concomitant rebirth that A and his associates seek aesthetically. For just as recollection of her father is responsible for Antigone's death, so A's recollection of her murders him, that is, he perceives there is no escape from the terrible isolation that grips his soul.[16]

Capturing certain subjective elements and states through art, however, can be difficult, if not impossible, to do. It has already been shown how, in the aesthete's view, the quality of sensuousness, an inward determination, can be represented only in music. As A moves on to a presentation of the other three "brides of sorrow" who suffer from unhappy love, a similar aesthetic problem presents itself. In this instance the issue revolves around the possibility of giving an aesthetic representation of the reflective sorrow they bear. Employing a distinction between poetry (*Poesi*) and art (*Kunst*) borrowed from Lessing, the aesthete characterizes art as lying in the qualification of space and expressing repose, poetry as lying in time and therefore expressing movement. Moreover, he claims, "the subject for artistic portrayal must have a quiet transpar-

16. In a passage deleted from a draft of the essay, A states, "And just as it went with Hercules, so it goes with me. It was predicted to him that he would not be murdered by a living person but by a dead one; thus, the recollection of her murders me" (EO, 1:544).

ency so that the interior rests in the corresponding exterior. The less this is the case, the more difficult becomes the task for the artist, until the distinction asserts itself and teaches him that there is no task for him at all." Applying this principle to the inner emotions of joy and grief, the aesthete suggests that joy can be portrayed artistically much easier than sorrow. "Joy is communicative, sociable, open, wishes to express itself," he points out, whereas sorrow is "silent, solitary, and seeks to return into itself" (EO 1:169). This is not to say that sorrow cannot be represented artistically, but at a certain stage in its evolution the contrast between the inner and the outer is so great that it becomes impossible for art to represent it. That stage or type of sorrow that resists artistic representation is reflective sorrow, a form of grief in which the external appearance of the individual provides no more than a hint, if that much, of the inner presence of sorrow. Furthermore, this type of sorrow "does not have inner stillness but is constantly in motion," so that it "is not at one with itself, does not come to rest in any one definite expression" (EO, 1:170). It is thus best dealt with through a poetic or psychological treatment, the aesthete concludes (EO, 1:172).

The only way such sorrow can be rendered visible in art, the aesthete suggests, is indirectly through pictures or sketches he calls "silhouettes" because they derive from the "dark side of life" and are not directly visible (EO, 1:172–73). By means of this device, the aesthete displays to the members of the *Symparanekromenoi* the inner sorrow of three literary characters: Marie Beaumarchais from Goethe's *Clavigo,* Donna Elvira from Mozart's *Don Giovanni,* and Margarete from Goethe's *Faust.* Their interest in sorrowful figures such as these is not motivated by mere curiosity about external and superficial matters but rather by a "sympathetic anxiety" that probes behind the outward appearances of these women to secret matters of the heart (EO, 1:176). This anxiety on the part of the society members is an indication that the hidden sorrow that so fascinates them in these women is really their own. Indeed, the lecturer implies as much at the conclusion of his salutatory remarks: "Although I designate them with specific poetic names, by no means is it suggested thereby that it is only these poetic figures who appear before you, but the names must be regarded as *nomina appellativa* [common nouns], and from my side there is nothing to hinder any one of you, if you feel inclined, from giving a particular picture another name, a more appealing name, or a name that perhaps comes more naturally to you" (EO, 1:176). Just as prolonged scrutiny of a face can sometimes lead to the discovery of a second face that is a "mirror of the soul" (EO, 1:175), so this probing beneath the surface portraits of these women characters reveals the hidden faces of the members of the society and mirrors the state of their own souls. The presence of a hidden face, the lecturer suggests, is generally a sign that the person has become "an emigrant who has withdrawn from the exterior face in order to watch over a buried treasure" (EO, 1:174).

In the cases of the three women characters, the imaginative peering into their souls through screens reveals a retreat into inwardness for the purpose of nursing sorrow over unhappy love affairs. Each has been jilted by her lover, and each is plagued by a question that gives her soul no rest. For Marie Beaumarchais, it is a question of deception: Was he a deceiver or was he not? To love, deception is an absolute paradox that cannot be thought but nevertheless must be entertained. By the same token, reflection can never resolve the issue, for only a determination of the will that places the individual under ethical categories will bring it to an end. Marie Beaumarchais cannot make that movement and thus is locked into a perpetual restlessness of reflective sorrow over the loss of her lover. For Donna Elvira, the paradoxical question is not so much whether she has been deceived—it is quite evident to her that she has—but whether she can love Don Juan even though he has deceived her. Torn between a powerful hate that requires revenge and a boundless love that has cost her everything, even her eternal happiness, Donna Elvira is likened to a person shipwrecked at sea who cannot decide in the face of imminent destruction what it is that should be saved (EO, 1:204). For Margarete, the simple maid seduced by Faust, the question of deception takes on an absolute character by her feeling of being nothing over against Faust's overwhelming superiority. Not only has she loved him with all her soul, he was the vital force through which she came into being and upon which she depends for her continued existence. To admit his love was a deception would mean a lapse back into nothingness for her, since she has no independent existence apart from him. Thus she is caught up in a basic mood of weakness and powerlessness that is total and unmitigated.

These four brides of sorrow provide very different but equally poignant images whose reflective sorrow we may, like the members of the *Symparanekromenoi,* sympathetically enter into and perhaps, like them, identify with in the recognition of our own hidden faces in their silhouettes or, in the case of Antigone, in the epic and dramatic conflict that brings about her death. Certainly the type of voyeurism practiced by the association is not limited to a few odd recluses but may be observed in society at large in the widespread fascination with the private lives of others exploited by the media today. If these classical literary figures do not interest us, then there are many others whose secrets are cunningly extorted every day for us to read about and view and whose sorrows we may parasitically dwell upon in an effort to conceal and perpetuate our own.[17]

TWO REARED ON ROMANCES

Comic relief from experimentation with unhappiness and sorrow is provided for us next by A's review of the French dramatist Scribe's one-act play *The First Love.* Here we meet two poetic figures, Emmeline and Charles, who illustrate the results of having been nurtured on romantic novels: either a sinking into a state of illusion in which one is hidden from oneself, as in the case of Emmeline, or a gaining of a talent for mystification by which one can hide oneself from others, as in the case of Charles (EO, 1:250). The condition of an inner hiddenness thus persists in these romantic characters, but here it is masterfully brought to light through "situation comedy"—the use of an accidental (yet necessary) occasion as a means of unfolding and revealing in dramatic action and dialogue the personalities of the poetic characters. Emphasizing the importance of an occasion for an artistic production, the aesthete claims that it is what determines the "true esthetic value" of every literary work (EO, 1:236). An occasion is important to a production because it is "the final category, the essential category of transition from the sphere of the idea to actuality." It is through an occasion, then, that an aesthetic idea is brought into contact with actuality and becomes real. In itself, the occasion is nothing and acquires its significance only "in relation to that which it occasions," but without it nothing happens (EO, 1:238). As our aesthetic critic aptly puts it, "A creation is a production out of nothing, but the occasion is the nothing that lets everything come forth" (EO, 1:236). It thus makes an ideal category for the operation of romantic irony in a work of art because it "often plays the absolute master; it determines the outcome; it makes the product and the producer into something or nothing, whatever it wishes" (EO, 1:234). Even the poet who produces a work of art is subject to the power of the occasion, which like a strange force of fate arbitrarily determines the significance or insignificance of the work.

17. The use of the terms "voyeurism" and "parasitism" to describe the activity of the *Symparanekromenoi* have aptly been suggested by George Connell, who uses them in his analysis of A's addresses to that society (*To Be One Thing,* 64).

As reported in his review, A uses the occasion of a stage performance of Scribe's play as an occasion for romantically recollecting his own first love—or what he thought was first love—and poetically reliving it, just as on a previous occasion that love was rekindled when he attended another performance of the same play and met her there. Although A seeks in this manner to renew his first love, confident that "the poetic power of this play will prompt the love in my breast to spring forth," he does not actually want to renew his relation to her but prefers instead to feel the beauty of loving her at a distance (EO, 1:241, 242). Even when he was experiencing love for the first time, he admits, they saw each other infrequently and felt more comfortable and closer when they were apart (EO, 1:240). In this, he sees a similarity between his situation and that of heroes in novels and comedies and thus likes to think of himself as a poetic character and as leading a poetic life. What he really hopes to recover and reexperience poetically is his youth and the spontaneous passion of love, which he expects to burst forth forcefully like the snap of a passionflower or the popping of the cork on a bottle of champagne (EO, 1:241).

A's former love had informed him on another occasion that he was not her first love, since her present fiancé held that honor. She thus bears a resemblance to the character Emmeline, who espouses the romantic dictum that "the first love is the true love, and one loves only once" (EO, 1:254). Emmeline is convinced that she loves her cousin Charles, whom she has not seen since she was eight years old, and she holds fast to this illusion during the course of a comic mix-up in which Charles courts her under another name and is roundly rejected. When it is at last revealed to her who he is and that he is already married, she agrees to marry another man who had pretended to be Charles. She will marry him, however, not out of love—for an "ideal" Charles remains her first and only love—but to be obedient to her father's wish and to get even with the real Charles for having been untrue to her. For his part, Charles, who has squandered his money and become dissolute, thinks he can hide his identity and ingratiate himself to his uncle in the disguise of a respectable man. The man whose identity he assumes is the man who is passing himself off as Charles in order to court Emmeline. In the end both Charles and Emmeline effect the opposite of what they sought, so that the play ends in irony. Emmeline's illusion, however, remains intact, as she looks to the future still in search of the ideal Charles who was her first and only love. Thus it is not a real man but an ideal one she has created in her own imagination whom she thinks she loves.

Just as the production of Scribe's play provides an occasion for the aesthete to recall and relive his first love poetically, so several subsequent fortuitous events—the finding of a copy of the play in the study of a friend he is visiting, the meeting with his first love again, the spilling of ink on an acquaintance's manuscript, necessitating the substitution of one of his own for publication—occasion the writing and publication of his review. The review, in turn, becomes an occasion for us to recollect our first loves, to try to recapture the primitive immediacy of those experiences, and perhaps to cause them to blossom forth again. But more than that—if we are not caught in the same illusion as Emmeline or do not practice the art of mystification like Charles—it offers an occasion for the enjoyment of romantic irony in and through these characters and the dramatic situations concerning them.[18] As A points out, almost every situation in the play constitutes "an infinitely witty mockery" of Emmeline's sentimentality and Charles's mystification. As the play progresses, the dramatic situations become more and more ludicrous, so that, as A rightly observes, the play revolves around nothing (nonsense) and comes to nothing (EO, 1:261). The aesthetic critic advises us, however, that "to enjoy the irony in this play contemplatively, one must not read it but see it . . . again and again," since, according to his aesthetic theory, "the performance is itself the play," which cannot be truly understood apart from its theatrical presentation (EO, 1:277, 239). In order to catch the full play of irony within the drama and especially as it draws to a close, we would need, then, to see an actual stage performance of it. Since that is not immediately possible, the aesthete provides for us a description of the ironic moment at the end of the play: "When the curtain falls, everything is forgotten, nothing but nothing remains, and that is the only thing one sees; and the only thing one hears is a laughter, like a sound of nature, that does not issue from any one person but is the language of a world force, and this force is irony" (EO, 1:273).

18. Scholars differ on the interpretation of *The First Love* as an ironic work. Ronald Grimsley, in *Søren Kierkegaard and French Literature* (Cardiff: University of Wales Press, 1966), 112–29, thinks Kierkegaard regards the work as an ironic treatment of romantic love. But Mackey, *Kierkegaard: A Kind of Poet,* 11; Connell, *To Be One Thing,* 80–81; and Jørgensen, *Kierkegaard som Kritiker,* 159, attribute the ironic stance to A, who is a romantic ironist. Since Judge William in volume 2 of *Either/Or* also interprets Scribe as a critic of romantic love and marriage (see EO, 2:18, 300, 325–26), it is likely that this interpretation also reflects Kierkegaard's point of view, as Grimsley suggests. But that does not rule out an ironic interpretation on the part of A too. The difference is that Judge William (and perhaps Kierkegaard) does not agree with Scribe's view of romantic love, whereas A does. Thus, while the work in itself may be ironic as well as trivial, it provides an occasion for A to engage in the practice of romantic irony. In fact, he admits that the work is trivial if given a moralistic interpretation, but when interpreted ironically it is shown to be a masterpiece (EO, 1:255).

In his view, however, the play constitutes an "infinite jest" that does not end (and thus is fragmentary) but is merely terminated arbitrarily (EO, 1:258, 277). For according to A's interpretation, Emmeline's illusion does not end at the conclusion of the play but simply turns in a different direction, toward the future rather than the past, so that it is possible to imagine an infinite number of dramatic confusions that might arise concerning her.

It is this endless quality of situation comedy, together with the constant motion of reflection directed toward it, that makes it an appropriate medium for aesthetic enjoyment in a contemplative manner. The more reflection uncovers in comic situations, the more infinite the comic situation becomes, the aesthete claims, and the dizzier and more mesmerized the spectators become in the process. They cannot stop thinking about it because they keep expecting something more ludicrous to happen (EO, 1:263). Because of the transparency of comic situations, less self-activity is seemingly required of the spectator in modern comedy, A claims, so that the spectators, "free from care, can enjoy, can absorb undisturbed, the dramatic life" (EO, 1:247). But in another sense, more is required of them, since closer attention must be given to details and greater absorption of the spectator into the drama potentially occurs in comedy than in tragedy. "The comic is commonly thought to be more a matter of the moment than is the tragic. We laugh at it and forget it, whereas we often turn back to the tragic and become immersed in it," A observes (EO, 1:262). But he wants to claim just the opposite, that the comic, when properly done, tempts us to become more absorbed in the situation than does tragedy (EO, 1:262–263). It thus provides an ideal artistic medium for endlessly losing ourselves in an ironic, romantic fashion in the infinite possibilities of imaginative characters and situations such as those in *The First Love.*[19] No wonder, then, that situation comedy is so popular as a medium of entertainment on television today! While we may not be able to see a stage performance of *The First Love,* we have plenty of comic substitutes available to us through which to lose ourselves in the nonsensical world of comedy and thus continue right on in the romantic style of living poetically.

19. The fact that *The First Love* was translated into Danish by J. L. Heiberg, who was himself a dramatist of vaudevilles and in his aesthetic theory placed comedy at the apex of dramatic form, suggests that he may indirectly be the target of irony in A's review (albeit perhaps unintentionally on A's part) inasmuch as situation comedy is elevated and presented here as a medium of romantic irony, thus revealing the aestheticism of Heiberg as being romantic as well as speculative in nature. On Heiberg's theory of comedy, see Paul Rubow, *Heiberg og Hans Skole i Kritiken* (Copenhagen: Gyldendal, 1953), 51–59, and Fenger and Marker, *The Heibergs,* chaps. 4–6.

THE ENGLISH TOURIST AND THE ROTATION ARTIST

In a philosophy of life based on the aesthetic, enjoyment is the highest principle, boredom the root of all evil.[20] Children at play, for example, get along well as long as they are enjoying themselves, but they become unruly when they get bored. As our aesthetic critic A sees it, all people are bores in one way or another; either they bore themselves, as in the case of the nobility, or they bore others, such as the crowd, or people in general, do (EO, 1:288). In the aesthete's view, the paradigms of boredom are the English, a people with a talent for indolence unparalleled in nature. In them boredom is not merely an inborn talent but an "acquired immediacy" born from a misguided effort to find diversion (EO, 1:290). The English seek relief from boredom in an eccentric or extensive manner by traveling from place to place. When the English tourist tires of one place, he or she moves on to another in an endless process of change. Like an "apostle of empty enthusiasm," the English tourist reacts to everything with a single interjection—Ah! or Oh!—that unites and neutralizes both admiration and indifference in the same breath with a concealed boredom (EO, 1:209).

Since boredom is the root of evil, the natural thing is to try to overcome it, but that must be done in a considered manner, in accordance with some principle, A claims (EO, 1:291). In a reflective venture in the theory of social prudence, therefore, he offers such a principle in a discourse on the notion of "rotation." By this he does not mean "changing the soil," that is, constantly moving to a different place in the manner of the English tourist; rather, he advocates a method of rotation that consists in "changing the method of cultivation and the kinds of crop" in an intensive, self-limiting manner. "The more a person limits himself, the more resourceful he becomes," A points out, so that, by becoming a "meticulous observer" of the world, one is able to find amusement in anything, no matter how trivial or monotonous (EO, 1:292).

The principle of limitation thus constitutes, in A's opinion, "the sole saving principle in the world," through which rotation may be developed into an art. Whereas, in his estimation, the extensive method of the English is "vulgar and inartistic," his method enables us "to live artistically" by abandoning hope and cultivating the arts of remembering and

20. In a parody of the biblical creation story, A suggests that boredom can be traced back to the beginning of the world, when the gods created human beings because they were bored and brought boredom into the world through Adam and Eve, who also were bored and whose descendants spread boredom throughout the world as a result of their dispersion after building the tower of Babel to amuse themselves (EO, 1:286).

forgetting (EO, 1:292).[21] These two arts, he suggests, are integrally connected in that "the more poetically one remembers, the more easily one forgets; for to remember poetically is actually only an expression for forgetting." The reason for this is that in a poetic remembrance the experience has been transformed so as to lose all its painful aspects (EO, 1:293). In remembering poetically, then, one forgets that which is painful in life. This mode of remembering, however, requires some care in the way one lives and enjoys life. We must learn to keep our enjoyment under control, so as not to indulge in an experience too long or allow it to acquire too strong a hold on us; otherwise the experience will be too intense to forget and will leave only a feeling of satiation to remember. Similarly, in developing the art of forgetting, we must learn to forget the pleasant as well as the unpleasant, since a pleasant experience, "as a bygone, has an intrinsic unpleasantness with which it can awaken a sense of loss" (EO, 1:294). Friendship and marriage must be guarded against also, as it is essential never to stick fast in relationships and to be able to discard them at will. We need to vary the soil to a degree by having contact with more than one person, but always in such a way that we have "enough reserve speed to run away from them" (EO, 1:296, 298). It is also recommended that one avoid taking official posts that make one "a tiny little cog in the machine of the body politic" and thus not in control of one's own life (EO, 1:298). Engagement in aimless pursuits, control of moods, and the practice of arbitrariness in one's activities are also important aesthetic talents to cultivate in this mode of living artistically. Arbitrariness in particular requires that we not "run wild" in the enjoyment of anything but derive an accidental kind of satisfaction from it by engaging in an unconventional practice such as reading the end of a book first (EO, 1:299). The degree of consistency with which one holds fast to arbitrariness reveals whether one is "an artist or a bungler," A maintains (EO, 1:300). The net result of all this, he suggests, is that we shall be able to realize complete freedom and self-control in our lives.

The English tourist, as the paradigm of boredom, and the rotation artist, which the aesthete recommends each of us become, represent opposite ends of the spectrum in the romantic view of life. Through the first, we catch the predominant mood of the romantic attitude toward life and a common way of reacting to the boredom often experienced in life. In the second, we find a more sophisticated solution to boredom in the detachment and freedom of romantic irony. Both express the roman-

21. "Not until hope has been thrown overboard does one begin to live artistically," A claims, for "as long as a person hopes, he cannot limit himself" (EO, 1:292).

tic mentality, but only in the latter do we achieve the radical freedom that constitutes the ideal of the romantic mode of living poetically. For an example of the consummate expression of that freedom, let us rotate our kaleidoscope once more to observe and imaginatively experience the rotation artist's theory put into practice in a figure who is a master artist and more in the romantic mode of living poetically.

THE EROTICIST AND HIS PROTÉGÉ

The final romantic figures A brings before us are an aesthete by the name of Johannes, who specializes in the seduction of young girls, and, indirectly through him, a female figure named Cordelia Wahl, a young girl of seventeen who has been marked as his next victim. A character of A's own creation (although he claims only to be the editor of the seducer's diary found in a secretary drawer), the seducer figure introduced here is designed to provide an appropriate literary treatment of a Don Juan at the reflective level and perhaps to serve as a contrasting analogue to the sensual hero of Schlegel's infamous novel *Lucinde.*[22] Although previous literary interpretations of Don Juan are criticized by A in his essay on the musical-erotic, he does not rule out the possibility of interpreting the Don in literary form. A reflective seducer such as he presents to us here constitutes, he claims, the only significant literary interpretation of Don Juan in contrast to a musical one (EO, 1:107). This interpretation pres-

22. In using the form of a diary instead of the novel to cast the figure of the reflective seducer, A's representation stands in contrast to Schlegel's *Lucinde* in form as well as in content. In a note to a passage from a draft of *The Concept of Anxiety,* Kierkegaard makes a reference to "The Seducer's Diary" in *Either/Or,* suggesting that anyone who "looks at it closely . . . will see that this is something quite different from a novel, that it has completely different categories up its sleeve" (JP, 5:5730). Thus, in labeling "The Seducer's Diary" a novel, as Aage Henriksen does in *Kierkegaards Romaner,* or in associating it with novelistic form, as John Vignaux Smyth does in *A Question of Eros,* 243, interpreters miss the significance of the diary form of the work. It is *Either/Or* as a whole, not one of its parts, that is properly viewed as a novel. Entitled "*Commentarius perpetuus,*" or "Running commentary," by the seducer (EO, 1:303), the diary—supposedly the fourth in a series of such commentaries—reflects the secretive, restless, unfinished, unsatisfied character of the romantic lifestyle of the reflective seducer. It thus constitutes, like a novel, a form by which the fragmentary character of his life and art may be represented. But unlike a novel, which is properly situated in a historical setting, the diary format allows a freer, more poetic, "subjunctive," rather than "indicative," rendering of the seducer's experiences, which enables him to live poetically in a double sense, both immediately and reflectively, and to allow "the possibility of any and every interpretation" (EO, 1:304, 374).

ents him as an intensive seducer rather than an extensive one, that is, as one who elicits an internal opposition in the victim of seduction, rather than external obstacles from the environment, to conquer. The mode of treatment in this instance centers around a portrayal of the craftiness with which the seducer wins over his victim and carries out the seduction. Unlike the musical Don Juan, this seducer is much more interested in the art of seduction—the method of conquering—than in the act of seduction, the experience itself. Thus in his diaries we are made privy to the inner machinations of his mind as he plots and executes the seduction of a young girl. The "strategic principle" by which he accomplishes it is the category of the interesting, which he employs in a plan to maneuver her into an "interesting situation" set up to take her by surprise. It is the interesting means by which the seduction is carried out, not some interesting feature of the girl herself, that gives him enjoyment.

Far more than Julius—the sensual hero of Schlegel's *Lucinde,* who Kierkegaard says in *The Concept of Irony* is "no Don Juan" but "a personality ensnared in reflection" (CI, 308)—the calculating seducer of *Either/Or* illustrates the extreme to which sensuality in the absence of any moral restraint at the reflective level may go. By virtue of the degree of consciousness and intellectuality such a figure displays, he properly falls under ethical categories but is not ethical; indeed, as the pseudonymous editor of the diary observes about him, "even the expression 'the conscience awakens' is too ethical to use about him; conscience takes shape in him merely as a higher consciousness that manifests itself as a restlessness that does not indict him even in the profound sense but keeps him awake, allows him no rest in his sterile restlessness" (EO, 1:308–9). The reflective seducer is described by A as a person whose "life has been an attempt to accomplish the task of living poetically" by imaginatively reproducing in his diary his sensual experiences as a "literary venture" (EO, 1:304, 310). By reflectively distancing himself from them in this way, he is afforded, in addition to the immediate personal pleasure of sensual satisfaction, a second enjoyment, the enjoyment of himself aesthetically and objectively as an aesthetic personality in the situation of seduction (EO, 1:305). The seducer thus epitomizes the romantic mode of living poetically in that he reproduces himself poetically for the purpose of aesthetic enjoyment rather than for personal development. In projecting himself poetically this way, his personality becomes "volatilized" in the enjoyment of the situation, and actuality becomes "drowned in the poetic" for him (EO, 1:301). With ironic detachment he transcends and cuts himself off from actuality, its only significance for him being to serve as a temporary stimulus to sensual experimentation and reproduction of the same in poetic form. Even the seduction with which he occupies himself in actuality is elevated to an art through the ingenuity and design of its execution. Like an artist who paints a picture of his beloved, or a sculptor who fashions a likeness of his, the seducer admits that what he is doing is "shaping for myself a heart like unto hers" (EO, 1:389). He does not actually want her heart, but only to develop her to the point of a resistant submissiveness to him. Once he has succeeded in artfully seducing a girl, he even more artfully tries to extricate himself from the relation: "To poetize oneself into a girl is an art; to poetize oneself out of her is a masterstroke" (EO, 1:368).

But Johannes is more than a master seduction artist; indeed, he claims not to be a seducer at all but rather an *eroticist,* a person who, according to his definition, "has grasped the nature and the point of love, who believes in love and knows it from the ground up," and who also knows that "the highest enjoyment imaginable is to be loved, loved more than anything else in the world."[23] For the eroticist, love is the absolute, but in Johannes's view it is a shortlived experience that must be carefully cultivated and controlled for maximum enjoyment. In his opinion, "no love affair should last more than a half year at most and . . . any relationship is over as soon as one has enjoyed the ultimate" (EO, 1:368). Unlike "vulgar seducers," who deceptively entice girls with false promises of

23. In "Seven Seducers: A Typology of Interpretations of the Aesthetic Stage in Kierkegaard's 'The Seducer's Diary,'" an essay by Bradley R. Dewey forthcoming in *International Kierkegaard Commentary: Either/Or I,* ed. Robert L. Perkins (Macon, Ga.: Mercer University Press, expected 1995), it is puzzling that while Johannes has been variously interpreted as a sensualist, immoralist, sinner, cog, child, artist, and as Kierkegaard himself in the role of a cad (to employ Dewey's classifications), his own self-characterization as an eroticist has virtually been overlooked as a principal category of interpretation. John Vignaux Smyth, in *A Question of Eros,* associates Johannes with an "erotic aesthetics" that has its conception in the eros and irony of Socrates, who is himself described as an eroticist, or amorist, in an intellectual sense in *The Concept of Irony* (CI, 191). But Smyth is more interested in spelling out the implications of "Kierkegaard's erotic conception of irony for aesthetics as such" than he is in elucidating the eroticism of Johannes (224). What he most perceptively brings out in Johannes's erotic aesthetics is the indeterminacy of the erotic, which is identified with the feminine and with truth and beauty, which the ironist playfully attempts to master (251). Another scholar who notes Johannes's claim to be an eroticist is Stephen Dunning, in his *Kierkegaard's Dialectic of Inwardness,* 54 (see also 69). But Dunning interprets Johannes fundamentally as a deceiver, seeing him as a representative of absolute deception in the Hegelian dialectical framework that informs Kierkegaard's thought. Deception is certainly a characteristic of Johannes and figures importantly in his eroticism, but it does not encompass the whole of his conception as eroticism does. The only other scholar I have found who consistently interprets Johannes as an eroticist is Knud Hansen, in *Ideens Digter,* 25–32. Hansen suggests that it is not sensuality but erotic ecstasy that Johannes seeks in relation to women, who function merely as external incitements to the awakening and culmination of ecstasy in him (26).

marriage, the eroticist makes no promises but receives everything as a gift of freedom, Johannes points out (EO, 1:367–68). "Only in freedom is there love; only in freedom are there diversion and everlasting amusement," he proclaims, for otherwise the girl will fall "like a heavy body" as a burden and obligation upon him (EO, 1:360–61).

To bring about this freedom requires a special kind of artfulness, a "discerning touch" that knows how to evoke devotedness along with freedom (EO, 1:342). "The majority enjoy a young girl as they enjoy a glass of champagne, at one effervescent moment" that corresponds to rape, Johannes observes (EO, 1:341–42). By contrast, the eroticist is able to enjoy more and to make the experience more interesting for himself by artfully developing a girl within herself. He may employ as techniques in this educative process deception, dissimulation, psychological conflict, irony, erotic stimulation, anything that will aid her development. Essentially, however, his method is passive.

> The art is to be as receptive as possible to impressions, to know what impression one is making and what impression one has of each girl. In that way, one can be in love with many girls at the same time, because one is in love in a different way with each one. To love one girl is too little, to love all is superficiality; to know oneself and to love as many as possible, to let one's soul conceal all the powers of love inside itself so that each receives its specific nourishment while the consciousness nevertheless embraces the whole—that is enjoyment, that is living. (EO, 1:361)

To this end Johannes undertakes, and recollects in his diary, the education of Cordelia Wahl in the art of erotic love. Unlike other young girls he has loved in the past, Johannes senses something special about this one. She is lovely, lively, passionate, innocent, imaginative, proud, full of confidence, ripe for an awakening to love. Much to his surprise, she also stirs up in him the passion and rapture of erotic love, which he had not expected to experience again and which necessitates all the more his breaking the relationship with her once he has accomplished his objective. That consists first of all in implanting himself in her life and becoming engaged to her even though she does not love him. Cultivating friendship with a timid young man whom he accompanies to her home and encourages as her suitor in order to arouse within her first the possibility of love and then a distaste for it, Johannes succeeds in ingratiating himself with her aunt, with whom Cordelia lives and whose advice she follows when he surprises them all with a declaration of love and petition for engagement. Then her education begins in earnest as she learns to love him with all the powerful force of erotic love and in learning to love comes to love him doubly so because she has learned to love from him (EO, 1:377). Patiently, cautiously, Johannes cultivates love in her through a series of letters. "When she has received a letter, when its sweet poison has entered her blood, then a word is sufficient to make her love burst forth," the eroticist proclaims. But he also prefers the technique of letters because "in a letter one can more readily have free rein; in a letter I can throw myself at her feet in superb fashion etc.—something that would easily seem like nonsense if I did it in person, and the illusion would be lost. The contradiction in these movements will evoke and develop, strengthen and consolidate, the erotic love in her—in a word: tempt it" (EO, 1:386). He uses the letters at first to develop her mentally in the power of imagination so as to help her discover and make a leap into the infinite: "What she must learn is to make all the motions of infinity, to swing herself, to rock herself in moods, to confuse poetry and actuality, truth and fiction, to frolic in infinity. Then when she is familiar with this tumult, I shall add the erotic; then she will be what I want and desire" (EO, 1:392). Then, to evoke the erotic in her, he switches from letters to notes and with these arouses her to the level of a naïve erotic passion.

But the eroticist has a higher form of the erotic than this in mind for his protégé. What he wants to develop in her is a reflected passion that is bold and free as well as "definite, energetic, determined, dialectical" (EO, 1:412). Having cultivated her passion within the bounds of the universal through an engagement, he now seeks to make her bored and dissatisfied with this convention and thus lead her to break the engagement herself in order to go beyond the boundary of the universal in the expression of a devoted yet free love that recognizes no earthly bounds. As Johannes puts it, "The point now is to guide her in such a way that in her bold flight she entirely loses sight of marriage and the continent of actuality, so that her soul, as much in pride as in her anxiety about losing me, will destroy an imperfect human form in order to hurry on to something that is superior to the ordinarily human" (EO, 1:428). The moment she gives herself to him in freedom and total devotion, however, everything is over. He is rejuvenated and ready to move on to another young girl in waiting; she is relativized and made weak and insignificant by her deflowering. For as the eroticist interprets woman's essence, she is a "being-for-others" whose value is instantly deflated in the moment of her birth and baptism as a woman (EO, 1:429). Like the other brides of sorrow who are victims of seduction, Cordelia is unable to find rest in recollection, and like them, she oscillates between hatred and forgiveness, blaming him and blaming herself, innocence and guilt. But being more highly developed in reflection than they, she is able to recall the experience with greater clarity and understanding. Through Johannes she has learned to love, but also through him she has learned the irony of erotic love, which is what he ultimately sought to teach her.

As an eroticist, Johannes is the consumate aesthete, a prospect so terrifying in its ultimate implications that even A is frightened by the shadowy, dreamlike relation of this character to his own being. Surely we too find him repulsive, whether we identify with the victim of psychological manipulation and subliminal control described in the diary or with the perpetrator of those *actiones in distans* (actions at a distance) who has gone so far astray in his own inner being that there is little or no chance of exit from the self-entrapment in irony and moral bankruptcy concealed there. Yet the flight into boundless freedom that both Johannes and Cordelia represent is an alluring one that constitutes the essence of the romantic mode of living poetically and that makes it ever attractive. Cordelia describes her reaction to Johannes in a letter to A that likens him to a "matchless instrument" of music (an appropriate medium for expressing "the demonic," we may recall): "With an indescribable but cryptic, blissful, unnameable anxiety, I listened to this music I myself had evoked and yet did not evoke; always there was harmony, always I was enraptured by him" (EO, 1:310).

THE IRONIC GLANCE BACKWARD

Having exhausted the possibilities put before us by the romantic poet and literary critic, let us now terminate this poetic expedition and reflect a moment on what we have seen through the kaleidoscope of A's papers. Having encountered in them quite an assortment of literary figures through whom we have experimented with living poetically in a romantic fashion, we must consider where all this has taken us. What has been gained? Who or what, if anything, have we become in the process? Do the range of attitudes, actions, moods, and emotions refracted through these figures correspond to our own? Do they offer appealing possibilities that we want to adopt as our own lifestyles? Or do they present possibilities that are best experienced aesthetically, at a distance, merely as interesting possibilities, not as viable alternatives for real life? Does not each one fall short in one or several ways, so that we are glad to move on to another alternative as the kaleidoscope turns? Does not all this leave us in an endless round of becoming in which we are potentially both all and nothing, ironically negating and being negated in our own existence as an expression of the infinite jesting with which we play? Are we not ourselves representatives of the fragmentariness of life portrayed in *Either/Or* and thus just as much a variation of the pattern as the characters we have viewed? Have we been aesthetically enjoying only ourselves all this time, or is the concept of self effectively nullified too, as Kierkegaard claims in his critique of romanticism?[24] These are some of the nagging questions we are left to ponder and play with in the aftermath of our experiment.

Certainly our aesthetic experience has been enriched through this romantic experimentation, and we can see the importance of aesthetic theory for determining and interpreting how a mood or idea may best be artistically represented. It is apparent that A's papers contain no systematic aesthetics, but there are certain characteristic aesthetic ideas that inform the way he sees the figures he puts before us and wants us to see them too. We can even detect, to a certain extent, an aesthetic development from the lyrical to the epic to the dramatic in the literary fragments that make up the total work. The figures portrayed in the "Diapsalmata" and "The Musical-Erotic" belong to the lyric stage; those in "The Tragic in Ancient Drama," "Silhouettes," and "The Unhappiest One" reflect the epic in their substantiality and restlessness; and those in "The First Love" obviously belong to the dramatic.[25] But in "Rotation of Crops" and "The

24. See, for example, CI, 298, where Kierkegaard accuses the romantic ironists of lacking any notion of an *an sich,* or essential self, to become, so that they become whatever they become, rather than become themselves. If this is true, a strong similarity may be noted between romanticism and postmodernism, which also denies any perduring idea of a self. On the relation between romanticism and postmodernism, especially postmodern French feminism, see my article "The Philosophical Affirmation of Gender Difference: Kierkegaard Versus Postmodern Neo-Feminism," *Journal of Psychology and Christianity* 7 (1988): 18–26, and the Epilogue below. As I see it, Kierkegaard's critique of romanticism applies equally to postmodernism and thus has special relevance for philosophy today.

25. Both Connell, *To Be One Thing,* and Dunning, *Kierkegaard's Dialectic of Inwardness,* see a Hegelian dialectical development in *Either/Or* I from immediacy to reflection to a synthesis of these in the mediation of subject and object (Connell) or in a unity in absolute contradiction (Dunning). Dunning also sees a dialectic of music-drama-poetry as constituting "one expression of the fundamental structure of *Either/Or*" (58). The fundamental dialectical framework they perceive corresponds to the genre development of the lyric-epic-dramatic suggested here, especially as that development is interpreted by Heiberg, whose aesthetics Kierkegaard and A are following and who was himself a Hegelian, although he reverses Hegel's scheme of genre development from the epic (objective) to lyric (subjective) to a dramatic synthesis of these (see Chapter 1). But the underlying dialectical structure they find in *Either/Or* is not adequate for an interpetation of volume 1 or of the book as a whole, especially if it is seen as a

Seducer's Diary" our editor/author transcends the traditional trilogy of genres and the ordering of them as set forth by the eminent Danish aesthetician Heiberg by ending with two prose forms, the essay and the diary. The figures portrayed through these forms contain a higher level of reflectivity than the dramatic personae, and through that reflectivity a greater control and recollection of immediacy. The use of these forms also serves to suggest that the traditional formulation is not an exhaustive one and that the dramatic is not the highest in the process of aesthetic development. From a romantic standpoint, the highest is not to be found in any single element but in the whole, which in romantic literature is the *Roman,* or arabesque novel, composed of a mixture of genres. In a journal entry relating to *Either/Or* Kierkegaard observes that "the only thing this work lacks is a narrative, which I did begin but omitted, just as Aladdin left a window incomplete" (JP, 5:5628).[26] Thus, even as a whole, the novel *Either/Or* remains true to its romantic, fragmentary character and leaves a window of possibility open for more poetic experiments by those of us who are imaginative enough to venture through it.

Roman that is fragmentary in structure. Dunning misses the epic quality of several of the figures and interprets the "Diapsalmata" as lying outside the aesthetic structure noted above, whereas they clearly belong to the category of the lyric. Furthermore, the "poetic" category under which he classifies "The First Love," "The Rotation Method," and "The Diary of the Seducer" is, in Kierkegaard's usage, a broad one that can be applied to any work of art, whether it be music, poetry, prose, painting, sculpture, or drama.

26. Cf. JP, 5:5866, where Kierkegaard identifies "Guilty"/"Not Guilty" in *Stages on Life's Way* as the missing narrative.

4

The Highest in Aesthetics

In contrast to the romantic pattern of living poetically—with its infinite variation of design using an array of characters depicted according to a corresponding romantic aesthetics of representation in volume 1 of *Either/Or*—an ethical pattern of living poetically is etched in volume 2. Unlike the romantic design, which experiments with a multiplicity of possible self-identities, this pattern is modeled on a single paradigmatic figure within the context of an ethical-existential aesthetics that stands in continuity with the religious, or Christian, alternative to the romantic mode of living poetically outlined in *The Concept of Irony.* The figure in which the pattern is exemplified in this instance is that of a married man, Judge William, the pseudonymous "author" of two long epistolary essays in this volume. Capitalizing on the possibility of a play on words in Danish, the judge maintains that it is as a "married man" (*Ægtemand*) that one proves oneself to be a "genuine man" (*ægte mand*) in the trials of life (EO, 2:125).[1] He thus mounts a concerted effort in the form of two "letters" to his friend, the romantic aesthete of volume 1, to make a convincing case for the aesthetic validity of marriage and the need for a balance between the aesthetic and the ethical in the development of personality.

In these letters, Judge William argues not only that the aesthetic is preserved and ennobled in the ethical but also that it receives its highest

1. That Judge William takes an androcentric view of human authenticity is obvious from this equation, but he does attempt to temper his patriarchal mentality later on. How successful he is in that remains to be seen.

aesthetic, or poetic, expression in that form of life. In what he modestly suggests may be regarded by his friend the aesthete and the "priests of esthetics" as "a poor married man's trivial offering on the altar of esthetics" (EO, 2:136), he constructs the rudiments of an existential aesthetics that views existence in an aesthetic light and, conversely, directs attention to the aesthetic as it appears in existence rather than in works of art. In order to engage the ethical mode of living poetically imaginatively and reflectively, therefore, we must attend to the ethical-existential aesthetics within which it is understood and represented. According to Judge William, however, to engage the ethical mode truly, it must be actualized in our lives, not merely entertained as a poetic possibility in the manner of the romantic mode of living poetically. Hence, in our present posture of viewing—through a kaleidoscope, as it were—the ethical as an alternative pattern of living poetically, we remain essentially in the romantic mode, but it may be hoped with enough "artistic earnestness" to be moved further to ethical action.

In order to establish the ethical as a poetic mode of living, Judge William must first show how the ethical is constituted by the aesthetic or is itself essentially aesthetic and poetic. That requires a reconsideration of what the aesthetic is. Focusing, like classical aestheticians, on the concept of the beautiful and its embodiment in concrete form, Judge William, in his first letter to the romantic aesthete, identifies two ideals that in his view constitute the aesthetic. Next, he tries to clear up a common misunderstanding, a confusion of the aesthetic with what can be aesthetically portrayed in artistic productions. He then shows how that form of the aesthetic which is not susceptible to artistic portrayal may nevertheless be aesthetically portrayed in human life, with the result that the categories of repetition and time receive different and greater significance than is found in the historical development of aesthetics, particularly in romantic aesthetics. In his second letter to the aesthete, Judge William develops a theory of self-identity appropriate to an ethical mode of living poetically, and in the closing pages of this letter he returns to the concept of beauty and further works out an aesthetics of work, talent, marriage, and friendship as ethical expressions of the beautiful in contrast to a romantic understanding of these concepts. Following the progression of the judge's thought on these issues, let us examine more closely the alternative mode of living poetically he proposes within the context of an ethical-existential aesthetics.

In conformity with the classical tradition of aesthetics, Judge William seems everywhere to assume an association of the aesthetic and aesthetics with beauty, since he frequently refers to the concept of beauty and to the aesthetically beautiful in talking about the aesthetic. Unlike most aestheticians, however, he is primarily interested in determining what constitutes the aesthetic or aesthetically beautiful *in life* rather than in works of art. Within this sphere, the aesthetically beautiful subject matter with which he is specifically concerned is not the beauty of nature but the beauty of human life and human relationships. In this context, the aesthetic is first of all identified with erotic love by Judge William, who regards it as "one of the most beautiful things in life" and as constituting the aesthetic ideal in immediate form (EO, 2:37). However, as indicated in the title of his first letter, "The Esthetic Validity of Marriage," Judge William is primarily concerned to show the aesthetic nature of marriage, which in his view is constituted by erotic love, contains the same aesthetic elements as are found in that love, and is even more aesthetic than erotic love because it contains more of those elements. In addition, and perhaps even more decisively for his aesthetics, marriage contains another element that is lacking in erotic love—an historical, or acquired, element that constitutes a second aesthetic ideal, making it "ideal in a double sense" (EO, 2:93, 96). To understand the concept of the aesthetic as it functions in an ethical mode of living poetically, therefore, we must examine these two forms of the aesthetic ideal.

THE IMMEDIATE AESTHETIC IDEAL

Instead of constructing an imaginary example with which to represent the aesthetic beauty of marriage, Judge William (although himself an imaginary character) proposes to refer from time to time to his own marriage as a model. According to him, his wife, who happens to be physically beautiful (except for her nose), shares the same aesthetic feeling of love and devotedness toward him as he does for her. Although the judge does not presume to set forth his own marriage as normative, he finds aesthetic treatments of love and marriage in literature generally untrue and unsatisfactory. On the one hand, novels about love over the centuries have tended to glorify marriage by having the story end in a happy marriage, as if all the struggles and difficulties of life were then over; but "precisely this is the corruption, the unhealthiness in these books, that they end where they should begin," the judge complains (EO, 2:17). A genuine aesthetic element may be observed in such works inasmuch as "love is situated in striving," he admits, but a defect is evident even here in that striving is centered in overcoming external opposition, which is not its proper dialectic, as he explains more fully later on (EO, 2:18). On the other hand, in his view modern literature no longer really believes in love (EO, 2:18–19); thus love is shown to be an illusion and is ridiculed, as can be observed, for example, in the dramatic works of Scribe, such as *The First Love* (one of the aesthete's favorite works we may recall). Working against the literary stream, therefore, the judge seeks to establish—or reestablish—by rational argument and personal exemplification in his own life not only the aesthetic validity of marriage but also that of love.

Beginning, then, with an analysis of erotic or romantic love, the judge emphasizes first of all its immediate, natural character and beauty, which derives from its being based partly on "sensuous beauty" and partly on "the beauty that can be conceived through and in and with the sensuous." Given this association of erotic love with the sensuous and beauty, it is easy to see why Judge William identifies it with the aesthetic, which is etymologically related to the Greek word for sense perception and traditionally associated with the beautiful. However, he goes on to point out that erotic love is not merely sensuous, since it contains a consciousness of the eternal, which gives it nobility and distinguishes it from lust (EO, 2:21). Whereas the merely sensuous is momentary and in its more refined expression makes the moment of enjoyment into a "little eternity" or a "sensuous eternity" in "the eternal moment of the embrace," the true eternal factor in romantic love "rescues it first out of the sensuous," he claims (EO, 2:22). Thus, while the judge admits that "romantic love is rather overworked these days," he has "a certain faith in the truth of it" and "a certain respect for it." He finds beauty in the predestined drawing power of romantic love, exclaiming, "Is it not indeed beautiful to imagine that two beings are intended for each other!" And he finds beauty as well in what he regards as its religious sanction: "How beautiful it is that the God who is spirit also loves the earthly love" (EO, 2:20).

In partial agreement with the modern literary viewpoint, however, the judge also regards the eternal factor in romantic love as illusory and presumptive, since it is based on nothing more than the conviction of the lovers that "in itself their relationship is a complete whole that will never be changed" (EO, 2:21). This is the weakness, the fatal flaw, in romantic love against which modern literature has unleashed its devastating and sometimes amusing ironic polemic. But, in the judge's considered opinion, modern literature has nothing to put in its place or, rather, goes off reflectively in two directions, neither of which is acceptable to him, because the first is immoral and the second "misses out on what is more profound in love" (EO, 2:22). The first path is one of indulging in a transitory sensuality antithetical to marriage, a sensuality that knows what "the most beautiful moment" is (surely an allusion to Schlegel's *Lucinde*)[2] and is satisfied with that; or, in its more respectable form, the parties enter into marriage as a temporary civil arrangement until someone more attractive comes along (EO, 2:23). The other path moves in the opposite direction toward a neutralization of the sensuous in a marriage of convenience based on calculation and involving only the "prose of love," that is, such matters as social and economic considerations (EO, 2:23, 27). In contrast to these paths, both of which effectively annihilate love, Judge William holds that romantic love may be delivered from its "illusory eternal" or transient nature and given a deeper erotic or sensuous expression, as well as greater beauty, by being assumed, transfigured, and ennobled in a marriage that has its center and authority in the religious (EO, 2:29–30).

The notion of a "higher concentricity" in which love and marriage are referred to God and oriented in a religious perspective appears frequently in the judge's first letter (see, e.g., 43, 47, 55, 57, 89, 94). It is, I believe, an integral factor in his thought that should not be overlooked or minimized.[3] For he is concerned not only to establish the aesthetic validity of the ethical in marriage but also to show how the aesthetic, ethical, and religious may be united and regarded as "three great allies" in the personal life and its social relations (EO, 2:147). It is not marriage per se that secures and ennobles romantic love, as Judge William has

2. Cf. *Friedrich Schlegel's Lucinde and the Fragments,* where the hero Julius writes "A Dithyrambic Fantasy on the Loveliest Situation in the World" to his beloved Lucinde (46–50). This situation, which occurs in "the most beautiful world," the world of love, is sexual intercourse, more particularly the playful situation in coitus when the man and woman reverse positions and roles: "One above all is wittiest and most beautiful: when we exchange roles and in childish high spirits compete to see who can mimic the other more convincingly, whether you are better at imitating the protective intensity of the man, or I the appealing devotion of the woman" (49). Although Julius describes their relation as a "marriage," it is not a marriage in any worldly, conventional sense but rather a timeless, eternal union of their spirits (47–48). In many passages *Lucinde* reflects the illusory eternity of love that Judge William and modern literature criticize in romantic love. To be consistent with the modern ironic critique of love, Julius's glorification of love would need to be interpreted ironically, as Kierkegaard apparently does here and in his earlier treatment of Lucinde in *The Concept of Irony,* where the same charge of immoral sensuality is brought against the work. It is not at all clear, however, that Schlegel intended the glorification of love in this work to be taken ironically, and other interpreters, including Firchow, take him to be quite serious in setting forth a religion of love in it.

3. Recent studies that tend to downplay or discount the significance of the religious in Judge William's thought include Dunning, *Kierkegaard's Dialectic of Inwardness,* 85, 101; Mackey, *Kierkegaard: A Kind of Poet,* 61; and, to a lesser extent, Mark C. Taylor, *Kierkegaard's Pseudonymous Authorship,* 224–30. For a more positive appreciation, see Connell, *To Be One Thing,* 151–52.

already shown in his critique of secular forms of marriage; only those marriages that take their point of departure in the saying of vows before God, in recognition of the authority and power of the divine in their lives, have the possibility of doing so. "Just as nothing is impossible for God, so also nothing is impossible for the religious individual either," Judge William claims (EO, 2:30). Thus, in the higher unity of the religious, romantic love is able to pass through reflection without losing its immediacy or sensuous character and in marriage becomes a unity of contrasting elements: sensuous yet spiritual, necessary yet free, momentary, or instantly present, yet eternal (EO, 2:30, 60). Judge William admits that first love or immediate love contains these opposite elements too, but in it spirit and freedom are expressed in a "psychical" manner, that is, in terms of a naturally given mental consciousness, and with less self-consciousness or clarity about oneself in one's inward infinity or freedom (EO, 2:61). In marriage, the sensuous and spiritual stand in greater contrast to each other, and spirit is given higher expression than in immediate love. Since marriage is more spiritual, it is also more aesthetic. "The higher the heaven is over the marriage bed, the better, the more beautiful, the more esthetic it is," Judge William proclaims (EO, 2:61). Sensuousness too acquires greater aesthetic significance through contrast with the spiritual factor in marriage, for now it exists as an element in relation to spirit, not merely as an animal instinct, which otherwise "would be the most esthetic," Judge William claims (EO, 2:61).

Here the aesthetic in both love and marriage is defined not merely in terms of the sensuous but as a *unity* of contrasting elements—for example, sensuousness *and* spirit. In this conception of the aesthetic, spirit is not something that stands over against or in contrast to the aesthetic, as in the romantic aesthete's view; rather, spirit is a constitutive element of the aesthetic that gives it greater beauty and significance. This understanding of the aesthetic as a synthesis of immediacy and reflection, sensuousness and spirit, necessity and freedom, derives from Schiller and receives further development in Hegel's view of the aesthetic ideal as the embodiment of spirit, or idea, in sensuous matter. But Hegel views intellectual contemplation as eventually delivering the idea from sensuous reality and thus signs the death warrant of poetry, since that is transcended in a more adequate realization of spirit in religion and philosophy.[4] Judge William, in contrast to Hegel, sees the sensuous and

4. See Hegel's *Aesthetics* 1:10–11, where he speaks of art as "a thing of the past." See also Karsten Harries, "Hegel on the Future of Art," *Review of Metaphysics* 27, no. 4 (1974): 677–96.

the aesthetic as preserved, transfigured, and given higher poetic expression in the ethical and religious personal life.

A second aesthetic element present in both love and marriage and closely associated with spirit is infinitude, a factor that Judge William, in agreement with Hegel (see EO, 2:474 n. 66), specifically identifies with the aesthetic, saying in one passage, "The esthetic consists in its [love's] infinitude, but the unesthetic consists in the impossibility of finitizing this infinitude" (EO, 2:58)—and in another, "The same esthetic element implicit in first love must then also be in marriage, since the former is contained in the latter, but, as described above, the esthetic consists in the infinitude, the apriority, that the first love has" (EO, 2:60). Connected with this feature is the element of striving, identified earlier by Judge William as the genuine aesthetic element in novels about love. But what is this aesthetic infinity after which love strives, and how does it constitute the spiritual side of the aesthetic? The judge identifies it with the eternal, that elusive quality that immediate love presumes to have but in fact lacks (EO, 2:61). Based in part on sensuous beauty and in part on a transcendent beauty conceived in and through and with the sensuous, immediate love, in a Platonic fashion, strives for that beauty, that infinity, that eternity, which would make it a complete whole. But, it fails. It fails because the infinity it seeks is conceived quantitatively rather than qualitatively, as in Don Juan's 1,003, or because the infinite is conceived externally and abstractly in terms of obscure forces rather than in its true form, which Judge William identifies as an interior infinitude or freedom that is acquired and becomes concrete in a marriage referred to God (EO, 2:58, 61).

Although the judge declares himself against female emancipation, which he views as "one of the many unbeautiful phenomena of which the men are guilty" (EO, 2:22), he nevertheless describes the freedom attained in marriage as one that emancipates both man and woman from a patriarchal mentality.[5] By referring the marriage to God, man is freed from a false pride that leads him to try to conquer and assert superiority

5. On the question of freedom in marriage, cf. Birgit Bertung, *Om Kierkegaard Kvinder og Kærlighed—en studie i Søren Kierkegaards kvindesyn* (Copenhagen: C. A. Reitzels Forlag, 1987), who argues that Judge William espouses a Hegelian view of the family and freedom that involves a relinquishment of personal autonomy in marriage and thus a loss of freedom rather than an affirmation of it. As she sees it, true freedom is found only in free love or a love that is not bound by the conventions of marriage—a view she thinks Kierkegaard indirectly advocates in opposition to Hegel. But that, of course, is to fall back into a romantic view of love and marriage that both Judge William and Kierkegaard reject. For a fuller critique of Bertung's book, see my review in *Kierkegaardiana* 15 (1991): 153–57.

over woman, and woman is freed from a false humility that causes her to surrender and submit herself to him as if she were nothing (EO, 2:61). In thankfulness to God they are thus mutually enabled to receive and devote themselves to each other in a more aesthetic manner. "It is truly far more beautiful to take the beloved as a gift from God's hand than to have subdued the whole world in order to make a conquest of her," Judge William contends (EO, 2:57). Moreover, "the freer the individual is, the more esthetically beautiful is the marriage," he claims (EO, 2:94).

Just as there is or should be a union of sensuousness and spirit in marriage, there exists, then, a close bond between the erotic and the religious and between marriage and the religious. In this regard Judge William is particularly concerned to point out the essential relation between the erotic and Christianity, on the one hand, and between marriage and Christianity, on the other. In an apparent reference to the aesthete's claim, in his essay on the musical-erotic, that the sensuous is "excluded" by Christianity (EO, 1:61–62), Judge William denies that the beautiful and the sensuous are negated or annihilated in Christianity (EO, 2:48–49). While admitting that the Christian God and Christianity are spirit and that spirit and the flesh stand in discord with each other in this religion, he stresses that the flesh is not identical to the sensuous but rather is to be understood as selfishness (EO, 2:36, 49). Thus "the joy and fullness that are in the sensuous in its innocence can very well be caught up in Christianity," Judge William claims (EO, 2:49). In another passage he notes that "it would indeed be beautiful if the Christian dared to call his God the God of love in such a way he thereby thought of that inexpressibly blissful feeling, that neverending force in the world: earthly love" (EO, 2:30). And he concludes that "if marital love has no place within itself for the eroticism of first love, then Christianity is not the highest development of the human race" (EO, 2:31). In Judge William's opinion, however, marriage provides the connecting link between the erotic and the religious inasmuch as it contains, or should contain, both of these elements. Furthermore, in his view, "marriage belongs essentially to Christianity," more so than in paganism and Judaism, which have failed to perfect it despite the sensuousness, beauty, and idyllic character of marriage in these religions (EO, 2:28). Although Judge William asks the aesthete to grant him this point without demonstration, he does offer one item of support for his claim, namely, the observation that sex differences are more deeply reflected in Christianity than in these other religions, enabling woman ("the other sex") to attain her full right as a separate and independent being (EO, 2:29).

A third feature that marriage shares with immediate love and that makes it aesthetic is that it has its teleology in itself.[6] Just as immediate love has no inherent "why" or purpose other than its own existence and self-enjoyment, so too marriage lacks any rationale or intention beyond itself. Although Judge William recognizes that marriage is often entered into for such purposes as developing character, having children, or having a home, all of which may be regarded in themselves as good and beautiful, he looks upon marriages contracted solely for such purposes as being not only mistaken in making "a particular feature of the marriage the purpose for marriage" but also immoral, irreligious, and unaesthetic (EO, 2:65, 72, 78, 88). In contrast to the many finite "whys" that may be chosen for marrying, Judge William stresses instead the beauty of those marriages that "have as little 'why' as possible," for in his view "the less 'why,' the more love," which is the only true "why," or constituting element, of marriage (EO, 2:32, 63). Since the lack of any finite purpose is what constitutes the aesthetic in love, this same condition constitutes the aesthetic in marriage based on love, enabling it to hide within itself a multiplicity of finite objectives without being determined by them (EO, 2:88). However, unlike immediate love, which contains the aesthetic in the form of an immediate infinity and "moves only in an external medium," marriage is subject to a "law of motion" that gives it the possibility of inner movement and promise for the future (EO, 2:94). In it first love has a "forward thrust"[7] and is an "infinite impulse," or propelling power, that is continually unfolding and rejuvenating itself, "maintaining a fresh current" in the present (EO, 2:39, 67). It thus has constancy and continuity as well as possibility and is historical in that it undergoes a process of inward assimilation and development in time.

THE HISTORICAL AS AN AESTHETIC IDEAL

It is precisely this historical element in marriage that, in Judge William's opinion, gives it an additional aesthetic character lacking in erotic love

6. Here again Judge William relies on Hegel's conception of the aesthetic. According to Hegel's *Aesthetics,* one of the common ideas of art is that "it has an end and aim in itself" (1:25). See 41–55 for an extended discussion of this idea. Hegel rejects both imitation of nature and moral improvement as the aim of art. On the latter point Judge William stands closer to Schiller but does not see moral improvement as an external aim.

7. Here I prefer the more literal translation of the Danish *det Fremadskyndende* by Lowrie over the Hong translation of it as "the motivating." Cf. SV 2:37, and *Either/Or,* vol. 2, tr. Walter Lowrie (Princeton: Princeton University Press, 1972), 40.

and makes it more beautiful than that love, leading him to declare that marriage, not erotic love, "is really the poetic" (EO, 2:96). This is the second aesthetic ideal consisting in something that is *acquired* rather than naturally or immediately given. Judge William writes:

> And now I turn everything around and say: The esthetic is not in the immediate but in the acquired; but marriage is precisely that immediacy which contains mediacy, that infinity which contains finitude, that eternity which contains temporality. Thus, marriage proves to be ideal in a double sense, both in the classical and in the romantic sense. When I say that the esthetic consists in the acquired, it does not at all mean that it lies in the mere striving as such. This is indeed negative, but the merely negative is never esthetic. When, however, it is a striving that in itself has content, a struggle that in itself has the victory, then in this duplexity I have the esthetic. (EO, 2:94–95)

Let us pause here to consider more closely what the judge is saying in this important passage. Thus far the aesthetic in both love and marriage has been defined in terms of an immediate aesthetic ideal characterized by three factors: (1) a unity of opposite elements consisting of sensuousness and spirit, necessity and freedom, the momentary and the eternal; (2) infinitude; and (3) an immanent teleology. Now Judge William also defines the aesthetic ideal conversely in terms of a mediacy, finitude, and temporality that is *acquired* through striving. The former factors give marriage aesthetic ideality in a romantic sense, the latter in a classical sense.[8] But neither of these is sufficient in itself to define the aesthetic. The romantic impulse toward infinite striving is negative or abstract, lacking substantial content or actuality. Classicism, by contrast, has content and is concrete but does not grasp the aesthetic ideal in all its infinity. Judge William's point seems to be, then, that the aesthetic consists in a combination of the two, an infinite striving that is not negative but acquires content in the process of striving in history.

But, we may ask, what is this historical element, this content that distinguishes marriage and makes it so aesthetically beautiful? In Judge William's view, two kinds of striving in the life of an individual determine two kinds of history: an external history, in which one lacks that for which one strives, or is prevented from possessing that which one has, because of

8. On the distinction between the classical and the romantic in Kierkegaard's thought, see JP, 3:3796–3823; 5:5135.

external obstacles, so that history becomes an arena for overcoming obstacles and acquiring what one lacks; and an internal history, in which external trials are transformed into an internal struggle through a process of "transubstantiation," or inward change, in the way one understands and meets them (EO, 2:124, 134).[9] In the latter form of history one already has that for which one strives, and gains lasting possession of it through a course of development or steady acquisition of it.

To further elucidate this distinction between two kinds of striving or history in the life of the individual, the judge contrasts two types of personality formation: the conquering nature and the possessive nature (EO, 2:131). The conquering individual may triumph over others and acquire many possessions but does not really possess them, because no deeper appropriation is made of them. The possessive individual, like the conqueror, is victorious over obstacles and in this sense has a conquering disposition too, but this person conquers more like a farmer than a warrior, by planting and reaping rather than by lording it over others. Thus the possessive individual does not merely conquer but has some end result, some lasting consequence of his or her actions. The judge identifies the conqueror with the natural or immediate personality who has only an external history; the possessive individual is associated with the person who has an acquired, or internal, history.

REPRESENTATION OF THE AESTHETIC IDEAL

The artistic significance of these correlations, as Judge William sees it, is that "true art goes in the direction opposite to that of nature, without therefore annihilating it, and likewise true art manifests itself in possessing and not in making a conquest" (EO, 2:131). In this connection, the judge points out a common misunderstanding with respect to the way the aesthetic is perceived and represented artistically. A great many people tend to confuse the aesthetically beautiful with what can be represented with aesthetic beauty in poetic reproductions, he thinks, and thus they seek aesthetic satisfaction in such aesthetic endeavors as reading a book or viewing a work of art. Relatively few, however, are able to see and enjoy "the esthetic as it is in existence" or, conversely, "existence in an esthetic

9. In several of Kierkegaard's early writings the term "transubstantiation" is used instead of "transfiguration" to indicate the inward change that takes place in a person via the ethical and/or the religious. See Chapters 1 and 2.

light" (EO, 2:133). This aspect of the aesthetic, he contends, cannot be represented in poetic reproductions because these concentrate the extensive in the intensive, in the moment, and are incapable of representing that which has its reality essentially in temporal succession. The judge duly notes that historically the development of the aesthetically beautiful has been away from static spatial determinants and toward an orientation in time, as in the transition from sculpture to painting, but he maintains that none of the arts can adequately represent temporal movement (EO, 2:136). Music takes place in time but is constantly vanishing. Poetry, the highest of the arts, accentuates the significance of time but nevertheless is compelled to concentrate in the moment.

By this measure, external history can be represented in artistic and poetic productions, since it culminates in an intensive moment of victory in comparison with which the historical strife encountered along the way has little importance, and it is that final moment which is the subject of artistic portrayal. But internal history—the process of inward blossoming in which such qualities as humility, patience, faithfulness, and long-suffering are acquired and possessed through steady acquisition over the years—is incommensurable with poetic representation or at most can only be hinted at in artistic reproductions. It is essential to humility, for example, that it remains constant; there is no ideal moment of humility that can be represented, for "its true ideality consists not in its being ideal at the moment but in its being continuous." Likewise, in regard to love and marriage, the judge maintains that "romantic love can be portrayed very well in the moment; marital love cannot, for an ideal husband is not one who is ideal once in his life but one who is that every day" (EO, 2:135).

The question persists, then, whether the aesthetic ideal of internal history can be represented aesthetically, since traditional forms of art are inadequate to express it. The judge's answer is that it can be represented, but only existentially, that is, by living it: "Everything I am talking about here certainly can be portrayed esthetically, but not in poetic reproduction, but only by living it, by realizing it in the life of actuality" (EO, 2:137). In another passage he reiterates to the aesthete that "although this cannot be portrayed artistically, then let your consolation be, as it is mine, that we are not to read about or listen to or look at what is the highest and the most beautiful in life, but are, if you please, to live it" (EO, 2:139).[10]

10. As a point of continuity with the existential aesthetics prefigured in *From the Papers of One Still Living*, it is interesting to note that in the margin of the draft of Judge William's

In the judge's view, this has the greatest significance for aesthetics, since it is only by portraying the ideal in personal existence that the aesthetic ideal becomes truly reconciled with life in a congruence of ideality and actuality. Insofar as poetry and art are representations of life, the judge admits that in a sense they provide such a reconciliation; but in another sense, he says, "they are enmity to life, because they reconcile only one side of the soul" (EO, 2:137). That is, they provide a reconciliation in the realm of ideality but not in the realm of actuality. When the aesthetic ideal is portrayed existentially, the personal life itself becomes a mode of artistic representation, giving expression to those qualities of the spiritually qualified aesthetic that other forms of poetic reproduction can only hint at—qualities such as constancy and faithfulness in love, which require daily repetition in existence to acquire. In this way the ethical mode of living poetically provides not merely a semblance of the ideal, as in the Platonic theory of imitation, but a reduplication of it in time and actuality.

REPETITION AND TIME

In this form of aesthetic reduplication the category of repetition acquires quite a different meaning than it has in the romantic mode of living poetically, where repetition is understood as an expression of boredom and habit in contrast to the category of the interesting, the favorite aesthetic principle of the romantic poets, by which a multiplicity of new data is continually selected for poetic experimentation. Judge William strenuously objects to the identification of repetition with habit, which he regards as evil and thus as something that ought to be changed (EO, 2:127). The way to counteract boredom and habit in marriage, he claims, is not by changing partners or by distancing oneself from the beloved so as to maintain interest, mystery, and secretiveness but by developing a shared history and a shared consciousness, or mutual understanding, characterized by sincerity, self-giving, and openness. In Judge

---

statements on living the aesthetic ideal, Kierkegaard writes, "Thus it reverts to epic again, has the scope of the epic but not the lyrical impatience of drama, but it is not the immediate externality that is at one with the external, and therefore it is a higher kind of epic. Here everyone becomes his own troubador and can await the explanation, the transfiguration an eternity will give" (EO, 2:378). Once again, then, the ethical is associated with the epic in Kierkegaard's writings.

William's opinion, understanding is "the life principle of marriage" and "the absolute condition for preserving the esthetic in marriage" (EO, 2:116, 117). Without it marriage is neither beautiful nor moral. With it repetition in the ethical sphere becomes a forward movement in which one constantly repeats what one already possesses in the form of love, faithfulness, patience, and so forth, and thereby gains content and continuity in the midst of the ongoing flux of life.

Time also acquires a different and greater significance in this form of aesthetic reduplication than it has in romantic and other forms of aesthetic representation. For instead of seeking to kill time in order to capture eternity or, conversely, collapsing eternity into a moment of time, the ideal married person seeks to preserve eternity in time and time in eternity. "The married man who does this," Judge William proclaims, "is truly living poetically" and is the "true victor" over time (EO, 2:138). To that person time is not an enemy to be fought against but a medium for living in eternity and for prolonging that state with each stroke of the clock. This is done by daily realizing in ethical repetition those qualities such as love, faithfulness, constancy, humility, patience, long-suffering, tolerance, honesty, and so forth, that constitute the eternal in the individual and that have within them the qualification of time, that is, the condition that their veracity consists in being continually realized in time rather than once and for all (EO, 2:139). In the end, the married person is seemingly no further along than when he or she began, since the object of this mode of living poetically is continually to acquire that which is already possessed. Yet the progression of time in it is a growing one in which the original datum is not merely preserved but increased. Moreover, in marriage, the judge claims, the individual is able to stand in a right relation to time by sustaining a relation to the past in recollection and to the future in hope while living in the present. In this way one is able to gain "truth and substantive continuity" (EO, 2:142).

Those individuals who have the aesthetic ideal in themselves, not merely a representation of it in a poetic product apart from themselves, thus succeed in living aesthetically or poetically to a high degree. In the judge's view, however, the highest ideal of aesthetics is realized when the individual feels him- or herself to be a character in a drama composed by God, where the performer, "as the experienced actor who has lived into his [or her] character and his [or her] lines," is indistinguishable from the prompter, having assimilated the prompter's words as his or her own. Only the person who in this manner is at once "poetizing and poetized" (*paa eengang digtende og digtet*), both the producer and artistic product of poetic endeavor, has realized the highest in aesthetics (EO, 2:137).[11]

CHOICE OF THE SELF

Unlike the romantic mode of living poetically, where the poet plays a variety of roles, experimenting with different identities in a drama of the poet's own making, in this divine drama the ethical individual has a single role and a single identity, or self, already assigned, to choose and to reduplicate poetically in existence. Having shown in his first letter to the aesthete the aesthetic validity of marriage as a mode of living poetically, Judge William proceeds to impress upon him in a second letter the importance of choosing oneself in one's eternal validity as a unified personality containing a balance of aesthetic and ethical factors. Accusing the romantic aesthete of being a "nonentity" who becomes something only in relation to others and then only through deception, that is, through the donning of a mask, the judge reminds him that "there comes a midnight hour when everyone must unmask" (EO, 2:159–60). This unmasking reveals a disintegration of the aesthetic personality into multiplicity and thus the annihilation and loss of the self. (A recurrent theme in the judge's second letter is the gospel theme of the futility of gaining the whole world and losing oneself [EO, 2:164, 167, 169, 176, 178].) Judge William thus urges the aesthete to choose the ethical and, with it, himself. One cannot be indifferent toward this choice or indefinitely postpone it by continually and abstractly deliberating on the matter as a thought experiment. To ignore it or put it off is already to make an unconscious decision in favor of the romantic-aesthetic mode of identity, or rather, it is to express a preference for the romantic-aesthetic; for properly speaking, the judge maintains, "an aesthetic choice is no choice." "On the whole," he goes on to state, "to choose is an intrinsic and stringent term for the ethical" (EO, 2:166). To choose, then, is to choose the ethical.

But how is one to choose? If we cannot legitimately "try out" the

11. Here I again follow the older Lowrie translation (140), slightly amended to give a more precise rendition of the Danish, in preference to the Hong translation of this phrase as "creating and created," which does not as clearly convey the artistic connotation of the Danish. Although Judge William uses only the masculine gender in referring to the individual, for the sake of inclusiveness I use the feminine gender as well.

ethical mode in a romantic experimental fashion by entertaining it imaginatively or reflectively as a possibility, how are we, along with the aesthete, to make the movement into the ethical stage? On the surface the ethicist might say that the answer to this question is simple and obvious: find someone to love and get married, thereby entering into the existential framework in which the qualities distinguishing the ethical life can be acquired and possessed through repetition. But the judge addresses this question at a more fundamental and far deeper level, in terms of an inward, psychological course of action. He tells the romantic aesthete that what he must do is despair. This comes at first as a surprising, even shocking, response, for the judge regards anyone who lives aesthetically on an immediate, abstract level as already being in despair. The romantic-aesthetic life-view—or, more accurately, what resembles a life-view—is one of despair in that its egoistic, hedonistic philosophy of enjoyment does not penetrate beyond the immediate level of personality to an awareness of any higher form of existence. At its most reflective level of development, this view of life becomes conscious despair in the recognition of the vanity of all things. But it is precisely at this point that it becomes incumbent upon the aesthetic individual to carry through with despair, that is, to despair absolutely, for in despairing absolutely, the judge thinks, we come to choose ourselves in our absolute, eternal validity as the specific, concrete individuals we already essentially are and have as our existential task to become (EO, 2:192, 208, 211, 213–14). Failure to carry through with despair results in a form of poet-existence that, like Socrates hovering above the world in a basket, remains midway between the finite and the infinite, the actual and the ideal, because the individual does not carry the image of the ideal within him- or herself as a task to realize in the realm of actuality. In agreement with the viewpoint expressed by Kierkegaard in *The Concept of Irony,* the judge asserts that "the true ideal is always the actual," not some poetic ideal beyond the world (EO, 2:210). Accordingly, he emphasizes that true choice is to choose oneself concretely, that is, to posit and take responsibility for oneself in the realm of actuality as a product, or, what amounts to the same thing, to produce oneself (EO, 2:251).

For Judge William, however, to produce oneself does not mean to create oneself. In *The Concept of Irony* Kierkegaard makes a distinction between poetically producing or creating oneself, as the romantic ironist seeks to do, and allowing oneself to be poetically produced in a synergistic fashion through cooperation with the divine in a Christian mode of living poetically. Judge William makes a similar distinction between creating the self and choosing the self (EO, 2:215). In his view, to produce oneself through choice of the self is not to create oneself but only to give birth to oneself (EO, 2:251, 259). Since that which is chosen already exists as a potentiality within the individual, it is not created by the individual but rather is received from God. In the birth of the self, then, the individual is the same as before yet becomes another through a metamorphosis in which the finite, individual personality is interpenetrated with the infinite and the universal (EO, 2:177, 251, 255–56). This infinitizing and universalizing of the self involves a movement toward realizing the possible self, or ideal self, as the goal of ethical action. It thus constitutes the role of imagination in the ethical sphere, which is indeed an important and indispensable aspect of the aesthetic dimension of the ethical individual.[12] But it is not so much imagination or reflection as it is the "art of willing" that is crucial for Judge William in the process of giving birth to the self (EO, 2:163, 169, 206, 252, 262). Anyone who has the will can do so, even in the context of the most insignificant of life situations, where every person has "a dancing place," as it were; and "if he himself so wills his dancing can be just as beautiful, just as gracious, just as mimetic, just as dramatic as the dancing of those to whom a place has been assigned in history" (EO, 2:252–53).

Over against the romantic-aesthetic mode of self-identity, or, more accurately, nonidentity, Judge William thus envisions an ethical-aesthetic form of self-identity that stands in sharp contrast to it: whereas the romantic-aesthetic sports with multiple self-identities through experimentation, the ethical-aesthetic acquires a single, unified, concrete, and constant personality through earnestness of spirit and inwardness; whereas the romantic-aesthetic claims total poetic license or freedom to create the self as the individual pleases, the ethical-aesthetic sees the self as a product of divine creation that the individual gives birth to or posits through choice and ethical striving; whereas the romantic-aesthetic practices hiddenness and mystification, making life a masquerade, the ethical-aesthetic requires revelation of oneself and openness to others as well as transparency to oneself; whereas the romantic-aesthetic is fragmentary, one-dimensional, and eccentric, seeking self-identity through something outside itself, the ethical-aesthetic is integrated, balanced, and concentrically oriented in relation to the divine; whereas the romantic-aesthetic thrives on possibility as a means of enjoying freedom and diversity and thus

12. For a good interpretation emphasizing the role of imagination in the judge's conception of the constitution of the self, see Gouwens, *Kierkegaard's Dialectic of the Imagination,* 191–211. See also Ferreira, *Transforming Vision,* 57–68. Ferreira insightfully points out the connection between imagination and reflection in Judge William's thought, revealing the latter to be a form of *action* as well as imagination in the process of choosing the self.

avoiding boredom in life, the ethical-aesthetic views possibility as a task, the task of making the self concrete in the exercise of a positive freedom that must also be distinguished from the abstract, negative freedom of the romantic-aesthetic; whereas the romantic-aesthetic personality develops like a plant, with necessity and in terms of that which the individual is immediately, the ethical-aesthetic personality undergoes a development through personal, civic, and religious stages, having one's teleology in a full realization of oneself within the context of the social environment in which one lives.

From this brief account of Judge William's extensive discussion of self-identity, it should be apparent that his theory of selfhood fits into and should be interpreted in the context of the aesthetic—or, more precisely, the ethical-aesthetic—framework articulated in his first letter to the romantic aesthete. Thus, when the judge contrasts, as he often does in the second letter, an ethical life-view and mode of living with an aesthetic one, this should not be read as a wholesale rejection of the aesthetic or simply as a subordination of the aesthetic to the ethical, although that language is sometimes used, as when the judge speaks of "dethroning" the aesthetic or of retaining it "relatively" in the absolute choice of the ethical (EO, 2:177, 226). Such terminology is used by Judge William to indicate the inclusion and place of the aesthetic as a nonabsolute element *within* the ethical, in which it "means something different from what it means for one who lives only esthetically" (EO, 2:226). The ethical is thus understood by him as incorporating the aesthetic in itself in such a way as to embody "the true art of living," manifesting in that life true beauty for the first time (EO, 2:226, 256, 271). For in the judge's view, "only when life is considered ethically does it take on beauty," and "only when a person himself lives ethically does his life take on beauty" (EO, 2:271).

THE AESTHETICS OF WORK, TALENT, MARRIAGE, AND FRIENDSHIP

In view of Judge William's identification of the ethical with beauty, it is quite fitting that in the closing pages of his second letter he returns to the concept of beauty and works out in this context an aesthetics of work, talent, marriage, and friendship in the ethical. Defining the beautiful in terms of his previous characterization of the aesthetic as that which has its teleology in itself, the judge tries to show the romantic aesthete, who presumably also subscribes to this definition, that beauty, so defined, is a category of the ethical and cannot without logical contradiction be applied to poetry, art, nature, or the immediately aesthetic individual in any essential way (EO, 2:272–73). For in the romantic aesthete's conception of the beautiful, as Judge William understands it, beauty is attributed to the individual in his or her distinctive, accidental, and even insignificant characteristics, and the individual is understood in an organic manner as an element of the whole. "But if a person is merely an element, then he does not have his teleology within himself but outside himself," the judge objects (EO, 2:273). "Even if the whole is beautiful," he goes on to point out, "the parts in themselves are not beautiful." Only when the individual is understood as being both an element and the whole, the judge contends, is that person considered according to his or her beauty. But that is the same as considering the individual ethically, he claims, because the individual is then considered according to his or her freedom and not merely according to necessity, which would be the case if the individual were only an element.

Furthermore, the judge charges that the aesthete's view of the beautiful lacks movement, since "beauty in nature simply is" and any mental activity involved in the interpretation of a work of art resides in the individual and not in the work of art itself. Thus, insofar as the aesthete can claim that beauty has its teleology within itself, this must be understood only negatively, that is, as saying "that the beautiful does not have its teleology in something else." Consequently, in the judge's opinion, this conception of beauty lacks a positive teleology, which he identifies with an "inner teleology" or "immanent teleology" that involves movement, history, freedom, and thus the ethical. By immanent teleology Judge William is quick to point out that he does not mean self-centeredness or self-sufficiency of the individual but rather a movement toward the self as the goal of a striving that moves in freedom from the individual to the world in a positive relation and then back again to the individual in a process of total concretion. "Only here," Judge William declares, "can we speak of beauty" (EO, 2:274). And only here can we look at ourselves and at others with an eye toward discerning individual beauty. For according to the judge's aesthetic judgment, the individual is seen in his or her beauty only when that person is seen as both an individual human being and the embodiment of the universally human (EO, 2:275). To realize the universal in the particular constitutes "the true art of living" and secures the "victory of the beautiful" in life (EO, 2:256, 276). Through faith in this victory one is able to see the beauty of life, which is joyful, triumphant, and strong, in contrast to the "sadness and gloominess that are inseparable from the beauty of all nature and art" (EO, 2:276).

Far from depriving us of beauty, then, Judge William claims that the ethical bestows a positive and higher beauty on the relationships of life, especially in those "mixed territories" where either an aesthetic (romantic) or an ethical view of life-relationships is possible (EO, 2:323). To conclude his discussion of beauty as an ethical category, the judge examines four such areas concerning the aesthetic status of work, talent, marriage, and friendship as these are manifested in the life of a typical yet concrete individual he identifies anonymously throughout the discussion as "our hero." This individual is portrayed as one who appeals alternately to an aesthete and to an ethicist for advice on how to order his life with respect to mundane matters such as making a living, as well as on personal matters such as love and friendship. Although the cards are stacked against the romantic-aesthetic interpretation in this contest of life-views, since Judge William is prejudiced toward the ethicist's point of view, it nevertheless provides a good setting for further development of his own ethical-existential aesthetics. For the judge's main objective is to show that the ethical does not lie outside the aesthetic but provides the highest and best expression and interpretation of it.

WORK

Turning first to the area of work, Judge William argues for the aesthetic validity of this traditionally ethical category over an aesthetic interpretation of it. Although the aesthete may claim that the person who has plenty of money and does not need to work is more independent and therefore more beautiful than the person who must work for a living, the judge claims just the opposite, that it is more liberating and beautiful for a person to provide for him- or herself and to acquire what he or she needs through work than to get it by an accidental condition, such as playing the lottery, or by virtue of providence, as the lilies and birds do in being free from care and anxiety (EO, 2:278, 282). The judge offers two rationales for his viewpoint. First, work expresses a universal human requirement. Every individual has a duty to work for a living, he asserts; thus, the person who does not work is an exception and in this respect is inferior, rather than superior, to others. From an ethical standpoint, having money by virtue of preferential treatment is a humiliation that places a greater, rather than lesser, demand upon the individual to work for a living (EO, 2:281). Second, work is an expression of human perfection and thus of true beauty. The judge disparages the fictitious idea that a world in which the individual does not need to work would constitute a perfection of existence and counters it with the charge that this would instead constitute an imperfection. For the fact that human beings can and must work is what distinguishes them from other creatures and gives them their human dignity as well as a higher beauty. Thus, even if one is not compelled to work for the necessities of life, one still must be willing to work, because that is seen as "the most beautiful and most perfect thing" (EO, 2:289).

TALENT

A second gray area where, in the judge's judgment, an ethical view is preferable to a romantic-aesthetic one has to do with the interpretation of talent. In a romantic-aesthetic perspective, talent is understood as an accidental determinant that distinguishes those who have it from those who do not. It is thus an egoistic category by which human differences may be measured and accentuated in a quantitative and arbitrary manner (EO, 2:292). From an ethical-aesthetic standpoint, however, talent is seen as a calling, which in the judge's view every human being has. It thus is understood as standing within the universally human and is a way of placing the talented person essentially on the same level as all other human beings without annihilating their differences (EO, 2:292–93). This view of talent, the judge argues, provides a more significant expression for the relation of work to the whole personality of an individual and to other people, since a particular talent itself is not central but is taken up into and mediated by the higher concentricity of the universal, which provides a norm outside the individual as a guideline for accomplishing something with one's talents (EO, 2:293–94). To accomplish something, rather than simply to indulge in the aesthetic satisfaction of a talent, is an ethical requirement that again places every person on an essentially equal level. What every person can accomplish is his or her task, and in that every person can be said to accomplish equally as much as another, though their tasks may differ in specific respects. According to Judge William, therefore, one advantage the ethical-aesthetic view of talent has over the romantic-aesthetic view is that it accounts for the universal, not merely the accidental, in talent. Another is that "it shows the universal in its true beauty," for in the judge's estimation "talent is not beautiful until it is transfigured [*forklaret*] into a calling, and existence is not beautiful until every person has a calling" (EO, 2:293).

MARRIAGE

Regarding marriage as a third instance where the ethical provides a better aesthetic expression and interpretation of a life-relationship than the romantic-aesthetic does, Judge William follows up on his previous association of beauty with the universal by showing how these categories apply equally to marriage. Just as every person has, or should have, a calling, from an ethical standpoint every person has a duty to marry, the judge claims. Although, in his opinion, it is not sinful for a person to remain single unless that individual is responsible for it, he regards marriage as advantageous and superior to the single life and to any erotic relationship outside the marriage for several reasons (EO, 2:302, 305–6). First of all, from an ethical standpoint, marriage, like talent, must be understood as an expression of the universal rather than the accidental; that is, it puts emphasis on the ordinary, what may be said of or experienced by every couple, rather than the extraordinary, the differences that set an individual or couple apart from others. Although differences are not canceled in marriage, they become transfigured in the relationship, so that one is able to see the universal in the differences and to appreciate differences as differences without making them determinative. A second advantage of marriage, therefore, is that it makes the universal, that is, the marital relationship itself, not differences, the absolute. Whether a person is uncommonly beautiful is thus inconsequential in marriage, since there is essentially no difference from others at the fundamental level. On the matter of beauty, however, a third advantage shows itself in that marriage reveals the true beauty of love, which consists not in the accidental beauty of good looks characterizing the lover or object of love, but in a "historical beauty" of freedom, whose task is to fashion something great and beautiful out of the ordinary, not merely to develop the differences or out-of-the-ordinary features that distinguish a marriage or the individuals in a marriage (EO, 2:304–5).

In the course of reconsidering the ethical-aesthetic merits of marriage over the single life and over erotic relationships outside of marriage, Judge William also returns to the category of time, which acquires a positive and especially important significance in the ethical-existential aesthetics developed in his first letter. In line with his previous perspective, time is viewed here not as a burden or enemy to personal happiness but as a blessing and a category that acquires beautiful meaning through marriage (EO, 2:305–6). For instead of experiencing occasional moments of ecstasy in love, as in nonmarital erotic relationships, marriage infuses, the judge claims, a gratifying equality and steadiness into love-relations through its requirement of a daily presence to one another. This ability to make every moment, not merely special occasions, count in marriage is understood by the judge as poetic: "In its humble incognito, the prosaic marriage had concealed a poet who not only transfigured life on special occasions but was always present and by his cadences gave a thrill even to the more impoverished hours" (EO, 2:306).

According to the judge, however, it is the wife who most succeeds in making time so meaningful that it never drags in marriage. Woman, he claims, stands in a natural harmony with time and has a "secret rapport" with it that enables her always to be occupied without becoming tired or idle (EO, 2:307–8). She, therefore, may be regarded as the model poet, or artist, with respect to time, as the judge comes close to suggesting in this description of her in aesthetic terms: "It is as if what she is doing is a game, a dance, as if a game were her occupation. . . . What she does I cannot explain, but she does it all with a charm and graciousness, with an indescribable lightness, does it without preliminaries and ceremony, like a bird singing its aria. Indeed, I do believe that her occupation can best be compared to a bird's work, and yet her arts seem to me to be genuine magic." However demeaning and sexist this comparison of womanly busyness to that of a bird may appear to some, the judge, in typical chauvinistic blindness, intends it to be complimentary to woman and credits her with being able to explain "in the most interesting and beautiful manner" the question of time in a way that philosophers have never been able to do (EO, 2:308).[13] In his view, woman is able to do this because she has a native talent for comprehending the finite, whereas man is concerned with pursuing the infinite. Man is therefore dependent on woman's help in properly orienting himself in the finite, as is amusingly illustrated by the judge's story about the Orientalist whose wife blows away the grain of snuff he had mistaken for an unusual vowel marking (EO, 2:309–10). Although, in the judge's view, woman is limited in relation to ideas, receiving them "secondhand," that is, via man, he nevertheless contends that "she is man's deepest life" because of her ability to explain the finite (EO, 2:311). It is thus important for man to live in harmony with her and to preserve her femininity. Accordingly, the

13. The full extent of woman's positive significance for Judge William may be seen in his further interpretation of her as a symbol of the religious congregation and as a model of faith in her natural disposition to pray for others and to believe in the possibility of all things through God (EO, 2:313–16). Much later, in an edifying discourse published in 1850, Kierkegaard again presents woman as a "pattern of piety" in the example of the woman who was a sinner (Luke 7:37–50) in her sorrow over sin (*Training in Christianity and the Edifying Discourse Which "Accompanied" It,* tr. Walter Lowrie [Princeton: Princeton University Press, 1957], 261–71). In other works such as *The Concept of Anxiety* and *The Sickness unto Death,* however, woman's natural condition and tendencies are regarded as being on a lower spiritual level than those of man. See Chapter 5 and the Epilogue as well as my article "On 'Feminine' and 'Masculine' Despair," in *International Kierkegaard Commentary: The Sickness unto Death,* ed. Robert L. Perkins (Macon, Ga.: Mercer University Press, 1987), 121–34.

judge continues to look upon the emancipation of woman, which he sees as an attempt to define woman in terms of man and to make her into a sort of half-man, as a deplorable and wretched attack upon woman perpetrated by a bunch of males who are themselves only half-men out to corrupt woman and take advantage of her (EO, 2:311–12).

FRIENDSHIP

After eulogizing woman in a long digression set off by further reflection on the ethical-aesthetic significance of marriage and time, the judge turns at last to his final example of a life-relationship containing the aesthetic and the ethical, namely, friendship. From a romantic-aesthetic standpoint, as the judge understands it, friendship would appear to fall entirely within aesthetic categories as a form of relationship that belongs to youth, before love, or else to maturity, following upon a bad experience with love (EO, 2:316–17). In the latter instance the individual may be led to abandon erotic love for intellectual or prudential relationships based on contradictory feelings ranging from sentimentality to callousness and manifesting an unstable attitude that may be compared, in the judge's estimation, to a "magic picture," or kaleidoscope, constantly shifting from one picture to another through the arbitrary control of the viewer (EO, 2:318; cf. 258 and n. 95). From the judge's perspective, however, such relations should be regarded as abnormal, since friendship, in his view, properly commences in and through marriage and contributes to an ethical achievement of actuality (EO, 2:318, 322). Through the deep and full satisfaction found in marriage, the possibility of other deep and beautiful relationships is opened up to those who regard friendship ethically, that is, as a relationship based not on obscure feelings or indefinable sympathies but on a conscious bonding of kindred minds. The absolute condition for friendship is "unity in a life-view," the judge claims (EO, 2:319).[14] Moreover, this shared life-view, he adds, must be positive, not negative, as it is impossible to sustain friendship on the basis of a laughing or mocking attitude toward life (irony). What is required for friendship and a positive life-view, therefore, is seriousness, or earnestness, toward life. (Judge William's emphasis upon a positive life-view and earnestness is similar to that of Kierkegaard in *From the Papers of One Still Living* and *The Concept of Irony.*) "Not until friendship is looked at in this way does it gain meaning and beauty,"

14. Given this criterion for friendship, it is strange that the judge regards the aesthete to whom his letters are addressed a friend, for one of the main distinctions he wishes to make is the difference between an aesthetic and an ethical life-view.

the judge proclaims (EO, 2:321). In another passage he reiterates, "If friendship is looked at in this way, one is looking at it ethically and therefore according to its beauty" (EO, 2:322). From his viewpoint, therefore, the true aesthetic significance of friendship is seen only in and through an ethical understanding of it.

JUDGING THE JUDGE

Judge William embarked upon a discussion of work, talent, marriage, and friendship to show the ethical significance, and ultimately the highest aesthetic significance, of these aspects of life. As he himself expresses it in the conclusion of this discussion, "What I wanted to do was to show how the ethical in the mixed territories is so far from depriving life of its beauty that it expressly gives it beauty" (EO, 2:323). On the basis of a close analysis of the text, we have seen that in the course of this discussion as well as in his previous remarks on the relation between the aesthetic and the ethical, these categories properly belong together and are not antithetical to one another except insofar as one attempts to define the aesthetic from a romantic-aesthetic perspective devoid of ethical and religious elements. When those elements are introduced, the aesthetic takes on a much richer meaning than it has in the common identification of it with the sensuous and quite a different interpretation than it has in romantic aesthetics, at least as Judge William understands this school of aesthetics, where it is associated with the particular, the extraordinary, and the interesting. In identifying the aesthetic with beauty, beauty with the universal, and the universal with its highest ethical embodiment in the particular, Judge William's ethical-religious aesthetics stands squarely in the idealist tradition and appropriates several of its categories of interpretation in characterizing the aesthetic. Within that tradition, however, his own small offering on the altar of aesthetics is not as trivial or insignificant as he so modestly suggests, for it shifts the focus of aesthetic reflection in at least three important ways: (1) by transferring categories normally applied to art to the realm of personal existence and interpreting that existence aesthetically; (2) by emphasizing the historical, not merely the immediate, as an aesthetic ideal; and (3) by orienting aesthetics in an ethical-religious framework. The first of these modifications Judge William shares with romanticism, since it too introduces a type of existential aesthetics with its notion of "living poetically." In contrast to romanticism, however, Judge William formulates an alternative understanding of living poetically informed by the second and third features mentioned above. These give greater depth not only to Judge William's understanding of the aesthetic but also to his view of personal existence, which is seen as incorporating the aesthetic, ethical, and religious in a unified form of subjectivity and self-identity. Moreover, his ethical-religious aesthetics is congruent with Kierkegaard's initial attempts to formulate an existential aesthetics in *From the Papers of One Still Living* and *The Concept of Irony* and in fact represents a further development of the basic ideas introduced in those works.

There are, however, various points on which Judge William's views may be criticized. In particular, one may take exception to his stereotyped view of woman (and man), even though it is appreciative of her, and one can note a glaring inconsistency in his opposition to the emancipation of women in an existential aesthetics that otherwise emphasizes their freedom and independence. In addition, one may regret his failure sufficiently to appreciate the validity of the single life, as opposed to marriage, which, as we have seen, is presented by him as a universal duty. Furthermore, one may be disturbed by his rather undialectical and overconfident understanding of the religious as legitimating the ethical as he sees it. It is especially this last objection that is brought to bear against the judge in the sermon that concludes volume 2 of *Either/Or.* Although Judge William believes that the Jutland pastor's homily concurs with his own views and expresses them even better than he himself is able to do, he does not see (or does he?) that the thrust of the sermon has the effect of relativizing his own position, since its central theme is the claim that "in relation to God we are always in the wrong." In a note accompanying the sermon and addressed to the romantic aesthete, Judge William writes, "I have read it and thought about myself, read it and thought about you" (EO, 2:338). We have no way of knowing what Judge William has in mind concerning himself or the romantic aesthete in this statement, but if he has taken the sermon to heart with respect to his own conduct and position, then he recognizes the limitations of his viewpoint and his failure to embody entirely and at every moment in his own life the ethical-aesthetic ideal he sets forth. There is some evidence in his letters that the latter at least is the case, for he admits as much in several places. Just as Judge William insists at the outset of his first letter that his own marriage is not normative, so he maintains at the end of the second that he lacks "full power of attorney" to represent ethics, being nothing more than a witness and speaking with authority only about what he has experienced (EO, 2:323). But even if, as an imperfect witness of the ethical, Judge William is in the right over against the romantic aesthete, the thrust of the sermon is that he will wish not to be so for the sake of his friend, and this wish is granted by acknowledging that in relation to God he is always in the wrong. Thus, even though the judge is, from Kierkegaard's standpoint, "unconditionally the winner" of the contest between contrasting life-views and modes of living poetically in *Either/Or,* his advantage is nullified before God, and the possibility of a still higher viewpoint is opened up (EO, 2:431; JP, 5:5804). That is provided in a quartet of pseudonymous poetic works that round out the first phase in Kierkegaard's attempt to construct a positive view of the poetic in the form of an existential aesthetics. It is to these works that I turn next to show how this existential aesthetics is carried forward in the context of the religious.

5

Dancing Lightly in the Sphere of the Religious

The first phase in Kierkegaard's attempt to formulate a positive conception of the poetic in the form of an existential aesthetics culminates in the publication of four pseudonymous works concerned with the religious sphere of existence: *Repetition* by Constantin Constantius (1843), *Fear and Trembling* by Johannes de Silentio (1843), *Philosophical Fragments* by Johannes Climacus (1844), and *The Concept of Anxiety* (1844) by Vigilius Haufniensis. The translators/editors of the new English editions of *Repetition* and *Fear and Trembling* have described these books as Kierkegaard's "two most poetic writings" (FT/R, xvi), but all four may be regarded as poetic, or aesthetic, writings inasmuch as the use of pseudonyms as authors is itself a poetic device designed to distance Kierkegaard from the specific viewpoints voiced in each work. Moreover, the pseudonymous authors also engage in the art of poetizing in the form of "experiments," or imaginary constructions.[1] Constantin Constantius subtitles his work "A Venture in Experimenting Psychology" and interests himself in the imagi-

1. For a discussion of the term *Experiment,* generally translated as "imaginary construction" by the Hongs, see the historical introduction to FT, xxi–xxxi, and the editorial note on the subtitle ("A Venture in Experimenting Psychology") of R, 357–62. See also Howard V. Hong, "*Tanke-Experiment* in Kierkegaard," in *Kierkegaard Resources and Results,* ed. Alastair McKinnon (Montreal: Wilfred Laurier University Press, 1982), 39–51, and Robert L. Perkins, "Comment on Hong," in ibid., 52–55.

nary construction of a case study of a melancholy young man seeking an ethical-religious repetition that will allow him to marry. Johannes de Silentio subtitles his work "Dialectical Lyric," emphasizing the poetic and passionate as well as reflective manner in which he attempts to depict Abraham, or the knight of faith, as a paradigm of the religious. Similarly, Johannes Climacus characterizes his thought-project as "A Poetical Venture" exploring the differences between the Platonic and Christian conceptions of knowing and existing in the truth. Like Constantin Constantius's book, Vigilius Haufniensis's work is psychologically oriented, but a prerequisite of the psychological observer, the author claims, is a "poetic originality" that enables the psychologist to fashion whatever examples or imaginary constructions he or she needs to draw observations "entirely fresh from the water" rather than from "literary repertoires" served up as "half-dead reminiscences" (CA, 54–55). While Constantin Constantius regards himself "a prose writer" in contrast to the young man, who is a poet, Johannes de Silentio denies being either a philosopher or a poet and describes himself instead as a mere "supplementary clerk" who seeks "in a poetic and refined way" to perform the neglected poetic task of speaking in honor of the passion of faith (R, 218; FT, 7, 32, 90). For his part, the other Johannes—Johannes Climacus—openly admits to being a poet and further confesses that he has plagiarized his poem from the deity, who must be regarded as the true author of the poem, or, more precisely, "the wonder" that is poetized in his thought-project (PF, 35–36).

Another poetic feature these works share is the use of the metaphor of dancing in relation to the religious.[2] After encountering a "thunderstorm" that leads him to believe that he has experienced a religious repetition, the young man in *Repetition* becomes inebriated by the thought of totally abandoning himself to the religious idea and giddily offers, among other toasts, "three cheers for the dance in the vortex of the infinite," which he is about to begin in service to the idea (R, 221–22). Similarly, Johannes de Silentio uses the image of a ballet dancer to characterize and contrast the movements of the knight of faith and the knights of infinite resignation (FT, 40–41). The knight of faith, like the knights of infinite resignation, makes the movement of infinity in the resignation of finitude; but unlike the knights of infinity, the knight of

2. The metaphor of dancing is also used by Judge William in *Either/Or* II to characterize the art of the lowliest of individuals who has the will and discipline to live ethically (EO, 2:252–53), and to describe the artistic activity of woman with respect to her occupation in time (EO, 2:308).

faith is able to do it "with such precision and assurance that he continually gets finitude out of it." Although the knights of infinite resignation also "come down" again after having made an upward leap into infinity, "every time they come down, they are unable to assume the posture immediately, they waver for a moment, and this wavering shows that they are aliens in the world," Johannes claims. By contrast, the knight of faith performs this downward movement so gracefully, he contends, that the dancer seems instantaneously to be standing and walking and thus able "absolutely to express the sublime in the pedestrian" (FT, 41). *Philosophical Fragments* does not follow up with the metaphor of dancing in its characterization of faith, but Johannes Climacus does describe himself as having trained himself "always to be able to dance lightly in the service of thought, as far as possible to the honor of the god and for my own enjoyment" (PF, 7). Like Simon Stylita, the proposed pseudonymous author of *Fear and Trembling* in an early draft, who is described on the title page as a "Solo Dancer and Private Individual," Johannes Climacus dances alone; or more precisely, he has the thought of death as a dancing partner, since he stakes his life on his thought-project rather than claim any scientific-scholarly authority for it (FT, 243; PF, 5–8, cf. 185). Trained in physical fitness as well as in psychology, Vigilius Haufniensis claims that "the psychological observer ought to be more nimble than a tightrope dancer in order to incline and bend himself to other people and imitate their attitudes" (CA, 54–55). More important, in the conclusion of his study Vigilius claims that "whoever has truly learned how to be anxious will dance when the anxieties of finitude strike up the music," for in his view anxiety becomes a saving phenomenon through faith (CA, 155, 161). In all four works, then, the relation of the individual to the infinite or the religious is signified through the artistic metaphor of dancing, which suggests the possibility of construing this relation in terms of a religious aesthetics, or an aesthetics of faith, in continuity with the existential aesthetics outlined in Kierkegaard's previous works. Although the image of dancing is not widely employed in any of the four books under consideration here, it provides an artistic metaphor by which to highlight what I see as an important aesthetic and poetic dimension of the religious as that is conceptualized in the first phase of Kierkegaard's authorship.

In the context of the present investigation of the poetic in Kierkegaard's thought, the primary question I shall pose and ponder in relation to the four works at hand, therefore, is not whether they are poetic—that becomes obvious in the course of examining them—but whether they advance a view of the religious that is fundamentally poetic. We have seen previously in *The Concept of Irony* that Kierkegaard initially defines the religious aesthetically as a form of self-enjoyment in one's inner infinity, which constitutes the truly poetic in human life. And in *Either/Or* II we have seen also that a religious orientation figures importantly in the ethical-existential aesthetics developed in that work. Is this ethical-religious aesthetics sustained in these early pseudonymous works dealing specifically with the religious? Does Kierkegaard indirectly offer through these new pseudonyms a higher view of the religious that transcends the ethical-religious perspective of Judge William's existential aesthetics? Although these works are united in a common effort to depict, or come close to depicting, the sphere of the religious, each work has its own particular concepts, themes, and concerns to explore poetically. Focusing on each one individually, therefore, I shall examine their respective poetic representations of the religious as they present it, with an eye toward discerning any aesthetic or poetic features of the religious that are suggested and toward determining the congruence of these with the existential aesthetics already developed in the early writings of Kierkegaard.

ON THE BOUNDARY OF THE RELIGIOUS IN *REPETITION*

I begin with *Repetition* because, although published on the same day as *Fear and Trembling*, it was finished first and uses the figure of Job to fight out "the disputes at the boundaries of faith," whereas *Fear and Trembling* presents Abraham as an exemplar of faith (R, 210).[3] We must

3. Cf. Mark Lloyd Taylor, "Ordeal and Repetition in Kierkegaard's Treatment of Abraham and Job," in *Foundations of Kierkegaard's Vision of Community,* ed. George B. Connell and C. Stephen Evans (Atlantic Highlands, N.J.: Humanities Press, 1992), 33–53. Taylor argues against the common practice of considering *Repetition* first and as a forerunner of *Fear and Trembling;* he points out that Kierkegaard generally discussed them in reverse order, using *Repetition* to safeguard a misunderstanding of *Fear and Trembling* in aesthetic or ethical terms. Oddly, Taylor then proceeds to consider *Repetition first,* giving an account of the category of repetition introduced by that book, before turning to an examination of the category of ordeal, which the two books treat in common. Nevertheless, Taylor claims that *Repetition* is a repetition of *Fear and Trembling* in veiled form, that is, indirectly through its use of the category of the comic, and that both books point beyond themselves to the problem of sin as the decisive expression of a religious mode of existence. He thus makes a rather strong admonition against the common practice of distinguishing between Job and Abraham on the basis of faith, claiming that "it just will not do to say that the Job of *Repetition* represents the boundary of faith, while Johannes' Abraham represents its center" (47–48). But, as I show below, *Repetition* itself makes the claim that Job's position is on the boundary of faith; and although neither work can

remember at the outset of our inquiry that the "author" of this text is not a religious person; rather, he is an ironist who seeks aesthetically to illumine the category of repetition—which is preeminently a religious category—through the opposite categories of jest and despair (R, 314). Thus we cannot entirely trust his understanding of the religious, but that is not to say he grasps nothing about it. Constantin Constantius describes himself as a Stoic whose distinguishing quality in the sphere of freedom is that of sagacity (R, 301, 320). Constantin possesses enough sagacity to discern that the young man hoping for repetition does not get it and that it is too transcendent a category for his own life, which observation at least establishes that he knows what repetition is not. But let us not put the cart before the horse. Or, to use one of Constantin's examples, let us not be like "an inquisitive female reader who reads the end of every book" to find out how things work out before commencing to read the beginning (R, 225). As Constantin points out, there is an art to being a good reader (and presumably a good writer too).

Constantin begins his poetic experiment[4] with a narrative report (part 1) introducing the concept of repetition and the young man imaginatively constructed to illustrate it negatively. This report also includes a detailed description of an investigative trip that he, Constantin, supposedly made "to test the possibility and meaning of repetition" in his own life (R, 150). Distinguishing repetition, which he classifies as a category of modern philosophy,[5] from recollection, the category of the Greeks,

be taken to provide, either directly or indirectly, a final or completely adequate description of faith, the faith of Abraham is surely closer to the center than that of Job. Taylor concludes that "one could view *Fear and Trembling*... as completing *Repetition*... only by mistaking the indirect method of communication employed by Johannes and Constantin" (48). But such a conclusion does not necessarily follow from the order of discussion of them in Kierkegaard's writings or from the fact that they share a common subject matter. *Fear and Trembling* may just as easily be seen as a repetition of *Repetition* as vice versa (especially since *Repetition* was written first) without jeopardizing the indirect character of either work. Moreover, since *Repetition* is concerned primarily with the problem of the aesthetic and *Fear and Trembling* is focused more on the problem of the ethical, it makes sense conceptually to treat *Repetition* first.

4. As a poetic work, *Repetition* defies classification, since Constantin claims that "it is not a comedy, tragedy, novel, short story, epic, or epigram" (R, 226). If we accept the author's view of the work, then Aage Henriksen's classification of it as a short novel is not appropriate (see *Kierkegaards Romaner,* 7–14, 87–131). Perhaps the best classification of it is as an *allegory* inasmuch as Constantin claims to be "writing in such a way that the heretics are unable to understand it" and does so by cloaking the seriousness of his project in jest.

5. Although Constantin presents repetition as a category of modern philosophy, he states that "the only modern philosopher who has had an intimation of this is Leibniz" (R, 131). What he means, then, is that "repetition is the new category that will be discovered" in modern

Constantin characterizes repetition as a forward movement, recollection as a backward movement; or, to be more precise, they are the same movement (since what is repeated or recollected has been) but in opposite directions (R, 131). Life is a repetition, Constantin declares, and in agreement with the existential aesthetics of Judge William in *Either/Or,* he sees repetition as constituting "the beauty of life" (R, 132, 149). Moreover, like Judge William, he associates repetition with earnestness and actuality, poetically illustrating and distinguishing it from hope and recollection through the figure of woman: "Hope is a lovely maiden who slips away between one's fingers; recollection is a beautiful old woman with whom one is never satisfied at the moment; repetition is a beloved wife of whom one never wearies, for one becomes weary only of what is new" (R, 132–33). But when the young man mentioned above reportedly comes to Constantin for counsel concerning an unhappy love affair, instead of advising him to marry the girl he loves, Constantin encourages him conversely to break off completely with her after making himself into a contemptible fellow in her eyes by behaving in an inconstant, nonsensical, inconsistent, passionless, inattentive, and unpleasant manner toward her (R, 142). In this way Constantin jestingly suggests that the young man can break through the state of melancholy and poetic confusion he has gotten himself into over this affair and become a real man and a true poet with respect to love: "Only he who actually can love, only he is a man; only he who can give his love any expression whatsoever, only he is an artist" (R, 145). But even though the young man initially approves of Constantin's plan and expresses a willingness to adopt it, he does not have the strength or courage for this sort of deception, admitting in his first letter to Constantin that "unfortunately, I was not the artist with the strength for such a performance or the perseverance" (R, 144–45, 190). Nor does he, in Constantin's opinion, understand or believe in the concept of repetition. So for the time being, he remains in the contradictory moods of melancholy longing and recollection, unable to break off with the girl yet essentially finished with her.

Thus far we can detect two forms of the poetic being illustrated in this work: one is associated with immediacy, romantic longing, and recollection awakened in the young man by the girl, who serves as the occasion

philosophy (R, 148). Although Constantin here contrasts repetition with recollection, he later contrasts it with mediation, the Hegelian category of reconciliation with which repetition, in his view, has been mistakenly identified (R, 148–49). On the contrast with mediation, see especially André Clair, "Médiation et répétition: Le lieu de la dialectique kierkegaardienne," *Revue des sciences philosophiques et théologiques* 59 (1975): 38–78.

for his becoming a poet; the other is a more reflective and sophisticated form of artistry that Constantin identifies with the truly poetic and that he apparently associates with repetition. But neither qualifies as truly poetic from Judge William's standpoint, and it remains to be seen whether the latter should be regarded as constituting a religious form of artistry. In addition to these expressions of the poetic, Constantin characterizes his own role of observer as an art, stating that "when an observer fulfills his duties well, he is to be regarded as a secret agent in a higher service, for the observer's art is to expose what is hidden" (R, 135). Seeking in this instance to expose the meaning and possibility of repetition, Constantin the artist decides to experiment on himself by taking a trip to Berlin, where he hopes to repeat and enjoy just as much as the first time the same living conditions, sights, and entertainments of that city. Disappointed at finding changes at his former lodgings, he goes to the theater, a particularly suitable setting, he thinks, for momentarily and imaginatively repeating through mood, for the sake of comic effect, the shadow-existence, or projection, of a variety of possible self-identities of the personality in childhood (R, 154–58).

That is best accomplished, Constantin maintains, through the genre of farce, which is unpredictable in its effects upon the viewer, since these depend upon the individual's own self-activity in determining what mood or moods will be evoked in response (R, 159–60). Farce thus has the advantage of eliciting, like childhood, the possibility of all moods, not just one fixed mood; and for that reason, in Constantin's view, it is preferable to tragedy, comedy, or light comedy for generating comic effect, since these produce a more restricted and uniform mood (R, 158, 162). Farce also has an accidental character that makes it particularly suitable for comically representing in the form of an "accidental concretion" the abstract impressions and categories (for example, man and woman in general) typical of childhood (R, 158). To be successfully performed, however, farce requires a small cast of very talented actors whom Constantin describes as "generative geniuses," "children of caprice, intoxicated with laughter," and "dancers of whimsy." "They are not so much reflective artists who have studied laughter as they are lyricists who themselves plunged into the abyss of laughter and now let its volcanic power hurl them out on the stage," Constantin observes. Depending upon improvisation in the moment and possessing inexhaustible comic resources for eliciting laughter without effort, these comic genuises know no limits in their hilarity (R, 161). Farce thus seems to be an ideal genre for the romantic aesthete seeking a childish, immediate, momentary enjoyment of an infinity of possibility, but a poor one for generating repetition.[6] And indeed, that is what Constantin discovers when he goes to the theater in Berlin, for he does not experience repetition. Either things are not the same as before, and hence there is no repetition; or else that which is the same has become jaded and stale, quickly making him weary and bored and thus providing a repetition of the wrong sort. So he returns home, only to find that there, too, repetition is not possible, since everything has been turned upside down by his servant. This leads him temporarily to abandon the category of repetition in favor of the Heraclitean view that life is a stream. As a symbol of the nonrepetitive transcience of life suggested by this viewpoint, he adopts the stagecoach horn, an instrument that cannot be counted on to produce the same note twice (R, 174–75).[7]

In part 2 of the book, however, Constantin has clearly abandoned the Heraclitean theory and no longer denies the reality of repetition, though he recognizes that it is a religious movement that is too transcendent for him. Our interest is thus turned once again to the young man, whose belief in the possibility of repetition has been strengthened by reflection on the figure of Job. In a series of confidential letters to Constantin, the young man develops an interpretation of Job as an example of repetition because, after having lost everything through a testing, or an ordeal, he is blessed by God and receives everything double. Since Job exhibits "the colossal revolt of the wild and aggressive powers of passion" in his dispute with God, he lacks the composure of a hero of faith. Thus the young man does not make that claim for him; rather, he suggests that "Job's significance is that the disputes at the boundaries of faith are fought out in him." Job's category is that of ordeal, which the young man claims is not "esthetic, ethical, or dogmatic" but transcendent, placing the individual "in a purely personal relationship of opposition to God" (R, 210).

The young man is empathetic with Job because, like Job, he thinks that he is in the right in his own personal dilemma regarding the young girl he has jilted, and he feels no guilt toward her, though he does have sympathy for her pain (R, 138, 191, 201). Having given up hope of ever realizing his love in marriage, he is convinced that it can happen only by virtue of the absurd. Thus he awaits the "thunderstorm" that will enable

6. On farce as a parody of repetition, see especially Louis Mackey, "Once More with Feeling: Kierkegaard's *Repetition,*" in *Points of View,* 79–81.

7. On the significance of the stagecoach horn for Constantin, see especially David Cain, "Notes on a Coach Horn: 'Going Further,' 'Revocation,' and Repetition," in *International Kierkegaard Commentary: Fear and Trembling and Repetition,* ed. Robert L. Perkins (Macon, Ga.: Mercer University Press, 1993), 335–58.

him to gain an ethical repetition in marriage. When the thunderstorm comes, however, it does not bring the kind of repetition he had expected, for he learns that the girl has married another man. This leads him to think that he has experienced a spiritual repetition in which he is healed and reunified as a self. In place of the girl he has received himself back again.

But has he? This self-interpretation of the young man is contested in the concluding letter to the reader from Constantin Constantius. Even though he admits that the young man's soul has gained "a religious resonance," that the joy he experiences "is grounded in a religious mood," and that "he is sustained by something inexpressibly religious," Constantin nevertheless claims that "the religious founders" in the young man because he is a poet; and what he gains again is not himself in the actuality of repetition but himself as a poet recollecting the actuality of a love relation that is essentially past (R, 228–29).[8]

This seems to place the poetic and the religious at odds with each other, and indeed, Constantin states that if the young man "had had a deeper religious background, he would not have become a poet" (R, 229). The figure of the poet nevertheless plays an important transitional role in the movement to the religious, and that, it seems to me, is the main point Constantin Constantius wishes to make in the final section of the book. Anticipating *Fear and Trembling*, what he wishes to call attention to is "the legitimate exception" to the universal (R, 227); and with that, we move beyond the existential aesthetics of Judge William, rooted as it is in the universal, to a far more controversial and perhaps more deeply aesthetic and poetic form of existential dialectic. But first the legitimate exception must be distinguished from the illegitimate exception. Constantin suggests this can be done by determining the exceptional individual's relation to the universal: whereas the illegitimate exception seeks to bypass the universal, the legitimate exception wrestles with the universal and by thinking through his or her own existence with intense passion also thinks and explains the universal, thereby becoming reconciled to it (R, 226–27). In Constantin's estimation, the poet constitutes such a legitimate exception, for the poet stands in conflict with life and finds reassurance or legitimation only after initially losing in this conflict (R, 228). Such a poet, however, is quite different

8. For a contrary reading that assumes the young man does realize repetition, see M. Jamie Ferreira, "Repetition, Concreteness, and Imagination," *International Journal for Philosophy of Religion* 25, no. 1 (1989): 3–34. I am inclined to agree with Constantin Constantius on this question.

from the romantic poets whose irony toward actuality was found to be unwarranted by the young Kierkegaard. Presumably not every poet would qualify, then, as a legitimate exception. In Constantin's view, however, the poet who qualifies as a legitimate exception constitutes the transition to the religious exception, the subject of the next book, *Fear and Trembling.* It is to this work that we must turn, therefore, to explore the aesthetic implications of the religious sphere proper in the figures of the religious exception and the knight of faith.

FAITH AS A WORK OF ART IN *FEAR AND TREMBLING*

"It is commonly supposed that what faith produces is no work of art, that it is a coarse and boorish piece of work, only for the more uncouth natures, but it is far from being that. The dialectic of faith is the finest and the most extraordinary of all" (FT, 36). With these words Johannes de Silentio introduces in his "Preliminary Expectoration" the artistic framework within which he understands the phenomenon of faith. We have already seen how he uses the metaphor of a ballet dancer to illustrate the ease and agility with which the knight of faith, in contrast to the knights of infinite resignation, makes the movements of faith. The knights of infinite resignation are dancers too, but not nearly so adept or at ease as the knight of faith in relating themselves to the world. In this section I explore the deeper existential aesthetics implied by the use of such artistic imagery with respect to faith and the knight of faith.

Let us begin by taking a closer look at the knight of faith as poetically portrayed by Johannes de Silentio. Unable through thought to grasp the movements of faith—because they are, in his view, paradoxical—Johannes undertakes to become the poet of faith by imaginatively describing these movements, even though he cannot make them himself. Although he has never encountered "a single authentic instance" of a knight of faith, he can "very well imagine" what one would be like, he says (FT, 38). The portrait Johannes draws of the knight of faith bears a striking resemblance to the "bourgeois philistine," which suggests that the knight of faith has an aesthetic appearance: "He finds pleasure in everything, takes part in everything, and every time one sees him participating in something particular, he does it with an assiduousness that marks the worldly man who is attached to such things" (FT, 39). Like the bourgeois philistine, the knight of faith belongs entirely to the world but nevertheless may be distinguished from such a person by the fact that the knight of faith does everything by virtue of the absurd. Having given up the finite through infinite resignation, the last stage before faith, the knight of faith receives it back again (the true repetition) in faith by virtue of the absurd. What appears to be impossible is made possible by the fact that for God all things are possible.

For Johannes, the drama and pathos of the knight of faith are exemplified in the figure of Abraham, whose command from God to sacrifice his beloved son Isaac places him in a dreadful ordeal and state of contradiction as a test of faith. In the "Exordium" with which the book begins, Johannes imaginatively explores several responses Abraham might have made with respect to this command, but in the main body of the book he focuses on the biblical account that portrays Abraham as a man of faith who did not doubt. Like the imagined knight of faith, Abraham is not a figure Johannes can understand or imitate, but he stands in awe and admiration of the man and furthermore is appalled by him. For what if Abraham were mistaken in trusting the voice he thought was the voice of God? By what right does he make himself an exception to the universal? One may well understand how an individual might sacrifice him- or herself for the sake of the universal (the tragic hero for example), but how can a person offer up his or her own beloved son? In Johannes's opinion, the action Abraham proposed to carry out must be regarded either as an act of murder or as a religious sacrifice, an expression of the highest egotism or of absolute devotion to God.

In order to bring out the intensely pathetic and unmediated paradoxical nature of faith, Johannes focuses dialectically on three *problemata* raised by the story of Abraham: Is there a teleological suspension of the ethical? Is there an absolute duty to God? Was it ethically defensible for Abraham to conceal his understanding from Sarah, from Eliezer, and from Isaac? My object here is not to examine these problems per se.[9] Rather, within the context of Johannes's discussion of these issues I shall focus more specifically on the aesthetic implications of three claims put forth in Johannes's view of faith: (1) faith is the paradox that the individual is higher than the universal (the religious exception); (2) faith is a passion in the form of a second immediacy or new interiority; and (3) faith, speaking only divine language or "in tongues," is cloaked in secrecy and silence.

9. For a range of critical interpretations of *Fear and Trembling*, see Robert L. Perkins, ed., *Kierkegaard's "Fear and Trembling": Critical Appraisals* (University: University of Alabama Press, 1981), and idem, ed., *International Kierkegaard Commentary: Fear and Trembling and Repetition.* See also Mackey, "The View from Pisgah: A Reading of *Fear and Trembling*," in *Points of View*, 40–67, and Edward F. Mooney, *Knights of Faith and Resignation: Reading Kierkegaard's "Fear and Trembling"* (Albany: State University of New York Press, 1991).

The first of these claims is advanced in problems I and II. Johannes begins by identifying the ethical with the universal, which admits of no exceptions. If an ethical individual asserts him- or herself over against the universal, then that individual, from an ethical standpoint, must be accounted as having sinned and is placed in a spiritual trial from which extrication is possible only through repentantly surrendering to the universal (FT, 54). In that case there is nothing higher than the universal, and the action of the individual amounts to what Hegel has termed a "moral form of evil" (FT, 54).[10]

There is another form of affirmation of the individual that Johannes does not mention but that should also be taken into account here inasmuch as Judge William in *Either/Or* contrasts the ethical as the universal to the individualism of the romantic ironists. This form of the individual stands outside the ethical, not within it as an instance of moral evil, and thus belongs to what the judge identifies as the aesthetic stage of life. Being premoral or amoral in this stage of development, the aesthetic individual does not fall under ethical categories and cannot, properly speaking, be said to be sinning, although at a reflective level such an individual may be aware of the ethical and for that reason, from an ethical standpoint, may be accounted as sinning, even though he or she has not yet chosen the ethical.

From an ethical standpoint, then, Johannes's claim that the single individual is higher than the universal appears to be either an instance of moral evil in which the individual transgresses the moral law or else an expression of reflective aestheticism in which the individual asserts him- or herself without regard to the moral law. Clearly, Johannes understands Abraham's ordeal as posing an ethical dilemma rather than an aesthetic one, but in affirming the individual over against the universal, he implicitly raises the question of aestheticism too. For just as the knight of faith has the appearance of a bourgeois philistine, who is an aesthete at heart, so the single individual who constitutes a religious exception to the universal resembles the aesthetic individual in the affirmation of a radical subjectivity that does not recognize the claims of the ethical. But unlike the aesthetic individual, who corresponds here to what Constantin Constantius would regard as an illegitimate exception, Abraham does not bypass the universal; he only suspends it by virtue of a higher rela-

10. See Hegel's *Philosophy of Right,* tr. T. M. Knox (Oxford: Clarendon Press, 1958), 86–104. The translators/editors of *Fear and Trembling* rightly point out that the phrase "moral form of evil" is not included in the table of contents to the English translation of this work, but it does appear in the table of contents to this section in the German edition of Hegel's works.

tion, in the form of an absolute duty to God, that is not identical to the universal or one's duty to others. The ethical is thus relativized but not rejected in and through this relation. Indeed, Johannes even claims that the ethical is given expression in the single individual's or religious exception's God-relation, but it receives "a completely different expression" in converse, paradoxical form, that is, in the form of "an expression opposite to that which, ethically speaking, is duty" (FT, 70). This means that love for a son, for example, may appear ethically as hate. In Johannes's opinion, this is precisely what happens in the case of Abraham. In being willing to sacrifice Isaac, Abraham does not give up his love for his son or become indifferent to him. On the contrary, as Johannes understands the situation, it is imperative that Abraham love Isaac, even more than before, and with his whole soul.

> The absolute duty can lead one to do what ethics would forbid, but it can never lead the knight of faith to stop loving. Abraham demonstrates this. In the moment he is about to sacrifice Isaac, the ethical expression for what he is doing is: he hates Isaac. But if he actually hates Isaac, he can rest assured that God does not demand this of him. . . . for it is indeed this love for Isaac that makes his act a sacrifice by its paradoxical contrast to his love for God. . . . Only in the moment when his act is in absolute contradiction to his feelings, only then does he sacrifice Isaac. (FT, 74)

Central to Abraham's act of sacrifice, then, is the passion of love, an absolute love for God, on the one hand, and a relative—though intensified, total, and ethical—love for Isaac, on the other.

Being a passion, Abraham's love may also be characterized as fundamentally aesthetic. Judge William identified love (in that instance, erotic love) with the aesthetic, which is taken up and ennobled so as to become a "second immediacy" in the ethical by being concentrically oriented in a relation to God. Johannes does not use this expression with respect to Abraham's love, but he does apply it to the paradox of faith.[11] Like love, faith is also understood by Johannes as a passion. Following Lessing, who wrote that "the passions make all men equal again," Johannes views passion as "that which unites all human life" (FT, 67). Every human being possesses passion, or the capacity for passion, which

11. One should note here that Kierkegaard also characterizes faith as a second immediacy, or primitivity, numerous places in his journals. See JP, 1:9, 49, 84, 85, 214, 235, 972, 1032; 2:1101, 1123, 1215, 1335, 1942, 1943; 3:3560, 3561; 5:6135.

is part of the immediate, natural, interior, aesthetic makeup of human existence. In Johannes's view, passion constitutes the essentially human, which cannot be learned or passed on from one generation to another but must be developed by each generation primitively or afresh. Among the passions, faith, in his view, is the highest (FT, 121). It is Johannes's contention, however, that faith, though a passion, is not identical with the first immediacy of the aesthetic. Faith is not an "esthetic emotion" or a "spontaneous inclination of the heart," he says, but rather a "new interiority" and a "later immediacy," that is, a form of immediacy or spontaneity that Kierkegaard describes elsewhere as being acquired after reflection by virtue of a relation to God (FT, 47, 69, 82; JP, 5:6135).

Johannes is particularly concerned to make this point about the immediacy of faith against Hegel, who holds that the outer is higher than the inner, and thus the ethical, which in his view comes to expression in the external realm (family, civil society, state), is higher than the aesthetic—the internal realm of passion, feeling, and mood. Over against Hegel, Johannes wants to claim, first of all, that the paradox of faith "is an interiority that is incommensurable with exteriority" inasmuch as outwardly it cannot be distinguished from bourgeois philistinism and in some instances, such as the ordeal of Abraham, even transgresses the universal. Second, he wants to claim that faith is not the aesthetic or immediate in the sense that Hegel understands it to be, for that would put faith "in the rather commonplace company of feelings, moods, idiosyncrasies, *vapeurs* [vagaries], etc." (FT, 69).[12] For this reason Johannes emphasizes that "faith is not the esthetic, or else faith has never existed because it has always existed" (FT, 82). Rather, in Johannes's view, faith is a passion or interiority that is acquired unexpectedly by virtue of the absurd, that is, after all human reflection, effort, and expectation have been exhausted. Faith presupposes the movement of infinity, which also requires passion; but the movement of infinity is something the individual can make him- or herself, whereas the movement of faith is not.

The fact that Johannes identifies the aesthetic here with the first immediacy of natural capacities and inclinations should not be allowed to obscure, however, the fundamentally aesthetic nature of faith insofar as it is a passion or a form of immediacy. Just as Judge William viewed the aesthetic ideal as something that is acquired as well as immediate, consti-

12. For a good illustration of Hegel's view of faith, see FT, 350 n. 7. For more extended treatments of the relation between the inner and the outer and faith as a form of immediacy in Hegel and Kierkegaard, see Dunning, *Kierkegaard's Dialectic of Inwardness,* 119–25, and Perkins, "Abraham's Silence Aesthetically Considered."

tuting the ethical as a higher form of the aesthetic, so faith acquired by virtue of the absurd may be regarded as a higher form of the aesthetic. Unlike Judge William, however, Johannes de Silentio does not make this claim for the religious, perhaps because he wants to safeguard against further confusion of faith with a first immediacy. But we can legitimately make it for him, I think, provided the distinction between first and second immediacy is properly taken into account.

Another aesthetic feature of the religious is that of hiddenness, or secrecy. In problem III, however, Johannes seeks to distinguish religious secrecy from aesthetic secrecy. Thus we are faced with the same problem here as previously: the religious has the appearance of the aesthetic but is qualitatively different from it. Insofar as the religious is characterized by secrecy, however, it is fundamentally aesthetic. If its secrecy is not the same as what is ordinarily understood as aesthetic secrecy, must we not then understand a higher expression of the aesthetic as being implied in religious secrecy?

Johannes begins his consideration of this problem by first drawing a distinction between the aesthetic and the ethical. The ethical is the universal (a claim stated at the beginning of each problem, but each time with different consequences) and as such demands disclosure; by contrast, "the single individual, qualified as immediate, sensate, and psychical, is the hidden." According to Hegelian philosophy, once again the target of criticism by Johannes, there is no justified hiddenness. Thus Abraham's failure to explain his action to others is indefensible from an ethical and/or Hegelian standpoint and appears to be an instance of aesthetic hiddenness. Inasmuch as Hegel regards Abraham as the father of faith, however, Johannes finds his philosophy to be "a little bemuddled" on this issue (FT, 82). Either Abraham stands as a single individual and the father of faith above the universal, or else his faith and silence must be regarded as an expression of the aesthetic immediacy Hegel disdains. Either the religious or the aesthetic. That seems to be the nature of the either/or we face in the religious sphere.

In order to show the "absolute dissimilarity" between aesthetic hiddenness and the paradox of faith, Johannes decides to pursue the whole question from a purely aesthetic standpoint (FT, 82, 85). He begins by orienting his inquiry in the context of the category of the interesting—a category identified earlier in *Either/Or* as the central category of romantic aesthetics. Johannes situates his discussion in this category because he regards it as the category of the turning point in history (the present age) and as a border category between aesthetics and ethics (FT, 82–83). Thus he does not disdain the category in the manner it was ironically treated in *Either/Or,* and he even puts in a good word for it, suggesting that "to become interesting, to have an interesting life, is not a handicraft task but a momentous privilege, which, like every privilege in the world of spirit, is purchased only in severe pain." Over against the artistic posturing of Johannes the Seducer, whose category was the interesting aesthetically pursued in a demonic, destructive fashion, Johannes de Silentio nominates Socrates as exemplar of an ethical form of the interesting rooted in suffering: "Thus Socrates was the most interesting man who ever lived, his life the most interesting life ever led, but this existence was alloted to him by the god [*Guden*], and inasmuch as he himself had to acquire it, he was not a stranger to trouble and pain."[13] As a border category, then, the category of the interesting may take either an aesthetic or an ethical form. Inasmuch as Johannes's aesthetic inquiry "must constantly wander into the territory of ethics" and "must seize the problem with esthetic fervor and concupiscence" (FT, 83), it also straddles the border between ethics and aesthetics and thus is aptly associated with the category of the interesting.

To draw the contrast between Abraham's silence and aesthetic hiddenness as sharply as possible, Johannes makes use of an interesting assortment of poetic examples: the story, reported by Aristotle, of a bridegroom who refuses at the last moment to get married, because of a prophecy of calamity delivered to him by an augur; the report of how Queen Elizabeth sat silent for ten days, biting her finger, after learning about the deception that led to the execution of her beloved Essex as a sacrifice to the state; the legend of Agnes and the merman, slightly modified to make the merman demonically incapable of seduction, repentance, and disclosure in relation to the innocent maid; the biblical story of Tobit's marriage to Sarah, seven times widowed in the bridal chamber and thus heroic in the humility with which she receives sympathy and healing from God; the character Gloucester from Shakespeare's *King Lear,* who in contrast to Sarah becomes "the most demonic figure Shakespeare has depicted," because he could not accept sympathy for his deformities; the figure of Faust, interpreted here sympathetically as a tragic hero who hides his doubt in self-sacrifice and compassion for the universal.[14]

With the exception of Gloucester, each one of these examples centers

13. On the category of the interesting, and especially on Socrates as embodying an ethical form of the interesting, see Perkins, "Abraham's Silence Aesthetically Considered."

14. For an examination of several of these figures in more detail, see Louise Carroll Keeley, "The Parables of Problem III in Kierkegaard's *Fear and Trembling,*" in *International Kierkegaard Commentary: Fear and Trembling and Repetition,* ed. Robert L. Perkins, 127–54.

around or involves a love-relation between a man (or in one case, a merman) and a woman in which the aesthetic feature of silence figures prominently as a problem and a source of inner suffering for the personage portrayed. To that extent they provide an array of aesthetic analogies to Abraham. But in Johannes's opinion, none of these examples is truly analogous to Abraham inasmuch as all of them can be explained and understood in terms of aesthetics (the aesthetic hero who can speak but will not) or ethics (the tragic hero who sacrifices him- or herself for the universal). By virtue of the deviation from the universal that each displays, however, they do provide an indication of "the boundary of the unknown territory" that is the paradox of faith (FT, 112). The demonic figure in particular bears a resemblance to the paradox in that the single individual enters into an absolute relation to the demonic just as the knight of faith enters into an absolute relation to the divine. Unlike the demonic figure, however, Abraham cannot speak—a factor that distinguishes him from both the aesthetic hero and the tragic hero of ethics. Abraham cannot speak because he cannot explain in an understandable manner, first of all, the nature of the ordeal he faces, involving as it does the ethical as a temptation, and second, the movement of faith he makes in believing by virtue of the absurd that he will receive Isaac back after having given him up as a sacrifice to God (FT, 115). When he does speak, as when he replies to Isaac that God will provide a lamb for the burnt offering, his words are ironic, for he knows that Isaac is going to be the sacrificial lamb and that he, Abraham, is willing to sacrifice his son at God's demand (FT, 118–19). Irony here thus becomes a mode of divine speech, like speaking in tongues, (FT, 114, 119). Insofar as Johannes is able to understand Abraham at all, he realizes that he, and the present generation as well, does not have the courage to speak and act as Abraham did. Nevertheless, in his view the task of coming to faith remains the highest for every generation and is enough to occupy every individual for a lifetime. From his standpoint, it is presumptuous, then, to want to "go further" than faith by transcending it in Hegelian (or any other form of) philosophical comprehension. Indeed, Johannes suggests that just as the disciple of Heraclitus attempted to go further by denying motion and thus regressed to the Eleatic thesis that Heraclitus had abandoned, the paradox of faith is similarly denied by attempts to mediate it (FT, 123).

In spite of the fact that Johannes continually contrasts Abraham not only to ethics but also to aesthetics, I have tried to show that the paradox of faith as described by him nevertheless has an aesthetic character, evident in the claim of the superiority of the single individual to the universal in relation to God, in the characterization of faith as a passion in the form of a second immediacy, and finally in the silence or religious secrecy that both links and separates Abraham from the aesthetic and tragic heroes of classical literature. These features, together with the poetic characterization of faith as a work of art and the artistic metaphor of the knight of faith as a ballet dancer, suggest that the religious sphere as presented in *Fear and Trembling* is paradoxically rooted in the aesthetic and poetic, even though it is sharply distinguished from the aesthetic as that is commonly understood and expressed in human life.

There is another determinant of the religious that is only briefly mentioned in *Fear and Trembling* but that in a certain sense provides an analogy to Abraham as well as to the aesthetic examples presented by Johannes (FT, 112). This determinant is the paradox of sin. Like faith, sin is described by Johannes as being a later immediacy (FT, 98). Thus it is not directly analogous to the aesthetic. But in Johannes's view sin cannot explain Abraham any more than aesthetic immediacy does, for Abraham was a righteous man and did not become the single individual through sin (FT, 99, 112). There is a resemblance between Abraham and the sinner, however, inasmuch as both are single individuals who stand higher than the universal. But Abraham stands higher in the direction of the paradox of faith, whereas the sinner stands higher in the direction of the demonic paradox (FT, 98–99). Therein lies the analogy between the single individual in sin and the aesthetic figures discussed by Johannes, several of whom were demonic. The paradox of sin, however, is only intimated in *Fear and Trembling.*[15] For an indication of the role sin and its predisposition in anxiety play in the early existential aesthetics of Kierkegaard, I turn finally to *Philosophical Fragments* and *The Concept of Anxiety.* Like *Repetition* and *Fear and Trembling,* these two works are companion volumes, published within a few days of each other in 1844.[16] *Philosophical Fragments* appeared first (June 13), and *The Concept of Anxiety* followed four days later (June 17). Although from the standpoint of conceptual analysis it might be preferable to consider *The Concept of Anxiety* first, since anxiety is a precondition of sin, I follow the order of publication in examining them, allowing the Christian con-

15. As in often the case in Kierkegaard's writings, what is to become a major theme in the next work is briefly introduced or hinted at in the preceding one. Such is the case with the subject of sin in *Fear and Trembling.* For a discussion of the hidden role of sin in this work, see Ronald M. Green, "Deciphering *Fear and Trembling*'s Secret Message," *Religious Studies* 22 (1986): 95–111.

16. Of course *Concluding Unscientific Postscript,* which appeared two years later, may also be regarded as a companion to *Philosophical Fragments* inasmuch as it is a "postscript," or sequel, to that work and is by the same pseudonymous author.

cept of sin to emerge in distinction to its Socratic, or idealist, counterpart before examining the psychological precondition of its appearance in human life.

DIVINE POETRY IN *PHILOSOPHICAL FRAGMENTS*

In the thought-project hypothesized by Johannes Climacus in *Philosophical Fragments* two artistic, or poetic, modes of acquiring truth and self-knowledge are contrasted with each other. One is the Platonic mode, which assumes that the individual stands in an immanent relation to truth and acquires self-knowledge through a recollection of truth that is within the individual but has been forgotten. The model for this mode of acquiring truth is Socrates, who consistently "remained true to himself and artistically exemplified what he had understood" by practicing the art of "midwifery," or assisting in the birth of self-knowledge in others as a means of acquiring it for himself (PF, 10).[17] In this form of artistry, it is assumed that the teacher and the pupil stand in an equal and reciprocal relation to one another, each acting as an occasion for the birth of self-knowledge in the other (PF, 24). The other artistic mode is the Christian, although it is not explicitly identified as such by Climacus and the artistry involved in this instance is the result of divine, rather than human, activity. In this mode the individual is deemed not to be in possession of truth, which has been lost due to sin, an act for which the individual is responsible and needs divine assistance in order to be delivered from the bondage incurred by it. Truth is thus acquired in a decisive moment of time via a relation to a teacher who in this instance is not simply another human being like Socrates but the god or eternal truth itself that has appeared in a moment of time. In this mode of learning the truth, the teacher not only serves as the occasion for the discovery of the individual's state of sin or untruth but also gives the individual the requisite condition for being reborn in the truth. The teacher thus plays a far more decisive role in the life of the individual in the Christian mode than in the Socratic. In this mode the pupil owes the teacher everything, whereas in the Socratic the pupil owes the teacher nothing. Moreover, in the Christian mode the condition of sin creates a disparity between the teacher and the pupil, or the god and the individual, which makes equality and mutual understanding between them im-

17. On the artistic character of Socrates' life, see also JP, 6:6360, and Chapter 7 below.

possible. Motivated by love for the individual, however, the god desires equality and understanding with the learner, for "only in love is the different made equal," and "only in equality or in unity is there understanding" (PF, 25).

But how might this be brought about? To find a possible solution to this dilemma, Johannes enlists the services of the poet, or rather, he himself undertakes the role of the poet and composes a love poem, or love story, using the erotic love relation between a king and a maiden as a metaphor for the divine-human relation.[18] Erotic love provides an apt analogy in this instance because, like the Socratic relation between teacher and student, it assumes equality between lovers or at least seeks to establish equality between unequals as its goal. The Christian love relation also seeks to make unequals equal. Its goal, then, is the same as the erotic and the Socratic but is achieved in a different way. In his love poem Climacus imagines two possible ways of bringing about this equality between unequals: either by ascent of the beloved to the status of the king or god or by descent of the king or god to the level of the beloved. The first option is rejected because it is essentially deceptive, making the beloved appear to be something she or he is not or else resulting in the glorification of the god rather than the beloved and thus thwarting the god's aim. The second path of unity is thus chosen because it is one that will not only establish equality between the lovers but also bring the beloved into the unity of truth. Unlike Socratic midwifery, which is an "assisting love" that enables the learner to give birth to him- or herself in the recollection of truth, the god's love not only assists the learner in coming to know the truth but also is a maternal "procreative love" that gives birth to the learner in the form of a rebirth or recovery of being in truth (PF, 30–31). The god's love is a suffering love as well, for in order to bring about this rebirth the god appears in history in the form of a servant who must "suffer all things, endure all things, be tried in all things, hunger in the desert, thirst in his agonies, be forsaken in death," so as to become "absolutely the equal of the lowliest of human beings" (PF, 32–33).

18. On the characterization of Climacus's parable as a love story, see Robert C. Roberts, *Rethinking Kierkegaard's "Philosophical Fragments"* (Macon, Ga.: Mercer University Press, 1986), 45–54. For other studies focusing on *Philosophical Fragments,* see C. Stephen Evans, *Passionate Reason: Making Sense of Kierkegaard's "Philosophical Fragments"* (Bloomington: Indiana University Press, 1992); idem, *Kierkegaard's "Fragments" and "Postscript";* H. A. Nielsen, *Where the Passion Is: A Reading of Kierkegaard's "Philosophical Fragments"* (Tallahassee: University Presses of Florida, 1983); and Paul Müller, "The God's Poem—the God's History," in *Kierkegaard—Poet of Existence,* ed. Birgit Bertung (Copenhagen: C. A. Reitzel, 1989), 83–88.

Johannes Climacus openly admits that this love poem is not a product of his own creative imagination but rather is plagiarized. In this instance, however, the plagiarized poem does not belong to another human being but to the deity. Thus it is a divine poem, not a human poem. Indeed, Climacus suggests that such a poem would never even occur to a human being, for "presumably it could occur to a human being to poetize himself in the likeness of the god or the god in the likeness of himself, but not to poetize that the god poetized himself in the likeness of a human being" (PF, 36). This poetic possibility would not occur to anyone, Climacus suggests, because a human being would have no way of knowing that the god had need of him or her without some indication from the god. From an Aristotelian-Christian standpoint, the godhead has no need of anything outside itself. If the god is moved, therefore, it must not be from any external need but rather from an internal need such as love (PF, 24). The thought that the divine could have need of human beings in this manner and is moved out of love strikes wonder in the heart of Climacus, leading him to declare at last that "the poem was so different from every human poem that it was no poem at all but 'the wonder' " (PF, 36). The divine poetry of the Incarnation thus goes beyond human imagination to include that which is unimaginable from a merely human point of view.

According to Plato and Aristotle, philosophy begins in wonder, not with doubt (as modern philosophy would have it). With a single word, therefore, Climacus makes a transition from the realm of imagination to the realm of thought and enlarges the scope of incomprehensibility of this divine poem to include thought as well as imagination.[19] Consequently, in the "Metaphysical Caprice" that follows, he explores the implications of the divine poem, or "wonder," for thought. Extending the analogy of love to the realm of thought, Climacus underscores the importance of passion and paradox for thought as well as for love: just as passion is essential for being a lover, so too thought includes passion; and just as erotic love paradoxically wills the downfall of self-love in love for the beloved, so the understanding in paradoxical passion seeks its own downfall in the collision of thought with that which it cannot think or comprehend (PF, 37, 39, 48). The object of thought in this instance is the god, who is unknown and absolutely different from human beings because of their sin. Since thought cannot think or comprehend that which is absolutely different, the tendency of thought is to confuse this difference with likeness, that is, to construe the divine in likeness to the

19. On this point, see Evans, *Passionate Reason,* 46.

human or, vice versa, the human in likeness to the divine. If the absolute difference of the human in relation to the divine is to be known, then, it must come from the god, who reveals this absolute difference to human beings in the consciousness of sin. But the god also desires to annul this absolute difference in absolute equality (PF, 47).

Herein lies the absolute paradox for thought. The appearance of the deity in time in the form of a servant is inconceivable and incomprehensible to the understanding, which feels threatened by as well as attracted to this paradox and thus responds to it in one or the other of two opposite forms of passion: offense or faith. As Climacus sees it, offense is essentially passive and constitutes a poetic response to the paradox in that it is "an acoustical illusion," that is, a mimicking, parroting, or caricaturing of what the paradox announces about itself, namely, that it is absurd to that which stands outside the paradox, although in itself it is not absurd but true (PF, 49, 51–52).[20] When the understanding declares the paradox to be foolishness, therefore, this is merely an echoing of the paradox's counterclaim that the understanding is absurd because it does not recognize the truth of the paradox but gives an "erroneous accounting" of the paradox as the absurd (PF, 51–52). If, on the other hand, the understanding recognizes that it cannot understand the paradox and accepts the paradox as a paradox, a mutual understanding is achieved and the condition for understanding the truth is given in a third factor, the happy passion of faith.

As Climacus understands it, faith is not a form of knowledge or an act or product of the will but an eternal condition received in the moment of encounter with the absolute paradox in time, making faith along with the absolute paradox a wonder, or paradox, that cannot be understood or canceled by thought (PF, 62, 65).[21] This eternal condition enables the

20. That the absolute paradox is not in itself absurd but only appears to be so from the standpoint of the offended consciousness or to someone who stands outside of faith is supported in the reply of Kierkegaard to a critique of *Fear and Trembling* by Theophilus Nicolaus (Magnus Eiríksson) that was never published (PAP, X^6 B 64–82). Portions of this reply are translated in JP, 1:9, 10, 11, 12; 6:6598, 6601; and in an article by Cornelio Fabro, "Faith and Reason in Kierkegaard's Dialectic," in *A Kierkegaard Critique,* ed. Howard A. Johnson and Niels Thulstrup (New York: Harper & Brothers, 1962), 156–206. For a discussion of this issue, see my article "Echoes of Absurdity: The Offended Consciousness and the Absolute Paradox in Kierkegaard's *Philosophical Fragments,*" in *International Kierkegaard Commentary: Philosophical Fragments,* ed. Robert L. Perkins (Macon, Ga.: Mercer University Press, 1994).

21. For a position arguing that Kierkegaard, or Climacus (no distinction is made between them here), is a volitionist in matters of belief and faith, see Pojman, *The Logic of Subjectivity,* 87–117. Pojman notes Climacus's claim that faith is not an act of will, but then proceeds virtually to ignore that claim in his insistence on choice and freedom of the will as determinative for belief and faith in Kierkegaard's thought. While I would not deny that these are

believer to make a decision, or resolution of the will, affirming that the god has come into existence contrary to all human understanding and expectation (PF, 62, 64, 84). Although Climacus downplays the significance of historical data as a basis for faith, claiming that every believer comes to faith in the same way, through a transhistorical personal encounter with the god in servant form, he does want to claim that the divine poem presented in his thought-project is not a fiction but rather is rooted in history. In fact, Climacus goes so far as to claim that "Christianity is the only historical phenomenon that despite the historical—indeed, precisely by means of the historical—has wanted to be the single individual's point of departure for his eternal consciousness, has wanted to interest him otherwise than merely historically, has wanted to base his happiness on his relation to something historical" (PF, 109).

To illuminate and underscore the importance of the historical in Christianity, Climacus inserts an orchestral "Interlude" between chapters, suggesting the passage of time between the Christ event and the present age. In this interlude Climacus conducts a rigorous analysis of the concepts of coming into existence, the historical, the past, and apprehension of the past in order to establish that historical coming into existence takes place in freedom rather than out of necessity (PF, 74–75).[22] Furthermore, he wants to claim that all historical coming into existence is characterized by a certain illusiveness or deceptiveness inasmuch as it

---

important aspects of Climacus's (and Kierkegaard's) thought, I would not ignore Climacus's statement that "all human willing is efficacious only within the condition" (PF, 62), or, as the older Swenson translation puts it (better, I think), "all human volition has its capacity within the scope of an underlying condition" (*Philosophical Fragments,* 2d ed., translated by David F. Swenson and revised by Howard V. Hong, with a new introduction and commentary by Niels Thulstrup [Princeton: Princeton University Press, 1962], 77). Pojman's interpretation has generated considerable reaction. For arguments countering his views, see David Wisdo, "Kierkegaard on Belief, Faith, and Explanation," *International Journal for Philosophy of Religion* 21, no. 2 (1987): 95–114; C. Stephen Evans, "Does Kierkegaard Think Beliefs Can Be Directly Willed?" *International Journal for Philosophy of Religion* 26, no. 3 (1989): 173–84; M. Jamie Ferreira, "Kierkegaardian Faith: 'The Condition' and the Response," *International Journal for Philosophy of Religion* 28, no. 2 (1990): 63–79; idem, *Transforming Vision,* which develops a mediating, nonvolitional position between volitionalism and antivolitionalism, emphasizing the role of the imagination in Kierkegaard's thought; and Robert L. Perkins, "Kierkegaard: A Kind of Epistemologist," *History of European Ideas* 12, no. 1 (1990): 7–18. See also Pojman's response to Wisdo, "Kierkegaard on Faith and Freedom," *International Journal for Philosophy of Religion* 27, nos. 1–2 (1990): 41–61, and my review of Ferreira's book in the *Søren Kierkegaard Newsletter* 25 (1992): 5–8.

22. For a closer study of these categories, see Charles Magel, "An Analysis of Kierkegaard's Philosophic Categories" (Ph.D. diss., University of Minnesota, 1960). See also Evans, *Passionate Reason,* 119–42.

can never be sensed immediately but only after the fact (PF, 81). With respect to the absolute paradox, this means that the god's historical coming into existence in the form of a servant, like any other historical fact, is not accessible to immediate cognition and thus is a matter of faith or belief. Beyond this, however, Climacus claims there is another sort of faith that is appropriate only in relation to the absolute paradox. This form of faith is characterized by Climacus as faith in an eminent sense in distinction to the ordinary kind of faith that obtains with respect to all historical coming into existence (PF, 87). The content of faith in an eminent sense is not that the god exists, which in Climacus's view is a qualification of the god's eternal essence, but rather that the god has come into existence, which is a historical fact based upon a self-contradiction, since the divine, properly speaking, does not come into existence, that is, is not subject to spatial-temporal determinations but exists eternally (PF, 87). The absolute paradox, therefore, is not a simple historical fact for which being a contemporary would be an advantage in apprehending it; rather, in Climacus's view the absolute paradox must be regarded as an absolute fact in the sense that it is an historical fact that is not subject to the apportionment of time in relation to it (PF, 99–100). In other words, those who live closer to the historical moment of the god's coming into existence possess no advantage over those of a later time. In Climacus's view, therefore, there is no such thing as a disciple at second hand. Historical reports may serve as an occasion for receiving the condition of faith from the god, but they are not decisive for that event. Climacus does admit, however, that at least a bit of historical information is needed as an occasion for faith: "Even if the contemporary generation had not left anything behind except these words, 'We have believed that in such and such a year the god appeared in the humble form of a servant, lived and taught among us, and then died'—this is more than enough" (PF, 104).

Although Climacus's thought-project is poetical, being an imaginative construction that explores as an alternative to a Socratic form of artistry the possibility of acquiring self-knowledge and truth through a divine poem that transcends human imagination and thought, the project and its poem nevertheless give considerable emphasis to the historical character of the absolute paradox and its encounter by individuals in the context of time and history. In this emphasis upon the historical, Climacus stands in continuity with Judge William's existential aesthetics. But in the latter's view it is assumed, in agreement with the Socratic perspective, that the individual has an immanent ability to realize selfhood and to actualize the eternal in the context of social relations.[23] Climacus's project, therefore, may be viewed as making an advance not only upon Socrates but also upon the immanent ethical-religiousness of Judge William and even upon Kierkegaard's earlier synergistic view of faith in *The Concept of Irony.* For if faith is a work of art, as Johannes de Silentio has claimed, it is not a product of human artistry but rather of divine craftsmanship by the god in time in the form of a lowly carpenter who is the equal of none, yet all.

DANCING IN AND OUT OF STEP IN *THE CONCEPT OF ANXIETY*

The final work in the first phase of Kierkegaard's authorship brings us back to the problem of sin to consider it from a psychological perspective. Being a psychologist, Vigilius Haufniensis, the pseudonymous author of *The Concept of Anxiety,* is somewhat uncomfortable in dealing with the subject of sin because he is of the opinion that sin cannot be explained and thus is not an appropriate subject for treatment in psychology, ethics, metaphysics, aesthetics, or indeed any science, since science by definition is ideal, or conceptual, and disinterestedly concerned with explaining the causes or underlying principles of things.[24] As Vigilius sees it, sin is properly the subject of the sermon, an art form that in his view has fallen into low regard lately (CA, 15–16). "But to preach is really the most difficult of all arts and is essentially the art that Socrates praised, the art of being able to converse," he observes (CA, 16). The sermon, like Socratic dialogue, has existential appropriation as its aim; thus it may be regarded as the art form appropriate to an existential aesthetics at the religious level.

That Vigilius subscribes to an artistic understanding of life is indicated in a passage, excised from the final text, in which he states that "each

23. While it is true that for Judge William the self is regarded as received from God, in his view this gift takes the form of an immanent potentiality, within the personality, that may be realized through choice and ethical action (EO, 2:177). However, the judge does recognize the effect of hereditary sin, which keeps human beings from becoming completely transparent to themselves (EO, 2:190).

24. The term "science" is used by Vigilius, in the broad sense that prevailed in the nineteenth century, as applying to any discipline that purports to speak ideally or conceptually about the world. Thus the term is not limited to empirical studies as it is in English-speaking countries today.

person should be concerned about himself and about transforming his life into a beautiful, artistically finished whole." As Vigilius sees it, this constitutes the meaning of life, and "every science should direct itself to this task" (CA, 192). Nevertheless, in the final text Vigilius emphasizes that each science must recognize its limitations and stay within the bounds of its proper subject matter; otherwise conceptual confusion and falsification will result. When sin is treated under the science of aesthetics, for example, Vigilius contends that a change of mood occurs and the concept of sin is altered. In place of its proper mood, which is earnestness (more on that later), aesthetics substitutes either light-mindedness, treating sin as comic, or melancholy, regarding it as tragic (CA, 14–15). In either case, Vigilius claims, the concept of sin is changed, becoming something that is conceptually annulled (*ophævet*) rather than existentially overcome (*overvundet*), in accordance with its true conception.[25] Likewise, when sin is treated under psychology, the mood becomes one of "persistent observation" rather than "the victorious flight of earnestness out of sin," and the concept of sin is altered to become a state that is continually annulled as a possibility, whereas the true conception of sin is that it is not a state but an actuality that should be continually overcome (CA, 15).[26]

Since ethics is that science which projects for human beings the ideal task of becoming a true and whole personality and assumes this task can be realized, it might appear that the concept of sin properly falls under the domain of ethics. But Vigilius finds a difficulty here too, claiming that sin is precisely the concept upon which ethics becomes "shipwrecked" in the discovery that sin is not an accidental phenomenon in the individual but a much deeper presupposition that goes

25. This distinction indicates the fundamentally existential context within which the concept of sin is properly dealt with and understood in contrast to a conceptual framework such as that of Hegel, in whose thought the concept of annulment, or negation (*Aufheben*), is central. Thus the specific target of Vigilius's critique here is Hegel. On the concept of *Aufheben* in Hegel's thought, see CA, 225, editor's note 16, where it is pointed out that the term means both to "abolish," or "do away with," and to "preserve," or "maintain," thus resulting in the double consequence that "what is annulled is at the same time preserved," which is an inappropriate consequence with respect to sin.

26. The text is somewhat ambiguous on this point in that the intended referent of the possessive pronouns in the sentence "Its idea is that the concept is continually annulled [*Dens Idee er, at dens Begreb bestandig ophæves*]" is unclear. I take "its" here to refer, not to sin, as the preceding sentence might suggest, but to psychology; otherwise the sentence would be inconsistent with the distinction between "annulled" (*ophævet*) and "overcome" (*overvundet*) previously drawn in the text and in my account above (CA, 15; SV, 4:287). At a later point in the text Vigilius clarifies why sin is not a state: he defines a state as "a becoming by necessity," as in the case of the history of a plant, whereas sin occurs in freedom (CA, 21).

beyond the individual to include the whole human race (CA, 19–20). In Vigilius's opinion, therefore, the science that comes closest to explaining sin is dogmatics, which unlike ethics takes the actuality of sin as a starting point and seeks to explain it by presupposing it (which is really no explanation) in hereditary sin as the ideal possibility of sin. With the introduction of dogmatics comes a new ethics having, as its object, consciousness of the actuality of sin within a dogmatic perspective. In this form of ethics the actuality of sin is explained by reference to hereditary sin, and the ethical task is seen as moving from actuality to ideality rather than from ideality to actuality, as projected in the first ethics (CA, 20–21, 23).

In Vigilius's view, the science of psychology is closely related to dogmatics in that it is able to treat the possibility of sin, even though it cannot deal with the actuality of sin. But whereas dogmatics is concerned with the *ideal* possibility or presupposition of sin in hereditary sin, psychology focuses on the *real* possibility of sin determined as that psychological condition within a person which predisposes him or her to sin (CA, 23). This condition is identified in psychology as anxiety, an antipathetic-sympathetic phenomenon that according to Vigilius appears in two forms: the anxiety of innocence, or the anxiety through which sin is first posited by a qualitative leap; and the anxiety of sinfulness, or the anxiety that enters the world in and with sin in quantitative increments in the individual (subjective anxiety) and in the creation (objective anxiety) (CA, 54, 56). My object here is to examine these two forms of anxiety with an eye toward discerning, on the one hand, the aesthetic and poetic character of anxiety and, on the other hand, its relation to spirit, in order to determine whether the integral relation between the aesthetic, the poetic, and the ethical-religious projected in Kierkegaard's earlier writings is sustained in this final pseudonymous work of the first phase of his authorship.

THE ANXIETY OF INNOCENCE

Let us begin our analysis, then, with the anxiety of innocence. According to the biblical account of the fall of humanity, Adam and Eve existed in a state of innocence before the Fall, which introduced sin into the world. Innocence, it might appear, is synonymous with the aesthetic concept of immediacy inasmuch as both refer to an original natural condition of some sort. But Vigilius refuses to identify the two, claiming that innocence is an ethical concept, whereas immediacy is a concept that belongs to logic (CA, 35). According to Hegel, immediacy is something that should be annulled (*aufheben*), whereas it would be unethical,

Vigilius points out, to say that about innocence.[27] Innocence is neither a state of imperfection that should be left behind nor a state of perfection that, if lost, should be regained (CA, 37). Rather, it is a psychic state of ignorance in which human beings, theoretically at least, may well have remained. The annulment of immediacy occurs through an immanent movement within mediacy or reflection, or it may be understood as an immanent movement within immediacy itself, since, according to Hegel, mediacy is implicit in immediacy. The loss of innocence, by contrast, is a transcendent movement that brings about a different quality of being, that of guilt. Just as Adam and Eve lost their innocence through guilt, so every individual loses innocence in the same way.[28]

Properly speaking, then, innocence, not immediacy, constitutes the primal aesthetic state of existence, and the loss of the aesthetic in this sense is not necessarily something to be desired. But innocence is an ambiguous state in that it constitutes not merely the natural psychic condition of human beings but also contains within itself the possibility of spirit, or freedom.[29] Spirit is that power by which human beings freely integrate or unite themselves as a synthesis of the psychical (soul) and the somatic (body), the eternal and the temporal, so as to become, as Vigilius puts it, "a beautiful, artistically finished whole" (CA, 192). Spirit is present in innocence in the form of anxiety, a psychological state of anticipation in which human beings are vaguely aware of the possibility of being able to act in freedom. This is a possibility to which they react with both desire and fear, since that which they are able to do is unknown and the unknown can be both attractive and terrifying. In this state spirit is "dreaming" or merely potential, and it dreamily projects the possibility of its actuality in anxiety (CA, 41). As Vigilius analyzes it, however, anxiety, or the possibility of freedom, has a dizzying and weak-

27. Strictly speaking, Vigilius points out, it is logically incorrect to say that immediacy is annulled, since for Hegel the immediate does not exist but is an abstract nothing that comes into existence as that which is annulled through the appearance of mediacy or reflection (CA, 35, 37).

28. The burden of part of the first chapter of *The Concept of Anxiety* is to show that Adam is not essentially different from the race, so that what holds for Adam holds for the race, and vice versa. This is necessary in order to avoid the "fantastic beginning" of the human race that would follow from placing Adam outside of history (CA, 25).

29. For a fuller treatment of the concept of freedom in *The Concept of Anxiety,* see Gregor Malantschuk, *Frihedens Problem i Kierkegaards Begrebet Angest* (Copenhagen: Rosenkilde & Bagger, 1971). For an enlightening discussion of the concept of freedom in relation to free will, the synthesis of the self, spirit, and the eternal, see Maurice Carignan, "The Eternal as a Synthesizing Third Term in Kierkegaard's Work," in *Kierkegaard Resources and Results,* 74–87, as well as Peter Carpenter's "Comment on Carignan," in ibid., 88–91.

ening effect upon human beings, so that when they first act, the result is the positing of sin and guilt rather than the actualization of spirit. This act, however, is ambiguous in that the individual is innocent as well as guilty, for anxiety appears as an alien power that takes hold of an individual, making that person in one sense unaccountable for his or her action yet in another sense personally responsible for it because the individual consents and acts out of desire as well as fear. As Vigilius sees it, anxiety is not the cause of sin but merely the psychological presupposition or precondition of sin. Sin is posited by a qualitative leap, that is, by an inexplicable movement in freedom from one state, or quality of being, to another (CA, 61). Ironically, then, the act by which spirit first posits itself as freedom results in the contradiction of spirit, or freedom, in sin.

Just as spirit is potentially present in innocence before the Fall, so also generic or sexual difference, in the form of sensuousness defined as a sexual drive, is contained there as a possibility that is made actual in the Fall. With the positing of sin, then, sexuality is also posited. Not only that, sexuality, or sensuousness, is posited as sinfulness.[30] Vigilius repeatedly contends that sensuousness as such is not sinful, but it becomes sinful in the qualitative leap of the individual into sin (CA, 49, 63, 68, 73, 76, 79, 80). Why this is so is never explicitly stated in the text, but in a marginal note to an excised passage where the claim is once again repeated, we may find a reason in Vigilius's statement that "the sexual is the sinful only to the extent that the drive at some moment manifests itself simply as drive in all its nakedness, for this can occur only through an arbitrary abstraction from spirit" (CA, 195). From Vigilius's standpoint, then, sensuousness and spirit are not inherently opposed; indeed, they must not be if it is the task of spirit to bring about a synthesis of the somatic (the bodily) and the psychic (soul, or the mental-emotional dimension in human beings). Nevertheless, Vigilius holds that the sexual in the form of the erotic is neutralized and suspended by spirit in Christianity, rendering the pagan ideal of the erotic comic in its light-minded identification of spirit with the beautiful and of beauty with the union of the psychic and the somatic (CA, 69). This suspension does not mean, Vigilius points out, that the sexual or the erotic is annihilated in an outward sense or that it is suspended simply because it is sinful; rather, it is reduced to a matter of indifference and ultimately forgotten in the transfiguration of the erotic wholly into spirit, where sexual differences are transcended and spirit is qualified "not merely as that which constitutes the synthesis" but simply as spirit (CA, 80). Here we have a determination of spirit

30. On this issue, see Nordentoft, *Kierkegaard's Psychology,* 56–60.

that is certainly higher than that recognized by Judge William in *Either/Or,* where sensuousness and spirit are seen as being fully compatible with one another and together give definition to the aesthetic in both immediate and historical form. Furthermore, it is higher than Vigilius's own working definition of spirit in terms of its constituting activity in relation to the synthesis of body and soul. Indeed, it is an ideal conception of spirit that for all practical purposes is irrelevant to existence, since every individual, as long as he or she lives, is never simply spirit but is always in the process of becoming such through the constituting activity of spirit: positively through faith or else negatively through anxiety and sin.

Vigilius's association of sensuousness with sinfulness is coupled with the further controversial claim that woman is more sensuous (and therefore more sinful?) than man and has more anxiety than he (CA, 64).[31] This claim is based aesthetically on the stereotyped notion of woman's ideal physical beauty, on the one hand, and ethically on her capacity for procreation, on the other. Neither of these constitutes a compelling justification for this claim inasmuch as Vigilius regards the facial beauty of man as more spiritual than that of woman and woman does not procreate alone (CA, 65–66). The claim is made even more problematic by the parallel contention of Vigilius that man is "more qualified as spirit" than woman (CA, 67). Does this mean that woman is less spiritual because she is more sensuous and anxious? If so, that would seem to undermine Vigilius's earlier analysis of anxiety as the harbinger of spirit and his correlation of the two in the statement, "The less spirit, the less anxiety" (CA, 42). In correspondence with that claim we would expect him to say, "The more anxiety, the more spirit," but such a correlation is not forthcoming. Perhaps the reason it is not can be found in a passage excised from the final text, in which Vigilius states, "Were she [woman] more spiritual [than man] she could never have her culmination point in another. Spirit is the true independent" (CA, 189). Since woman's being, in his view, culminates substantially in procreation, she cannot be as spiritual or as independent as man. But these are merely quantitative differences; from a religious standpoint, Vigilius claims, woman is essen-

31. On this issue, see Howard P. Kainz, "The Relationship of Dread to Spirit in Man and Woman, According to Kierkegaard," *Modern Schoolman* 47 (1969): 1–13; Christine Garside, "Can a Woman Be Good in the Same Way As a Man?" *Dialogue* 10 (1971): 534–44; Gregor Malantschuk, "Kierkegaard's View of Man and Woman," in *The Controversial Kierkegaard,* tr. Howard V. Hong and Edna H. Hong (Waterloo: Wilfrid Laurier University Press, 1980), 37–61; Bertung, *Om Kierkegaard Kvinder og Kærlighed,* 36–42; and my review of Bertung's book in *Kierkegaardiana* 15 (1991): 153–57.

tially identical with man inasmuch as both are essentially defined as spirit, in which the sexual difference disappears (CA, 66, 189). Nevertheless, it appears that woman, because of her physical nature, is precluded from becoming that which she essentially is, and thus does not really have the possibility of spiritual independence claimed for her in the religious. Thus, Vigilius's view of woman, like that of Judge William, is inconsistent and sexist.

THE ANXIETY OF SINFULNESS

The second form of anxiety identified by Vigilius is the anxiety of sinfulness, or anxiety resulting from the first sin, the loss of innocence through the anxiety of innocence. As Vigilius sees it, the transition between these two expressions of anxiety is historical, but it must also be understood as a state, a moment of repose in which time and eternity intersect so as to bring about a synthesis of psyche and body within the context of another synthesis, that of the temporal and the eternal (CA, 85, 88).[32] In this moment spirit, or the eternal, is present, giving to time as a succession of moments a significance that was lacking before, and establishing temporality, a division of time into past, present, and future. In this division the eternal—viewed Platonically, in its timeless perfection, as the present with no past or future—appears as the future and thus as the possible.

It is in relation to the possibility of sin in the future as well as to the actuality of sin or the annulled possibility of spirit in the past that anxiety reappears after freedom succumbs to sin in the first instance. This form of anxiety differs from the first in that there is now something definite about which to be anxious. This anxiousness has to do with the possibility and actuality of a quantitative progression of sin in the individual (subjective anxiety) and in the creation (objective anxiety) rather than with the qualitative leap into sin, although every appearance of sin, whether through the first positing or through a subsequent repositing, always enters by way of a qualitative leap. I have designated this second form of anxiety as the anxiety of sinfulness, since Vigilius distinguishes sin, which enters by way of a qualitative leap, from sinfulness, which accrues quantitatively in the individual and in creation throughout gen-

32. The claim that this transition is a "state," which Vigilius has previously defined as "a becoming by necessity" (CA, 21), may seem inappropriate inasmuch as the transition of which he speaks here takes place "in the sphere of historical freedom" (CA, 85). Vigilius may be guilty of using the term loosely in this context, but I think not, since there is no movement in the moment of transition itself and one gets out of it through a leap, that is, in the exercise of freedom rather than by an immanent or necessary process of movement in the transition itself.

eration (CA, 47). This form of anxiety expresses itself in terms of an anxiety about evil, on the one hand, and about the good, on the other (CA, 113, 118). Anxiety about evil manifests itself in the attempt to negate the unwarranted actuality of sin either through sophistry and self-deception or through the forming of a consciousness of sin in repentance, neither of which, in Vigilius's view, is successful in eradicating sin, since the first desires the removal of sin only to a certain degree and the second cannot cancel sin but only sorrows over it (CA, 113–15).

It is anxiety about the good, however, that Vigilius is primarily concerned to elucidate. He equates this expression of anxiety with the demonic, and thus his account bears a close relation to the earlier treatment of the demonic in *Fear and Trembling,* where the demonic is considered in analogy with and in contrast to the paradoxes of sin and faith. There the demonic appears in certain aesthetic figures who, like Abraham, do not speak; but unlike Abraham, who cannot speak, they do not speak because they will not. In *The Concept of Anxiety* this aesthetic silence, or muteness, on the part of a demonic individual is described as "inclosing reserve," or the attempt of the individual to close him- or herself off from others and become incommunicado, closed up within her- or himself (CA, 123).[33] As Vigilius sees it, this is actually impossible, since freedom always retains a relation to the good (the good in this instance signifying disclosure, which Vigilius regards as "the first expression of salvation"), even when it is entangled in anxiety and bound up in the unfreedom of sin (CA, 123, 127). The demonic individual is thus characterized by Vigilius in a Pauline-Augustinian fashion as having two wills, one that wills revelation but is impotent and subordinate to the other, which wills inclosing reserve. Ironically, however, the more the weak will is suppressed, the more likely the individual in inclosing reserve is to reveal involuntarily through a sudden declaration of words or through what we would today call "body language"—a revealing facial expression, glance, or touch—that which he or she wishes to conceal (CA, 129). Vigilius likens this sort of involuntary disclosure to "comic ventriloquism," in which all sorts of ridiculous, trivial, puerile, and petty matters are shown to make up the content (or, more precisely, the contentlessness) of inclosing reserve (CA, 129, 133). From an aesthetic standpoint, however, the demonic is best represented artistically, Vigil-

33. On the demonic in *The Concept of Anxiety,* see Ronald L. Hall, "Language and Freedom: Kierkegaard's Analysis of the Demonic in *The Concept of Anxiety,*" in *International Kierkegaard Commentary: The Concept of Anxiety,* ed. Robert L. Perkins (Macon, Ga.: Mercer University Press, 1985), 153–66. Hall is particularly concerned to show the significance of the demonic, in Kierkegaard's thought, for discerning the communal dimension of the life of faith.

ius claims, through the comic medium of mime, since the demonic is essentially mimical (mute) and sudden (lacking continuity) (CA, 132–33).[34] Since communication is the expression for continuity, the sudden (or discontinuity) finds expression in opposite form, in the nonverbal medium of mime, through the mimicking of continuity in boredom, or monotonous sameness, thus revealing the contentless and boring character of the demonic.

In contrast to this demonic inclosing reserve Vigilius also calls attention to a "lofty inclosing reserve" such as that nurtured in the parent-child relationship—for example, in the parental task of helping the child become independent, a task that is very difficult indeed. Here, Vigilius observes, "the art is that of constantly being present, and yet not being present, so that the child may be allowed to develop himself, and at the same time one still has a clear view of the development. The art is to leave the child to himself in the very highest degree and on the greatest possible scale, and to express this apparent relinquishing in such a way that, unnoticed, one is aware of everything" (CA, 126). This sounds very much like the maieutic art by which self-knowledge is elicited from the student by the teacher, and indeed, in a later passage Vigilius makes specific reference to Socrates, indicating that "his irony was precisely inclosing reserve, which he began by closing himself off from men, by closing himself in with himself in order to be expanded in the divine, who also began by closing his door and making a jest to those outside in order to talk in secret." But this sort of irony, or inclosing reserve, is not demonic or negative in the sense that Hegel (and Kierkegaard, in *The Concept of Irony*) thought it to be. Although Vigilius credits Hegel with being the first to explain irony in terms of the negative, he nevertheless contends that "he [Hegel] did not know much about irony" (CA, 134).

Instead of being merely a negative phenomenon, irony (or inclosing reserve) in the Socratic sense is an expression of what Vigilius calls earnestness. Since earnestness is an existential concept that cannot be apprehended essentially in the form of an abstract definition, Vigilius

34. The prototype of the demonic, of course, is Mephistopheles, whom Vigilius describes as essentially mimical, in contrast with Don Giovanni, who is essentially musical. In *Either/Or,* however, music is presented as the medium of the demonic, and Don Giovanni is seen as the representative of demonic sensuousness. The pseudonyms thus appear not to be in agreement with one another on this matter. But this apparent discrepancy may be resolved by keeping in mind the distinction between the immediate demonic and the reflective demonic in *Either/Or.* Music is an appropriate medium for expression of the immediate demonic but not the reflective demonic, which requires speech or, better, the negation of speech (noncommunication) in silence.

declines to define it, but he does identify it as being synonymous with three concrete factors in the healthy individual: certitude, inwardness, and disposition (CA, 146–48). Certitude and inwardness are those qualities within a person by which truth is brought forth and acknowledged in such a way as to permeate that individual's whole being. Thus they constitute a concrete, rather than an abstract, form of subjectivity, or self-consciousness, and understanding and are attained through action rather than through contemplation (CA, 141–43). For example, certitude about the existence of God is gained not by occasionally concerning oneself with rational proofs or demonstrations of God's existence but by continually living with that thought. "To live in a beautiful and intimate companionship with this conception truly requires inwardness, and it is a much greater feat than that of being a model husband," declares Vigilius in an obvious put-down of Judge William's ethical conception of inwardness (CA, 140). On the other hand, he also takes a poke at religious piety, suggesting that the pious person who lacks inwardness is comical, just as a bowlegged man who wants to act like a dancing master but does not know how to dance is comical. Carrying the analogy of dancing a bit further, Vigilius characterizes the spurious pious person as someone who knows how to beat time but is not able to get in step, that is, he or she is unable to make the religious absolutely commensurate to life, so as always to have it with him or her, but understands it as applying only to certain occasions and moments of life (CA, 141). Inwardness is further identified by Vigilius, this time in agreement with Judge William, as the factor of the eternal in human beings. Here the eternal is understood, like inwardness itself, concretely rather than abstractly; in metaphysical, aesthetic, and aesthetic-metaphysical perspectives, the eternal is understood abstractly: it is viewed negatively as the boundary of the temporal, or as imaginatively and dreamily present or anticipated in poetry and art, or as comically preserving the temporal in itself.[35]

35. Vigilius specifically has in mind here first of all a statement by Kierkegaard's deceased friend and teacher, Poul Møller, who wrote that "true art is an anticipation of the blessed life" (CA, 253 n. 61). Vigilius rejects this claim because, in agreement with Kierkegaard's assessment of romantic poetry in *The Concept of Irony,* poetry and art in his view provide a reconciliation of the temporal and the eternal only in the imagination, not in actuality. In a play on words, he observes that "they may well have the *Sinnigkeit* [thoughtfulness] of intuition but by no means the *Innigkeit* [inwardness] of earnestness" (CA, 153). The other intended target is Hans Martensen's Hegelian tendency to give superiority to the comic in an aesthetic-metaphysical viewpoint that swallows up the temporal in the eternal (CA, Supplement, 207). In Vigilius's view, the temporal is permeated and preserved in the eternal (understood here in the sense of Platonic timelessness), but with no trace of the comic, since that is strictly a temporal category express-

The other factor with which earnestness is identified is the psychological factor of disposition, which is a determinant of immediacy and thus is aesthetic in character. But earnestness is not simply identical with disposition; it is, rather, "a higher as well as the deepest expression for what disposition is," Vigilius explains (CA, 148). Disposition is something one is born with, whereas earnestness is an "acquired originality" that results from becoming concerned about oneself (CA, 149). It thus bears a close resemblance to the second immediacy of faith in *Fear and Trembling* and to the acquired aesthetic ideal of inward history of which Judge William speaks in *Either/Or* II. It also resembles the concept of repetition; in fact, Vigilius explicitly identifies earnestness with repetition. Like Judge William, he distinguishes repetition from habit in that the latter signifies the disappearance of the eternal or self-consciousness in one's actions, whereas the former is precisely that historical process by which it is acquired and preserved (CA, 149; cf. 210 and EO, 2:127). Using the example of the weekly recitation of common prayer in church to illustrate the difference, Vigilius observes, "Earnestness alone is capable of returning regularly every Sunday with the same originality to the same thing." This is because the object of repetition is not the action that is repeated but rather a repetition of the earnestness or original spirit with which it is done. Finally, earnestness becomes an expression for personality itself, since in Vigilius's view "only an earnest personality is an actual personality" (CA, 149).

Earnestness, inwardness, certitude, and disposition are thus synonymous and interrelated concepts that together give definition and content to the existential dialectic in which spirit is brought forth and posited in freedom. In Vigilius's view, anxiety is ambiguously related to this process inasmuch as it is both the possibility of freedom and unfreedom, or sin. Even in the act of positing itself as unfreedom, freedom is present and contains the possibility of spirit within itself. Thus anxiety may be regarded indirectly as a positive phenomenon, even when it issues in the negativity of sin and unfreedom, for not ever to have been anxious is equivalent to spiritlessness. The task, therefore, is not to avoid anxiety but rather to become educated by it. "Whoever has learned to be anxious in the right way has learned the ultimate," Vigilius declares (CA, 155). This consists in learning how to relate oneself correctly to actuality through possibility. We have seen previously how Kierkegaard and

---

ing contradiction, whereas "in eternity all contradictions are canceled and the comic is consequently excluded" (CA, 154; cf. 207).

Judge William criticize the romantic mode of living poetically because of its ironic negation of actuality and experimental orientation of existence in possibility. Like the romantics, Vigilius affirms a positive role for possibility in the life of the individual, but as he sees it, the infinite possibility of all things in possibility, rightly understood, allows us to perceive the lightness of actuality in contrast to the heaviness of possibility (CA, 156).[36] For the perspective of possibility, including as it does both the terrible and the joyful, the good and the bad, enables us to realize that our various anxieties about what has happened or may happen in the realm of the finite are weak and pale in comparison to what they might be when construed from the perspective of the infinity of possibility. Actuality is never as terrible or as good as that which may be envisioned in possibility, Vigilius seems to be saying.[37] But until one has learned to face the possible, one cannot rightly or without anxiety face and accept actuality. Employing once again an artistic metaphor to make this point, Vigilius states, "Whoever performs on the stage of the theater of life is like the man who traveled from Jericho and fell among robbers. Whoever does not wish to sink in the wretchedness of the finite is constrained in the most profound sense to struggle with the infinite" (CA, 160). In this way, anxiety and possibility may become a "magic picture," or kaleidoscope, as well as, like controlled irony, a serving spirit to faith, taking away that which it has brought forth and leading to the formation of an inner certainty that anticipates infinity without being overwhelmed by it (CA, 157, 159). Far from regarding anxiety as something from which to shrink back or avoid, then, the person who has been educated by possibility or anxiety "bids it welcome, greets it festively, and like Socrates who raised the poisoned cup, he shuts himself up with it and says as a patient would say to the surgeon when the painful

36. Vigilius's association of lightness with actuality and heaviness with possibility is, he suggests, a reversal of the usual associations drawn between these terms. An interesting use of these images may also be found in Milan Kundera's novel *The Unbearable Lightness of Being*, tr. Michael Henry Heim (New York: Harper & Row, 1984), briefly treated by M. Jamie Ferreira in "Repetition, Concreteness, and Imagination." According to Ferreira, Kundera's perspective is rooted in the Nietzschean idea of the necessity of eternal return, which places a weight of unbearable responsibility upon human action in contrast to the weightless shadow existence of life in a world without eternal return. The weight of existence in eternal return is not necessarily a negative value for Kundera, however, since he questions the traditional idea that heaviness is deplorable, while lightness is splendid. Vigilius, by contrast, accepts the traditional evaluation of these images and affirms a lightness of being and a repetition in actuality posited through freedom.

37. I disagree with this contention, since it seems to me that actuality often brings us far more than we ever dreamed was possible, both in terms of the good and the bad. But I agree that possibility may serve to temper our anxieties.

operation is about to begin: Now I am ready" (CA, 159). It is in this spirit that Vigilius concludes his psychological investigation, suggesting that "whoever has truly learned how to be anxious will dance when the anxieties of finitude strike up the music" (CA, 161).

CODA

In keeping with the spirit of dancing lightly in the realm of the religious, the spirit that characterizes these final writings in the first phase of Kierkegaard's authorship, let me briefly recapitulate the themes introduced by the four pseudonymous works just examined. In *Repetition* and *Fear and Trembling* the theme of the religious exception emerges in the transitional figure of the poet and in its prototype, the knight of faith, both of whom are dancers in the realm of the religious. But whereas the poet becomes intoxicated in the infinite and is unable to experience repetition in actuality, the knight of faith is a master artist equally at ease in the realm of the finite and in the realm of the infinite. The knight of faith thus takes on an aesthetic appearance that is indistinguishable from bourgeois existence and romantic aestheticism in outward form but is qualitatively different from them in the inward expression of the aesthetic in a religious form of individualism, immediacy, and secrecy that constitutes faith and makes it a work of art. The author of *Philosophical Fragments* dances to a somewhat different tune as he poetically explores alternative artistic modes of acquiring truth, the Socratic and the Christian, in an attempt to show that the latter is the product of divine poetry or craftsmanship rather than human imagination and thought, thus providing a historical as well as transcendent basis for faith in the appearance of the god in time. *The Concept of Anxiety* further develops already familiar themes in its emphasis upon inwardness, earnestness, repetition, possibility, and the synthesis of sensuousness and spirit in freedom. But it also introduces a new theme in the concept of anxiety as a saving phenomenon in the service of faith. Here we find, I think, the ultimate expression for what it means to dance lightly in the realm of the religious: to be able to express the religious joyfully in every aspect of our daily life (or, as Johannes de Silentio states, to be able to express "the sublime in the pedestrian") while entertaining an infinity of possibility without undue anxiety. For readers familiar with Nietzsche, the metaphor of dancing lightly undoubtedly brings to mind the image of Zarathustra the tightrope walker through whom a god dances in the affirmation of life.[38] Zarathustra's god, however, is identical with the higher self, or the overman, which only the noble and strong can become. The god of whom Kierkegaard's pseudonyms write, by contrast, is not an immanent divinity within the elite but a transcendent deity whose paradoxical coming into existence creates an identity in the sense of equality with every human being, even the lowest. In this instance, therefore, those who have occasion to dance are not merely the privileged few but all who are willing to accept the gift of faith and rejoice in it.

These four early works bring to a conclusion what I have distinguished as the first phase in the development of Kierkegaard's concept of the poetic in the form of an existential aesthetics. I have argued and sought to demonstrate that in this phase Kierkegaard begins to formulate a fundamentally positive conception of the poetic as integrally connected with the ethical and the religious in the personal life. This connection first becomes apparent in *From the Papers of One Still Living,* where Kierkegaard associates the aesthetic categories of the lyric and the epic with existential categories and sets forth the notions of an epic development, or life-development, and a positive life-view as aesthetic criteria for becoming an authentic poet in the form of a poetic writer of novels. This existential and ethical-religious conception of the poetic emerges even more clearly in *The Concept of Irony,* where he sketches in contrast to German romanticism a Christian mode of living poetically in which the religious is understood aesthetically as a form of self-enjoyment in one's inner infinity and the truly poetic is identified with the religious. Through a kaleidoscope of possibilities, in the form of representative figures to illustrate and experiment with the romantic mode of living poetically, in volume 1, and with the articulation of an ethical-religious, or existential, aesthetics of love, marriage, work, talent, and friendship in volume 2, the contrast between these two modes of living poetically is sharpened in *Either/Or,* and a unified ethical-aesthetic conception of self-identity emerges in contradistinction to a romantic-aesthetic masking of the self in experimentation with multiple identities. As the existential, or ethical-religious, aesthetics introduced in these early works is developed more specifically in a religious context in the works considered in the present chapter, it is apparent that through the image of the dance and other poetic as well as aesthetic features, the pseudonymous authors of these works continue to envisage the reli-

38. See Friedrich Nietzsche, *Thus Spake Zarathustra,* tr. Walter Kaufmann (New York: Viking, 1966), 14, 41.

gious, or faith, as an aesthetic and poetic phenomenon. Although the category of actuality, or the realization of the ethical-religious ideal in actuality, remains the decisive category for distinguishing between an ethical-religious and a romantic-aesthetic conception of the poetic in the first phase, in the present chapter we have also seen that the category of possibility—for example, in the form of anxiety (when rightly educated in it)—plays an important role in enabling us to relate ourselves to actuality properly and in establishing the poetic character of the religious sphere and faith. Since the poetic is identified first and foremost with the realm of ideality or possibility, the ethical-religious is determined by how it relates itself not only to actuality but also to possibility, or that ideality which is to be actualized in the personal life.

6

Away from the Poetic?

> Just as for the Jews fertility was the epitome of the highest blessedness, so is the poetic for every [human being] in whom something higher stirs, and yet Rachel deservedly upbraided God, saying: If this is what being pregnant means, why did I get this way? (JP, 1:1027n)

In spite of the positive conception of the poetic advanced in Kierkegaard's early works, his writings abound with statements critical of poetry, often leaving the impression that he and his pseudonyms are opposed to the poetic. Although negative remarks about poetry can be found throughout the literature, they are especially prominent in several works that belong to what I have distinguished as the middle period of his authorship (1845–48): *Stages on Life's Way* (1845), *Concluding Unscientific Postscript* (1846), *Works of Love* (1847), and *The Point of View for My Work as an Author* (1848). These works declare, for example, that a union between the aesthetic and the ethical is a "misalliance" (SLW, 442); that a poetic relation to actuality is a "misunderstanding" and a "retrogression" (CUP, 1:388); that "religiously the pathos is not a matter of singing praises and celebrating or composing song books but of existing oneself" (CUP, 1:388); that the poet cannot help one to understand life (WL, 63); and that one must move away from the poetical to a religious, more specifically a Christian, mode of life (PV, 74).

What are we to make of such declarations? Do they reflect some deep ambivalence toward poetry now asserting itself in Kierkegaard's writings? Is some glaring inconsistency in his thought evidenced here? Has he simply changed his mind about poetry, coming now to recognize dangers and limitations of it unforeseen earlier? Can we explain them by attributing a negative attitude toward poetry to his pseudonyms while identifying the earlier more positive posture as his own? Or do they perhaps represent Kierkegaard's own view of poetry in contrast to the ethical-religious conception of the poetic developed by the pseudonymous authors of phase one?

Clearly the procedure of trying to distinguish between Kierkegaard's own views and those of his pseudonyms to account for differences of viewpoints—often a dubious or ambiguous practice anyway—will not suffice in this instance. For negative statements about poetry appear in pseudonymous writings as well as in works issued under Kierkegaard's own name as author, just as earlier the notion of living poetically in an ethical-religious manner was advanced in both pseudonymous and non-pseudonymous writings. It is equally clear, however, from the presence of a positive conception of poetry in the early writings, that the negativity toward poetry in Kierkegaard's writings must characterize only one aspect of his thought, not the total viewpoint that a random sampling of statements on poetry might lead one to believe. Moreover, the negative attitude prominent in the productions of the middle period of his authorship does not constitute a complete departure from his earlier perspective. For on the one hand, a number of statements can be explained as presupposing a romantic conception of poetry that he continues to oppose, and on the other hand, evidence of a continuing underlying positive stance toward the poetic can be detected in these and other works of the middle period.

THE LIMITS AND DANGERS OF POETRY

Before blithely dismissing this negative phase or attempting to determine its congruence with a continuing positive perspective of the poetic, we need to examine it more carefully. Are there some inherent conditions or characteristics of poetry or artistic imagination as a medium that make it inadequate for relating to reality? Or is it only a particular form of poetry—for example, romantic poetry—that must be rejected? What is the nature of poetry? What are its limits and dangers, if any? A number of problematic features of the poetic are indicated in Kierkegaard's writings. Kierkegaard's awareness of some of them is apparent from the time of his earliest journals and writings, and they form the basis for his critique of romanticism in that period. These are reiterated in the later works and others are added to the list as the stages of life are further delineated in relation to one another. Essentially, however, the objectionable characteristics of poetry, as Kierkegaard and his pseudonyms see them, especially in the writings from the middle period of his authorship, can be stated in a series of propositions formulated from the literature and summed up as follows.

1. *Poetry transfigures actuality and therefore cannot give a true or adequate representation of it.* This perception has its source in the premodern suspicion of poetic imagination as an imitative faculty.[1] This suspicion appears very early in Kierkegaard's thought, constituting one of the first statements about poetry in his journals: "All poetry is a *glorification* (i.e., transfiguration) [*Forklarelse:* transfiguration] of life by way of its clarification [*Forklarelse*] (in that it is explained, illuminated, developed, etc.)" (JP, 1:136). In this passage, the transfigurative quality of poetry is seen as a characteristic of all poetry, not just a particular form of it; and as the duplex meaning of the Danish word for transfiguration indicates, it is associated with the attempt of poetic language to render an explanation or clarification of life. But in the process of clarifying or illuminating life, poetry inadvertently glorifies it, makes it appear better than it really is. That is the effect of the unhappy poet's attempt to express his suffering in *Either/Or* I: his words of woe become music to the ears of others, bringing them enjoyment, with a desire for more, rather than a true communication of the suffering he experiences. This perception also underlies Kierkegaard's critique of poetry in *The Concept of Irony,* but there he seems to have in mind romantic poetry in particular and counters the phenomenon of transfiguration in romantic poetry with the notion of a transubstantiation of the given actuality by the truly poetic, which is identified with the religious. In *Concluding Unscientific Postscript,* however, Kierkegaard's pseudonym Johannes Climacus contrasts existential, or religious, pathos, which in his view consists essentially in suffering, with aesthetic, or poetic, pathos, where suffering, he claims, is seen as the result of external misfortune and thus as something accidental (CUP, 1:387, 431–34, 445). According to Climacus, the poet, like the religious individual, suffers but cannot comprehend the actuality of suffering as essential to existence. The poet thus seeks to find ease from suffering by anticipating via poetry a happier, more perfect condition in life in which suffering has been overcome. In Climacus's view, however, the actuality of suffering consists precisely in

1. On the premodern understanding of imagination, see Kearney, *The Wake of Imagination,* 37–152.

the persistence of suffering in relation to the religious telos of eternal happiness (CUP, 1:443). Poetry thus gives a "foreshortened perspective" of actuality that should never be used in religious discourse, because it is deceptive and illusory (CUP, 1:441, 445). This point of view is reiterated by a later pseudonym, Anti-Climacus, who likens poetry to "an actor dressed in rags" (PC, 188). Even though the imagination may try to represent the sufferings of actuality, it cannot succeed, he claims, because it constructs a picture of perfection in which suffering is "mitigated, toned-down, foreshortened" (PC, 187). The picture it renders is thus very different from the actual situation of being dressed in rags.

2. *Poetry deals only with ideality or possibility and is therefore indifferent to actuality.* Another aspect of the inability of poetry to represent actuality adequately is indicated in the claim that poetry deals with a conceived actuality rather than the given, empirical actuality. Poetry is the medium of ideality, of possibility, and thus teaches without reference to actuality. It may try to look like or play the role of actuality, but in doing so it is being unpoetic (CUP, 1:319). As Aristotle pointed out in his *Poetics,* the function of poetry is to represent what might be, rather than what has been (chap. 9, 1451a, 36–38). Kierkegaard takes this view of the poetic in his early journals and writings, associating it with the "subjunctive," and it continues to be viewed in that light in later works. In *Concluding Unscientific Postscript,* for example, poetic pathos is described as "the pathos of possibility" (CUP, 1:389). Aesthetically and intellectually considered, possibility is higher than actuality, since knowledge and understanding are acquired by transforming actuality into possibility, that is, by forming a concept of it (CUP, 1:318). The only actuality to which one can have more than a cognitive, abstract relation is one's own actuality, and even that is known to oneself in the form of a conceived actuality, or possibility, before it becomes actual, Climacus claims (CUP, 1:320).

The problem with art, poetry, and abstract thought, Climacus thinks, is that they are essentially disinterested in, indifferent to, or detached from existence (CUP, 1:313).[2] The subjects with which they are concerned, such as the good and the beautiful, are abstract ideas that have only a conceptual existence or exist only in the sense of being thought (CUP,

2. As noted in the Prologue, the notion of disinterestedness as a principle or criterion of aesthetic experience goes back to the eighteenth-century aesthetics of Shaftesbury, Hutcheson, and Kant. Kant regards disinterested satisfaction in judgements of taste to be of "capital importance," arguing that "everyone must admit that a judgment about beauty, in which the least interest mingles, is very partial and is not a pure judgment of taste" (*Critique of Judgment,* 39).

1:329). Furthermore, the aesthetic and intellectual spheres deal only with the universal, not the particular, and must abstract from existence, which involves particularity, in order to conceptualize anything. They are concerned with "humanity in general," not the existence of a particular individual (CUP, 1:330). From an aesthetic point of view, the existence of the poet is nonessential or accidental in relation to the artistic product of the poet. It is the poem, not the poet's existence, that is important. Whether the poetic production influences the poet's mode of existence is a matter of indifference. Indeed, from an aesthetic point of view the highest pathos is for the poet to do whatever is necessary to produce a work of art—to annihilate or demoralize oneself, even to sell one's soul to the devil if need be (CUP, 1:390). "For the poet, actuality is merely an occasion that prompts him to abandon actuality in order to seek the ideality of possibility," Climacus maintains. Thus he concludes that poetic pathos is "essentially fantasy" (CUP, 1:388). By contrast, from an ethical standpoint the existing individual is obliged to take an interest in existence, that is, to be passionately concerned about his or her own existence. Indeed, this interest in existing is what constitutes the actuality of the individual, for as Climacus sees it, subjectivity, or "an interiority infinitely interested in existing," *is* actuality (CUP, 1:325, 343). At the same time, subjective passion is an "idealizing passion," a passion that brings one into relation to a goal or eternal ideal toward which one strives in life (CUP, 1:312). This ideal is the individual's own actuality, or a realization of the ideal within the individual him- or herself. Ethically considered, actuality is higher than possibility, and the existential task is to move from possibility to actuality rather than vice versa (CUP, 1:320). If the individual fails to make this movement, his or her life becomes poetic, fantastic, unreal.

Since poetry is indifferent to existence, the particular, it likewise cannot deal with the religious, especially the Christian form of religiousness. As Climacus defines it, Christian faith, like the ethical, requires a passionate interest, but a passionate interest in the actuality of another rather than oneself: "To be infinitely interested and to ask about a reality that is not one's own is to will to believe and expresses the paradoxical relation to the paradox" (CUP, 1:323). Whereas the ethical is concerned only with the existing individual's own actuality, the actuality with which faith is concerned is the God-man. Furthermore, it is concerned with the particularity of that figure—the fact that God has actually existed as an individual human being—rather than the abstract, logical question of the possibility of a unity of the divine and the human in him. While faith is analogous to the ethical in having an infinite interest, then, it differs from the ethical in the focus of that interest. But it is united with the ethical in opposition to poetic indifference to actuality.

3. *Poetic or aesthetic pathos takes one outside oneself so as to lose oneself in the ideality of the possible.* "The majority of [human beings]," Kierkegaard writes in a journal entry of 1847, "are like a railway car detached from the locomotive—they are far beyond themselves, and in actuality they are far behind" (JP, 1:1049). There are a number of ways by which we can transcend ourselves—through imagination, feelings, thought, speech. Imaginative or poetic pathos is a mode of self-transcendence by which we can relate ourselves to ideality, but the problem with this mode of transcendence, as Kierkegaard and his pseudonyms see it, is that it does not relate us to ideality in such a way as to permit its conception of the ideal to transform our existence in a decisive way. In aesthetic or poetic pathos, Kierkegaard's pseudonym Johannes Climacus observes, "the individual abandons himself in order to lose himself in the Idea" (CUP, 1:387). Another pseudonym, Frater Taciturnus, in *Stages on Life's Way,* points out in this regard that "it is not wrong of the spectator to want to lose himself in poetry; this is a joy that has its reward, but the spectator must not confuse theater and actuality, or himself with a spectator who is nothing more than a spectator at a comedy" (SLW, 461).

Poetic pathos thus runs the danger of self-abandonment. We may form a correct conception of the ideal this way, but if we fail to relate that ideal to our existence so as to transform it absolutely, that is, to begin to embody that conception in our own being or actuality, then our relationship to the idea is not an ethical one. Thus Climacus distinguishes between a purely poetic, or aesthetic, form of pathos and an existential, or ethical, form (CUP, 1:387). Existential pathos is essentially concerned with bringing the idea, or abstract conception, of ideality into relation to the individual's existence so as to transform it into the actuality of the conception. Aesthetic pathos moves in the opposite direction, away from the individual's existence to the possibility of the ideal. In view of this distinction, Climacus declares, "If one wants ethically to establish a poetic relation to actuality, this is a misunderstanding and a retrogression" (CUP, 1:388). This holds in the religious sphere as well, since it is imperative for the religious to pass through and preserve the ethical in itself. From Climacus's standpoint, therefore, a religious poet stands in an "awkward position" in relation to the religious inasmuch as such a poet stands in only an aesthetic relation to it via the imagination (CUP, 1:388). The religious poet is thus characterized by Climacus as a "runaway poet" who has deserted the aesthetic sphere for the religious without speaking the language of that sphere (CUP, 1:390).[3] Ethical-religious pathos consists in action, in existing, rather than in poetic productivity. Any poetic production on the part of a religious personality stands in an accidental, rather than an essential, relation to that individual's mode of existence, whereas from an aesthetic standpoint, just the opposite holds: the poet's mode of existence is a matter of indifference, and it is the poetic production that is all important.

4. *Poetry may be used as a means of distancing ourselves from a life-relationship, thereby falsifying the ethical element in it.* If poetry leads us to abandon ourselves, it may also provide an avenue by which to remove ourselves from actual relationships with others. By reflecting about love in a poetic fashion, for example, we can avoid making a resolution that would lead to decisive ethical action in regard to a love relation, and the relation itself takes on the appearance of being "a casual happening and a mere problem for thought."[4] Taking Goethe's portrayal of himself in *Aus meinem Leben* as paradigmatic of this sort of "poetizing," Kierkegaard's ethical spokesman Judge William, in *Stages on Life's Way,* criticizes the poet for distancing himself from life-relationships by rationalizing his breach and withdrawal from them in poetic form (SLW, 149–54). From the ethicist's standpoint, this sort of poetizing is really unpoetic because it invalidates marriage, which, as is pointed out in *Either/Or,* he regards as more poetic than erotic love and the single life. "If that poet-existence in *Aus meinem Leben* is poetic, then goodbye to marriage, which then at most becomes a refuge for the declining years," Judge William further laments in *Stages On Life's Way* (SLW, 155). Kierkegaard may well have thought of his own accounts of his breach with Regine Olsen as an effort to poetize his love-relation to her in this fashion. The young man in *Repetition* also falls into this category, as does the Quidam, or anonymous experimental subject, in *Stages on Life's Way,* who poetically agonizes in his diary over whether he is guilty or not guilty in breaking off a love-relationship. Recollecting his past relationship with his beloved, Quidam writes:

3. In characterizing the religious poet as a "runaway poet," I am using the translation from the older English edition of *Concluding Unscientific Postscript,* tr. David F. Swenson and Walter Lowrie (Princeton: Princeton University Press, 1941), 349. The new Hong edition describes him as "a poet escaped from the esthetic" (CUP, 1:390).

4. Here I follow Walter Lowrie's translation of *Stages on Life's Way* (New York: Schocken Books, 1967), 153. Compare the Hongs' version, which tends to downplay the lightness of the falsification (CUP, 1:155).

> A year ago I escorted her home in the evening. There was no one else who could be asked to do it. In the company of several others, I walked happily along at her side. And yet it seemed to me that I was almost happier in my hiding place; to come so close to actuality, yet without actually being closer, results in distancing, whereas the distance of concealment draws the object to oneself. What if the whole thing were an illusion? Impossible. Why, then, do I feel happier in the distance of possibility? (SLW, 205)

Seeking to put the actuality of his love-relationship behind him, Quidam further states, "Now . . . I want to reflect on the relationship as if I were only an observer who has to file his report" (SLW, 236). Quidam, like Kierkegaard, claims a religious justification for the breach of his love-relationship and thinks that he is truly in love with the girl he has abandoned. But because of Quidam's inability to resolve the state of suspension in which he is held by reflection on the issue, Frater Taciturnus, the pseudonymous creator of this imaginary figure, describes him as being a "demoniac character in the direction of the religious" (SLW, 398). Thus, like the young man of *Repetition,* he becomes a poet, not an authentic religious personality, by this action.

5. *Poetry deals essentially with immediacy and is undialectical within itself.* The absolute subject of poetry is the immediate passion of love. As long as that passion is present—even if the love becomes unhappy because of some external obstacle that prevents it from being consummated—poetry is in its element, although it may contain a relative reflection on how to deal with and overcome the impediment. If, however, that love becomes unhappy by virtue of some contradiction or opposition arising from within a lover, poetry cannot grasp such a duplex situation and must relinquish the matter to be dealt with by a higher passion, a sense of and passion for the infinite. Such a situation is the subject of Frater Taciturnus's experiment in imaginary construction in *Stages on Life's Way.* There the unhappy lover Quidam holds fast to his love, faces no external threats to its realization in marriage—indeed, he will be threatened with a loss of honor if he does not realize it—yet cannot realize it. In this situation, Frater argues, it is incumbent upon the individual to move beyond poetry to infinite reflection and the religious, where the immediate passion of love is brought into relation to "the idea," or God, and through that relation, to itself (SLW, 414). By becoming doubly or dialectically reflective in this way, the

individual gains a freedom and clarity, or transparency, in relation to him- or herself that is not possible in poetry and immediacy as such:

> The idea is also in immediacy; the poet does indeed see it, but for his hero it does not exist, or in his relation to it he is not in relation to himself. For this very reason he is not free in his passion. That is, freedom does not at all mean that he is to give it up, but freedom means that in order to hold on to it firmly he uses the passion of infinity by which he could give it up. Such a thought the poetic hero cannot think at all, and the poet does not dare to have him think it, for then he immediately ceases to be a poetic character. (SLW, 414)

When love becomes dialectical in this fashion, it means that "the time of poetry is over" and "immediacy is at an end," Frater maintains (SLW, 412). The task then becomes to win and to hold fast to the religious through infinite reflection. In becoming dialectical in himself, Quidam differs from the usual poet in the expression of poetic passion, but in his inability to come to a religious resolution concerning the matter, he becomes extremely dialectical and consequently demonic, that is, unwilling to relate himself to himself in the religious idea (SLW, 427).

6. *Poetry is unparadoxical in that it cannot be both tragic and comic simultaneously.* "To be able to stick to one thought, to stick to it with ethical passion and undauntedness of spirit, to see the intrinsic duplexity of this one thought with the same impartiality, and at one and the same time to see the most profound earnestness and the greatest jest, the deepest tragedy and highest comedy—this is unpopular in any age for anyone who has not realized that immediacy is over" (SLW, 415). In line with his critique of the reflective limitation of poetry, Frater Taciturnus levels another charge against poetry on aesthetic grounds, namely, that it cannot deal with a duplexity of comic and tragic genres simultaneously. This charge is directed particularly against romantic poetry, which in his view puts the two together only in the form of contrast and succession so as to resolve one another (SLW, 417).[5] Basic to both tragedy and comedy is the element of misunderstanding, which in poetry is usually

5. On the unity of the tragic and the comic in *Either/Or* I and *The Concept of Irony,* where romanticism is portrayed, see John D. Glenn, Jr., "Kierkegaard on the Unity of Comedy and Tragedy," *Tulane Studies in Philosophy* 19 (1970): 41–53.

attributed to some external interference by a third party or event; when that factor is eliminated, then understanding can proceed in either a comic or tragic mode. But if one encounters a situation such as Frater Taciturnus projects in his imaginary construction—that of a relation between two heterogeneous individuals, a man and a woman whose lives are oriented toward different categories (his toward the religious, hers to the aesthetic) but who nevertheless love one another—then misunderstanding between them has its source in the relationship itself, in the union of two heterogeneous natures that essentially clash and thus fundamentally misunderstand each other in a number of ways. In the case of the imaginary couple Frater has in mind, they are characterized by several important differences. The young man is reserved and melancholy in anticipation of the higher life of the religious, toward which he is bound; she, by contrast, is immediately open and lighthearted. He is essentially a "self-thinker," concerned with understanding his existence in relation to ideas; she is not. In accordance with the respective categories in which they live, he is dialectical in an ethical manner, and she is immediate on an aesthetic level, so that their conceptions of suffering are entirely different. In sympathy for her, he is moved to break off their engagement, while she, out of an instinct for self-preservation, in an innocent sort of self-love, tries to bind him by taking advantage of the ethical element in their relationship.

Such a situation, Frater claims, is at once comic and tragic. "The tragic is that two lovers do not understand each other; the comic is that two who do not understand each other love each other" (SLW, 421). When this situation is resolved in a tragic mode—which in Frater's opinion involves a higher passion than the comic—it constitutes the beginning of a dialectical form of religiousness "for which immediacy is over" (SLW, 422). Unlike the illusory aesthetic ideality of a poetic view, the religious ideality expressed in this situation has its ground in actuality, in an act of freedom whereby, by virtue of a relation to God, the man chooses the tragic side of the situation (he breaks off with her because of their heterogeneity), even though he sees the comic side of it (he still loves her). However, insofar as Quidam only approximates the religious, not having fully attained repose in it, his life-view is demoniacal and remains dialectical and illusory in an aesthetic-ethical manner. Thus only the possibility of the religious, not the religious itself, is presented in Frater's imaginary construction. Were he actually able to present that actuality, his thesis would be refuted, for the construction is itself a form of poetry, the entertainment of a conceptual possibility that he has said poetry, by its inability to deal with paradoxes, cannot entertain. But the thesis is at least compromised, it seems to me, in that Frater is able to present and to grasp, he thinks, the unity of the tragic and the comic in an imaginary construction. Yet he admits that he cannot conceive whence the young man gets the new and higher passion of religiousness that issues from the unity of the two genres (SLW, 435). Thus the religious remains beyond poetic grasp, even when it is the subject of poetic experimentation.

7. *Poetry is defective in that the aesthetic outcome it shows is only external, not internal.* Another claim Frater Taciturnus makes against poetry concerns its attempt to show a visible, external result in aesthetic productions. This is particularly characteristic of tragedy, he thinks, since that genre, unlike comic poetry, relies on history for its content (SLW, 437). In attempting to make everything visible, poetry assumes, like Hegelian philosophy, that the outer is commensurable with the inner and that the latter can be shown outwardly (SLW, 441).[6] In Frater's view, however, this constitutes an imperfection, rather than the perfection, of the aesthetic, since there are realms of experience that are not conducive to denouement in final and visible results. "It goes without saying that when it comes to the religious," Frater points out, "such categories of actuality as the one that the outer is the inner and the inner the outer are in relation to the religious the inventions of Munchhausens who have no understanding whatever of the religious" (SLW, 428). The religious, he contends, properly "lies in the internal" and is indifferent to the external sphere, its outcome being assured only inwardly through faith (SLW, 441–42). Moreover, the religious cannot be made visible in an external result, because it is never finished in time; its outcome is thus constantly being deferred (SLW, 443–45). The ethical likewise resists external depiction of its results or, rather, demands a result with such boundless speed that it cannot be depicted (SLW, 441). Thus when an aesthetic production presents the good triumphing over evil, for example, this represents a misalliance of aesthetic and ethical categories (SLW, 442). The ethical seeks instead an alliance with the religious, where it undergoes development in the realm of inwardness. Unlike poetic representations, which in Frater's opinion are more naturally aligned with (Hegelian) philosophy in its attempt to obtain and quantify a positive infinity in a finished system, the ethical-religious is related to a negative infinity, that is, to an infinity that is never completely captured

6. On the relation of the inner and the outer in *Stages On Life's Way,* see Dunning, *Kierkegaard's Dialectic of Inwardness,* 125–40.

and expressed in an individual's entire lifetime (SLW, 443–44). Thus Frater cautions us that "it is up to us human beings to be careful not to become all too positive" and claims that for finite beings, which all of us are, "the negative infinity is the higher, and the positive is a dubious reassurance" (SLW, 444). Since Frater's own poetic, or imaginary, construction is, by his own testimony, incomplete, it bears a likeness to the ethical-religious that is unusal in poetry, but for that very reason it serves to compromise his thesis about poetry or else must be seen as perpetrating the same sort of "misalliance" to which he is opposed.

8. *Poetry can make no use of repentance.* Since poetry cannot represent inwardness, it cannot appropriate the category of repentance, which belongs to the ethical sphere and the realm of inwardness in a person. Insofar as the young man of Frater's imaginary construction has not withdrawn into repentance, admitting his guilt in relation to the woman he loves, he does not represent ethical inwardness in this respect. There is instead a demonic trait in him that resists the religious and leads him to deceive her, letting her think that he is guilty even though he is unclear in himself on that score (hence the ambiguous title of his diary, "Guilty?"/"Not Guilty"). Still less is he able to move beyond repentance, to let it go, so that he may be healed by the religious through the forgiveness of sin.

Another poetic character in which repentance is dialectically prevented from constituting itself is Hamlet, a figure Frater considers in a "side-glance" at Shakespeare's play in a short appendix to his discussion of repentance (SLW, 452–54). Just as some aesthetic productions unite the aesthetic and the ethical in a misalliance, in Frater's opinion Shakespeare's dramatic masterpiece confuses the aesthetic and the religious in an inappropriate manner. Characterizing the play as a "religious" drama, Frater declares its only fault to be "that it did not become that or, rather, that it ought not to be drama at all" (SLW, 453). If Hamlet is interpreted religiously, then his doubts and misgivings must be understood as religious doubt, which he in fact lacks (cf. JP, 2:1561). In Frater's opinion, therefore, Shakespeare has failed to endow his hero with the necessary presuppositions for a religious interpretation of the figure, and if he had, Hamlet must then act in ways that make him an inappropriate subject for dramatic treatment. For either he must be portrayed as succumbing to his religious doubt in inaction, in which case "his unpoetic doubts and misgivings in the psychological sense become a remarkable form of dialectical repentance, because the repentance seems to come too early," or else he must be given the "demonic power resolutely and masterfully to carry out his plan" and then be permitted to "collapse into himself and into the religious until he finds peace there" (SLW, 453–54). In either case, repentance cannot be successfully portrayed externally in the context of dramatic conflict and action.

9. *Poetry cannot explain life or, rather, explains things in riddles, which is really to explain nothing.* Perhaps the most devastating criticism of the poet and poetry in the writings of the middle period comes not from a pseudonym but from Kierkegaard himself, in *Works of Love,* where he conducts a running diatribe against the poet and the poetic interpretation of love in the midst of a Christian exposition of love and the works of love.[7] "Christianity knows far better than any poet what love is and what it is to love," Kierkegaard proclaims; in fact, in his view they explain things in opposite ways, so that "it is an impossibility to love according to both explanations simultaneously" or to understand life by placing their explanations together (WL, 36, 63). The poet, Kierkegaard claims, understands and explains everything in riddles, that is, in terms of obscure forces in things themselves; Christianity, by contrast, explains everything by reference to something higher, that is, God or the eternal (WL 45, 63; cf. CUP, 1:443–44). Thus the poet, who is the priest of immediate, spontaneous love, tries to make love secure by having lovers pledge and swear their love forever on the basis of love itself, whereas in Christianity love is secured by swearing by the eternal or the duty to love (WL, 45). The poet *celebrates* love in the forms of erotic love and friendship, which are preferential; Christianity *commands* love in the form of love of the neighbor and requires self-renunciation (WL, 35, 65). The poet sings of loving the beloved only, in distinction to and above all others, even more than oneself; Christianity teaches us to love all humankind as neighbors and to love them as we love ourselves (WL, 35–36, 63, 80). The poet advocates a poetic love that is secretly a form of self-love, the intoxication and identification of the "I" in an "other-I," or "other-self"; by contrast, Christian neighbor love is love of the "other-you," or a true other distinct from oneself (WL, 66–67). The poet understands love and friendship as good fortune for which one is grateful; Christianity understands them as containing an ethical task, that is, a duty to love (WL, 64).

These are but a few of the ways, in Kierkegaard's view, that Christian-

7. On the poetic in *Works of Love,* see also my article "Forming the Heart: The Role of Love in Kierkegaard's Thought," in *The Grammar of the Heart,* ed. Richard Bell (New York: Harper & Row, 1988), 234–56.

ity and the poet differ in the understanding and explanation of life and love. Although admitting that a poet may be a Christian, Kierkegaard nevertheless insists that "*qua* poet he [the poet] is not a Christian." Kierkegaard further distinguishes the godly, or religious, poet from the secular, or usual, poet and recognizes the former as constituting a "special case" or exception in relation to the poetic (WL, 60). But with respect to religious poets, he also points out:

> These do not celebrate erotic love and friendship; their songs are to the glory of God, songs of faith and hope and love. Nor do these poets sing of love in the sense a poet sings of erotic love, for love to one's neighbor is not to be sung about—it is to be fulfilled in reality. Even if there were nothing to hinder the poet from artistically celebrating love to one's neighbor in song, it is quite enough that with invisible letters behind every word in Holy Scriptures a disturbing notice confronts him—for there it reads: go and do likewise. Does this sound like an artistic challenge, inviting him to sing? (WL, 60)

As a poet, the religious poet, like the secular poet, thus stands in tension with the ethical task of love but is distinguished from the secular poet by the fact that the religious poet recognizes that task first and foremost as a commandment to be fulfilled in the life of the poet, not merely as something to be sung about.

What then of the ordinary poet and of poetic celebrations of love? Shall the poets be banished, as Plato would have it, and erotic poems of love no longer be recited? Kierkegaard concludes in *Works of Love* that it would do little good to rid the world of poets so long as people continue to understand existence as they do. Neither does he admonish Christians to shun poetry. A good poet may still be read and admired, but one must know how to distinguish between the Christian and poetic life-views and understand everything differently from the poet (WL, 60–61).

From this series of propositions about poetry abstracted from Kierkegaard and his pseudonyms, it is apparent that the poetic by itself is insufficient and even dangerous when adopted as a mode of life. Far from orienting us properly in existence, it directs us out of actuality, distorts the actual, and leads us to self-abandonment in the ideal. It may be used as a foil for avoiding relations with others and is inadequate for representing and dealing with the complexities those relations sometimes pose. In a number of respects it stands in tension and contrast with the ethical and the religious, making an alliance with those spheres appear inappropriate. While these charges are in some instances brought specifically against romantic poetry, they range beyond that to include poetry in general. Although a number of them are voiced only by Kierkegaard's pseudonyms, particularly Johannes Climacus and Frater Taciturnus, they express reservations within the authorship that must be taken seriously. But they must also be considered in light of a positive stance toward the poetic that continues in the works from the middle period and that serves to temper this negative phase in the authorship and to place it in the context of an overall positive perspective of an existential aesthetics that preserves the poetic in, and unites it with, the ethical and the religious. It is to instances of this perspective in the literature of the second phase that I now turn.

POSITIVE VIEWS OF THE POETIC IN THE SECOND PHASE

Several works during the period 1845–48, including *Stages on Life's Way* and *Concluding Unscientific Postscript,* which are the major voices of the negative impulse toward poetry that comes to the fore in the literature of the second phase, indicate that Kierkegaard and his pseudonyms continue to maintain a positive stance toward the poetic in this period in spite of the dangers and limitations of poetry recognized in the authorship. In the remainder of this chapter I consider instances of this positive stance in *Stages on Life's Way* and three other works of this period: *The Crisis and a Crisis in the Life of an Actress* (1848), *Two Ages* (1846), and *The Book on Adler* (1846). The next chapter is devoted to an examination of aesthetic categories in the existential dialectic of *Concluding Unscientific Postscript.*

THE POETIC IN MARRIAGE

In contrast to Frater Taciturnus's negative assessment of poetry in *Stages on Life's Way,* the poetic continues to have an advocate in this work in the thought of Judge William, who earlier set forth and exemplified an ethical mode of living poetically in *Either/Or.* In conformity with his previous perspective, Judge William continues in his "Reflections on Marriage" to view marriage as poetic, describing it in aesthetic terms as being both epical (because of its responsibility) and idyllic (because of its happiness) (SLW, 117). He also continues to see marriage as constituting the "deepest, highest, and most beautiful expression of love" and laments the fact that poets do not depict married couples in conversation, making it appear "as if a married couple were not just as poetic as a couple of lovers" (SLW, 127–28, 147). Just as lovers become poetic through their love-relation, the "quiet and contended security of married life" receives "poetic articulation" through humor, a necessary ingredient of marriage if one is to be a good husband (or wife, we may assume), the judge contends (SLW, 128–31).

Another way the aesthetic continues to manifest itself in marriage is through woman's beauty, which according to Judge William increases, rather than decreases, over the years as a result of marriage: "As a bride, woman is more beautiful than as a maiden; as a mother she is more beautiful than as a bride; as a wife and mother she is a good word in season, and with the years she becomes more beautiful" (SLW, 140). The reason for this is that in her roles as wife and mother woman has her life in actuality, that is, in the concreteness of everyday life, where her love "is an inexhaustible source of inwardness" in its boundless dedication to her children (SLW, 134). In line with his earlier emphasis on giving expression to the poetic ideal in the actuality of everyday life, the judge regards mother love as being just as beautiful in its everyday manifestations as on critical occasions; indeed, he goes on to observe, "it is actually essentially beautiful in the routine of everyday life, for there it is in its element" (SLW, 138). Just as the woman who is a wife and mother becomes more beautiful in the happiness to be found in marriage, so also she becomes more poetic than a young girl if she is unhappy or suffers a time of grief: "Let the young girl lose her beloved, let her grief be ever so deep, let her dwell in the memory of him—her grief is still abstract, likewise her memory. For this daily requiem for the dead, which is the occupation of the grieving wife, the young girl lacks the dedication and the epic presuppositions" (SLW, 141–42).

How are we to reconcile these opposing voices of Judge William and Frater Taciturnus in *Stages on Life's Way?* Or are they irrreconcilable? Perhaps a measure of harmony may be found by considering a crucial point in Judge William's analysis of love and marriage, namely, the importance of forming a resolution that issues in a new immediacy that is both ethical and religious. To the immediacy of falling in love, the judge maintains, reflection must be added in the form of a resolution that focuses the love-relation in the direction of concretion in the actuality of marriage (SLW, 160). Ordinarily "reflection is immediacy's angel of death," he observes, but in the ideality of this resolution not only is the immediacy of falling in love preserved, but a new immediacy is gained that corresponds to it (SLW, 157, 162). The resolution responsible for bringing about this concretion is described by the judge as "a religious view of life constructed upon ethical presuppositions" (SLW, 162). Consequently the new immediacy issuing from this resolution is a religious immediacy whose resolve is to achieve three things: to hold fast to love through the imperative of duty and the avoidance of criticism, to triumph over dangers and spiritual trials by believing in God, and to form a relationship with God through faith and the resolution (SLW, 163–64).

Although Judge William envisions the application of this resolution and new immediacy within the context of marriage, he is willing to admit the possibility of there being a legitimate exception to the universal as proposed in *Repetition* and *Fear and Trembling.* "From the essentially religious point of view, it cannot be denied that it makes no difference whether or not a person has been married," he concedes (SLW, 172). But he is suspicious of those who would bypass the reality and temporality of marriage by withdrawing into a religious abstraction that relates itself to God alone. Thus, if there were to be a legitimate exception, in the judge's view that person would have to meet the following criteria: (1) the individual must have experienced a real falling in love; (2) the individual must be a married person; (3) the individual must continue to love life; (4) the individual must feel the break with the universal as a fatality and horror for which he or she is punished with suffering; (5) the individual must comprehend the break in such a way as to be hurled out into new, more horrible peril as a "rebel against the earthly"; (6) the individual must comprehend and accept the fact that no one can understand him or her, and he or she must feel "the torturing of misunderstanding" in this situation (SLW, 176–81).

These criteria provide a basis for assessing whether Quidam of Frater Taciturnus's imaginary construction qualifies as a legitimate religious exception and for determing whether Frater's account of the religious agrees with that of the judge. Since Quidam obviously does not meet the judge's second criterion—namely, that he already be a married man—it is apparent without measuring him against the remaining criteria that he would not qualify as a justified religious exception from the judge's point of view. Nevertheless, Frater does share the judge's view of the religious as a new and higher immediacy or passion characterized by reflection (SLW, 399, 406). Frater describes the form of reflection appropriate to the religious as "infinite reflection," which he defines as "immediacy's transparency to itself," or that whereby immediacy relates itself to itself in the idea or God-relationship (SLW, 414). But whereas Judge William sees the truly poetic as coming to expression in the new immediacy of marriage and the religious, Frater, like Hegel, speaks of the time of poetry as being over when the immediate infinity is grasped by the infinite reflection of the religious (SLW, 412). While Frater has essentially the same view of the religious as Judge William, then, he lacks a sense of the aesthetic character of the religious that is implied in the definition of it as a higher *passion* or as a new *immediacy.* Thus, instead of becoming a true poet by virtue of having chosen the religious, in Frater's view Quidam becomes a poet precisely because he does not resolve reflection in relation to the religious. For Frater, poetry is limited to first immediacy or to the inability via infinite reflection to make a final break with that immediacy, whereas for Judge William the poetic is given a higher amd more authentic expression in the second immediacy of the ethical-religious. We may recall that Johannes de Silentio in *Fear and Trembling* similarly characterizes faith as a second immediacy and as a work of art. There is, then, an essential continuity between these pseudonyms on the fundamentally aesthetic (immediate, passionate) nature of the religious, but not on the role of the poetic in the religious. Since Frater Taciturnus is a later pseudonym than the other two, it might be thought that his viewpoint should be regarded as a higher one than theirs, and in its understanding of the essential element of suffering in the religious, it surely is. But inasmuch as the poetic is seen as having an integral relation to the religious in later writings, Frater's viewpoint cannot be regarded as final on this issue.

ETHICAL METAMORPHOSIS IN THE AESTHETIC

In a note to his discussion of womanly beauty in *Stages on Life's Way,* Judge William praises a prominent actress of the time, Madame Nielsen, for her ability to express the essentially feminine in every period and role of her life as an actress (SLW, 131–32). In a similar discussion in *The Crisis and a Crisis in the Life of an Actress,* a piece of aesthetic criticism published under the pseudonym Inter et Inter, Kierkegaard describes two kinds of metamorphosis of an actress: one that recollects feminine youthfulness through potentiation, or "a more and more intensive return to the original condition," and one that is a process, a metamorphosis of continuity and perfectibility that involves a steady transformation through the years (CLA, 90). The first is illustrated by an actress (Madame Heiberg) who ventures to portray Juliet again fourteen years after her debut in that role. Although this actress lacks something of the immediacy of her youthful performance, she is a more developed, cultivated, and refined actress in the later production, bringing to it an ideality that illumines femininity in a way that was not present in her youthfulness. By contrast, the second kind of metamorphosis is illustrated by an actress (Madame Nielsen) who assumes older roles as she grows older and performs each with the same perfection as in her youth. This form of metamorphosis, the author suggests, "has an especially ethical interest," which makes it appealing to the ethicist (Judge William) and provides him with an ally and a better proof of his theory than he himself presents (CLA, 90). The author does not elaborate on why this is so, but we may surmise that it is because the second form of metamorphosis illustrates concretely in a dramatic context the elements of steady transformation, continuity, process, and perfectibility that are central to the judge's existential aesthetics. The author praises both actresses for their ability to resist the power of time, and in keeping with the principle of aesthetic distance previously established in the authorship, he does not commend one over the other. The second, however, is commensurate not only with Judge William's existential aesthetics but also with Kierkegaard's earlier emphasis on self-development as a prerequisite for authentic poetic productivity in an epical mode. Although the first type of artistic transformation may also be said to involve self-development in that the actress possesses a maturity in later life that was lacking in her youth and is able to bring that to bear in her interpretation of youthful roles, the second type involves a greater correspondence between the dramatic roles performed and the stages of the actress's own personal development in life. Thus we may regard it as providing a dramatic correlate to the correspondence between the life and art of the creative artist called for in Kierkegaard's first book, *From the Papers of One Still Living.*

LITERATURE ON THE BOUNDARY OF THE AESTHETIC

Another literary work published by Kierkegaard under his own name in this period, *A Literary Review,* or *Two Ages* (1846), also sustains a connection between the aesthetic and the ethical-religious by recognizing a form of aesthetic literature that lies on the boundary of the aesthetic, oriented in the direction of the religious.[8] In particular, Kierkegaard has in mind two novels by the celebrated author Madame Thomasine Gyllembourg: *A Story of Everyday Life* and *Two Ages.* The first had received a favorable review, in passing, much earlier in *From the Papers of One Still Living* and is again praised in the later review for the closeness with which, unlike most poetry, it portrays actuality while maintaining aesthetic distance in the understanding of actuality

8. For a collection of secondary studies of this work, see Robert L. Perkins, ed., *International Kierkegaard Commentary: Two Ages.* Unfortunately, none of these studies focuses on the poetic or literary aspects of the book, but they do illumine its social criticism very well.

(TA, 14). So close is the author to actuality that one finds it difficult to tell whether the stories are "fact or fiction," Kierkegaard contends, and instead of love, marriage, family, and so forth, being cast in a misleading light, as is often done in novels, they are clarified and made endearing to the reader in this work (TA, 17). Although *A Story of Everyday Life* does not portray the pain of actuality, which in Kierkegaard's view finds its reconciliation and reassurance only in the categories and ideality of the religious, the novel nevertheless contains "a certain religious tinge," he claims, in that it has a commonsense view of life "mitigated and defined by persuasive feeling and imagination" (TA, 21). Moreover, for the single individual it provides a form of consolation and healing that is congruent with the more decisive categories of the religious.

Kierkegaard also praises this book because it is the fruit of a "second maturity" that corresponds, in a literary context, to the "second immediacy" of religious faith. Reaffirming after eight years (seven at the time of writing) the same aesthetic criteria for authentic novel writing as were set forth in his first review, *From the Papers of One Still Living,* Kierkegaard notes that the author has taken time to acquire a mature life-view before writing, with the consequence that the novel is not simply an element in the author's self-development but is "a work of interiority" resulting from his (her) already mature life-development.[9] Neither is the success of the novel due merely to the author's immediate "genius, talent, or virtuosity"; rather, the possibility of the author being able to produce such a work of art is, in Kierkegaard's view, a reward from God for his (her) having won "something eternal" in a life-view (TA, 15). Although the author's life-view is not, strictly speaking, a religious life-view, it nevertheless is representative of a type of life-view that is lacking in novelists in general, Kierkegaard thinks, inasmuch as it attempts to explain life in terms of a totality rather than as a series of everyday events and experiences that make the novel end up in a "trackless maze" (TA, 18).

Perhaps the most distinctive feature of the author's book, from Kierkegaard's point of view, is the fact that the author seeks to *persuade,* or guide, the reader into actuality rather than to inspire, or transport, the reader away from actuality through imagination, the latter being the practice of the poet (TA, 18–20). Persuasion is not only a difficult rhetorical device but also a "beneficent art" that this author has per-

9. Although *A Story of Everyday Life* was written by a woman, it was published anonymously, as were all the novels of Madame Gyllembourg. Respecting her anonymity, Kierkegaard pretends the author is a male and thus uses masculine third-person-singular pronouns to refer to "him."

fected not by a discursive discussion of the qualities and actions he (she) wishes to recommend to others but by simply portraying or letting them happen, Kierkegaard observes (TA, 19). In this way the reader is led into the world creatively supported by the life-view of the author, which is the world of actuality defined in terms of love, marriage, family, and civil and religious life, such as the one envisioned by Judge William in *Either/Or* II (TA, 19–20). In *A Literary Review,* however, it is clear that Kierkegaard, at this stage in his authorship, understands that *both* the aesthetic and religious relations to actuality lead the individual away from actuality, the first into the medium of imagination, the second into the eternity of the religious; and both become strangers and aliens to actuality, but in quite different ways (TA, 20). Whereas the aesthetic individual becomes alien to actuality by being absent from it, the religious individual becomes an alien within the realm of actuality. For the religious, unlike the aesthetic, constitutes for the individual a new beginning in the form of a life qualitatively different from the happy or despairing immediacy of the old. In Kierkegaard's view, the author of *A Story of Everyday Life* provides support for this transition by offering "a place of rest" in actuality in the process of moving to the decisive categories of the religious (TA, 20–21).

The later novel, *Two Ages,* which is the primary work examined in this review, also gives, in Kierkegaard's estimation, a "balanced and dignified faithful reproduction of actuality" and an "authentic portrayal of great passions" in the faithful constancy of love in domestic life (TA 33, 39). The same life-view is sustained in this novel as in *A Story of Everyday Life,* but what primarily distinguishes it from other novels, in Kierkegaard's judgment, is its transparent depiction of the totality of the age as reflected in domestic life (TA, 32). The novel is organized in two parts: the first part depicts an age of revolution, more specifically the period of the French Revolution; the second part portrays the present age. The author, Kierkegaard claims, does not directly describe or illustrate the present age but rather illumines it indirectly through its reflection, or mirroring, in domestic life in contrast to that of the age of revolution (TA, 41). According to Kierkegaard's analysis of the author's portrayal, the age of revolution is characterized by passion, form, culture, a sense of propriety, revelation, and decisive action (TA, 61–68). The characteristic that stands out among these, however, is passion, without which everything becomes meaningless, devoid of character, stagnant, and crude, Kierkegaard claims (TA, 62). Employing a nautical simile to describe passion, he writes, "All passion is like sailing: the wind must be sufficiently forceful to stretch the sail with one *uno tenore* [continuous] gust, there must not be too much flapping of the sails and tacking before reaching deep water, there must not be too many preliminaries and prior consultations. It is a matter of passion getting the power and dominion to take complete control of the unprepared" (TA, 43). The art with respect to passion is to be able to "let go with passion" as in the experience of falling or being in love, which Kierkegaard regards as the "culmination of a person's purely human existence" (TA, 43, 49). Although individuals in the present age may also experience love, as depicted in the novel, this age is characterized, in contrast to the age of revolution, as being essentially "a sensible reflecting age, devoid of passion, flaring up in superficial, short-lived enthusiasm and prudentially relaxing in indolence" (TA, 68). Just as the mastery of the author is displayed in the impartiality with which he (she) describes these two ages and gives each side its due, Kierkegaard claims only to be depicting the present age rather than judging it in his analysis (TA, 34–35, 110). He nevertheless manages indirectly to indict the present age for its apathy, prudentiality, and envy in the forms of individual selfishness and social leveling carried out with the aid of the press and the creation of the abstract phantom of the "public" (TA, 81–110). Very ingeniously, then, in this review Kierkegaard uses his role as literary critic to sound off as a social critic as well. Not only does he acknowledge and approve the existence of aesthetic productions that avoid the tendency of poetry to lead us away from actuality and that are congruent with the religious, he also acknowledges a social role for art in the criticism of modern culture.[10]

ESSENTIAL AUTHORS VERSUS PREMISE-AUTHORS

The final work to be considered in this chapter is *The Book on Adler,* a work completed in 1846 and extensively revised in subsequent years

10. Charging Kierkegaard with being "reactionary" and "regressive" in his social criticism, Terry Eagleton, in *The Ideology of the Aesthetic,* a Marxist interpretation of aesthetics, reads Kierkegaard as fostering a "strident subjectivism" that is abstract and "bereft of all history and culture," resisting any form of social integration (191–92). Nothing could be further from the truth, as any discerning reader of *Two Ages* and *Works of Love,* among other works in the Kierkegaard corpus, can testify. Eagleton's description of Kierkegaard more nearly fits the romantic ironists against whom Kierkegaard directed much of his authorship. The same or similar criticisms of Kierkegaard from a Marxist perspective may be found in Theodor W. Adorno, *Kierkegaard: Construction of the Aesthetic,* tr. and ed. Robert Hullot-Kentor (Minneapolis: University of Minnesota Press, 1989), and in Steven Best and Douglas Kellner, "Modernity, Mass Society, and the Media," in *International Kierkegaard Commentary: The Corsair Affair,* ed. Robert L. Perkins (Macon, Ga.: Mercer University Press, 1990), 23–61. For a critique of Adorno's book, see Robert L. Perkins's review in the *Journal of Aesthetics and Art Criticism* 43 (1990): 262–63.

but never published in its entirety.[11] In the first introduction to this book, a distinction is drawn between two kinds of authors: an essential, or true, author and a premise-author, or fake writer. The fact that a person writes and publishes something does not necessarily make that person a real author, Kierkegaard contends, for the writer may well have a premise and a purpose that lead him or her to engage in literary productivity, but if the writer lacks a conclusion or clear conception of what he or she wants to achieve by writing, that individual cannot be said to be a true author (OAR, 3–4, 6). Just as the fact that a life comes to an end does not necessarily mean that it has reached a conclusion, so a book also may end without reaching a conclusion. From an aesthetic as well as an ethical standpoint, Kierkegaard suggests, to be without a conclusion is a failing, not a virtue, for it reveals that one has not taken time to acquire a life-view by which to understand oneself and the world. A life-view, or total perspective of life, then, is what provides a conclusion both to the life of the individual and to a work of art. Unlike a premise-author, who is only outwardly directed toward addressing some social or religious problem that he or she has not thought through, the essential author possesses a life-view by which he or she first becomes inwardly directed or attentive to achieving self-understanding within the context of that perspective (OAR, 6). Only then does the essential author begin to write, and only that which has been personally understood by the author is explained in his or her writing (OAR, 7). The essential author feels a need to communicate him- or herself, either for the gratification of sharing that which the author has personally understood or for the sake of a consciously assumed ethical task (OAR, 8). This type of writer thus may be regarded as a teacher whose writing is "nourishing" or upbuilding of the reader (OAR, 9). By contrast, the premise-author, pretending to be something he or she is not (that is, a writer) and lacking a life-view to give meaning to what is written, has no real need to write or anything essential to communicate (OAR, 8). This author's writings thus may be characterized as destructive, or "devouring," because they merely make an outcry and raise doubts without having a solution for the problems discussed (OAR, 6, 9).

Once again, as in *From the Papers of One Still Living,* Kierkegaard affirms the necessity of having a life-view as a criterion for authentic

11. A small portion of *The Book on Adler,* "On the Difference Between a Genius and an Apostle," was published in *Two Minor Ethico-Religious Treatises* under the anonym H. H. in 1849. An English translation of the 1846 manuscript, with some revisions from later years incorporated, is available under the title *On Authority and Revelation* (OAR). This text will be used here for references to *The Book on Adler.*

writing; only this time it is applied more generally to the art of writing and is not limited to novel writing. Not only that, he sustains in this work the same view of poetic communication as before: "The art of all communication consists in coming as close as possible to [actuality], i.e. to contemporaries who are in the position of readers, and yet at the same time to have a viewpoint, to preserve the comforting and endless distance of ideality" (OAR, 9). This dialectic of closeness and distance in communication applies not only to poetic communication but to existential communication as well, or perhaps it would be more accurate to say that existential communication is a form of poetic communication, or vice versa, that poetic communication is or should be a form of existential communication. For in Kierkegaard's view, the content of the essential author's writing has an integral meaning for his or her own life as well as, potentially at least, for that of the reader.

In *The Book on Adler* Kierkegaard uses this distinction between the essential author and the premise-author in scrutinizing the writings of Magister Adolph Adler, a learned Hegel scholar and a clergyman of the Danish state church who claimed in his writings to have had a vision in which Jesus Christ appeared to him and dictated some new doctrines for him to write down. Adler was charged by church authorities with being in a confused state of mind and consequently was deposed from his pastoral position. At first refusing to admit to these charges, Adler later acquiesced and modified his claim to have received new revelations from Christ. He then retired to the country, where he wrote four more books, in which he made no further mention of having received a revelation and instead talked much about the nature of a genius, with the implication that he was to be regarded as one.

Adler's situation provided Kierkegaard with a concrete case study by which he could examine the concepts of authority and revelation and the difference between a genius and an apostle. In Kierkegaard's opinion, Adler exhibited almost all possible confusions with respect to the concept of revelation and showed by his indecisiveness that he did not understand its significance for himself, his authorship, or others. He thus typifies the premise-author described above. Were he a true author, the fact of having received a revelation would be that to which he would hold fast and which would fix for him an understanding of himself and his task as well as form the essential content of his writing. Instead of taking time to understand himself, however, Adler immediately burned his Hegelian books and jumped into print, becoming literarily productive about that which had been entrusted to him.

Although Kierkegaard concluded that it was highly doubtful Adler had received a genuine revelation (or if he had, he was too confused to understand the significance of the event), Kierkegaard did admit that Adler was an exceptional individual who had been deeply moved by his religious experience. Thus Kierkegaard was willing to grant that Adler was a genius, albeit a deranged genius, but not an apostle. The distinctiveness of a genius, Kierkegaard points out, lies in an individual's exceptional ability to think or create; genius is thus an aesthetic (immediate, natural) and immanent (determined by what one is in oneself) category (OAR, 105–6). "The genius may well have something new to contribute," Kierkegaard concedes, "but this newness vanishes again in its gradual assimilation by the race" (OAR, 105). The distinctiveness of an apostle, by contrast, resides in the fact that this individual has received a special call that "stands paradoxically outside his personal identity with himself as the definite person he is" and that confers upon him the authority to proclaim to others the revelation he has received (OAR, 106). Apostleship is thus a transcendent category that makes the apostle paradoxically different from others and heterogeneous to the universal or established order. In this heterogeneous capacity, however, the apostle seeks to become a reformer, not an enemy, of the established order by reflectively bringing its fundamental presuppositions into question and introducing a new point of departure via the essential paradox of the Christ. Unlike the new vision of the genius, this paradox cannot be anticipated by or assimilated into the world but forever remains "equally new, equally paradoxical," to every age (OAR, 107).

Kierkegaard's dual distinction between a premise-author and an essential author, on the one hand, and between a genius and an apostle, on the other, raises certain questions for the interpreter. First of all, we must ask whether these are parallel distinctions, that is, whether the premise-author corresponds to the genius and the essential author to the apostle. Although Kierkegaard regarded Adler as a premise-author and a (deranged) genius, that does not mean these categories are necessarily correlative. A genius might well be an essential author, such as Kierkegaard himself, who considered himself to be a genius and certainly thought of himself as an essential author, though not as an apostle, since he wrote without authority. Thus one may be an essential author without being an apostle. However, the reverse possibility does not obtain, for a true apostle, in Kierkegaard's view, is qualitatively different from a premise-author like Adler, whose mental confusions and subsequent actions concerning whether he did or did not receive a revelation strongly indicated to Kierkegaard that he was not an apostle called to introduce a new point of departure to the present age.

A second issue raised by Kierkegaard's distincitions concerns the role of the artist in relation to the categories of genius and apostle. In a provocative article on *The Book on Adler,* Stanley Cavell has suggested that serious art today "is produced under conditions which Kierkegaard announces as those of apostleship, not those of genius."[12] Cavell does not exactly identify the artist with the apostle, since in his view the concept of an apostle, as well as the concept of revelation, is "forgotten, inapplicable," in the present age, but he does claim that the modern artist has taken the place of the apostle and plays a similar role in relation to the age.[13] From Kierkegaard's point of view, however, that is surely too much to claim for the artist, who properly falls under the immanent category of a genius rather than an apostle. Although there may be some similarities between an artist and an apostle, these may obtain between a genius and an apostle as well and are at least in part attributable to the fact that the serious artist, like an apostle, may be regarded as an essential author or the equivalent in other artistic mediums. It may well be that we lack an apostle in the modern age, but we should not for that reason confuse the category of an apostle with that of an artist or genius or elevate the artist to the vacant position of apostleship. Although Kierkegaard maintains a positive view of the poetic in *The Book on Adler* in the recognition of an authentic writer, or essential author, who may be either a genius or an apostle, he also makes a clear distinction between the aesthetic and the religious, particularly as that applies to the transcendent category of an apostle.

These examples from the literature of the second, middle phase in Kierkegaard's authorship clearly show that Kierkegaard and certain of his pseudonyms continue to recognize a legitimate role of the poetic in both existential and aesthetic contexts in spite of the dangers and limitations of poetry pointed out in writings of this period. In existence, the poetic is manifested in marriage and in the new, or second, immediacy of the religious. Aesthetically, authentic expressions of the poetic may be

12. Stanley Cavell, "Kierkegaard's *On Authority and Revelation,*" in *Kierkegaard: A Collection of Critical Essays,* ed. Josiah Thompson (Garden City, N.Y.: Doubleday, 1972), 389. The similarities Cavell sees between the artist and the apostle include the following: (1) being "pulled out of the ranks by a message which [one] must, on pain of loss of self, communicate"; (2) undergoing a period of silence until one finds one's own way of communicating that message; (3) having no proof of authority or genuineness other than one's own work; (4) becoming repulsive in order to avoid being attractive to others; (5) denying one's own "personal or worldly authority"; and (6) receiving a "call," although in the case of the artist there is "no recognized calling" in which that call can be exercised (391).

13. Ibid., 392.

seen in dramatic performances, novel writing, and other forms of writing by a true, or essential, author. However, these examples by no means exhaust the possibilities of an authentic expression of the poetic in existence or in art. For a much deeper understanding and appropriation of the poetic in an existential context, let us turn to the existential aesthetics of Johannes Climacus in *Concluding Unscientific Postscript* before making a final assessment of the negative criticisms of poetry that characterize, to a considerable extent, the attitude toward the poetic in the second phase, or middle period, of Kierkegaard's authorship.

7

The Art of Existing

By far the most important indication of a continuing positive stance toward the poetic in the writings of Kierkegaard's middle period, or what I have identified as the second phase in the development of his understanding of the poetic, is to be found in *Concluding Unscientific Postscript.* In this work the existing individual, exemplified by the figure of the subjective thinker, and existential striving itself are understood as incorporating the poetic and as being essentially artistic. Moreover, the stages of existential development in the life of the individual are analytically expanded to include the aesthetic categories of irony and humor as existential determinants that serve as boundary zones, or stages of transition, between the aesthetic and the ethical (irony), on the one hand, and between the ethical and the religious (humor), on the other. In addition, these existential determinants play an important role within the ethical and the religious, appearing as the mask, or incognito, through which ethical and religious inwardness is given expression in the external realm. Irony and humor are likewise integrally related to the aesthetic genres of the tragic and the comic, which are also regarded in the *Postscript* as existential categories and seen as being present in every stage of life. My task in this chapter, therefore, is to examine these various aspects of the poetic in the existential dialectic delineated by the *Postscript* and to show how they contribute to the continued development of an existential aesthetics in Kierkegaard's thought in spite of the critique of poetry contained in this and other works of the middle period. Dividing my examination into two parts, I consider first the artistic character of the subjective thinker and second the role of irony, humor, the tragic, and the comic as existential determinants in the art of existing.

THE SUBJECTIVE THINKER AS ARTIST

In the course of an extensive discussion of the figure of the subjective thinker in *Concluding Unscientific Postscript,* Johannes Climacus, the pseudonymous author of the work, makes the following statement: "The subjective thinker is not a scientist-scholar; he is an artist [*Kunstner*]. To exist is an art [*At existere er en Kunst*]" (CUP, 1:351; SV 7:304).[1] In view of the strong contrast between existential pathos and aesthetic pathos drawn in the work and noted in the previous chapter, this statement comes as quite a surprise. It is clear from Climacus's statement that he intends to distinguish the subjective thinker, whose thought is directed inward to the thinker's own existence, from an objective thinker, who is essentially disinterested in existence and abstracts from it in order to consider everything as a cognitive possibility. This contrast is well drawn in the work and will not be elaborated here.[2] What is much less apparent and does need some explication, however, is the sense in which the subjective thinker may be regarded as an artist.[3] Consideration of this matter is made even more pertinent and complicated by the fact that Climacus not only distinguishes the subjective thinker from a scientist or objective thinker but also from a poet: "The subjective thinker is not a poet even if he is also a poet" (CUP, 1:351). In Climacus's view, being a

1. An earlier version of this section was published under the same title in *History of European Ideas* 12, no. 1 (1990): 19–29.

2. For recent discussions of the distinction between subjective and objective reflection in the *Concluding Unscientific Postscript,* see Evans, *Kierkegaard's "Fragments" and "Postscript,"* 95–135, and Pojman, *The Logic of Subjectivity,* 22–75.

3. Very little attention has been given to the description of the subjective thinker as an artist in the secondary literature on *Concluding Unscientific Postscript.* Although Louis Mackey, in *Kierkegaard: A Kind of Poet,* devotes a long chapter to the philosophy of Johannes Climacus (see 133–94), he does not explore the image of the subjective thinker as an artist—a curious omission given the poetic emphasis of the work. C. Stephen Evans, in *Kierkegaard's "Fragments" and "Postscript,"* briefly refers to the "existential artist" and to the ethical as an art form in his discussion of ethical existence, but he does not elaborate further the artistic character of the subjective thinker and the ethical (86). David Gouwens, in *Kierkegaard's Dialectic of the Imagination,* devotes a whole chapter to imagination and the subjective thinker (95–127) and in the course of this discussion briefly touches on the subjective thinker as artist.

poet, or creative artist who produces a work of art, is an accidental feature of a subjective thinker. Essentially, a subjective thinker is an existing individual whose reflection is focused on existential problems pertaining to the individual's own personal existence. In this respect the subjective thinker stands in sharp contrast to both the objective thinker and the poet, whose reflection and products of the imagination have validity quite apart from any significance these may have for their lives. Indeed, with respect to the poet, Climacus states, "That a poet, for example, does not allow himself to be influenced by his own poet-production is esthetically quite in order or is a matter of complete indifference, because esthetically the poet-production and possibility are the highest." For the subjective thinker, however, quite the opposite holds. From an ethical standpoint the thinker's mode of existence is of infinite importance, and any poetic productivity that may result is a matter of indifference. In fact, Climacus suggests that "ethically it would perhaps be the highest pathos to renounce the brilliant poet-existence without saying a single word" (CUP, 1:390).

This being the case, how are we to understand the subjective thinker as an artist? In what sense is it appropriate to use an aesthetic category, an artistic metaphor, with reference to the subjective thinker? And what does this add, if anything, to our understanding of the ethical demand to be subjective thinkers in our respective occupations and endeavors in life?

We may begin to discern why Climacus characterizes the subjective thinker as an artist by looking at the personal characteristics and form of communication associated with this figure. Besides being essentially inner-directed in reflection, the subjective thinker is described by Climacus as being "bifrontal," or both positive and negative, comic and tragic, and as manifesting passion, action, and a simultaneity of imagination, thought, and feeling in existence. Let us briefly consider each of these factors, beginning with the personal characteristics indicated above and concluding with an examination of the subjective thinker's form of communication.

THE BIFRONTAL CHARACTER OF THE SUBJECTIVE THINKER

The subjective thinker is first introduced by Climacus in the context of a discussion of a series of theses possibly or actually attributable to Lessing, one of the foremost philosophers and aestheticians of the eighteenth century whose thought figures importantly in Climacus's reflection. One of the theses attributed to Lessing by Climacus is the following: "*In his existence-relation to the truth, the existing subjective thinker is just as negative as positive, has just as much of the comic as he essentially has of pathos, and is continually in a process of becoming, that is, striving*" (CUP, 1:80). Inasmuch as the subjective thinker is involved in a process of becoming, which is a synthesis of the negative and the positive, that which counts as positive in the sphere of thought (certainty in sense perception, historical knowledge, and speculative results) amounts, in Climacus's opinion, to no more than "approximation-knowledge" and therefore is false and deceptive as well as illusory, because it "fails to express the state of the knowing subject in existence." This state is characterized by a pervading negativity or lack of certainty that is part of the very structure of existence. For as Climacus sees it, certainty can be had only in the infinite, where he as an existing subject cannot remain but only continually arrive. "Nothing historical can become infinitely certain to me except this: that I exist . . . which is not something historical," he claims (CUP, 1:81). Only the infinite, then, constitutes the positive, and that is repeatedly given expression in the life of the existing subject through a continuous realization of inwardness, or subjective concern, that in turn enables the subject to become conscious of the negative, or the elusiveness of the infinite (CUP, I: 84–85). The infinite thus remains just as negative as positive in the existing subject, and the positive security that is gained is continually threatened by the possibility of death.

If the existing subject is a subjective thinker, the task of the subject as a thinker is to learn to think about existence in terms of a process of becoming that is uncertain and never finished and then to reproduce that in one's own existence. Climacus likens the ability of the subjective thinker to think in such an unfinished fashion to the artistic "style" of a creative writer: "This is similar to having style. Only he really has style who is never finished with something but 'stirs the waters of language' whenever he begins, so that to him the most ordinary expression comes into existence with newborn originality" (CUP, 1:86). In Climacus's estimation, the ability to think dialectically in this manner about the infinite in relation to one's own existential situation in the context of the ongoing activity of daily life is what distinguishes the cultivated personality from the uncultivated, or common lot of human beings, and is also what constitutes the art and difficulty of life.

> The thoroughly educated and developed individuality is known by how dialectical the thinking is in which he has his daily life. To have his daily life in the decisive dialectic of the infinite and yet to go on living—that is the art. Most people have comfortable

> categories for daily use and the categories of the infinite only on solemn occasions, that is, they never have them. But to have the dialectic of the infinite for daily use and to exist in it is, of course, the greatest strenuousness, and in turn the greatest strenuousness is needed lest the practice, instead of exercising a person in existing, deceptively trick him out of it. (CUP, 1:86n)

Another way of expressing the thesis that the subjective thinker is equally positive and negative is to say that the subjective thinker is just as sensitive to the comic as to the pathetic or tragic character of life (CUP, 1:87).[4] A comic-tragic apprehension of existence is integral to the makeup of the subjective thinker because existence itself is both pathetic and comic, being directed toward the actualization of infinitude in the pathos of infinite striving yet never able to finish (the tragic) or to give adequate expression to it in external form (the comic). "The truly comic is that the infinite can be at work in a human being, and no one, no one discovers it by looking at him," Climacus maintains (CUP, 1:91). It is this discrepancy or contradiction between the inner and the outer, the finite and the infinite, the temporal and the eternal that "lies at the root" of both the comic and the tragic (CUP, 1:89). Insofar as existence is continually characterized by this contradiction, the comic and the tragic are integral elements in existence as well as in the reflection of the subjective thinker.

Ordinarily, Climacus points out, these aesthetic elements are divided so as to appear separately in different persons, but the subjective thinker possesses both in equal proportions (CUP, 1:87). In this the artistry of the subjective thinker may again be distinguished from that of the poet inasmuch as, according to the view of Frater Taciturnus noted in the previous chapter, poetry cannot be both tragic and comic simultaneously. From Climacus's standpoint, however, the simultaneous presence of both factors in equal proportions in the subjective thinker is important for assuring the soundness of each. For the presence of one ensures the presence of the other, so that jest, for example, is not merely

4. That Climacus intends an identification of the pathetic with the tragic here is an interpretation on my part inasmuch as he does not explicitly equate the two. In identifying the comic and the tragic in the subjective thinker, however, he does imply an identification of the pathetic with the tragic when he states, "The relative difference between the comic and the tragic within immediacy vanishes in double-reflection, where the difference becomes infinite and identity is thereby posited. Religiously, the comic expression of worship is therefore just as devout as its pathos-filled expression" (CUP, 1:89). In other contexts the term "the pathetic," or "pathos," is used more broadly to connote simply an intensified form of passion, which is also characteristic of the subjective thinker.

jest but becomes the expression for the highest earnestness in a person. The individual set before us as an example of this sort of bifrontal contradiction is Socrates, who was a jester indulging in all sorts of frivolity while at the same time being deeply concerned about the divine and disciplining himself throughout life for the divine test (CUP, 1:89; see also 90n).[5]

PASSION

Of all the characteristics associated with the subjective thinker, priority is given to passion, a quality noted previously as lacking in the present age. "For a subjective thinker, imagination, feeling, and dialectics in impassioned existence-inwardness are required. But first and last, passion, because for an existing person it is impossible to think about existence without becoming passionate. . . . To think about them [existence issues] so as to leave out passion is not to think about them at all, is to forget the point that one indeed is oneself an existing person" (CUP, 1:350–51). The subjective thinker's own existence constitutes the highest interest or passion of that individual and thus forms the content of his or her reflection. But how does one think passionately about existence, especially if it is recognized that actuality, like the eternal, is elusive and cannot be grasped by thought except by nullifying it in abstraction? Climacus distinguishes between two ways of thinking about existence: one is to think in a disinterested fashion about something as a cognitive possibility in the medium of abstract thought; the other is to think with passion or personal concern in the medium of existence (CUP, 1:315–16). Every actuality other than one's own actuality is known only in the first manner, Climacus claims; the only actuality that can be known in the second manner is one's own existence, to which one is immediately and passionately, as well as cognitively, related (CUP, 1:316). Passion is generated by interpenetrating one's existence with reflection in such a way as to understand life as composed of oppositions, and oneself as existing in them in an unmediated manner—that is, without any final resolution of the various contradictions encountered in existence. Passion and reflection thus go hand in hand in the subjective thinker, forming a mutual fit. Climacus laments the loss of passion in a dialectical thought that has become disinterested (CUP, 1:385), since passion gives

5. Described by Climacus as "a solo dancer to the honor of the god" (CUP, 1:89), Socrates may also be considered the model for the pseudonyms and their imaginary constructions who characterize themselves as dancers (see Chapter 5). For in these instances, dancing, like jesting, may be understood as connoting earnestness in relation to the divine, not merely aesthetic frivolity.

tension to the contradictions discovered by subjective thought and intensifies the subjective thinker's concern about existing in them.

Passion is not only crucial for thought but also for existing, since in Climacus's view "existing . . . cannot be done without passion" (CUP, 1:311). A difficulty every individual faces in life is how to give continuity to one's existence. In Climacus's view, it is not possible to achieve an absolute continuity in existence, since that may be predicated only of the eternal. But an approximation of continuity or a "momentary continuity" may be had in the form of a "concrete eternity" within the existing individual, an eternity that is equivalent to a particular form of passion Climacus identifies as an "idealizing passion" in contrast to "earthly passion." "All idealizing passion is an anticipation of the eternal in existence in order for an existing person to exist," Climacus contends, whereas "earthly passion hinders existing by changing existence into the momentary." Idealizing passion helps the individual to exist by acting as a constraining or limiting factor, on the one hand, and as an impulse toward movement or an instigator of action, on the other (CUP, 1:312). The goal of this movement is continually to arrive at a decision and then to renew it, in much the same way as Judge William in *Either/Or* understands the daily renewal of inner history in repetition as providing continuity to the ethical life. The requirement of passion is what links the subjective thinker most closely to the poet but is also what further serves to establish a distinction between them. For the poet, too, passion is a sine qua non. As the pseudonym Frater Taciturnus most emphatically and succinctly states it in *Stages on Life's Way,* "Without passion no poet, and without passion no poetry" (SLW, 369). Both the subjective thinker and the poet, in contrast to an abstract thinker, possess a passion for the ideal. But whereas the poet invests that passion in imaginatively constructing a work of art that represents the ideal in something external to the poet's existence, the passion of the subjective thinker is directed inward toward fashioning the thinker's own existence into conformity with the ideal so as to make that existence a work of art. Contrasting the Greek subjective thinker to the artist who pursues an artistic career without any personal reflection, Climacus says, "I also know that in Greece a thinker was not a stunted existing person who produced works of art, but he himself was an existing work of art" (CUP, 1:303). In a related passage in his journals, Kierkegaard remarks, "That Socrates belonged together with what he taught, that his teaching ended in him, that he himself was his teaching, in the setting of actuality was himself artistically a product of that which he taught—we have learned to rattle this off by rote but have scarcely understood it" (JP, 6:6360). In a note to this passage, the English translators point out that Kierkegaard is using the term "artistically" (***kunsterisk***) here as derived from its Danish root ***kunne,*** "to be able," in the sense of "a being able, a making, a doing, an embodying in personal being of what he [the existential thinker] understands" (JP, 6:604 n. 2151).

Like the ethical individual who is at once "poetizing and poetized" in the divine drama in which that individual has an assigned role (see EO, 2:137, and Chapter 4 above), the subjective thinker thus may be understood as both an artist and a work of art, the producer and product of an idealizing passion that does not forget or lose the life of the artist in representing the ideality of the possible in an external form of art but is engaged in transforming the existence of the thinker/artist into the actuality of the ideal in the form of that which constitutes the essentially human (CUP, 1:356). In Kierkegaard's early writings such a transformation is characterized as a "transubstantiation," or inward change in the given actuality of the individual, in contrast to a "transfiguration," or abandonment of actuality in the realm of ideality that takes place in poetry. Although the former term is not used in *Concluding Unscientific Postscript,* it is consistent with the way the artistic transformation of the subjective thinker is understood and contrasted to the aesthetic pathos of the poet in that work.

ACTION

The characterization of the subjective thinker as the product of artistic endeavor as well as its artistic producer underscores another distinguishing feature of the figure, that of action. For the Greek thinker, Climacus maintains, "to philosophize was an act" (CUP, 1:331). Ordinarily thought is associated with the static sphere of the abstract, the possible, and the objective, where, in the view of Climacus, there is no movement or process of becoming. Readers of the *Postscript* will recall how mercilessly he criticizes and lampoons Hegel for having confused abstract thought with existence in such a way as to suggest that the latter can be conceived and embraced by thought. Every thought of action is only an anticipation of action, not the action itself, which belongs to the realm of the subjective. Yet there is, Climacus concedes, a *confinium,* or "twilight zone," between thought and action in which "the interest of actuality and action is already reflected."[6] Indeed, Climacus even goes so far as to claim that action itself is an internal decision, not an external act: "The

6. In referring to this *confinium* as a "twilight zone," I am following the translation of the older English edition of *Concluding Unscientific Postscript* by Swenson and Lowrie (302).

actuality is not the external action but an interiority in which the individual annuls possibility and identifies himself with what is thought in order to exist in it. This is action" (CUP, 1:339). Thus, from the moment when Luther, for example, decided with subjective passion to appear before the Diet of Worms, he may be counted as having acted. Any further deliberation on his part would have been regarded as a temptation.

The existential pathos of the subjective thinker, then, consists in action, which falls under the category of the ethical. This would seemingly place the subjective thinker in opposition to the aesthetic, where poetic pathos is defined as "the pathos of possibility" (CUP, 1:389). In associating the poetic with possibility, Climacus relies on the view of Aristotle as set forth in his *Poetics* (chap. 9). But there is also a passage in Aristotle's *Nicomachean Ethics* that provides a precedent for a distinction between the aesthetic and the ethical in terms of action (book VI, 4, 1140a, 1–23). Kierkegaard refers to this passage in his philosophical notes from 1842–43, noting that "with respect to the concept of poetry it would be good to point out how Aristotle distinguishes *poiein* and *prattein* and defines art" (JP, 5:5592). Kierkegaard does not elaborate further on this distinction, but in the text to which he refers, Aristotle associates *poiein*, or "making," with art, and *prattein*, or "acting," with practical wisdom. Practical wisdom here is similar to the ethical knowledge of the subjective thinker in that the person who possesses practical wisdom is, according to Aristotle, a thinker who is concerned with his own interests with respect to what is "good and expedient for himself" (book VI, 5, 1140a, 25–26; 8, 1142a, 1–2).

If the subjective thinker is understood on the basis of Aristotle's distinction between art and practical wisdom, however, this would militate against an understanding of the figure as an artist, since in Aristotle's view art is a matter of making rather than of acting. To the extent that the subjective thinker stands in contrast to the usual poet and the kind of aesthetic productivity with which that person is engaged, the distinction is a useful one for highlighting an important difference between them. But it does not allow us to see how the action of the subjective thinker, and thus the thinker's own person, can be understood in aesthetic terms.

For that, let us return briefly to Kierkegaard's first work, *From the Papers of One Still Living*, where he undertakes a literary assessment of Hans Christian Andersen as a novelist. One of the chief criticisms Kierkegaard levels against Andersen in this review is that Andersen lacks an epic development, which is essential for becoming a real personality as well as for being an authentic writer of novels. In this work the aesthetic category of the epic, involving as it does action and heroic striving toward a single goal or ideal in life, corresponds closely to the ethical stage of life. From this association of the epic with the category of action, I think the subjective thinker, whose internal action brings that individual under ethical qualifications, can also be construed in aesthetic terms as an artist, even if he or she never produces a work of art. For what is essential to both the artistic and personal development of an individual is the forming of an authentic personality through ethical, or epical, action.

THE SIMULTANEITY OF IMAGINATION, THOUGHT, AND FEELING

A fourth feature of the subjective thinker, and one that, according to Climacus, sets this type of thinker off sharply from the scientist or speculative thinker, is the coordination of imagination and feeling with thought. In the evolution of scientific or speculative reflection, Climacus claims, "the stages of imagination and feeling are left behind" and thought is considered to be the highest stage of human development (CUP, 1:344). In existence, however, Climacus maintains that this does not hold true, for there "the task is not to elevate the one at the expense of the other, but the task is equality [*Ligeligheden*], [simultaneity] [*Samtidigheden*], and the medium in which they are unified is *existing*" (CUP, 1:348).[7] From this standpoint, Climacus points out that it is just as bad for a thinker to lose imagination and feeling as it is to lose reason, and he laments the tendency of his generation to dismiss poetry as a transcended phase because of its close connection with imagination. "In existence," Climacus asserts, "it holds true that as long as there is a human being who wants to claim a human existence, he must preserve poetry, and all his thinking must not disturb for him the enchantment of poetry, but rather to enhance it" (CUP, 1:348). For Climacus, therefore, the aesthetic elements of imagination and feeling are essential ingredients in the makeup of the subjective thinker and are what partly determine that individual as an artist. Even if the subjective thinker is not a poet or artist in the usual sense, the poetic must be present and must contribute to the formation of a truly human life.

This positive role of imagination and the poetic is not developed in *Concluding Unscientific Postscript,* but it is spelled out in more detail in other works of Kierkegaard, for example, *Repetition* and *The Sickness*

7. In the new translation of *Concluding Unscientific Postscript* the Hongs translate *Samtidigheden* as "contemporaneity." Although the term is commonly translated that way, I prefer the equally common translation of it as "simultaneity," following here the older Swenson-Lowrie translation, which conveys a stronger sense of unified or coordinated action in the process of incorporating these factors.

unto Death.[8] In *Repetition* imagination is credited with being that which awakens an individual at a very early age to the possibility of personality. The self, or personality, appears in the imagination not as an actual shape but as a variety of shadows, all of which resemble the self and vie equally for constituting the self (R, 154). Constantin Constantius, the pseudonymous author of the work, points out that this "shadow-existence" requires satisfaction and that "it is never beneficial to a person if this does not have time to live out its life" (R, 154–55). He adds, however, that one must not make the mistake of living out one's life in it. That is the danger or temptation of imagination to which the later work, *The Sickness unto Death,* calls attention in its analysis of despair. In this work, which I examine more closely in the next chapter, imagination is again viewed as the capacity by which the self is reflected in its infinite possibility; in fact, Anti-Climacus, the pseudonymous author of the work, goes so far as to claim that imagination is the capacity by which all other capacities of the self, such as feeling, willing, and knowing, are constituted. But when imagination (*Phantasien*) goes wild, as it were, leading a person out into the infinite in such a way as to get lost there and to prevent the individual from returning to the finite self in the concrete, it becomes fantastic (*det Phantastiske*) and the self is volatilized (SUD, 30). The process of self-transcendence, or infinitizing of the self through imagination, is necessary and valid in itself but must be combined dialectically with a process of finitizing in the medium of actuality.

Insofar as the subjective thinker is characterized by imagination along with thought and feeling, imagination must function in the manner indicated above, in coordination with these other capacities. As an artist who employs imagination, however, the subjective thinker should not be understood in an Aristotelian manner as a poet or artist who makes or imaginatively constructs the self in the realm of ideality or in an illusory actuality. Since the subjective thinker is oriented toward existence, has the task of acquiring self-understanding in the process of existing, and is characterized by action, the ideality of the self must be reflected in the medium of existence, not merely in imagination. "To be an idealist in imagination is not at all difficult," Climacus points out, "but to have to *exist* as an idealist is an extremely rigorous life-task, because existing is precisely the objection to it" (CUP, 1:353). Moreover, since that which constitutes the ideal, or essentially human, is already given as a potentiality within the individual (either immanently, as supposed in Socratic

8. For more extensive treatments of Kierkegaard's view of imagination, see Gouwens, *Kierkegaard's Dialectic of the Imagination,* and Ferreira, *Transforming Vision.*

subjectivity and in Religiousness A, or via a relation to the eternal in time, as believed in Christianity), the subjective thinker does not possess the poetic license imaginatively to create or construct the self simply as she or he pleases. The function of imagination in the ethical-religious, therefore, is better understood as depicting or portraying the ideal self rather than imaginatively constructing, making, or creating it. That this is how Kierkegaard also understands the proper role of imagination in human existence will become evident in his later religious writings and journals, where he views his own task as a "poet of the religious" to be one in which he merely describes or portrays (*fremstille*) the existential ideals, not imaginatively constructs (*experimentere*) them.[9] Experimentation is a mode of poetizing characteristic of the German romantics that Kierkegaard strongly criticizes in *The Concept of Irony* and *Either/Or.* In the latter work, for example, Judge William maintains that "as soon as the ethical person's gymnastics become an imaginary constructing [*Experimenteren*] he has ceased to live ethically" (EO, 2:253). To be sure, some of Kierkegaard's own pseudonyms engage in a bit of imaginary constructing, but generally with quite a different aim than that of the German romantics. For the pseudonyms' experiments are designed in the interest of indirect ethical-religious communication rather than as the capricious and arbitrary forms of play with different possibilities of selfhood advocated, in Kierkegaard's view, by the German romantics.

THE ART OF COMMUNICATION

Last, an artistic character can be observed in the subjective thinker's form of communication, both in terms of the way in which the subjective thinker is related to the communication and the way in which it is presented to others. Inasmuch as the subjective thinker is an existing individual essentially interested in his or her own existence and making it the object of reflection, the type of reflection engaged in by the subjective thinker is different from abstract reflection in that it takes the form of a double reflection. As in other forms of reflection, the subjective thinker first thinks the universal. But in addition to this, the universal is related to and assimilated in the subjective thinker's own existence. Since personal appropriation in inwardness constitutes the goal of this

9. On experimentation and imaginary construction, compare my interpretation with Engebretsen, "Kierkegaard and Poet Existence with Special Reference to Germany and Rilke," 165–67, and with the Hongs' historical introduction and extensive note on the subtitle to *Repetition,* xxi–xxx and 357–62. See also my discussion of Kierkegaard as a religious poet in the next chapter.

type of reflection, it is impossible to communicate the truth of this mode of thinking directly to others or to communicate it truthfully without having first appropriated the content of that reflection in one's own existence. For an appropriate communication to be made, then, artistry is needed on the part of the subjective thinker: "Wherever the subjective is of importance in knowledge and appropriation is therefore the main point, communication is a work of art" (CUP, 1:79). In fact, "the more art, the more inwardness" in the subjective thinker, for the use of an artistic mode of communication ensures that the subjective thinker is concerned to preserve his or her own inwardness in the process of communication (CUP, 1:77). Just as inwardness itself is inexhaustible, so the subjective thinker's form of communication constitutes an "inexhaustible artistry" in the variety with which double reflection and its communication are carried out (CUP, 1:77, 80). Once again, the model for this form of artistry is Socrates, who by the practice of his "maieutic artistry" helped others to achieve the same point of view (CUP, 1:80, cf. PF, chap. 1).

In all indirect or artistic communication, the principle holds that "the reduplication of the contents in the form is the artistry, and the point is especially to abstain from all expressions of the same thing in an inadequate form" (CUP, 1:333). Thus the form, or style, of the subjective thinker's communication must reflect the content, or makeup, of that individual as a thinker. Inasmuch as the subjective thinker is an artist, the form will constitute an expression of that artistry as well as manifest it in the content of the communication. The subjective thinker's communication will take, then, an aesthetic form, but since the subjective thinker is not a poet or artist in the usual sense, it will not take that form directly. The same holds with regard to ethical, dialectical, and religious modes of communication. These are to a certain degree at the disposal of the subjective thinker but must be employed in a manner consistent with the concrete nature of the thinker's being and thought. The form of the subjective thinker "must first and last be related to existence," to the existence of the subjective thinker. This means that in presenting his or her thought, the subjective thinker "describes" (*skildrer*) and communicates his or her own self (CUP, 1:357). In this way the form of the subjective thinker becomes dialectically concrete and artistic—a "portrait of the artist" at home and at work, if you will, passionately, actively, imaginatively thinking in existence, relating the content of that reflection to daily life, and striving to exist in it.

However, Climacus points out that the subjective thinker, unlike the ordinary poet or artist, "does not have the medium of imagination for the illusion of esthetic production, he does not have the poetic repose to create in the medium of imagination and esthetically to accomplish something disinterestedly" (CUP, 1:357). The subjective thinker is not free, therefore, to present an imaginary, illusory self-portrait, using the variety of enhancing scenes and settings ordinarily employed in poetic construction. No, Climacus says, "the subjective thinker has only one setting—existence—and has nothing to do with localities and such things. The setting is not in the fairyland of the imagination, where poetry produces consummation, nor is the setting laid in England, and historical accuracy is not a concern. The setting is inwardness in existing as a human being; the concretion is the relation of the existence-categories to one another" (CUP, 1:357–58). In line with this aesthetic restriction upon the subjective thinker's communication, a presumably religious person who depicts eternal happiness "with all the allurement of the imagination" is later described by Climacus as "a poet escaped from the esthetic who wants to have citizenship in the religious without even being able to understand its native language" (CUP, 1:390). Since ethical-religious pathos consists in action, it would be more appropriate for the religious individual, he suggests, to describe instead what that person has suffered for the sake of eternal happiness.

In the final analysis, however, Climacus concludes that existential actuality (*Existents-Virkelighed*) can be communicated to another only in the form of possibility (CUP, 1:358; SV, 7:310). In order for others to form a cognitive and existential relation to the self-communication of the subjective thinker, therefore, the thinker must be careful to cast the communication in the form of the possible. This means that instead of giving a direct account of personal actions so as to become an object of admiration by others, the subjective thinker should present that which constitutes what is admirable in the universally human ideal to which the thinker is related and present that as an ethical requirement, as a challenge to the recipient to exist in it (CUP, 1:358–59). In presenting the universal human ideal as a possibility, the subjective thinker's communication conforms to the traditional concept of poetry as concerning itself with ideality, but there is an important difference here too, in that the ideal is set forth as an ethical requirement, not merely as an imaginative possibility.

The subjective thinker thus combines in communication, as well as in thought and existence, elements of the aesthetic and the ethical in such a manner that it is appropriate to speak of that figure as an artist, even though in some respects the artistry of the subjective thinker is quite different from that of the traditional poet, or artist. At the same time Climacus is critical of the poetic, therefore, he presents an alternative type of artistry in the figure of the subjective thinker. Seen in the context of both earlier and later works in the Kierkegaardian corpus, the subjective thinker as artist is both illumined by and conceptually consistent with a broader concern in the authorship to fashion the rudiments of an ethical-religious, or existential, aesthetics that unifies the aesthetic, the ethical, and the religious. This unity is not merely one that incorporates the aesthetic into the ethical and the religious, but is one in which the ethical-religious itself is understood in aesthetic terms as the truly poetic, the true ideality, the true reconciliation of ideality and actuality. Although other attempts have been made in modern and contemporary philosophy to formulate an existential aesthetics or philosophy of art that relates art to life, their emphasis has been primarily upon traditional art forms as media for expressing human feeling and meaning.[10] In the figure of the subjective thinker human existence itself becomes a mode of artistic endeavor and representation, giving expression to human ideals that other forms of poetic production can only hint at or give a semblance of in time. As thinking individuals, we are thus challenged by Climacus to don the artist's frock, take up our palettes, and sketch our own self-portraits in existence, reproducing in ourselves the human ideals toward which we strive.

10. On developments in modern and contemporary aesthetics, see Beardsley, *Aesthetics from Classical Greece to the Present,* 244–388; Richard Kostelanetz, ed., *Esthetics Contemporary* (New York: Prometheus, 1978), 19–35; and Arturo Fallico, *Art and Existentialism* (Englewood Cliffs, N.J.: Prentice-Hall, 1962), 1–17. Similar to Kierkegaard, but minus any a priori or fixed concept of the essentially human, or ideal, self, Nietzsche has been interpreted by Alexander Nehamas, in *Nietzsche: Life as Literature* (Cambridge: Harvard University Press, 1985), as trying "to create an artwork out of himself" by exemplifying the character type about which he writes (8, 39). Nietzsche's aestheticism, however, more closely resembles that of the German romantics whom Kierkegaard criticized than the ethical-religious alternative he offered to them. Indeed, Nehamas described Nietzsche as "the last romantic" (234). Also somewhat like Kierkegaard, Wilhelm Dilthey made "lived experience" the basis for art as well as religion and philosophy, but in his poetics it functions primarily as a source for poetic imagination and creativity in traditional art forms (see his *Selected Works,* vol. 5, *Poetry and Experience,* ed. Rudolf A. Makkreel and Frithjof Rodi [Princeton: Princeton University Press, 1985], 223–27). Heidegger as well sees an integral connection between poetry and human existence, but for him poetic creation through language is what enables us to live authentically in the world (see his *Poetry, Language, Thought,* 213–29). Somewhat closer to Kierkegaard but more explicitly using and inverting Dewey's association of art with experience, Joseph H. Kupfer, in *Experience as Art: Aesthetics in Everyday Life* (Albany: State University of New York Press, 1983), locates aesthetic values in the moral, social, and personal concerns of everyday life.

IRONY, HUMOR, THE TRAGIC, AND THE COMIC AS EXISTENTIAL DETERMINANTS

In continuity with the earlier pseudonymous authors in the Kierkegaardian corpus, Johannes Climacus views personal existence as developing through three stages: (1) the aesthetic, which has its telos in immediate enjoyment through the satisfaction and refinement of natural drives, passions, moods, talents, mental capacities, and inclinations; (2) the ethical, which has as its goal victory in the struggle to fulfill universal ethical requirements in the personal life of the existing individual; and (3) the religious, which has its telos in eternal happiness, a fulfillment that is only anticipated in existence through a relation to God characterized by persistent inner suffering due to the consciousness of guilt and sin. But while Climacus retains the three-stage schema of the earlier pseudonymous works, the structure of the stages in *Concluding Unscientific Postscript* corresponds more to a view of them diagrammed as follows: aesthetic / ethical-religious / Christian. The ethical optimism with which the existential task of self-transformation into conformity with the ethical ideal is begun flows progressively into a recognition of impotence in the existential pathos of immanent religiousness, or Religiousness A. Thus these two stages really belong together. Within this schema, dialectical opposition, or an either/or, occurs with respect to two factors, immediacy and immanence. In relation to immediacy, the dialectic is decisively with aestheticism, and the qualitative either/or may be diagrammed as: aestheticism / the ethical-religious and the Christian. Here Christianity stands in pathetic continuity with ethical-religious inwardness over against aesthetic immediacy. In relation to immanence, however, the dialectic occurs primarily between Christianity and the ethical-religious, and the qualitative either/or is inverted: aestheticism and the ethical-religious / the Christian.

Between the stages, Climacus also adds to his analysis two boundary zones, or transition spheres: irony, which falls between the aesthetic and the ethical, and humor, which comes between the ethical and the religious (CUP, 1:501–2). Irony and humor also function *within* the ethical and religious spheres as the disguise, or incognito, through which the ethical and immanent religiousness are given expression. Closely connected to irony and humor are the aesthetic categories of the comic and the tragic, which I have already considered briefly in relation to the figure of the subjective thinker. In this section, my task is to examine the way in which these four aesthetic categories function as existential categories or existential determinants that are essential, not accidental, to the art of existing.

IRONY AS AN EXISTENTIAL ART

Let us begin with irony. In *The Concept of Irony* we saw that irony originates in Socrates as an existential standpoint, not merely as a rhetorical device, and that the ironic standpoint is one of absolute infinite negativity toward actuality. Although Kierkegaard thought that Socratic irony was justified or warranted in its negation of the established order (whereas the irony of the romantics toward actuality as a whole was not), he nevertheless viewed irony as a standpoint that must be mastered—an art that Socrates never perfected. In the *Postscript,* however, a somewhat different assessment of irony and of Socrates is given.[11] Here irony is seen as an "existence-art" [*Existents-Kunst*], and Socrates is portrayed as the exemplar of it (CUP, 1:520; SV, 7:454). "Irony emerges," Climacus claims, "by continually joining the particulars of the finite with the ethical infinite requirement and allowing the contradiction to come into existence." To be an ironist, an individual must maintain an ironic stance toward every finite relativity, including his or her own existence; otherwise the individual becomes ironic in an illusory or spurious fashion on the basis of a supposed relative superiority of the individual's own position vis-à-vis that of others (CUP, 1:502). This total relativizing of the finite on the part of the ironist is an indication that the individual has made the movement of infinity. But the existential art of irony goes beyond this abstract movement to sustain an inner relation to the ethical requirement. In other words, the existential ironist is an ethicist who uses irony as an incognito. In Climacus's view, Socrates was an ironist and an ethicist in this sense. Accusing Magister Kierkegaard of presenting only one side of Socrates in his dissertation, Climacus offers a different definition of irony as "the unity of ethical passion, which in inwardness infinitely accentuates one's own *I* in relation to the ethical requirement—and culture, which in externality infinitely abstracts externally from the personal *I* as a finitude included among all other finitudes and particulars" (CUP, 1:503).

Here an ethical definition of irony accentuates the contradiction or

11. On the change in Kierkegaard's view of Socrates, see especially J. Himmelstrup, *Søren Kierkegaards Opfattelse af Sokrates* (Copenhagen: Arnold Busck, 1924). This change is prefigured in *The Concept of Anxiety,* where Socrates is presented as an example of "lofty inclosing reserve," or earnestness in relation to the divine, and it is already apparent in *Philosophical Fragments,* where Socrates is admired for his maieutic artistry and is portrayed as an exemplar of ethical concern in purely human relations.

discrepancy between the ironist's, or ethicist's, internal state and his or her external life in society. The art of the ironist in this circumstance is to conceal the internal so that it is not outwardly noticeable to others. The existential ironist thus takes on the appearance of aesthetic hiddenness just as Abraham does in *Fear and Trembling.* Being an ethicist, the existential ironist reveals him- or herself in and through the various tasks of everyday living, just as the immediate individual does; but what distinguishes the ethicist from others and makes that individual an ethicist (and ironist) is the inward movement of spirit by which the individual conjoins this external life with the infinite ethical requirement (CUP, 1:504). Irony, then, signifies the movement of the infinite within a person, and as such it is higher than and justified over against aesthetic immediacy (CUP, 1:520). But Climacus is careful to point out that only existential irony and the existential ironist are justified in relation to immediacy. In agreement with Magister Kierkegaard, he maintains that total irony (such as that practiced by the romantics) is, like all abstractions, "unauthorized in connection with every existence-sphere." Distinguishing the existential ironist from the abstract ironist, Climacus goes on to explain that "irony certainly is abstraction and the abstract compounding of things, but the legitimacy of the existing ironist is that he himself, existing, expresses it, that he keeps his life in it and does not dally with the grandness of irony and have his own life in philistinism" (CUP, 1:521). As Climacus sees it, then, irony not only constitutes an existential standpoint or abstract posture toward existence but is also an "existence-qualification"; that is, the legitimate ironist has his or her life in it (CUP, 1:503). As an existential determinant, irony is not only justified but also essential to the life of the individual inasmuch as it functions as the incognito through which the individual's inner relation to the infinite ethical requirement is given outward expression and protected from disclosure in the external realm.

HUMOR ON THE BOUNDARY OF THE RELIGIOUS AND AS HOLY JEST

Like irony, humor is also an existence-qualification, and just as Climacus speaks of existential irony, he also speaks of existential humor, but with more personal authority on this category, since he identifies himself as a humorist. And again like irony, humor seems to play a double role in the *Postscript.*[12] On the one hand, humor is said to lie on the boundary

12. On the role of humor, see Evans, *Kierkegaard's "Fragments" and "Postscript,"* 195–201. In his interpretation of the existence spheres Evans thinks of them not in terms of a fixed

between the ethical and the religious, where the humorist evokes contradiction by setting the God-idea into conjunction with other things but does not personally have a passionate relation to God (CUP, 1:505). On the other hand, humor is described as "the final *terminus a quo* in relation to the Christian-religious," which "terminates immanence within immanence," and as "the last stage in existence-inwardness before faith" (CUP, 1:291). It seems, then, that humor may function as a boundary category at two levels, between the ethical and the religious (the religious here being conceived in the widest sense as including Christianity but understood mainly in terms of immanent religiousness, or Religiousness A), and between Religiousness A and Religiousness B, or Christianity. Just as irony functions as an existential determinant between the aesthetic and ethical existence spheres as well as an incognito within the ethical, so too humor may be understood to function in a comparable manner both on the border of the religious and within the religious. In fact, Climacus appears to recognize a gradation or development of humor, since he also identifies an "immature humor" that is a

---

schema but rather as "existential possibilities that can be helpfully reflected on with the help of certain defining categories" (199). While it is helpful to relax the rigidity of the schema of the stages, or existence spheres, by thinking of them in this way, another solution, I suggest in what follows, may be found in thinking of humor in terms of a gradation, or range, of humorous standpoints and as operative on the boundary between immanent religiousness and Christianity as well as between the ethical and the religious. This way of understanding Climacus's view of humor is close to that of Julius Schousboe's *Om Begrebet Humor hos Søren Kierkegaard* (Copenhagen: Arnold Busck, 1925), which remains one of the most extensive treatments of the concept of humor in Kierkegaard's thought. Schousboe distinguishes two forms of humor in *Concluding Unscientific Postscript,* one forming a *confinium* to the religious and lying between the ethical and the religious, the other a *confinium* to Religiousness B and corresponding to Religiousness A. One problem in his account, however, is that he views Quidam, in *Stages on Life's Way,* as being representative of Religiousness A, which as the last stage of immanence becomes the *terminus a quo* in relation to Religiousness B, or Christian paradoxical religiousness. But Quidam can hardly be a paradigm of Religiousness A, at least as Frater Taciturnus interprets him, since he is a "demoniac character in the direction of the religious," not an authentic religious personality (SLW, 398). Thus he can be said to illuminate Religiousness A only negatively, if at all. Totally missing the element of humor in Religiousness A, Mark C. Taylor, "Humor and Humorist" in *Bibliotheca Kierkegaardiana,* vol. 3, *Concepts and Alternatives in Kierkegaard,* ed. Niels Thulstrup and Marie Mikulová Thulstrup (Copenhagen: C. A. Reitzels Boghandel, 1980), 220–28, views humor only as a boundary category between the ethical and Christian-religious stages, though he does place humor within immanent categories. Thus when Taylor goes on to discuss humor as the incognito of religious faith, he presumably means Christian faith, not Religiousness A, as Evans, Schousboe, and I interpret it. For other studies of humor in Kierkegaard, see Lloyd Ellison Parrill, "The Concept of Humor in the Pseudonymous Works of Søren Kierkegaard," (Ph.D. diss., Drew University, 1975), and Theresa H. Sandok, "Kierkegaard on Irony and Humor," (Ph.D. diss., University of Notre Dame, 1975).

parody of the religious.[13] This type of humor, he suggests, is nothing more than "a kind of flippancy" or "esthetic subtlety" that "skips past the ethical" and is very far from being true religiousness (CUP, 1:292). Humor on the boundary of the religious comes close to the religious and is often confused with it inasmuch as the humorist, like the religious individual, preceives suffering and its persistence as belonging essentially to existence rather than being something accidental, such as misfortune, which one seeks aesthetically to overcome. But in Climacus's opinion the humorist on this level does not comprehend the significance of suffering beyond this bare apprehension of its relevance to existence (CUP, 1:447). Instead of going on to seek an explanation of suffering, the humorist takes the opposite course of revoking its significance in jest by making light of the existential plight. Although the humorist, in perceiving the essentiality of suffering in existence, gives more significance to existence than the ironist does, existence for the humorist nevertheless lacks the significance it has for the religious individual, since the humorist, like the ironist, essentially opts for a retirement out of existence and into the eternal by way of recollection (CUP, 1:242).[14]

While jest is the expression for the humorist's revocation of the decisive significance of existence, there is another form of jesting that serves as a sign of the utmost earnestness toward existence, or what Climacus calls "holy jest" (CUP, 1:462, 471–72). This form of jest comes to expression in humor that is the incognito of the religious individual.[15] Characteristic of the religious personality as Climacus understands it is a consciousness of impotence, or the inability to do anything by oneself to transform one's existence into conformity with the ideal (CUP, 1:461, 484). In the world, however, it may appear that one has power to do many things. This contradictory state of affairs occasions the discovery of the comical on the part of the religious individual, for that person is able to enjoy the amusement of apparently having the power of accom-

13. Where Climacus himself fits on this scale is not entirely clear, since in one passage he denies being a religious individual, claiming to be solely a humorist, while in another passage he places himself on the boundary of the religious within immanence but seeking the Christian-religious (CUP, 1:501, 451). In still another passage he identifies his position as falling within the boundaries of Religiousness A (CUP, 1:557).

14. Although the existential ironist accentuates existence, Climacus points out that for Socrates, the exemplar of this form of irony, "existence in temporality has no decisive significance, because there is continually the possibility of taking oneself back into eternity by recollecting, even though this possibility is continually annulled because the inward deepening in existing fills up time" (CUP, 1:206).

15. In "A Glance at a Contemporary Effort in Danish Literature" Climacus also claims that "the highest earnestness of the religious life is distinguishable by jest" (CUP, 1:235).

plishing everything while inwardly understanding this to be an illusion (CUP, 1:462). This comic discrepancy between the religious individual's outward appearance and actual inner condition makes itself felt in a variety of ways, since the art of the religious individual is precisely to live so that "no one will detect anything in him." For as Climacus sees it, true religiousness consists in secret inwardness and has its criterion in invisibility (CUP, I:475).[16] Like the knight of faith in *Fear and Trembling*, the religious individual looks and acts like others, but that is an incognito by which inwardness is humorously concealed in order to protect it from direct expression and from the taint of worldliness (CUP, 1:500).[17] Like the knight of faith, the religious individual remains in the world rather than withdraws from it, but this apparent worldliness on his or her part becomes an incognito, or "veil," behind which the inward suffering and God-relation of true religiousness are ensured and safeguarded. The religious individual is also active in the world, but this outward activity is likewise transformed into an inward matter in the admission before God that one can do nothing of oneself (CUP, 1:506).

Using humor as an indirect mode of expression, the religious individual also appears outwardly to be a humorist but inwardly is not; on the contrary, Climacus claims that the religious individual is "infinitely higher than" and "qualitatively different from" the humorist (CUP, 1:501). One crucial difference between them is that the religious individual is earnest—that is, existentially committed to the religious ideal—whereas the humorist is not. Here again a characteristic noted earlier with respect to the subjective thinker comes into play, namely, that jest functions as the sign of earnestness and, in this instance, that humor functions as a sign of religiousness in the religious individual with humor

16. The characterization of religiousness in terms of hidden inwardness is something Kierkegaard later explicitly rejects in *Practice in Christianity* because it too easily becomes an excuse for the relaxation of rigorous striving in Christendom, where everyone is presumed to be a Christian in hidden inwardness (PC, 215–32). In place of hidden inwardness Kierkegaard begins to talk about the "inverted recognizability" of the Christian through external suffering brought about by opposition from the world (PC, 212, 215). But Christianity is still essentially inwardness for Kierkegaard, and he continues to speak of a true "concealed inwardness" in the form of "the suffering of real self-denial" on the part of true Christians (PC, 138–39).

17. Ideally, the religious individual would be so artful in disguising inwardness that not even the slightest hint of it would be apparent to others, but Climacus admits that "as long as the struggle and the suffering in inwardness continue he will not succeed in hiding his inwardness completely" (CUP, 1:501). It is this element of imperfection that distinguishes the religious individual of whom Climacus speaks from the knight of faith in *Fear and Trembling*, for Climacus claims that the knight of faith is presented in an illusory state of completeness and thus in a false medium, not in the medium of existence, where nothing is ever finished or complete (CUP, 1:500–501).

as an incognito. For the humorist, jest and humor signify nothing but themselves, or more precisely, they signify just the opposite of humor in the religious individual, namely, that the humorist does not maintain a decisive relation to God in jesting but on the contrary uses it as a way of distancing him- or herself from such a relation. Thus the humorist may reflectively comprehend the various movements of the religious sphere, such as resignation, suffering, and the consciousness of guilt, but in an impatient, childlike manner revokes them in the nonserious form of jest. By contrast, the religious individual with humor as incognito uses humor or holy jest precisely as a means to preserve and give indirect expression to these forms of pathos in his or her life.

Humor therefore may function in several different ways and on more than one level as an existential art. It should be noted, however, that Climacus restricts the expression of humor as an incognito of the religious to Religiousness A, or immanent religiousness, which serves as the *terminus a quo,* or presupposition, for defining Religiousness B, or the Christian paradoxical religiousness (CUP, 1:532n, 534–35, 556). In Climacus's opinion, humor is incapable of dealing with the "decisive Christian category of becoming a Christian"—that is, the consciousness of sin—because humor falls essentially under the category of recollection; it is "always a revocation" of existence "into the eternal by recollection backward," whereas Christianity is "the direction forward" that continually moves toward becoming and being a Christian (CUP, 1:602). Here Climacus is in essential agreement with the humorist Constantin Constantius's association of humor with recollection rather than the forward movement of repetition. Climacus's point is that humor assumes an essential relation to the eternal that is denied in Christianity on the basis of original sin, and thus it is an inappropriate category for the expression of Christian inwardness. It would seem, however, that humor in the form of "holy jest" might well be employed in Christianity inasmuch as the Christian's sense of contradiction in relation to the divine and his or her awareness of being unable to do anything without divine help are paradoxically heightened in Christianity.[18]

18. It is interesting that in Kierkegaard's early journals humor is seen as intrinsic to Christianity and that Christianity itself is regarded as the most humorous view of life, Hamann being the greatest humorist in Christianity (JP, 2:1681; cf. 2:1682, 1686, 1687, 1690). Even as late as 1849 he writes that "Christendom is waiting for a comic poet à la Cervantes, who will create a counterpart to Don Quixote out of the essentially Christian" (JP, 2:1762), and in *Judge for Yourself!* he uses the lilies and the birds jestingly to teach the God-fearing worker the earnestness of God as a coworker (JFY, 179, 183, 186). On religious or Christian humor in Kierkegaard's early journals, see Schousboe, *Om Begrebet Humor hos Søren Kierkegaard,* 122–43,

Another point of contention in Climacus's analysis concerns his claim that humorous revocation is a way of distancing oneself existentially from the divine. Certainly it may be that, but Climacus's own revocation at the end of the book suggests another possibility, namely, that the existential humorist may revoke his or her words in the interest of indirect communication. In an appendix to his book Climacus suggests that the whole work has been but an experiment or imaginary construction that is "about myself, solely and simply about myself" (CUP, 1:617). He does not claim to be an authority on the subject of Christianity and has but one opinion, namely, "that it must be the most difficult of all to become a Christian" (CUP, 1:619). He is thus qualified on the basis of his own self-reflection in the book to be only an apprentice, or learner. For this purpose he seeks a "teacher of the ambiguous art of thinking about existence and existing" who will allow him to ask questions and will go over everything until he has understood it, not simply learned by rote a paragraph a day (CUP, 1:622–23). Having found no such teacher, Climacus is reluctant to assume the role of teacher himself, as if a learner in the art of existing could teach anyone else. Climacus thus leaves his readers free to master the art of existing for themselves, just as he must do. Another possible interpretation of the revocation is that Climacus seeks to protect his own secret inwardness by cloaking his earnestness in jest. If that is the case, then his claim to be solely a humorist must be taken ironically—and humorously.

THE TRAGIC AND THE COMIC

It remains to be considered how irony and humor are related to the tragic and the comic as existential determinants in *Concluding Unscientific Postscript.*[19] We have already seen in this chapter's section on the

---

who distinguishes between three forms of humor in Kierkegaard's thought: religious humor, demonic humor, and sympathetic humor, the last being the view of humor set forth by Frater Taciturnus and Johannes Climacus.

19. On the comical, see Howard V. Hong, "The Comic, Satire, Irony, and Humor: Kierkegaardian Reflections," *Midwest Studies in Philosophy* 1 (1976): 98–105, together with discussions by Robert L. Perkins, "The Categories of Humor and Philosophy," ibid., 105–8, and Harold P. Sjursen, "The Comic Apprehension," ibid., 108–13; Masaru Otani, "The Comical," in *Bibliotheca Kierkegaardiana,* vol. 3, *Concepts and Alternatives in Kierkegaard,* ed. Niels Thulstrup and Marie Mikulová Thulstrup, 229–35; Douglas Langston, "The Comical Kierkegaard," *Journal of Religious Studies* 12, no. 1 (1985): 35–45; Andrew J. Burgess, "A Word-Experiment on the Category of the Comic," in *International Kierkegaard Commentary: The Corsair Affair,* ed. Robert L. Perkins, 85–121; and Lee Barrett, "The Uses and Misuses of the Comic: Reflections on the Corsair Affair," in ibid., 123–39. On the tragic, see Pierre Mesnard, "Is the Category of the 'Tragic' Absent from the Life and Thought of Kierkegaard?" in *A Kierkegaard Critique,* ed.

subjective thinker as artist that the tragic and the comic are regarded as integral features of the subjective thinker's existence, being expressions for that individual's awareness of the discrepancy or contradiction between the inner and the outer, the finite and the infinite, the temporal and the eternal in existence. Insofar as both the tragic and the comic are based on existential contradiction, they are the same, but they are also different from each other in that the comic involves a "painless contradiction," whereas the tragic has to do with "suffering contradiction" (CUP, 1:514). This difference is based on the fact that a legitimate comic apprehension cancels or knows a way out of the contradiction, whereas the tragic does not (CUP, 1:516, 523).

The comic is obviously closely related to humor in that it involves jest and laughter, but both irony and humor have a comic and a tragic side (CUP, 1:520–21). Of the two, Climacus claims to have particular expertise in the comic, boasting that "if there is anything I have studied thoroughly, from A to Z, it is the comic" (CUP, 1:483). This does not mean, however, that he considers the comic to be the highest standpoint; on the contrary, he ridicules Hegelian philosophy for giving "predominance to the comic" and seeks to relegate the comic to the religious in his account (CUP, 1:512). "On the whole," Climacus claims, "the comic is present everywhere, and every existence can at once be defined and assigned to its particular sphere by knowing how it is related to the comical" (CUP, 1:462; cf. 513 and 520). In his view, the various stages of existence may be ranked and legitimated according to whether they have the comic within or outside themselves, that is, by whether the contradiction is understood as due to internal or external conditions. The immediate consciousness has the comic outside itself and ranks at the lowest level; both irony and humor have the comic within themselves and consequently rank higher. Religiousness with humor as its incognito ranks still higher, although here the comic is a relative factor and the individual is legitimated by the passion with which the God-relation is sustained. At the apex is the hidden inwardness of religiousness, which in Climacus's view is inaccessible to comic apprehension precisely because it is hidden and cannot come into contradiction with anything outside itself (CUP, 1:522). From Climacus's standpoint, therefore, the religious stands higher than the comic, just as it is higher than humor, though the comic may legitimately be used by the

---

Howard A. Johnson and Niels Thulstrup, 102–15; Karsten Friis Johansen, "Kierkegaard on 'the Tragic,' " *Danish Yearbook of Philosophy* 13 (1976): 105–46; and Holler, "Kierkegaard's Concept of Tragedy in the Context of his Pseudonymous Works."

humorist against presumptuous forms of religiosity in which individuals view themselves on a comparative scale as being more religious than others (CUP, 1:462, 519–20, 523). In general, however, the rule for the comic is that "the lower can never make the higher comic" (CUP, 1:519); rather, just the opposite holds, namely, that it is the higher that makes the lower comic, for it is precisely by being able to assume a higher standpoint that a lower one is rendered comical and the contradiction at that level is canceled. Without such a higher standpoint, Climacus claims, a comic apprehension is illegitimate, for wherever a way out is not known or the contradiction is not annulled or corrected in something higher or the individual succumbs to despair, the comic is inappropriate (CUP, 1:520).

Since the religious has a higher standpoint than other levels of existence, even the comic, the religious individual more than anyone else will discover the comic, for "the more competently a person exists, the more he will discover the comic," Climacus claims (CUP, 1:462). If that does not happen, then the individual him- or herself becomes comical and loses the superiority of the religious standpoint. There is one contradiction, however, that is not canceled by the religious. This is the contradiction that the negative determinants (resignation, suffering, and guilt) of religious pathos in Religiousness A themselves signify, namely, the incommensurability between religious pathos and the absolute telos toward which it is directed. For while these determinants indirectly signify a positive relation to the eternal (and for that reason are not expressions of despair), they are at the same time negative expressions for the incompatibility or misrelation that exists between the individual and the eternal. Resignation forms the *initial* expression or religious pathos by establishing an absolute respect toward the eternal as one's absolute telos and by commencing the transformation of one's existence through a dying away from immediacy or attachment to selfish and worldly ends—an act that must be continually renewed, so that it seems no progress is ever made. Suffering forms the *essential* expression of religious pathos in that it signifies one's failure to make oneself over into conformity with the absolute telos or to find any satisfactory external expression for manifesting one's positive relation to the eternal. Guilt-consciousness forms the *decisive* expression for this pathetic situation, being an awareness of one's total incompatibility with or misrelation to one's absolute telos. Consciousness of this contradiction is further intensified in Religiousness B through the consciousness of sin, which posits a total breach, not merely an incompatibility, between existence and the eternal. However, a way out of this contradiction is projected in Christianity, or Religiousness B, through a relation to the deity or eternal in time. For here, it is claimed, the individual becomes "a new creature," and the possibility of eternal happiness is restored via a relation to the absolute paradox of the eternal in time. Thus, while Climacus seeks to restrict the concepts of the tragic and the comic, as existential categories, to the stages and boundary zones prior to and within religious inwardness, excluding the hidden inwardness of Religiousness A and B from accessibility to comic apprehension, it would seem that there is a legitimate comic dimension in Christianity, just as there would appear to be a place for humor in it. The appropriate comic apprehension in this instance is twofold: first, in relation to Religiousness A, whose contradiction is annulled by the recognition of an even deeper contradiction between the individual and the eternal in the consciousness of sin, and second, in relation to the consciousness of sin itself, which is paradoxically overcome in the forgiveness of sin and the rebirth of the Christian believer.

Although Johannes Climacus perhaps does not go far enough in recognizing a legitimate role of the comic in the sphere of the paradoxical religiousness of Christianity, the merit of his account lies in perceiving and delineating the essential roles that irony, humor, the tragic, and the comic play as existential determinants in the art of existing. In construing these aesthetic categories in existential terms, on the one hand, and in characterizing the subjective thinker and existential striving in aesthetic terms, on the other, Climacus works out a positive conception of the poetic in an existential context even as he is critical of poetry in those forms that abstract from existence. His perspective may thus be seen as standing in continuity with and providing a more developed formulation of the existential aesthetics that emerges in the first phase of Kierkegaard's writings. Far from simply advocating a move away from the poetic, then, *Concluding Unscientific Postscript* and other writings from the second, or middle, period of Kierkegaard's authorship may be seen as affirming and incorporating the poetic in an existential framework and as viewing existing itself as an art.

In light of the positive conception of the poetic that is sustained and further developed in these works, a final assessment may now be made of the negative criticisms of poetry that are evident in these and other works of the second phase, or middle period, of Kierkegaard's authorship. To recall these criticisms briefly, we have seen that poetry is charged with giving an untrue or inadequate representation of actuality, making it appear to be better than it is and thus presenting a deceptive and illusory picture of actuality; that as the medium of ideality and possibility, poetry is detached and disinterested in existence, the poetic product rather than the life of the poet being the most important thing; that poetry leads to self-abandonment in the ideality of the possible, taking us aesthetically away from actuality rather than leading us from possibility to actuality in the realm of the ethical; that poetry is a means of distancing life-relationships and avoiding ethical action; that poetry is undialectical and unparadoxical and thus unable to deal with internal contradictions or to unify the comic and the tragic elements that characterize the personal life; that in seeking to give visible and final external expression to its subject matter, poetry fails to recognize that there are realms of experience that are not conducive to external form and a final denouement; that poetry is unable to express repentance, which belongs to the realm of inwardness and is not conducive to representation in poetic form; and, finally, that poetry cannot explain life or, rather, explains it in a manner opposite from Christianity, thereby setting Christianity and the poetic in conflict with each other. To be sure, there are many examples of poetry to which these criticisms may be justly applied, especially if poetry is conceived in traditional form as external products of the creative imagination in the various media of the fine arts. But we have seen that it is possible, from the standpoint of Kierkegaard and his pseudonyms, to conceive the poetic in a different manner as an existential dimension or determinant of human life itself, not merely as external expressions or creations of the human spirit. We have seen that it is also possible, as demonstrated by Kierkegaard's own aesthetic writings as well as in the writings of others whose works are the subject of his literary criticism in this phase, to create external products of art that come close to reflecting actuality in an ethical-religious manner and that serve to direct us toward actuality rather than away from it in the realization of poetic ideality in our own lives. To see how Kierkegaard continues to employ the poetic to this end in his specifically religious writings, let us turn to the third and final phase in the development of the concept of the poetic in his writings.

8

Poet of the Religious

The third and final phase in the development of Kierkegaard's understanding of the poetic emerges in the journals and specifically religious writings of his later years. Described by some commentators as Kierkegaard's "second literature," these writings consist of a large group of titles that were penned and/or published between the years of 1849 and 1852, including *The Sickness unto Death* (1849), *Armed Neutrality* (1849), *Practice in Christianity* (1850), *For Self-Examination* (1851), and *Judge for Yourself!* (1851–52), as well as numerous religious discourses, newspaper articles, and a collection of pamphlets issued under the title *The Instant* (1855).[1] The majority of these works were published by Kierkegaard under his own name as author, but a few are still attributed to pseudonyms. Others were withheld from publication, for various reasons, and appeared in print only posthumously. In terms of form and content, the works constituting this considerable body of writings can be grouped generally into two categories: those designed to be edifying, instructive, or polemical concerning religious matters, and those intended to provide an explanation of the nature and purpose of the whole authorship from Kierkegaard's point of

1. On the designation of Kierkegaard's religious writings as his "second literature," see Elrod, *Kierkegaard and Christendom,* who credits Robert L. Perkins with the invention of this phrase (xi). For a complete list of Kierkegaard's works during this period as well as earlier, see Walter Lowrie, *Kierkegaard* (New York: Harper & Brothers, 1962), 2:605–18. An earlier version of this chapter appears under the title "Kierkegaard: Poet of the Religious," in *Kierkegaard on Art and Communication,* ed. George Pattison, 1–22.

view. Except for selected works such as *The Sickness unto Death* and *Practice in Christianity,* these writings may also be described as being, to a large extent, Kierkegaard's "forgotten literature," since they have been greatly understudied in comparison to his earlier pseudonymous literature. But if we are to arrive at a balanced and comprehensive understanding of his thought, these writings must also be taken into account. This is especially true with respect to Kierkegaard's views on the relation between the poetic and the religious, as some significant aspects of his thought on this subject come to the fore in the later literature and journals. For the most part, however, I examine these writings as a group rather than individually, since my objective here is primarily to illumine the essentially poetic nature of this literature as a whole.

KIERKEGAARD'S TASK AS A RELIGIOUS, OR CHRISTIAN, POET

Although negative remarks about poets and poetry can still be found in Kierkegaard's later writings,[2] it is clear from the journals of this period that Kierkegaard understood his role in writing the religious literature to be that of a poet, and the productions of these years to be a form of poet-communication. A survey of journal references to himself as a poet reveals that he identifies himself with this role far more frequently in this period than in earlier years.[3] Again and again he declares in the later journals that he is essentially a poet, and in several entries he describes himself more specifically as a "poet of the religious" and even more narrowly as a "Christian poet and thinker" (JP, 6:6511, 6521, 6391). On the surface, however, this observation seems to stand at odds with the characterization of the authorship put forward by Kierkegaard in *The*

2. See, for example, *The Lilies of the Field and the Birds of the Air: Three Godly Discourses* (discourses from 1849 published in English translation with *Christian Discourses*), where it is reiterated that the poet "cannot come to an understanding with the Gospel" and where the poet's life is seen as being one of despair (CD, 319–20). See also *The Instant,* where the poet is vilified as "the most dangerous" of men (AC, 201–2).

3. For a list of references to himself as a poet, consult the index to *Søren Kierkegaards Papirer,* vol. 14, under "Digter," 303–10. The references dating from the later period are far too many to list here, numbering ninety or more, whereas in only one entry prior to 1847 does he refer to himself as a poet (JP, 5:5748). In the early journals, references to the poet are in the third person and not directly about himself.

Point of View. There Kierkegaard divides his writings into two groups: the so-called aesthetic works of his early years and the religious works of the later period, with *Concluding Unscientific Postscript* being the point of transition between the two (PV, 22–43). Although his writings do fit rather neatly into such a grouping and classification, this way of construing the authorship makes it seem as if Kierkegaard began as a poet and later became a religious author, that he moved away from the poetic to the religious in accordance with the progression prescribed in *The Point of View* (PV, 74). But such a conclusion is precisely what Kierkegaard wishes to dispel in that work. Contrary to all outward appearances, Kierkegaard maintains in this accounting of the authorship that he was from the first a religious author, employing the aesthetic maieutically and dialectically (and thus in a sense deceptively) in service to the religious. This claim is supported by the publication of a number of edifying discourses parallel to the pseudonymous aesthetic works and issued under his own name as author. These provided, he contends, a clear testimony that he was a religious author from the beginning and betokened that the edifying is what should come to the fore: "I held out *Either/Or* to the world in my left hand, and in my right the *Two Edifying Discourses;* but all, or as good as all, grasped with their right what I held in my left" (PV, 20). Kierkegaard also explains that the little aesthetic book, *The Crisis and a Crisis in the Life of an Actress,* was issued along with the later religious writings as a sign that he was still aesthetically productive during this phase (PV, 14). Just as a religious intention was present in the early aesthetic writings, so too the aesthetic remained in the later religious works. Although Kierkegaard admits that he did not have from the beginning quite the clarity of aim and extent of design as suggested in *The Point of View* (PV, 72), his claim of a simultaneity of aesthetic and religious motivations in the authorship is substantiated not only by the continued production of explicitly aesthetic literature during this period but also by the poetic character of the religious writings themselves.[4]

In line with his general understanding of poetry as a medium for expressing ideality, Kierkegaard understands his task as a poet in the later writings to be that of bringing the religious ideals once again into view for his time. Believing that a radical "world-shift" had taken place, leaving his generation without a norm, he indicates in a journal entry of

4. For critical discussions of Kierkegaard's interpretation of his authorship in *The Point of View,* see Fenger, *Kierkegaard, the Myths and Their Origins,* 26–31, and Garff, "The Eyes of Argus."

1850 that the relation of human beings to the ideal needs to be redefined (JP, 2:1792). In light of this situation he goes on to conclude:

> Now there will be need for the presentation of the religious in poetic form. This is a step forward compared to what prevails now when meaninglessness and mediocrity actually have taken the place of the religious, so that the poet in the ordinary sense is even higher than the religious.
>
> In any case there no doubt must be something poetic in the religious domain, mainly just to get hold of existential ideals again and to encounter the existential ideals. (JP, 2:1792)

In contrast to contemporary pastors, who are authoritatively charged with proclaiming and expressing the religious ideals but instead relax the requirements and abolish the ideal, Kierkegaard sees religious poets such as himself as taking precedence. But they must have the ability to write in a way that will help people "out into the current" by creating a "pathos-filled impression of an existential expression of the ideal." The first and foremost task of the religious poet, then, is to create a "pathos for the existential" (JP, 6:6521).

In Kierkegaard's view, the highest existential ideality is to be a Christian. Thus, in his religious writings he is primarily concerned to portray, like an artist, the ideal picture of a Christian. But unlike an ordinary artist or poet, from whom Kirkegaard comes to distinguish himself in several respects, he sees his task as a religious poet to be one in which he merely describes (*fremstille*) the existential ideals, not imaginatively constructs (*experimentere*) them.[5] The religious ideals are already given or prescribed determinants for human existence, not possibilities created by the imagination of the poet. Moreover, as a Christian poet, Kierkegaard seeks to place the Christian ideals "into the situation of actuality" (AN, 36), not simply to present them, in the manner of an ordinary poet, as abstract possibilities or pure idealities. This means that the Christian existential determinants must be described dialectically on two levels, both in terms of their purely ideal definition and in terms of their highest or strictest expression in existence. Defined in purely ideal terms, the Christian life, as Kierkegaard sees it, is an entirely positive one, consisting of faith, hope, love, joy, forgiveness, consolation, new life, and blessedness. But in existence these positive determinants are coupled with and made recognizable through negative factors such as the conscious-

5. On this point, see also the previous chapter.

ness of sin, the possibility of offense, self-renunciation, and suffering. In existence, one does not come to have faith except through the consciousness of sin and the possibility of offense. Similarly, Christian love is expressed through self-renunciation, and joy is found in and through the strife of suffering in life.[6]

THE CHRISTIAN DIALECTIC OF INVERSION

In his journals Kierkegaard describes this positive-negative expression of Christianity as an "inverted dialectic" (*omvendt Dialektik*), or a "dialectic of inversion" (*Omvendthedens Dialektik*).[7] The formula of this dialectic is first stated in *Concluding Unscientific Postscript,* where it is seen as governing the religious sphere in general: "The religious continually uses the negative as the essential form. . . . The negative is not once and for all and then the positive, but the positive is continually in the negative, and the negative is the distinctive mark" (CUP, 1:524; see also 1:432, 532). In the later literature and journals Kierkegaard associates this dialectical formula specifically with Christianity and views it as the form by which every Christian determinant is expressed in existence. In his journals he states that "the formula for the Christian is: the Christian is always the positive, which is recognized by the negative" (JP, 1:760). Inversion is also seen as characteristic of Socrates, but in a qualitatively lower form than in Christianity, which in his view has "a developed philosophy of inversion" (JP, 4:4289).

In this inverted dialectic the Christian understanding of what constitutes the positive and the negative is seen to be diametrically opposite to that of an immediate, natural, merely human, pagan, or worldly understanding of these terms. What the world regards as positive, the Christian views as negative, and vice versa: what appears as negative to the natural understanding is seen as indirectly positive by the Christian. In his religious writings Kierkegaard devotes a number of discourses to the elucidation of this inversion, contrasting the Christian conception of poverty and wealth, lowliness and highness, weakness and strength, loss and gain,

6. For a fuller discussion of the nature and relation of these positive and negative determinants in Christian existence, see Sylvia Walsh Utterback, "Kierkegaard's Dialectic of Christian Existence" (Ph.D. diss., Emory University, 1975).

7. See JP, 1:760; 4:4680, 4782; 5:5997. See also 3:2525, 3329, 3349; 4:4666, 4696. For a more developed discussion of this form of dialectic in Kierkegaard's thought, see Sylvia Walsh Utterback, "Kierkegaard's Inverse Dialectic," *Kierkegaardiana* 11 (1980): 34–54.

misfortune and good fortune, to the worldly understanding of these conditions (CD, parts 1 and 2). In his view, the Christian is called upon to exercise "duplex thought" and "duplex vision," paradoxically seeing exaltation in lowliness, strength in weakness, and so forth (CD, 56; PC, 196; JP, 3:3664).

The process of reduplication or actualization of the Christian ideality in existence is also qualified by this dialectic of inversion. Instead of striving to express the positive determinants of Christian existence in a direct manner, the Christian procedure takes the form of an indirect, inverted dialectical movement in which one "works against oneself" (JP, 3:3661; JP, 6:6593; PV, 147n). Rather than striving directly to gain exaltation, for example, the Christian strives toward it by becoming lowly in the eyes of the world. From an ordinary human standpoint, Christian striving thus results in the opposite of the effect or condition desired. But from a Christian perspective, one works against one's goal only in the sense that one goes about achieving it in a manner opposite to what is commonly recommended and done. The consequence of this inverted procedure is that one brings upon oneself "double danger," or opposition from the world corresponding to the degree to which one succeeds in actualizing the Christian ideals (WL, 84, 86, 90–91, 186–89). Thus, the more one becomes a Christian, the worse it will go for one in the world, and the less one will appear to be achieving or embodying that for which one strives.

This dialectic of inversion is central to Kierkegaard's view of Christianity and to his polemic against the state church unleashed in his later literature. Kierkegaard's main critique of Christendom is that it has collapsed the Christian dialectic, viewing Christian existence directly and superficially in terms of the positive while virtually eliminating the negative factors that are essential to becoming a Christian. As a corrective to this one-dimensional perspective, he seeks to reintroduce the negative determinants through which the positive qualities of Christian existence should be expressed and recognized (FSE, 24). Being a poet unusually proficient in both dialectic and imagination, Kierkegaard claims to be peculiarly qualified for this task. Without modesty he asserts of himself, "I know with uncommon clarity and definiteness what Christianity is, what can be required of the Christian, what it means to be a Christian. To an unusual degree I have, I believe, the qualifications to portray this" (AN, 42). Aided by an imagination that in his case is not immediate but rather follows after reflection or the dialectical, Kierkegaard thinks that he can "grasp all the Christian qualifications in the most faithful and vital way" (JP, 5:6061).

THE ROLE OF IMAGINATION

In describing the Christian ideal existentially in terms of the dialectic of inversion described above, Kierkegaard seeks to mitigate as much as possible the gap between ideality and actuality that inherently obtains in poetry. One of the chief reservations about poetry expressed in the second phase of the authorship, we may recall, is that it does not give an adequate or true representation of actuality. This criticism is reiterated in the later religious literature—for example, in *Practice in Christianity*—where imagination is seen as constructing a picture of perfection that is remote from actuality in its inability to portray the suffering of actuality or the actuality of suffering except as something already completed and thus perfected, idealized, softened or toned down, and foreshortened (PC, 185–88). Imagination is thus likened to an "actor dressed in rags," which is totally different from being clad in rags in the everyday life of actuality (PC, 188). This viewpoint is graphically illustrated in a journal entry of 1850 concerning the illusory representation of Christianity in the medium of imagination.

> Take a stick. You hold it in your hand, and it is straight. Thrust it into the water and it looks broken. You pick it up again and say, "Yes, but good lord, it is still straight"—but please thrust it into the water again, and it will appear broken.
>
> This is the way rhetoricians and their ilk present Christianity. They take it out of the medium of actuality (they do not express it existentially), and therefore Christianity looks completely different than it truly is—please venture it existentially in the realm of actuality, and you will see that it looks completely different, that exaltation becomes abasement, etc. (JP, 2:1828)

To have Christianity only in the form of imagination is not to have it (JP, 2:1829), or even to have a true picture of its perfection, since that, Kierkegaard claims, involves continuous daily trials of actual suffering in the realm of actuality (PC, 186–87). Thus, even though as a religious poet Kierkegaard comes closer to depicting the Christian ideality under the conditions of actuality than the usual poet does, actual reduplication of the Christian qualifications or determinants in existence is still required. Without that, Christianity is merely mythology or poetry:

> Anyone whose life [*Leven*], whose existence [*Existeren*], is not characterized by the existence-form defined in the New Testa-

> ment thereby expresses—regardless of what his mouth babbles, declaims, assures—that for him Christianity is mythology, poetry.
>
> The existential is the characteristic that distinguishes between poetry and mythology—and Christianity. Indeed, the reason Christ proclaimed Christianity is discipleship or imitation [*Efterfølgelse*] was to prevent a merely imaginary relationship to the essentially Christian. (JP, 3:2805)

Imagination nevertheless plays an important role in bringing us to the point of reduplication in existence. As late as 1854, Kierkegaard observes in a journal entry:

> Imagination is what providence uses to take men captive in actuality [*Virkeligheden*], in existence [*Tilvaerelsen*], in order to get them far enough out, or within, or down into actuality. And when imagination has helped them get as far out as they should be—then actuality genuinely begins. (JP, 2:1832)

This positive role of imagination in luring us into actuality is described in some detail in *The Sickness unto Death*, where Kierkegaard's pseudonymous author Anti-Climacus examines it in relation to the task of becoming a self.[8] Being defined in part as a synthesis of the finite and the infinite, the self becomes itself, Anti-Climacus maintains, through "an infinite moving away from itself in the infinitizing of the self, and infinite coming back to itself in the finitizing process" (SUD, 30). In his view, imagination is the medium for the process of infinitizing in this dual movement. It is that by which the self reflects itself, that is, projects the possibility of itself to itself. In this sense, Anti-Climacus claims, imagination is identical to reflection and constitutes "the possibility of any and all reflection" by the self (SUD, 31).[9] In fact, imagination is so fundamental to the constitution of the self, he believes, that it should not be regarded as "a capacity" among others such as feeling, knowing, and

8. Cf. *Practice in Christianity*, where, in spite of Kierkegaard's criticism of imagination in this work, he sees the picture of perfection it renders deceiving us into truth by captivating and drawing us further and further into actuality and suffering in the desire to resemble the picture (PC, 188–90).

9. In advancing this understanding of reflection, Kierkegaard, or Anti-Climacus, appropriates the Augustinian-Cartesian concept of reflection as self-reflection, or self-mirroring. For a philosophical exposition of this concept of reflection and the history of its development in modern philosophy, for example, Hegel, see Rodolphe Gasché, *The Tain of the Mirror: Derrida and the Philosophy of Reflection* (Cambridge: Harvard University Press, 1986), 1–78.

willing, but as "the capacity *instar omnium*"—the capacity for all capacities (SUD, 30–31).[10] "When all is said and done," Anti-Climacus concludes, "whatever of feeling, knowing, and willing a person has depends upon what imagination he has" (SUD, 31). Whereas the young Kierkegaard in his dissertation had criticized German romanticism and the earlier Fichte for their views of the self-constructing, ruling power of the ego through imagination (CI, 290–93; 308n), now under the guise of a pseudonym he agrees with Fichte's fundamental position, following Kant's *Critique of Judgment,* that the basic categories of knowledge are derived from the imagination (SUD, 31).[11] However, Kierkegaard draws an important distinction between the imagination (*Phantasien*) and the fantastic (*det Phantastiske*), which continues to set his view of the imagination apart from the romantic tradition as he had earlier characterized it.

In *The Concept of Irony* the primary representative of romanticism whom Kierkegaard criticizes is Friedrich Schlegel, who in his *Dialogue of Poetry* defines the romantic as presenting "a sentimental theme in a fantastic form."[12] Although the fantastic is seen as closely related to the imagination in *The Sickness unto Death,* in the view of Anti-Climacus it generally leads us in the opposite direction from imagination—that is, away from ourselves rather than to ourselves—in an abstract kind of infinitizing that prevents the dialectical movement of returning to ourselves in finitude from taking place (SUD, 31). To become itself, the self must become concrete, which is to realize in existence a synthesis of the finite and the infinite, not merely one or the other of these dimensions. In fantasy, the self does not become itself but rather loses itself in infinitude, gradually becoming volatilized in an inhuman state of abstraction. In relation to the imagination, then, one might describe the fantastic as imagination gone astray or imagination gone wild, intoxicated, without recognition of any limiting factor or any necessity to relate itself to the realm of actuality. When the imagination or a capacity dependent upon it becomes fantastic in this manner, the self can be said to be in despair, the despair of infinitude, which is to lack finitude. Although Anti-Climacus does not explicitly draw a parallel here, this form of despair corresponds to the romantic poet's tendency to take flight into the infinite with an ironic stance toward actuality. Thus the central role Kierkegaard now

10. On the importance of imagination, in Kierkegaard's thought, as the fundamental capacity in human existence, see Gouwens, *Kierkegaard's Dialectic of the Imagination.*

11. On the importance of imagination in Kant and Fichte and the influence of the former upon the latter, see Kearney, *The Wake of Imagination,* 155–88.

12. Friedrich Schlegel, *Dialogue on Poetry,* 98.

envisions for imagination in the process of becoming a self differs significantly from the way it functions in romanticism, where the imagination, according to Kierkegaard's earlier analysis, becomes fantastic and the self is in despair.

Although one may fall into despair by exercising imagination in a fantastic fashion, to be deficient in imagination, and hence to lack infinitude, also constitutes a form of despair, the despair of finitude. In Anti-Climacus's opinion, this form of despair is characteristic of the secular mentality of his day in its narrow, limited conception of self-identity in terms of a mass society where one is a number, just one more copy of the others, rather than a unique self. Here the self loses itself by taking the prudent course of not venturing beyond a cozy life in finitude. Finding it easier and safer to be like others, it becomes absorbed in pursuing temporal goals that promise success in the world. As the medium of infinitizing, imagination is needed for the expansion of the self beyond finite horizons and for the differentiation of the self from others. It is thus a crucial capacity in the constitution of the self.

THE CATEGORY OF POSSIBILITY

Another aesthetic, or poetic, element closely related to imagination that receives emphasis in the final phase of Kierkegaard's authorship is the category of possibility. Throughout Kierkegaard's authorship, especially in the initial phase of it, primary emphasis is given to actuality as that to which one must properly relate oneself and that which one must realize, although this is accomplished in part by also sustaining a proper relation to possibility. One of the limitations of poetry is that it is concerned only with ideality and possibility and thus may lead one away from actuality. In *The Sickness unto Death,* however, the claim is made that both possibility and necessity (the given actuality or limitations of the self), like finitude and infinitude, are "equally essential" in the task of becoming a self (SUD, 35). Actuality is defined as the unity of possibility and necessity, and the self is seen in part as a synthesis of possibility (freedom) and necessity (limitation). Just as the self in despair can lose itself in infinitude, it can also run away from itself in possibility, so that it lacks necessity and becomes unreal in the illusion that everything is possible—a circumstance described earlier in *The Concept of Irony* as characteristic of romanticism (CI, 282). As elaborated in *The Sickness unto Death,* this situation is one in which "more and more becomes possible because nothing becomes actual." Rather than take time to actualize some of the possibilities manifested before it, the self becomes more and more intensively absorbed in them until finally it becomes "a mirage," unrecognizable to itself even in the mirror of possibility where it has become fantastically reflected (SUD, 36).

Possibility is nevertheless regarded by Anti-Climacus as "the ever infallible antidote for despair" and "the only salvation" of a person in that it constitutes the condition of faith (SUD, 38–39). As Anti-Climacus sees it, everything *is* possible, just as the romantics proclaimed, but only in the sense that *for God* or *with God* everything is possible. Whether one will believe that is the decisive question of faith. But faith, noetically equated here with belief, is dialectically defined in relation to this question. Faith comes to expression in the will to believe. But what one is asked to believe is that all things are possible for God—more specifically, that forgiveness is possible—precisely at that point when one is brought to the utmost extremity where, from a human standpoint, there seems to be *no* possibility. In a sense, faith is understood here as the inverse of human understanding and expectation, but it also incorporates that understanding as a dialectical factor in itself. That is, faith is not merely to believe, but to believe against the understanding. Whether one will believe that for God everything is possible, Anti-Climacus maintains, "is the very formula for losing the understanding; to believe is indeed to lose the understanding in order to gain God" (SUD, 38). Faith, then, is to fight for possibility, to have the will to believe in possibility, even though possibility seems impossible. One does not believe rightly or have a grasp of what is implied in a belief in possibility unless a sense of the impossibility of possibility is contained in that belief.

In accordance with the two-leveled conception of the Christian determinants advanced in Kierkegaard's specifically religious writings, this understanding of faith in terms of a dialectical procurement of possibility constitutes an existential, as opposed to a purely ideal, definition of faith. That is, it is a definition of faith as expressed in the process of striving toward selfhood in existence. Ideally defined, faith is that condition of the self in which despair is completely eradicated and the self in willing to be itself is grounded transparently in God. But in existence, faith is defined in relation to the negative and assumes a dialectical character, incorporating in its definition the element of negativity in the form of an antithesis to human understanding.[13]

13. On the definition of faith in terms of possibility, see my article, "Kierkegaard's Inverse Dialectic," 44.

A second way in which possibility figures importantly in Kierkegaard's understanding in the final phase of his authorship is in the virtual identification of possibility with God. Following through with what to him is the logical implication of his thought, Anti-Climacus asserts in *The Sickness unto Death* that "since everything is possible for God, then God is this—that everything is possible." This claim is put forth in the context of a discussion of the determinist, or fatalist, for whom everything is necessary and who consequently is in despair because of a lack of possibility. Likening personhood, which is a synthesis of possibility and necessity, to breathing, which involves inhaling and exhaling, Anti-Climacus describes the fatalist as an individual who cannot breathe, because that person has only necessity. Since only one of the conditions needed for respiration, or selfhood, is present, the fatalist has lost both self and God and is unable to pray. Praying is also likened to breathing by Anti-Climacus in that it requires both possibility and necessity, just as breathing needs both oxygen and nitrogen. "Possibility is for the self what oxygen is for breathing," Anti-Climacus goes on to complete the analogy (SUD, 40). Elaborating further on the importance of possibility, he says:

> In order to pray there must be a God, a self—and possibility, or a self and possibility in a pregnant sense, for God is that everything is possible or that everything is possible is God [*thi Gud er det at Alt er muligt, eller at Alt er muligt, er Gud*]; and only the person whose being has been so shaken that he became spirit by understanding that everything is possible, only he has anything to do with God. That God's will is the possible makes me able to pray; if it is merely the necessary, humanity is essentially as dumb as the animals.[14]

This is a remarkable passage that in its association of God with possibility offers an intriguing insight and basis for conceptualizing the divine in a poetic perspective. In fact, in a journal entry of 1854, Kierkegaard moves in just such a direction as he muses on God's role as creator.

> My thought is that God is like a poet. This is why he puts up with evil and all the nonsense and wretchedness and mediocrity of

14. My translation. See SV, 11:153, for the Danish text. In my opinion the older English translation of *The Sickness unto Death* by Walter Lowrie (Princeton: Princeton University Press, 1968) renders a more precise translation of the text quoted here than does the newer one by Howard and Edna Hong. My translation is close to Lowrie's but uses more gender-inclusive terminology.

> triviality, etc. The poet is related in the same way to his poetic productions (also called his creations). But just as it is a mistake to think that what a particular character in a poem says or does represents the poet's personal opinion, so it is a mistake to assume that God consents to all that happens and how. O, no. He has his own view of things. But poetically he permits everything possible to come forth; he himself is present everywhere, observing, still a poet, in a sense poetically impersonal, equally attentive to everything, and in another sense personal, establishing the most terrible distinctions—such as between good and evil, between willing according to his will and not willing according to his will, and so on.
>
> The Hegelian rubbish that the actual is the true [the identity of being and thought] is just like the confusion of thrusting the words and actions of the dramatic characters upon the poet as his own words and actions.
>
> But it must be kept clear, if I may put it this way, that God's wanting to work as a poet in this fashion is not a diversion, as the pagans thought—no, no, the earnestness lies in God's passion to love and to be loved, yes, almost as if he were himself found in this passion, O, infinite love, so that in the power of this passion he cannot stop loving, almost as if it were a weakness, although it is rather his strength, his omnipotent love. This is the measure of his unswerving love. (JP, 2:1445)

We cannot explore here the implications of this passage for Christian theology, but it provides a suggestive metaphor for the development of a theopoetics in which creation, like the poetic productions of the poet, may be understood in aesthetic terms as a work of art by God, in and through whom everything is possible.[15] Another striking feature of the passage is the way in which God is envisioned as a poet of love and

15. In distinguishing between God the poet and the world as a poetic production, Kierkegaard directs his comments against Hegel, but Schelling is also subject to attack on this score, especially since he too exploits the image of the objective world as a work of art in his aesthetics; only for him nature constitutes an unconscious "poetry of the spirit" that becomes conscious in human works of art. See Friedrich Wilhelm Joseph von Schelling, *System des transzendentalen Idealismus,* in *Werke,* ed. Manfred Schröter (Munich: Beck, 1956–60), 2:349. See also Megill, *Prophets of Extremity,* 16, and Kearney, *The Wake of Imagination,* 177–81. As Megill points out, Nietzsche also sees the world as a work of art, but in an "aesthetically self-creating" manner, not as a product of the divine. On the artistic character of the world in Nietzsche, see also Nehamas, *Nietzsche: Life as Literature.*

passion whose very essence is love. If God is possibility for Kierkegaard, so too God is love and love is God for him (WL, 124, 247, 335).[16]

Another consequence of Kierkegaard's identification of God with possibility is that it has the effect of infinitely expanding human potentiality and selfhood. In part 2 of *The Sickness unto Death,* Anti-Climacus brings this out in a distinction he makes between "the human self," whose criterion is the highest on a purely human scale, and "the theological self," whose criterion is God (SUD, 79). By becoming conscious of existing before God, the self gains an "infinite reality" that functions as its "qualitative criterion" (*Maalestok*) and ethical goal (*Maal*); together, these define what the self is—subject to the possibility of freedom not to become that which it essentially is. If God, the measure and goal of selfhood, is infinite possibility, then the self has the potentiality and responsibility to be that too.

CHRIST AS PROTOTYPE

But who can measure up to such a standard? Who can realize all that is required by Christian ideality? Even as a young man Kierkegaard recognized that we are generally no more than caricatures in relation to our ideals, that most people do not achieve the great and extraordinary ideals they project for themselves (JP, 5:5947). This perception becomes intensified in his later years. "No human being is sheer ideality or the ideal," he readily admits in a journal entry of 1848 (JP, 1:964). Only one person—Jesus Christ—has fully expressed the ideal in his life, but he is the God-man, not a mere man. However, since Christ is the incarnation of God, he constitutes the measure of human selfhood. In *The Sickness unto Death* Anti-Climacus states:

> A self directly before Christ is a self intensified by the inordinate concession from God, intensified by the inordinate accent that falls upon it because God allowed himself to be born, become [a human being], suffer, and die also for the sake of this self. As stated previously, the greater the conception of God, the more self; so it holds true here: the greater the conception of Christ,

16. On Kierkegaard's view of God as love, see my article "Forming the Heart: The Role of Love in Kierkegaard's Thought," 234–56, including references to other studies of love in his thought.

> the more self. Qualitatively a self is what its criterion is. That Christ is the criterion is the expression, attested by God, for the staggering reality that a self has, for only in Christ is it true that God is [humanity's] goal and criterion, or the criterion and goal. (SUD, 113–14)

Christ serves as the criterion and goal for human existence by being a model for imitation (*Efterfølgelse*).[17] In this he may be viewed as the equivalent, in a Christian perspective, to the Universal Forms that serve as a standard for poetic imitation in a Platonic view of art and reality. A similarity between the Christian and the Platonic may also be seen in that both perspectives regard imitation as imperfect in relation to the ideal model or standard. In Kierkegaard's view, the relation to the Christian ideality through imitation of Christ as paradigm is a complex, dialectical one characterized by inversion and a need for reliance on Christ as redeemer. In contrast to the medieval conception of the imitation of Christ, which in Kierkegaard's view held up Christ literally and directly as a prototype for humanity and assumed that we could actually achieve the ideal of resembling him, Kierkegaard maintains that the primary function of the prototype is to teach us how greatly we are in need of grace (JP, 2:1432, 1857, 1922; JFY, 193). Labeling the medieval view a youthful, even childish, naïve, and unrealistic conception of human ability, Kierkegaard suggests that the more "mature" we become religiously, the more we will feel how infinitely far we are from resembling the ideal and how qualitatively different the prototype is from the merely human. Then we do not dare to attempt to resemble it directly but become humbled by the ideal. It is just at this point that the role of Christ alternates to that of redeemer, offering grace for our imperfect striving: "When we are striving, then he is the prototype, and when we stumble, lose courage, etc., then he is the love which helps us up, and then he is the prototype again" (JP, 1:334; cf. 349 and 692 and 2:1863).

In Kierkegaard's understanding, then, Christ *is* the prototype for human existence, but not simply or directly a prototype. Insofar as he is humanity's redeemer, he is not in this respect an object for imitation at all. Moreover, in his fulfillment of the ideal, Christ stands at such an infinite distance from all human striving that all direct efforts at resem-

17. On Kierkegaard's view of the imitation of Christ, see Bradley R. Dewey, *The New Obedience: Kierkegaard on Imitating Christ* (Washington, D.C.: Corpus Books, 1968), and Marie Mikulová Thulstrup, "Efterfølgelsens dialektik hos Søren Kierkegaard," *Dansk teologisk Tidskrift* 21 (1958): 193–209.

blance fall infinitely short and are reduced to nothing. Effort toward reduplication of the Christian ideality through likeness to him thus once again has the consequence of working against oneself: the more one strives, the further from being like Christ one seems to oneself. And the more aware one becomes of Christ's heterogeneity, the more one must come to affirm and rely on grace rather than on one's own efforts. From a Christian standpoint, then, reduplication or imitation does not signify in the first instance the achievement of likeness to Christ but a growing realization of one's unlikeness to him. Only through Christ's help can we come to resemble him, but in order to reach the point where we realize our need for help, want it, and are willing to accept it, we must acquire a sense of our impotence and nothingness before God. This is what Christ as the prototype in the first instance is intended to accomplish. Imitation is thus used dialectically in Christianity to train us in the need for grace, so that we may learn to flee to it in faith and not use it in vain (JP, 2:1785, 1905, 1906; 1:692). The prototype represents the ideal for us, not as something we can directly or realistically expect to fulfill on our own but as that which we cannot fulfill. If Christ did not appear then in his other form as a savior, he would, as prototype, fall on us crushingly, requiring something we cannot become (JFY, 153). Thus, as Kierkegaard sees it, Christ never appears simply as the prototype but incorporates with this the grace whereby real imitation is made possible. For the gift of grace does not mean that imitation is thereby dispensed with; no, Kierkegaard says, "the prototype remains with his demand that there be a striving to be like him" (JP, 2:1432). The requirement of imitation is reintroduced after grace, but as an expression of gratitude rather than as a matter of law or works righteousness. As the prototype, Christ belongs to the proclamation of the law and even raises it to a higher level in requiring humanity to be like him. Because Christ fulfills the law, he can require the absolute of humanity. But by fulfilling the law, he also destroys it. By presenting himself as the prototype, he ransoms human beings from the law by causing them to flee to grace in an awareness of their inability to fulfill the law by their own efforts. Far from exempting them from striving, however, grace requires renewed earnestness in striving, which quickly leads once again to a need for grace: "Soon or immediately this striving, too, comes to need grace—and again grace—because after having received grace it is so imperfect" (JP, 2:1482; cf. 1472). Insofar as every person continually falls short of the ideal in striving, the dialectical alternation of Christ between the roles of prototype and redeemer is continually necessitated.

The effect of this dialectical process is a continually deepening understanding of our distance from the ideal and of our need for grace. Kierkegaard understands Christian striving not as a gradual achievement of perfection but inversely as a deepening recognition of the imperfection of our striving: "Every step forward toward the ideal is a backward step, for the progress consists precisely in my discovering increasingly the perfection of the ideal—and consequently my greater distance from it" (JP, 2:1789). If we are actually striving, however, from a Christian standpoint the emphasis falls not so much on actually fulfilling the ideal as on getting an impression of the requirement in all its infinitude, so that we are humbled by it and learn to rely on grace (JP, 1:993).

THE POET WHO FLIES TO GRACE

It is on the basis of this view of Christianity that Kierkegaard comes in his final years to understand his role as a Christian poet and to distinguish himself as a religious poet from the ordinary poet. While he fully understands that the existential task is to actualize the ideal rather than poetically to represent it, he believes that he has received permission from God to present the Christian ideal poetically in order to occasion, if possible, a "poetic awakening" in his readers (JP, 6:6337, 6528, 6727). Painfully conscious of his own falling short of the Christian ideality that he undertakes to present, however, he describes himself in his journal as "a poet who flies to grace" (PAP, X^6 B 215, pp. 340–41), and in *Armed Neutrality* he states:

> The one who presents this ideal must be the very first one to humble himself under it, and even though he himself is striving within himself to approach this ideal, he must confess that he is very far from being it. He must confess that he is related only poetically to this ideal picture or *qua* poet to the *presentation* of this picture, while he (and here he differs from the ordinary conception of a poet) personally and Christianly is related to the *presented* picture, and that only as a poet presenting the picture is he out in front. (AN, 37)

In another passage from the same work he says of himself, "I myself am brought to a halt by the ideal—not as if I had grasped it, not as if I were it, for I am so far from it that in a whole lifetime I very likely shall not finish the task of properly discovering and rightly presenting the ideal"

(AN, 38–39). In the journals of this period he repeatedly describes himself as a "penitent" in his own personal religious life (JP, 6:6195, 6206, 6261, 6317, 6325, 6327, 6364) and in a religious order of rank puts himself at the lowest level (PAP, X^5 B 153).

To underscore the fact that he is not the ideal he presumes to depict or an apostle or an extraordinary Christian who can authoritatively present it, Kierkegaard publishes two works of this period, *The Sickness unto Death* and *Practice in Christianity,* under the pseudonym Anti-Climacus, who is a Christian in a strict sense and thus qualified to present the requirements of the ideal. The invention of this pseudonym enables Kierkegaard to justify these writings as a form of ethical-religious communication and at the same time to see them for what they are, a kind of "poet-communication" (JP, 6:6528). From an ethical-religious standpoint, one may not communicate more than what one's own life conforms to (AN, 92; JP, 6:6528). If one seeks to communicate something higher, therefore, it must be made clear that the presentation is a poetic one. Kierkegaard thinks that can be done in either of two ways: by a statement on the part of the speaker indicating that the communication, although true, is poetic by virtue of the fact that he or she is saying it; or by the use of a pseudonym who can pose as a representative of the position being set forth (JP, 6:6528). Many times in his earlier aesthetic writings Kierkegaard had adopted a pseudonym for this purpose, but they always represented an existential position lower than his own. To him, Anti-Climacus represents a position so much higher than his own that he must stand related to it as a striver no less than others.

It is through the working out of this understanding of poetic communication that Kierkegaard comes finally to distinguish himself as a religious poet from the typical poet and to view his later religious writings as a form of poetry. To be a poet means that one has "one's own personal life, one's actuality, in categories completely different from those of one's poetical production," he candidly admits (JP, 6:6300); and in this respect Kierkegaard sees himself as being like other poets. But he also differs from them in several respects, which may be summed up as follows from the preceding discussion. First, he sees his poetic task as one of merely describing, not imaginatively constructing, the religious ideals. Second, unlike the usual poet, he is able to bring to bear a dialectical as well as imaginative understanding of the ideal. Third, he sees his task as providing an existential, rather than a purely poetic, portrayal of the Christian ideal. Fourth, he "is ethically aware that the task is not to poetize the ideal but to be like it" (JP, 6:6632). Fifth and finally, he does not merely present the ideal, like the ordinary poet, but is personally engaged in striving toward it (JP, 1:817; 6:6528). Without that, he believes, the poetic communication of the ethical-religious ideal is untrue. "It is a terrible thing for the requirements of the ideal to be presented by persons who never give a thought to whether their lives express it or not," he writes in his journal (JP, 6:6528). In this respect Kierkegaard sees himself as being much further along than the poet in general. As a poet who flies to grace, however, his own existential position is perhaps best portrayed in the dozen "penitential addresses," or "Discourses at the Communion on Fridays," that bring his authorship to its point of concentration and culmination in the confession and forgiveness of sin.[18] In the preface to the last of these, published in 1851, Kierkegaard states:

> A gradually progressing work as a writer which had its beginning in *Either/Or* seeks here its definite point of rest at the foot of the altar, where the author, who personally knows best his imperfection and guilt, does not by any means call himself a witness for the truth, but only a peculiar sort of poet and thinker who, "without authority," has nothing new to bring but would read the fundamental document of the individual, humane existence-relationship, the old, well-known, from the fathers handed down—would read it through yet once again, if possible in a more heartfelt way.[19]

In these heartfelt discourses we see Kierkegaard as a religious poet in the truest sense, both depicting the religious ideal and relating himself to it in an existential manner by humbling himself before God in the confession of sin and in the assurance of forgiveness in grace and love. As a form of religious poetry, however, they depict the situation of confession and forgiveness to which every Christian striver must continually return. Thus they are primarily intended to give *us* pause on the way to the altar, enabling us through the voice of the speaker to make our own confessions before God in secret (CD, 277). For Kierkegaard, I think, this is the

18. Seven of these discourses comprise part 4 of *Christian Discourses,* published in 1848, and three discourses published in 1849 appear with the current English edition of that work. Two more discourses published in 1851 are included in *For Self-Examination and Judge for Yourselves! and Three Discourses 1851,* tr. Walter Lowrie (Princeton: Princeton University Press, 1968).

19. *For Self-Examination and Judge for Yourselves! and Three Discourses 1851,* 5.

ultimate task and goal of the religious poet, and in that role he has served and continues to serve us well. Not only is his religious poetry eloquent and deeply heartfelt in the passion with which it presents the religious ideals, it also expresses those ideals in uncompromising and disquieting ways that prevent us, if we are honest, from appropriating them lightly or in vain.

Epilogue: Living Poetically in the Present Age

The notion of living poetically, as shown in previous chapters, is one that Kierkegaard first encountered in German romanticism and subsequently appropriated in his own early writings, giving an alternative meaning to the concept by construing it in an ethical-religious, or Christian, manner. Although the phrase "living poetically" later drops out of Kierkegaard's writings, the content of the concept of living poetically in an ethical-religious manner is sustained and further developed in the authorship in a number of ways. Central to that concept is the task of becoming oneself by relating oneself to an inward infinity in self-enjoyment, which constitutes the truly poetic and aesthetic. This idea receives further development in the authorship in the notion of inwardness, or earnestness toward life, understood as a process of infinite striving for wholeness, integration, and unity of the personality in all its dimensions, including the aesthetic and poetic as essential elements in the constitution of the self. An emphasis upon striving toward a goal in life, with the achievement of self-clarity, or transparency in the actualization of the self, as the substance of that goal, runs throughout the authorship, culminating where it began in a Christian understanding of the self that is formed through the grace of, and in cooperation with, the divine. Determined as spirit, or freedom, the self continually becomes and does not become itself in a process of infinite striving that repeatedly must pause for rest at the foot of the altar in the confession of sin and hope for forgiveness.

Even though this self-formation is a task that is never actually completed in the process of striving and has the infinity of the divine incarnated in Jesus Christ as its criterion and goal, it is essential from Kierkegaard's point of view that human striving not be aimless and abstract but rather informed by an ideal of wholeness that constitutes the self as a concrete actuality. Otherwise human existence remains fragmented even in its conception and lacks the synthesizing activity that provides unity and continuity as well as concreteness along the way.

From Kierkegaard's point of view it is also important that human striving be understood as a process of self-development rather than self-creation, with an appreciation of the given actuality and its potentialities, whether these be immediately implanted within us or acquired through a conscious relation to the divine. Even though the self is defined as spirit, or freedom, we do not create ourselves but rather in freedom develop or fail to develop that which we actually are and potentially can be. Along with an emphasis on self-development, we have noted too the continuing importance in Kierkegaard's thought of forming a positive life-view, or affirmative attitude, toward actuality as a means of understanding life artistically in terms of a totality that affirms every moment as an integral part of the whole. Equally important for becoming a self is the sustaining of a proper relation to possibility, which in Kierkegaard's view is a poetic feature that is virtually identified with God. When possibility is understood as having its source in the divine, then the infinity or possibility open to the self is not determined quantitatively in a multiplicity of roles as in a romantic mode of living poetically but rather qualitatively in terms of those characteristics such as love, faithfulness, and long-suffering that mark the presence of the eternal in human beings. Also essential to the development of a genuinely artistic or poetic life are the aesthetic elements of existential irony, humor in the form of holy jest, and a sense of the comic as well as tragic character of life—elements that give expression to the continuing contradiction between the actual and the ideal, the inner and the outer in the process of striving.

This mode of living poetically is one that, in Kierkegaard's view, is not elitist but a possibility and requirement for every human being, a mode that gives meaning and depth to our everyday life. If he is right, then it is incumbent upon us in concluding this investigation to consider at least briefly what it might mean to live poetically in an authentic fashion from a Kierkegaardian point of view in the context of the present age. As we have seen, Kierkegaard's thought was developed to a large extent in response to, and as a critique of, the prevailing literary, philosophical, social, and religious movements of his own time. In previous chapters I have noted how Kierkegaard both directly and indirectly subjects these movements to criticism, revealing the ironic negativity, isolation, anxiety and despair, lack of passion, aimless becoming, and bourgeois aestheticism he believed to be characteristic of his age. To a considerable extent, and perhaps in some instances to an even greater degree, these same conditions may be said to characterize the twentieth century as well. I cannot at this point enter into a full-scale analysis of these tendencies in the present age, but I do want to call attention to a cluster of issues that, in my view, contain some important implications for the project of living poetically in the present age. These issues have to do with the emerging attitude toward self-identity, gender differences, and the relation to the other in the recent movement that calls itself "postmodernism" or "deconstruction."[1]

Although some postmodern thinkers like to claim Kierkegaard as a precursor of their philosophies of difference, his thought constitutes in some fundamental ways a critique of postmodernism as well as of the Hegelian and early German romantic philosophies of the modern era.[2] Deconstruction in particular bears a close resemblance to the early German romantic mode of living poetically, as characterized by Kierkegaard, in the assertion of an endless process of experimentation and play with a multiplicity of interpretations and roles in language, or writing. This similarity suggests that deconstruction or postmodernism may be better viewed as a continuation of romanticism than as the beginning of a new era of thought. At least from Kierkegaard's point of view, I suspect, it would appear to be a more radical form of romanticism or perhaps the

1. Another term with which this movement is frequently associated is "poststructuralism." Although these terms are not synonymous—deconstruction is somewhat more narrowly construed as a method, or strategy, for destabilizing binary hierarchical oppositions constructed by modern society, whereas poststructuralism and postmodernism are vaguely and variously defined terms expressing the denial of linguistic forms and other "deep structures" embedded in things (poststructuralism) in an attempt to communicate in writing that which lies beyond language (*différance,* or otherness) but leaves its trace in the unconscious and on the margins of society (postmodernism)—for the purposes of the present analysis I treat them as a single phenomenon.

2. Kierkegaard has been assimilated into postmodernism in two ways. First, some Kierkegaard scholars influenced by the postmodern movement have begun to subject his writings to deconstructive analysis and to construe his thought in terms of a philosophy of difference. Second, selected features of Kierkegaard's thought, for example, the concepts of irony and repetition, have been appropriated as a point of departure for the deconstructive project itself, especially the overthrow of metaphysics and any form of foundationalism. For a critique of several postmodernist interpretations of Kierkegaard, see my review-essay "Kierkegaard and Postmodernism," 113–22. On the implied critique of postmodernism in Kierkegaard's thought, see also Hall, *Word and Spirit.*

culmination of that movement, neither truly postmodern in its continuity with the past nor truly modern in the ironic aestheticism with which it negates actuality.[3]

3. The relation of postmodernism to romanticism is a hotly debated subject in current literary and philosophical studies. Rodolphe Gasché, in *The Tain of the Mirror,* insists on a disassociation of the two, contending that early German romanticism sought (but failed to achieve) a dissolution or neutralization of opposing concepts in a unitary ground, whereas deconstruction, by contrast, not only does not seek such a totality but also calls into question the very possibility of totalization by postulating a nonfoundational, abysmal condition of both identity and difference in an unconditional heterology (*différance*), or system of indeterminate infrastructures that are preontological, prelogical, plural, decentered, and open. John McGowan, in *Postmodernism and Its Critics* (Ithaca, N.Y.: Cornell University Press, 1991), also views postmodernism as setting itself against a romantic vision of unity and social solidarity, but he detects a romantic, hierarchical, totalizing tendency in postmodernism itself in its privileging of pluralism over unicity as more inclusive of difference (12–13, 109–10). Ernst Behler, in *Irony and the Discourse of Modernity* (Seattle: University of Washington Press, 1990), takes the position, in conformity with my own, that "postmodernism is neither an overcoming of modernity nor a new epoch, but a critical continuation of modernism" in "radicalized, intensified" form, for example, in its use of irony (5). Art Berman, in *From the New Criticism to Deconstruction: the Reception of Structuralism and Post-Structuralism* (Urbana: University of Illinois Press, 1988), also recognizes the romantic character of deconstruction, for example, as it functions in Derrida's notion of the free play of language and in the emphasis on the autonomous subject in American literary criticism, in contrast to which Derrida holds, Berman claims, a deterministic, poststructuralist view of the subject as being constituted by language.

The issue is complicated by the fact that there are not only differing interpretations and assessments of postmodernism among scholars but also disagreements concerning the nature of romanticism, especially early German romanticism, which is the form of romanticism with which Kierkegaard is concerned. Some modern scholars, such as Gary J. Handwerk, in *Irony and Ethics in Narrative: From Schlegel to Lacan* (New Haven: Yale University Press, 1985), view the German romantics, for example, Friedrich Schlegel, in a more positive light than did Hegel and Kierkegaard, finding in their works an ethical irony in the form of intersubjectivity. (It should be noted, however, that intersubjectivity, or a relation to oneself via a relation to others, is not, from Kierkegaard's point of view at least, in itself ethical; everything depends on *how* one is related to others.) Like Gasché, Philippe Lacoue-Labarthe and Jean-Luc Nancy, in *The Literary Absolute: The Theory of Literature in German Romanticism,* tr. Philip Barnard and Cheryl Lester (Albany: State University of New York Press, 1988), interpret German romanticism as a perpetual attempt to present a totality or absolute in literature or, more precisely, in a *theory* of literature as a totalizing process that realizes itself in, yet continually transcends, any finite product of literature, which necessarily remains fragmentary or incomplete in its fragmentary completion as a work of art. Emphasizing the open-ended or never-ending elliptical character of the productive imagination in Friedrich Schlegel's early writings, Marcus Paul Bullock, in *Romanticism and Marxism: The Philosophical Development of Literary Theory and Literary History in Walter Benjamin and Friedrich Schlegel* (New York: Peter Lang, 1987), contests the interpretation of Walter Benjamin and scholars, such as Lacoue-Labarthe and Nancy, who were influenced by Benjamin's "messianic" view of romanticism in terms of a metaphysics of presence or a striving for completion and perfection. According to Bullock, the absolute for Schlegel corresponds to nothingness rather than presence, with the result that all representations are pure constructs and the notion of absolute truth is denied (100, 129, 131, 136). In like manner, Paul de Man, in *Blindness and Insight: Essays in the Rhetoric of Contemporary Criticism,* 2d ed., rev. (Minneapolis: University

Let me put some substance into these contentions by lightly sketching the program of deconstruction, whose chief architect, the French philosopher and literary critic Jacques Derrida, has aptly been described as a "supreme ironist" and "undoubtedly the most accomplished ironist of our age."[4] In essence, deconstruction is another name for irony, which Kierkegaard defines in *The Concept of Irony* as "infinite, absolute negativity" in its Socratic and romantic forms (although he later revises his understanding of Socratic irony, viewing it as an ethical category).[5] Like romantic irony, which engages in a perpetual process of positing and negating actuality, so that nothing is recognized as a complete and adequate realization of the infinite ideal toward which it strives, deconstruction is an endless process of textual dismantling and reinscription that seeks to undermine and displace established forms of literary and philosophical interpretation based on a metaphysics of presence or revelation of truth, calling into question by this practice the very notions of truth and fixed meaning. Subverting established hierarchical oppositions in texts by first reversing, then reinscribing them in such a way as to generate new concepts and interpretations that do not conform to an exclusive, hierarchical, binary mold as previously conceived, the strategy of Derrida and his

of Minnesota Press, 1983), views the dialectic of self-destruction and self-invention in Schlegel as "an endless process that leads to no synthesis" (220). While recognizing a unitive thrust in Schlegel's early writings, Ernst Behler, in "The Theory of Irony in German Romanticism," in *Romantic Irony,* ed. Frederick Garber (Budapest: Akadémiai Kiaidó, 1988), 43–81, agrees that in Schlegel's early writings there is no final synthesis, only a ceaseless process of oscillation between self-creation and self-destruction that constitutes the essential meaning of irony for him. It is in the use of irony in this manner that I am primarily interested in showing an affinity between German romanticism and postmodernism.

4. Megill, *Prophets of Extremity,* 260. Behler, *Irony and the Discourse of Modernity,* 104; Berman, *From the New Criticism to Deconstruction,* 214; and Richard Rorty, *Contingency, Irony, and Solidarity* (Cambridge: Cambridge University Press, 1989), who undertakes to defend ironism in this work (83, 94–95, 122–37), also note the importance of irony in Derrida, although Derrida does not use that term himself to characterize his deconstructive method.

5. Rodolphe Gasché, in *The Tain of the Mirror,* denies that deconstructive methodology is "nihilistic, destructive, or negative"; on the contrary, he maintains that it is "affirmative" in the sense that it "affirms the play of the positive *and* the negative, and thus it wards off the ethical temptation to liquidate negativity and difference" (154). Gasché understands negativity as a process of annulment, neutralization, or cancellation of oppositions in a unity he associates with German romanticism and, interestingly enough, with most deconstructive literary critics, who in his opinion harbor a misconception of deconstruction on this score (138). But romantic irony as Kierkegaard and some more-recent interpreters understand it is not a cancellation of opposites in a higher unity but rather the perpetuation of an endless process of oscillation between the positive and the negative such as Gasché ascribes to deconstruction. In Kierkegaard's view, this process constitutes "infinite, absolute negativity," since it allows nothing that is posited to stand; everything is arbitrary.

deconstructive colleagues is to put into play a multiplicity of interpretations, all of which—or, what amounts to the same thing, none of which—may be said to be true (although the reverse oppositions and new interpretations tend to be privileged over the old).

Deconstruction is more thoroughgoing than previous forms of romantic irony, however, in that it not only negates the established order and actuality as such but also the possibility of determining any underlying foundation or reality of that which appears, regarding concepts of "reality" in a poststructuralist fashion as the product of language or a chain of signification that is nonreferential or only self-referential.[6] Deconstruction also rejects the possibility of realizing any higher ideality, totality, or ultimate truth by which actuality is continually judged inadequate and negated in romantic irony, since these concepts are also regarded as constructs of language, which is always constituted in relation to *différance,* or what is not. Deconstruction further rejects the possibility of attaining self-identity in the form of an autonomous, unified self that is often associated with the romantic quest, although in Kierkegaard's view romantic striving resulted in the opposite of this goal, perpetuating fragmentation of the self rather than unifying it, and losing self-identity in experimentation and play with a multiplicity of roles rather than concretely realizing the self through a continuous actualization of the given potentialities of the self in an ethical-religious relation to others and to the divine.[7]

Deconstruction thus rejects the notion of any final, unified or closed system of truth or self-identity that may be attained in thought or imagination, substituting instead the epistemological principle of undecid-

6. On this issue, see especially Christopher Norris, *Derrida* (Cambridge: Harvard University Press, 1987), 142–44.

7. It should be noted, however, that according to Berman, *From the New Criticism to Deconstruction,* American deconstructionist literary critics (e.g., Paul de Man and J. Hillis Miller) differ from the French poststructuralist deconstructionists in retaining the romantic (and existentialist) quest for self-identity, although recognizing its ultimate unattainability due to the indeterminancy of linguistic meaning (cf. 223–74). Similarly, the American postmodern pragmatist philosopher Richard Rorty, in *Contingency, Irony, and Solidarity,* emphasizes the free, self-creating individual who recognizes the contingencies of human existence that distinguish that individual from others and who is ironic toward the past, "constantly playing the new off against the old" in an attempt to redescribe reality without claiming any final or true vocabulary that corresponds to the real (73–75). According to Judith P. Butler, in *Subjects of Desire: Hegelian Reflections in Twentieth-Century France* (New York: Columbia University Press, 1987), the French postmodern thinkers Lacan, Deleuze, and Foucault also understand the subject as "a projected unity, but this projection *disguises* and falsifies the mutliplicitous disunity constitutive of experience," so that the projected self becomes a "false construct imposed upon an experience that eludes the category of identity altogether" (185).

ability concerning the truth or falsity of anything. To inscribe this displacement, postmodern writers resort literarily to word play, parody, mime, preface writing, collage, and other techniques of writing to dislodge and negate the possibility of coming to or disclosing some original or definitive truth in a text or thesis. In the realm of postmodern art this viewpoint is reflected in an antirepresentationalism that undermines the distinction between the aesthetic and the unaesthetic, art and reality, copy and original. It replaces the notion of an original truth, idea, or reality that is re-presented or copied in art with that of a "mimesis without origin," that is, an endless play of copying that has no reference to an underlying reality beyond the images produced.[8]

Although Kierkegaard shares the postmodern suspicion of totalizing systems, of the ability of thought or imagination to comprehend human existence, which is never finished or complete as long as one is alive, he certainly does not share the postmodern conclusion that there is no truth or original meaning to which we may aspire in our cognitive, as well as existential, endeavors.[9] This difference is especially evident when we consider the implications of postmodern thought with respect to the project of selfhood. Unlike Kierkegaard, who believes in an originally given structure that defines the self, postmodernism rejects the notion of any determinate, proper, or ultimate self-identity, opting instead for a philosophy of difference that privileges the concept of "the other" over the concept of the self.[10] Just as there is no "correct" interpretation of a text in postmodernism, there is no true or originally given

8. For an excellent account of postmodern art, see Kearney, *The Wake of Imagination*, 251–358. See also Mark C. Taylor, *Disfiguring: Art, Architecture, Religion* (Chicago: University of Chicago Press, 1992). Taylor distinguishes between a "modernist" form of postmodernism that is really a "disguised modernism" in its "logo centric" (as opposed to "logocentric") attempt to realize a reconciliation with "the Real" through the figure, image, or sign rather than through the word or speech, and a deconstructive form of postmodernism that is subversive of both modernism and modernist postmodernism in its attempt to "figure the unfigurable" in a nontotalizing, nonintegrative, and nonreconciliatory fashion.

9. For Kierkegaard, the epistemological criterion of personal or subjective truth is edification, or that which builds up the human personality, such as love (JP, 4:4847; WL, 199–212). On edification as the criterion of subjective truth in Kierkegaard's thought, see Robert L. Perkins, "Kierkegaard: A Kind of Epistemologist."

10. Kierkegaard's concept of structure should not be confused with that of structuralism, which holds that the self is a linguistic construct, shaped by language, or the system of signs of the cultural system into which one is born. For Kierkegaard, the self is freely constituted in its given structure via a relation to the divine, not self-created as in German romanticism or determined by the social order as in contemporary structuralism. For a good overview and comparison of structuralism and poststructuralism, see Berman, *From the New Criticism to Deconstruction.*

structure that constitutes the self either; rather, the subject, or subjectivity, is regarded as constituted temporally in relation to otherness, or that which it is not, by the force of desire, which signals a gap or lack of self-identity, so that the "I" is constantly deferred.[11] Instead of becoming a self or adopting the project of self-identity, therefore, one postmodernist writer suggests that we think of ourselves as "personae," ironically donning masks to preserve nonidentity as we play various roles as actors on the stage of life.[12] Insofar as any concept of self-identity is operative in postmodern "serpentine wandering," as Mark C. Taylor characterizes the movement, it is one that remains open, undefined, and experimental, as in German romanticism.[13]

Such a view of self-identity is especially evident in the understanding of female identity emerging in postmodern feminist thought.[14] Since the question of woman's self-identity is a critical one in our time, it is appropriate here, I think, to illustrate the contemporary crisis of self-identity specifically from that perspective, although the discussion of female self-identity contains important implications for the forming of male self-identity as well. In what follows, I try briefly to show how the penchant of some postmodern French feminist writers to privilege difference between the self and the other—for example, woman and man—ironically results in a volatilization of the self in the other that corresponds to the romantic experimentation with self-identity so roundly criticized by Kierkegaard in his early writings.[15] In setting forth an alternative vision

11. On the concept of desire in contemporary French theory, see Butler, *Subjects of Desire,* 175–238. According to Butler, the role of desire in the constitution of the subject is especially important in the thought of Lacan, who associates it with the impossible recovery of a repressed preoedipal unity with the mother; Deleuze, who understands it as a nondialectical, multiple play of forces that cannot be synthesized in a higher unity; and Foucault, who regards it as the product of a discourse of repressive power relations that are constantly changing.

12. John D. Caputo, *Radical Hermeneutics: Repetition, Deconstruction, and the Hermeneutic Project* (Bloomington: Indiana University Press, 1987), 289–90. Caputo's suggestion sounds familiarly like the playacting of the romantic ironist as characterized by Kierkegaard in *The Concept of Irony* and artistically portrayed in the first volume of *Either/Or.* For a critique of Caputo's book, see my review-essay, "Kierkegaard and Postmodernism."

13. Mark C. Taylor, *Erring: A Postmodern A/theology* (Chicago: University of Chicago Press, 1984), 11, 15.

14. See, for example, Rosi Braidotti's characterization of postmodern feminist subjectivity, in the manner of Deleuze, as "nomadic," in *Patterns of Dissonance: A Study of Women in Contemporary Philosophy,* tr. Elizabeth Guild (New York: Routledge, 1991), 277–79, and in her more recent article "Embodiment, Sexual Difference, and the Nomadic Subject," *Hypatia* 8, no. 1 (1993): 1–13.

15. An earlier version of the following discussion was published under the title "The Philosophical Affirmation of Gender Difference: Kierkegaard Versus Postmodern Neo-Feminism." I

of self-identity and the concept of the other, Kierkegaard may also be seen to affirm difference, but within a common structure of selfhood and the more fundamental qualification of our common humanity.[16] These elements of commonality, I contend, provide a matrix for transcending gender differences and alienation between man and woman, self and others, without loss of individual uniqueness on the part of the self or the other. As I see it, such a matrix is lacking in postmodern French feminist thought (as well as in postmodern thought more generally) but is needed for a genuine affirmation of sexual differences, self-identity, and others, and thus for living poetically in an authentic fashion in the present age.

POSTMODERN FRENCH FEMINIST AFFIRMATIONS OF DIFFERENCE

In the resurgence of feminism in the first half of the twentieth century, Simone de Beauvoir, the foremost French feminist writer of the early post–World War II period, made the denial of any essential gender difference between women and men a fundamental tenet of her thought. Such differences as existed were, Beauvoir maintained, on the whole culturally determined and imposed rather than biologically given in the forms of feminine and masculine essences. Setting out to dethrone "the myth of femininity" in her now classic manifesto, *The Second Sex,* Beauvoir analyzed women's situation as one in which they are pressured either to comply with the inessential, inferior, submissive role of "the other" assigned to them by men or else to deny their sexual identity as women by adopting the ways of men.[17] Over against this unhappy pseudochoice, Beauvoir urged women, in the spirit of

---

wish to stress that my treatment of feminism is limited to only one school of that movement and does not apply to all forms of feminism. For a good introduction to the various schools of feminism, see Rosemarie Tong, *Feminist Thought: A Comprehensive Introduction* (Boulder: Westview Press, 1989).

16. For an opposite interpretation of Kierkegaard that sees him as emphasizing difference and as being "completely opposed to any notion of equality" (8), see Laura Lyn Inglis, "The Dialogue of Action: Søren Kierkegaard's Dialectical Conception of Ethics" (Ph.D. diss., Princeton Theological Seminary, 1981). Inglis views commonality as rooted in otherness, rather than vice versa.

17. Simone de Beauvoir, *The Second Sex* (New York: Random House Vintage Books, 1989), xix–xxxvi.

Sartrean radical freedom, to affirm themselves as equal, independent, and creative subjects without renouncing their womanliness. Although she rejected the notion of "equality in difference," an equal but separate status for women, she did affirm the possibility of "differences in equality," that is, distinctive ways of relating to their own bodies, to each other, and to children.[18] Thus Beauvoir was prepared to acknowledge the validity of some gender differences between women and men, but not gender essences defining different natures of males and females.

Seeking to reaffirm and preserve a more distinctive character for woman, some feminist thinkers in recent decades have placed greater emphasis on gender differences. In America, for example, the radical feminist philosopher Mary Daly, like Simone de Beauvoir, rejects the traditionally defined stereotype of femininity, but she thinks that by "spinning" threads of connectedness with their sisters, women can develop genuine differences from men that are not male-defined.[19] Also detecting "a different voice" of women in her studies of women's moral development, but one more in line with traditional conceptions of the feminine, Harvard psychologist Carol Gilligan emphasizes the importance of intimacy, relationships, and care for others in the formation of female identity.[20] By far the greatest emphasis on female difference, however, has come from a group of postmodern French feminist writers—for example, Julia Kristeva, Hélène Cixous, Catherine Clément, and Luce Irigaray—who are heavily influenced by poststructuralism and deconstruction.[21] Appropriating aspects of the analyses and strategies of such postmodern writers as Lacan, Derrida, Deleuze, and Foucault, they

18. Ibid., 731.

19. Mary Daly, *Gyn/Ecology: The Metaethics of Radical Feminism* (Boston: Beacon Press, 1978), 382.

20. Carol Gilligan, *In a Different Voice: Psychological Theory and Women's Development* (Cambridge: Harvard University Press, 1982), 17. See also idem, "Remapping the Moral Domain: New Images of Self in Relationship," in *Mapping the Moral Domain: A Contribution of Women's Thinking to Psychological Theory and Education,* ed. Carol Gilligan, Janie Victoria Ward, and Jill McLean Taylor, with Betty Bardige (Cambridge: Harvard University Press, 1988), 3–19.

21. For an introduction to postmodern French feminist thought, see Toril Moi, ed., *French Feminist Thought: A Reader* (Oxford: Basil Blackwell, 1987); Elaine Marks and Isabelle de Courtivron, eds., *New French Feminisms: An Anthology* (Amherst: University of Massachusetts Press, 1980); and Elizabeth Grosz, *Sexual Subversions: Three French Feminists* (Sydney: Allen & Unwin, 1989). In treating the postmodern French feminists as a group, I recognize that there are also important differences between them as individual thinkers, which a more detailed study would need to take into account. My objective here is only to highlight certain similarities among them with regard to the issue of female self-identity.

seek to reclaim a sense of female difference and self-identity through the nonexclusion and internalization of difference.[22]

In the analysis of this group of feminist thinkers, "the problem with Western literature, philosophy, and politics is not that it has asserted the difference of women from men, but rather that it has denied and repressed the specifically feminine."[23] According to the Lacanian psychoanalytic perspective that underlies much of postmodern feminist thought, at the root of the human psyche there is a traumatic sense of separation of the subject from itself and from others, reflecting and veiling the separation of the subject at birth from its mother. Desiring but forever barred from a return to primordial unity with her, the subject struggles to become an independent being by differentiating itself from everything other than itself. As this process takes place in man, woman (the mother) is pushed to the margin of his existence and excluded as "the other" (Cixous and Clément) or "the abject" (Kristeva) who threatens to engulf and return him to an original, primordial identity with her.[24] Unable to tolerate this otherness, he represses it to the level of the unconscious, reduces woman to sameness with himself by domesticating her into structures of symbolic order, or "language," established by him (including psychological, sociological, political, religious, and economic codes and systems of signification, which form the unconscious matrix out of which consciousness is shaped), and dominates over her. Although uniformity prevails at the conscious and social levels of existence, traces of the excluded and repressed other in the unconscious reveal an underlying metaphysical state of difference rather than identity, alienation rather than reconciliation, endless lack and desire rather than satisfaction and fulfillment in personal relations.

Instead of resigning themselves to this situation as generations of women have done, however, postmodern feminists make it an occasion

22. It should be noted that in France and America the postmodern feminist reaction to these male thinkers is not entirely positive, since they have been criticized for what are perceived to be masculinist and antifeminist features of their thought. For some recent critical assessments of these thinkers, see Jane Flax, *Thinking Fragments: Psychoanalysis, Feminism, and Postmodernism in the Contemporary West* (Berkeley and Los Angeles: University of California Press, 1990); Braidotti, *Patterns of Dissonance;* Alice A. Jardine, *Gynesis: Configurations of Woman and Modernity* (Ithaca, N.Y.: Cornell University Press, 1985); and Margaret Whitford, *Luce Irigaray: Philosophy in the Feminine* (London: Routledge, 1991), 123–35.

23. Jane Sawicki and Iris Young, "Issues of Difference in Feminist Philosophy," *Feminism and Philosophy Newsletter* (April 1988): 13–17.

24. Hélène Cixous and Catharine Clément, *The Newly Born Woman,* tr. Betsy Wing (Minneapolis: University of Minnesota Press, 1986); Julia Kristeva, *Powers of Horror: An Essay on Abjection* (New York: Columbia University Press, 1982).

for affirming, even flaunting, their difference and liminal position in the face of the phallocentric and patriarchal society that has marginalized woman's existence. Catherine Clément, for example, conjures up in her writing the figures of the sorceress and the hysteric—metaphors representing most graphically the exclusion of women in Western culture—as models of female liberation.[25] Reveling in the expression of a bisexuality through which they explore and identify in a romantic fashion with other personalities, both masculine and feminine, these women view female identity as being constructed through the experience of bodily pleasure—ecstasy, or *jouissance,* in autoerotic, lesbian, and heterosexual relations. "Femininity and bisexuality go together," declares Hélène Cixous, for woman more so than man is disposed to venture out of herself, to explore other possibilities of identity in the expression of a cosmic "libido of the other" that is diffused and infinitely changing.[26] Whereas man is self-absorbed, engrossed in a mirror economy of narcissistic self-love that seeks to protect and reinforce the traditional image of masculinity and male self-identity, woman seeks without self-interest to love, to love the other, to become the other, Cixous proclaims. Construing the meaning of bisexuality in terms of this "other-capacity" of woman, she writes, "Bisexual doesn't mean, as many people think, that she can make love with both a man and a woman, it doesn't mean she has two partners, even if it can at times mean this. Bisexuality on an unconscious level is the possibility of extending into the other, of being in such a relation with the other that *I* move into the other without destroying the other: that I will look for the other where s/he is without trying to bring everything back to myself."[27] Paradoxically, then, woman becomes herself by decentering, depropriating, depersonalizing, and diffusing herself in others in a kind of fluidlike intersubjectivity, especially with other women, with whom she retains and shares a primordial connection to the maternal source of life. In relation to men, however, sexual difference is never entirely overcome, always leaving a certain irreducibility or residue between them.[28]

25. Cixous and Clément, *The Newly Born Woman,* 3–39. Similarly, the American feminist philosopher Mary Daly exploits the metaphors of *spinster, lesbian, hag, harpy, crone,* and *fury*—all traditionally negative images associated with women—as patterns for women's journey to selfhood in *Gyn/Ecology.*

26. Cixous and Clément, *The Newly Born Woman,* 85, 88, 92.

27. Hélène Cixous, "Castration and Decapitation," tr. Annette Kuhn, *Signs: Journal of Women in Culture and Society* 7, no. 1 (1981): 41–55.

28. On this point, see especially Luce Irigaray, "And the One Doesn't Stir Without the Other," tr. Hélène Vivienne Wenzel, *Signs: Journal of Women in Culture and Society* 7, no. 1 (1981): 56–67, and idem, "Sexual Difference," tr. Seán Hand, in Moi, *French Feminist Thought,*

For Cixous, it is most of all in *writing* that woman becomes herself; thus she urges women to "write themselves," giving voice to their femininity through imagination as well as through their bodies. There are, she claims, not only physical and psychological differences between women and men but also distinctively feminine and masculine styles of writing, distinguished by differing ways of relating to the other and to the "law of return." Whereas woman is disposed to admit in her writing that there is an other, man, Cixous thinks, has difficulty in letting the other come through his. And whereas woman gives of herself without expectation of returning to herself, man seeks to gain more masculinity (virility, authority, power, money, pleasure) through his giving of himself. "Rare are the men able to venture onto the brink where writing, freed from law, unencumbered by moderation, exceeds phallic authority, and where the subjectivity inscribing its effects becomes feminine," Cixous contends.[29]

It is also in writing that love, in Cixous's view, becomes love of the other, for writing, she thinks, is what makes love other. Indeed, Cixous goes even further to proclaim of writing, "It is itself this love. Other-love is writing's first name."[30] For the woman who writes, however, this other-love is fleeting and unattached. "She will let nothing intervene in her fight, other than the 'natural' desire for 'a' man, whoever he is, without any preference, for she must not be *attached* to any man. Love for a unique one cannot occur." Like many men and women, Cixous views the sexes as being at war with one another: "For a free woman there can be no relationship with men other than war." Just as man has tried to conquer and dominate woman, so she now seeks to capture and dominate him, but with a difference: whereas he seeks to dominate in order to destroy, she dominates in order not to be dominated, "to de-

---

118–30. As Irigaray describes this process in *This Sex Which is Not One,* tr. Catherine Porter with Carolyn Burke (Ithaca, N.Y.: Cornell University Press, 1985), woman "herself enters into a ceaseless exchange of herself with the other without any possibility of identifying either" (31). See also her *Marine Lover of Friedrich Nietzsche,* tr. Gillian C. Gill (New York: Columbia University Press, 1991), 86.

29. Cixous and Clément, *The Newly Born Woman,* 118. As examples of male writers who exhibit this ability, Cixous cites Kleist and Shakespeare (98–99). Similarly, Julia Kristeva detects a feminine form of writing in what she calls "semiotic discourse," or writing in which unconscious maternal associations resurface. Among male writers in whom this appears, she cites Joyce, Mallarmé, and Artaud. I would add to this list D. H. Lawrence. On Lawrence, see my article, "Women in Love," *Soundings* 65 (1982): 352–68. On feminine writing in Kristeva's thought, see Toril Moi, ed., *The Kristeva Reader* (Oxford: Basil Blackwell, 1986), and Ann Rosalind Jones, "Writing the Body: Toward an Understanding of *l'Écriture féminine,*" in *The New Feminist Criticism,* ed. Elaine Showalter (New York: Pantheon Books, 1985), 361–77.

30. Cixous and Clément, *The Newly Born Woman,* 99.

stroy the space of denomination."[31] Cixous maintains that ultimately both man and woman "must kill warring power to liberate loving power" in themselves, but unfortunately she does not tell us how this can be done.[32] While her affirmation of female difference supports the liberation of women from male domination and the formation of a distinctive female self-identity, she does not envision "sorties" or ways out for women that heal the wound of alienation between woman and man or allow for a truly distinctive view of man (and others) as an other. For on the one hand, the internalization of otherness by extending or giving themselves in bisexual relations and writing does not involve any enduring relationships, commitment, or attachment to men as actual others by women, though it may enhance their sense of the masculine gender (assuming there is one).[33] And on the other hand, it appears that the other, particularly male alterity, is not really affirmed and respected as an independent other but rather is poetically explored as a possibility in the construction of women's identities and exploited as an object of sexual play for the sake of female bodily pleasure.

True to their deconstructionist roots, however, these postmodern French feminists are hesitant to encode female identity and femininity, purposely leaving them conceptually vague and undefined. Since, from their nominalistic viewpoint, there is no general woman, or one typical woman, the concept of female identity must be kept open and fluid to reflect the plurality, infinite richness, and incompleteness of woman's sexuality and being.[34] In a recent interview Julia Kristeva states, "I am in favour of a concept of femininity which would take as many forms as there are women."[35] Furthermore, in her view female identity is constantly reborn and remade; there is no continuity of identity or per-

31. Ibid., 116.

32. Ibid., 118.

33. Although the logic of the postmodern feminist view of female subjectivity supports such a conclusion, it is interesting that in her more recent writings Luce Irigaray does envision marriage between women and men, but in a form that preserves openness and fluidity of identity without transgressing the boundaries of the other. For a discussion of this point, see Christine Holmlund, "The Lesbian, the Mother, the Heterosexual Lover: Irigaray's Recodings of Difference," *Feminist Studies* 17, no. 2 (1991): 283–308.

34. Hélène Cixous, "The Laugh of the Medusa," tr. Keith Cohen and Paula Cohen, *Signs: Journal of Women in Culture and Society* 1, no. 4 (1976): 875–93, reprinted in Marks and de Courtivron, *New French Feminisms,* 245–64. See also Irigaray, *This Sex Which Is Not One,* which emphasizes the plural nature of woman's sexuality or eroticism and thus the indefinite or multiple character of her self-identity or, more accurately, lack of self-identity, since she is neither one nor two.

35. In Moi, *French Feminist Thought,* 114. See also Julia Kristeva, "Woman Can Never Be Defined," tr. Marilyn A. August, in Marks and de Courtivron, *New French Feminisms,* 137–41.

during idea of a self to which women should aspire. In the final analysis, therefore, the postmodern French feminist assertion of female difference ironically results in a negation of self-identity rather than an affirmation of it in the process of becoming.

KIERKEGAARD ON GENDER DIFFERENCE, SELF-IDENTITY, AND THE OTHER

At several points in previous chapters of this study we have seen that the possibility of independence and selfhood for woman is also rendered problematic in Kierkegaard's writings by the stereotyped and patriarchal view of woman he and his pseudonyms shared with his age. In two of Kierkegaard's later works, *The Sickness unto Death* and *Works of Love,* however, the concepts of selfhood and love are analyzed in such a way as to point beyond these limitations to a vision of both the self and the other, woman and man, as equal and independent subjects bound to one another and to the divine in a spiritual love that affirms both their common humanity and their differences. Focusing on these two works, I examine first of all the use of gender categories in *The Sickness unto Death* to show how the analysis of selfhood and despair in that work envisions a wholeness of identity as a self in both males and females that includes both "feminine" and "masculine" modes of relating to themselves, to the divine, and to others.[36] From this examination I also show how, on the basis of his analysis, postmodern French feminism would appear to be an expression of romantic aestheticism and despair rather than an authentic way of forming female self-identity. Next, I examine Kierkegaard's concept of the other in *Works of Love* to show how true otherness is viewed there as being based not on difference, as it is in postmodern French feminism and in postmodernism more generally, but rather on what is shared in common, namely, our common humanity.

GENDER DIFFERENCES AS MODES OF SELFHOOD AND DESPAIR

Kierkegaard affirms throughout his writings a given structure of selfhood, or personal identity, that is the task of every human being to realize in life, although that task is one that is never finished in the process of existing. In *The Sickness unto Death* this self is defined in

36. For a more extensive analysis of the use of gender categories in *The Sickness unto Death,* see my article "On 'Feminine' and 'Masculine' Despair."

spiritual terms as a conscious and dynamic relating to itself and to that power which establishes it as a synthesis of the finite and the infinite, the temporal and the eternal, necessity (given conditions and limitations) and freedom, or possibility (SUD, 13). Since no distinction is made between the sexes in this definition and the generic term "human being" (*Mennesket*) is used to refer to the person whose task is to become a self, both woman and man may be assumed to become and to be constituted as a self in the same manner. Within this common structure of selfhood, however, substantive differences may be observed in the ways woman and man are oriented toward themselves and falter on the pathway to selfhood by falling into despair. In initial agreement with the postmodern feminists, Kierkegaard, or Anti-Climacus, the pseudonym under which he pens this work, claims that woman's nature is characterized by devotedness [*Hengivenhed*] and givingness [*Hengivelse*].[37] She acquires her sexual identity as a woman by instinctively giving herself in devotion to others. Man, by contrast, is more self-contained and intellectual. Although he also gives himself to others, he has and retains a sense of self-awareness apart from that giving (SUD, 50). In Kierkegaard's view, then, woman and man exhibit different ways of acquiring their substantive, sexual identities. Her being is centered in relatedness to others, which I designate here for purposes of analysis "the feminine mode"; his is centered in the relation to himself, or what I call "the masculine mode."

According to Kierkegaard, however, neither mode is equivalent to the self or sufficient in itself to become a spiritually qualified self, although masculine self-consciousness corresponds more closely than feminine devotedness does to the definition of the self as a self-relation in *The Sickness unto Death*.[38] To become a self, one must be related not only to

37. Since Anti-Climacus represents a Christian viewpoint with which Kierkegaard agrees, I will depart from my previous practice of referring to the pseudonymous author and proceed to identify the views of this book as his own. Although the French postmodern feminists deny any form of female essentialism, claiming that femininity is an open and infinitely changing concept, they have sometimes been accused of assuming or reverting to an essentialism in their emphasis on the female body and in their characterization of woman as being disposed toward giving herself without reserve to others. For discussions of this issue, see Linda Alcoff, "Cultural Feminism Versus Post-Structuralism: The Identity Crisis in Feminist Theory," *Signs: Journal of Women in Culture and Society* 13, no. 3 (1988): 405–36; Diana J. Fuss, " 'Essentially Speaking': Luce Irigaray's Language of Essence," *Hypatia* 3, no. 3 (1989): 94–112; Maggie Berg, "Luce Irigaray's 'Contradictions': Poststructuralism and Feminism," *Signs: Journal of Women in Culture and Society* 17, no. 1 (1991): 50–70; and Jane Gallop, *Thinking Through the Body* (New York: Columbia University Press, 1988).

38. On the question whether the definition of the self in *The Sickness unto Death* includes relations to others besides God, see my article "On 'Feminine' and 'Masculine' Despair," 125–

oneself but also to the power that constitutes the self, that is, God. In relation to the divine, Kierkegaard maintains, "it holds for men as well as for women that devotion is the self and that in the giving of oneself the self is gained" (SUD, 50). Thus the feminine mode as well as the masculine mode is integrally involved in the process of becoming a true self, or religious personality. That both are needed is explicitly indicated in a late journal entry (1854) by Kierkegaard.

> In a certain sense woman is by nature better suited for essentially religious service, for it is a woman's nature wholly to give herself.—But on the other hand she does not explain anything.—An eminently masculine intellectuality joined to a feminine submissiveness—this is the truly religious. Woman's devotedness is essentially limited to interjections, and if it is more than that it is unfeminine. But on the other hand an eminent masculine intellectuality is directly related to an enormous selfishness which must be slain in submissiveness. (JP 4:5006)

In spite of the stereotyped and critical view of both sexes displayed in this passage, it is apparent that, from Kierkegaard's point of view, to become a self, or religious personality, both woman and man need to develop not only the natural inclinations, or tendencies, that constitute their respective sexual identities but also the qualities characteristic of the opposite sex. In other words, both the feminine and masculine modes of relating to oneself and to others are needed, in a manner comparable to what modern psychologists have identified as "psychological androgyny."[39] Failure to cultivate either of these in an appropriate

---

26, where I find Kierkegaard's position to be unclear and ambiguous on the matter. See also C. Stephen Evans, "Kierkegaard's View of the Unconscious," in *Kierkegaard—Poet of Existence,* ed. Birgit Bertung, 31–48. Evans argues that relations to other human beings must be assumed in Kierkegaard's definition inasmuch as his notion of the mature self presupposes a "pre-self" formed through relations with others.

39. See J. H. Block, "Conceptions of Sex Roles: Some Cross-Cultural and Longitudinal Perspectives," *American Psychologist* 28 (1973): 512–26; June Singer, *Androgyny: Toward a New Theory of Sexuality* (Garden City, N.Y.: Anchor Books, Doubleday, 1977); Barbara Lusk Forisha, *Sex Roles and Personal Awareness* (Morristown, N.J.: General Learning Press, 1978), 30–36, 87–105; Janet T. Spence and Robert L. Helmreich, *Masculinity and Femininity: Their Psychological Dimensions, Correlates, and Antecedents* (Austin: University of Texas Press, 1978), 109–10 (with other references favoring an androgynous approach to sexual identity); S. L. Bem, "The Measurement of Psychological Androgyny," *Journal of Consulting and Clinical Psychology* 42 (1974): 155–62; and Judith M. Bardwick, *In Transition: How Feminism, Sexual Liberation, and the Search for Self-Fulfillment Have Altered Our Lives* (New York: Holt,

manner results in despair, or a misrelation of the self to itself, to others, and to God.

Although, according to Kierkegaard's analysis, despair may be unconscious, lacking any spiritual awareness of the self, conscious despair appears in two forms: despair in weakness and despair in defiance. Despair in weakness is manifested as an unwillingness to become a self; despair in defiance consists in willing to become the self one wants to be rather than the self one is intended to be by God. Kierkegaard further distinguishes between these two forms of despair by identifying despair in weakness as "feminine despair," and despair in defiance as "masculine despair" (SUD, 49).[40] Although either form of despair may appear in both women and men, women are more inclined, he thinks, to manifest despair in weakness, or feminine despair, and men are more prone to defiant, or masculine, despair. Since women tend by nature to lose or abandon themselves in devotion to others, their despair is to lack a sense of self-identity apart from the object of their devotion (the masculine mode), so that a loss of that object also results in a loss of the self. Men's despair, by contrast, is characterized by an unwillingness to lose or submit themselves in devotion to God (the feminine mode). Their despair thus consists in an unwarranted self-assertion as autonomous beings over against God, whereas women's despair lies in an unwarranted self-abandonment in something or someone other than God. Woman's self is lost or displaced in a finite object outside herself; man's is inwardly misplaced in himself.

Although Kierkegaard's characterization of selfhood and despair in *The Sickness unto Death* is drawn in terms of traditional Western stereotyped views of masculine and feminine genders that are themselves highly questionable from a modern psychological point of view, it reflects the historical situation of women in his time as well as patterns of personal and social development many men and women are still encouraged and trained to follow.[41] An important distinction that emerges in his

---

Rinehart & Winston, 1979), 153–69, 177–78 (who, however, retains an appreciation for gender identity and differences).

40. For a somewhat more detailed analysis of these categories, see my article "On 'Feminine' and 'Masculine' Despair."

41. While definite physiological differences obtain between women and men, it is now widely recognized that psychological characteristics distinguishing them are largely culturally rooted rather than biologically determined. Indeed, many apparent differences turn out upon inspection to be mythical, the product of cultural stereotyping, rather than real. Thus far, psychological measurements devised for determining gender differences have shown only four such differences clearly to exist: males exhibit more aggression, better quantitative skill, and

analysis, however, is that sexual identity and self-identity are not one and the same, although they are certainly interrelated and interdependent concepts. Those qualities we naturally tend and/or are culturally conditioned to develop in order to establish our sexual identities as women and men may be characteristic of a particular sex but are not distinctive to either, nor are they sufficient in and of themselves to constitute the self, which requires a synthesis of factors established through a relation to the divine. The thrust of Kierkegaard's analysis, therefore, is to call into question the sufficiency of either mode of sexual identity as a form of self-identity and to show their potentiality as modes of despair. It thus serves to illumine some of the dangers and limitations of the traditional modes of sexual identity and points to a complementary wholeness of identity as a self toward which both women and men should strive. In this perspective the gender categories employed in Kierkegaard's description of selfhood and despair may be understood to function more as code words for the factors of individuality, or self-consciousness (masculinity), and self-giving, or relatedness (femininity), that are necessary for psychic wholeness than as expressions of essential gender differences between the sexes or of bisexuality in the makeup of the self.

Viewed from the standpoint of Kierkegaard's analysis of selfhood and despair, the feminine abandonment in the other advocated by the postmodern French feminists would appear to be a manifestation of feminine despair in which they lose themselves in identification with the other. Instead of giving themselves to a single object of devotion, however, they depropriate and diffuse themselves in a multiplicity of other personalities, seeking in this way to construct, in the manner of defiant despair, their identities as women in terms of the many possibilities with which they experiment poetically. In this, the French feminists may be seen to resemble the romantic poets characterized by Kierkegaard in *The Concept of Irony* as trying to create themselves by imaginatively playing or experimenting with various possibilities in life, like dramatic actors, each of whom plays a variety of roles. All things are possible for the

---

greater spatial visualization, whereas females excel in verbal ability. There is no evidence supporting gender differences in general intelligence, particularly the widely held notion that women are less intelligent than men. See Eleanor Emmons Maccoby and Carol Nagy Jacklin, *The Psychology of Sex Differences* (Stanford: Stanford University Press, 1974), 349–55. See also Anne Fausto-Sterling, *Myths of Gender: Biological Theories About Women and Men* (New York: Basic, 1986), and Sherrie Ortner and Harriet Whitehead, eds., *Sexual Meanings: The Cultural Construction of Gender and Sexuality* (New York: Cambridge University Press, 1981).

romantic ironists, we may recall, but because they flit from possibility to possibility, living "completely hypothetically and subjunctively," Kierkegaard contends, their lives lose concreteness and continuity (CI, 299, 301). Thus they do not become anything, least of all themselves, but merely play at becoming whatever they arbitrarily decide to become on any day or occasion.

Although, in Kierkegaard's view, possibility is an integral component in the composition of the self, one may fall into despair by getting lost in possibility and fantasy. That is one of the dangers of poetry and the chief fault of the romantic mode of living poetically. What is needed in this event is an antidote of necessity and finitude, that is, the recovery of a sense of one's given conditions and limitations as a human being. Since the postmodern French feminists recognize no given structure of selfhood and admit no boundaries or definition of their femininity, their despair may also be diagnosed as infinitude's or possibility's despair, that is, as a lack of a proper sense of finitude and necessity. Taking the female body as the starting point for the construction of female identity, they attempt to infinitize themselves through sensuality and imagination rather than to effect a synthesis of the finite and the infinite, possibility and necessity, the temporal and the eternal, and (I might add) individuality and relatedness in a proper construction of the self.

THE NEIGHBOR AS THE TRUE OTHER

Another way Kierkegaard differs from postmodern French feminism (and by extension, postmodernism in general) is in his concept of the other. Kierkegaard ponders the question of the other in *Works of Love,* a series of reflections on the biblical commandment "You shall love your neighbor as yourself" (Matt. 22:39). In his view, the other appears in true form only in the person of the neighbor. Establishing a conceptual identity between these two categories, Kierkegaard claims, "Neighbor is what philosophers would call the *other,* that by which the selfishness in self-love is to be tested" (WL, 27). As he sees it, Christianity presupposes self-love in human beings and seeks to bring about a transformation of that love, eradicating the element of narcissism or selfishness in it by requiring us to love others as neighbors. Although natural expressions of love in the forms of erotic love and friendship may appear to be unselfish love of others, in Kierkegaard's view these forms of love are secretly expressions of self-love. The beloved or friend is really an "other-I" or "other-self" with whom we unite to create "a new selfish self" based on our common likenesses and differences from others (WL,

66–69).[42] Erotic love-relations and friendships are formed on the basis of personal preferences and require mutuality and reciprocity in love, that is, the satisfaction of our needs and desires in return. Thus they are fundamentally selfish and need to be transformed.

In Kierkegaard's view, the transformation of self-love occurs in coming to love the other as a neighbor. Defined etymologically, the neighbor is the "near-dweller," a person who is or ought to be as near to us as we are to ourselves. As in erotic love and friendship, neighbor love also involves a duplication of the self in the other, but in such a way as to place demands upon ourselves rather than upon the other. Only in neighbor love, therefore, do we truly love the other as we love ourselves, that is, want for the other what we would want for ourselves. The neighbor thus constitutes the "first-*Thou,*" or "*other-you,*" who stands in relation to us as an independent subject rather than as a means of projecting our egos and satisfying our own selfish desires (WL, 66, 69).

Although one other person is sufficient to test our ability to love others in this way (and thus erotic love and friendship may become modes of neighbor love), Kierkegaard emphasizes that the concept of neighbor includes all human beings in their absolute equality before God (WL, 37, 72). The category of neighbor is thus equivalent to the category of human being, which in his view is the fundamental qualification of human existence. Elaborating on this qualification at some length, Kierkegaard writes:

> Everyone of us is a human being and at the same time the heterogeneous individual which he is by particularity; but being a human being is the fundamental qualification. No one should mistake his distinctiveness to the degree that he cravenly or presumptuously forgets that he is a human being. No one should be preoccupied with the differences so that he cowardly or presumptuously forgets that he is a human being; no man is an exception to being a human being by virtue of his particularizing differences. He is rather a human being and then a particular human being. (WL, 142)

Similarly, in another passage he states, "In being king, beggar, scholar, rich man, poor man, male, female, etc., we do not resemble each other—

42. For a more detailed account of Kierkegaard's analysis of erotic love and friendship in *Works of Love,* see my article, "Forming the Heart: The Role of Love in Kierkegaard's Thought."

therein we are all different. But in being a neighbor we are all unconditionally like each other" (WL, 97).

To love the other as a neighbor means, then, to love that person first of all as a human being, on the basis of our common humanity rather than out of personal preference. Second, it involves the exercise of an "eternal equality" in loving others (WL, 70). Although special relations are still permitted, Kierkegaard maintains that "Christianity has not come into the world to teach this or that modification in how you *in your particularity* should love your wife or friend but to teach how you *in your universal humanity* shall love all [human beings]" (WL, 143). He is quick to point out, however, that spouses and friends must not be made exceptions to this requirement but are to be loved first and foremost, like others, as neighbors rather than on the basis of their attractive features. Certainly persons in special relations are in some ways loved differently (e.g., erotically) from others, but fundamentally there is no difference in the way all persons are to be loved.

How, then, are distinctions or differences to be regarded? In one sense, Kierkegaard claims, Christianity disregards all distinctions, requiring us to look away from them or to lift ourselves above them in order to see the essential humanity of the other. Although every person is by virtue of his or her differences a particular individual, essentially each person is something other than that, namely, a human being. However, because of the differences, which form a disguise, this essential humanity is not seen. The task, therefore, is to allow the differences to "hang loosely" so as to perceive "in every individual that essential other person, that which is common to all men, the eternal likeness, the equality" (WL, 96). In another sense, however, Christianity "makes infinite distinctions in loving the differences," Kierkegaard claims (WL, 252). All persons should be loved according to their own individuality, as the particular persons they are rather than as we might wish them to be. Moreover, the only real benefaction we can give to others, Kierkegaard maintains, is to help them stand on their own as independent persons before God (WL, 258–59).

From this brief examination of Kierkegaard's concept of the other, we can see that for him true otherness is not determined by the *difference* between man and woman, self and others, as in postmodern French feminism, but rather is based on a fundamental *commonality* between them, namely, the fact that they are first and foremost human beings. To recognize the other as an other who is truly other than ourselves is to recognize and respect that person first of all as a human being like ourselves. Only then, in Kierkegaard's view, do we relate to others in a truly unselfish, self-giving manner without losing or projecting our own identities into them. Whether it is possible to love others unselfishly on the basis of difference rather than commonality is, it seems to me, an open question posed by postmodern French feminism in opposition to Kierkegaard. He may underestimate the capacity of the self in erotic love and friendship to love the other unselfishly, as an independent other, without expectation of reciprocity or a return to oneself. But given the postmodern French feminists' sense of being the other who is, to use Simone de Beauvoir's characterization, a "hostile stranger" to man and to the phallocentric symbolic order, there seems to be little basis in their thought for achieving a loving relation between woman and man based on difference.

From this examination it can also be seen that Kierkegaard's thought includes a strong affirmation of individuality and gender differences, but within a common structure of selfhood and a fundamental recognition of our universal humanity in love for others as neighbors. His thought thus provides a conceptual framework for transcending narcissism, alienation, and differences between man and woman, self and others, in a relationship of genuine love and reconciliation that recognizes the fundamental humanity and equality of all persons without denying either their individuality or their differences. His position may thus be characterized as a dialectic of commonality and difference and of individuality and relatedness in contrast to the nondialectical view of postmodern French feminism, which advocates a diffusion of the self in others, thereby confusing the self with others and volatilizing self-identity in difference and multiplicity. In their desire to find ways to give voice to woman's difference, the postmodern French feminists have been led to deny that which, from Kierkegaard's point of view, women need most of all to develop, namely, a strong sense of individuality and separate identity coupled with the love, care, devotedness, and giving to others that traditionally have been associated with their nature.[43] Although Kierkegaard's

43. Kierkegaard's thought thus may be seen to stand closer to the existentialist feminism of Simone de Beauvoir than to the postmodern French feminists, although Beauvoir, of course, denied the notion of a female essence, which Kierkegaard assumes. Beauvoir's description of the "woman in love" in *The Second Sex* provides a good illustration of precisely the loss of woman's self-identity in others that Kierkegaard identifies as feminine despair in *The Sickness unto Death.* It may be, however, that Kierkegaard does not sufficiently recognize or appreciate the degree to which self-identity and relatedness to others are interconnected in personal development, inasmuch as for him they seem to be separate categories. Claiming that "we know ourselves as separate only insofar as we live in connection with others," psychologist Carol Gilligan finds in women's development a fusion of separation and attachment, identity and intimacy (*In a Different Voice,* 63; see also 156, 159, 164). If that is true, she provides an

view of the self is dialectical in structure, this dialectical structure is one that seeks to affirm and synthesize rather than to exclude one term in relation to the other. Moreover, it is general enough to allow for specific gender, cultural, and racial differences to be taken into account in the process of becoming a self, so that each individual may find his or her own way to self-identity or selfhood within the context of a cultural environment politically and socially transformed so as to be conducive to the development of a wholeness of being in both women and men.[44]

Since the task of living poetically is intimately bound up with striving toward becoming a whole and integrated self in the context of social relations with others, it makes a great deal of difference how we understand ourselves as women and men and as human beings, or selves, if we are to be engaged in the practice of living poetically in an authentic manner. The existential aesthetics developed in Kierkegaard's writings has demonstrated that the poetic is an important aspect of human existence that needs to be incorporated and used in the process of striving, but in a wholesome and upbuilding way. Not just any relation to the poetic is conducive to the realization of the self or to an affirmation of others; only one that promotes the unity and independence of the self as well as the other and that respects our commonalities as well as differences as human beings in terms of sex, race, and other distinguishing features is conducive to such a realization. Thus we may say that, from a Kierkegaardian point of view, it is through an affirmation of the self as well as the other, of commonalities as well as differences, that an authentic mode of living poetically may be given expression in the present age.

---

important corrective to Kierkegaard in pointing to an interdependence of self-identity and relatedness in women. Although such an interdependence may be typical of women, it can be extended to males as well, for in them too identity and relatedness are undoubtedly interconnected, even if perhaps in a somewhat different way.

44. Although Kierkegaard did not work out an explicit political or social philosophy in support of the social implications of his thought, preferring instead to focus on the inward qualifications of an authentic human existence, there is ample evidence that a social critique, both direct and indirect, is contained in his writings. For studies focusing on the social dimensions of his thought, see Kirmmse, *Kierkegaard in Golden Age Denmark;* Elrod, *Kierkegaard and Christendom;* Robert L. Perkins, "Kierkegaard's Critique of the Bourgeois State," *Inquiry* 27 (1984): 207–18; and Merold Westphal, *Kierkegaard's Critique of Reason and Society* (Macon, Ga.: Mercer University Press, 1987).

Works Consulted

Adorno, Theodor W. *Kierkegaard: Construction of the Aesthetic.* Translated and edited by Robert Hullot-Kentor. Minneapolis: University of Minnesota Press, 1989.

Agacinski, Sylviane. *Aparté: Conceptions and Deaths of Søren Kierkegaard.* Translated by Kevin Newmark. Tallahassee: Florida State University Press, 1988.

Albeck, Gustav; Oluf Friis; and Peter P. Rohde. *Dansk Litteratur Historie.* Vol. 2, *Fra Oehlenschläger til Kierkegaard.* Copenhagen: Politikens Forlag, 1971.

Alcoff, Linda. "Cultural Feminism Versus Post-Structuralism: The Identity Crisis in Feminist Theory." *Signs: Journal of Women in Culture and Society* 13, no. 3 (1988): 405–36.

Allemann, Beda. *Ironie und Dichtung.* 2 vols. Neske: Pfullingen, 1969.

Allen, Jeffner, and Iris Marion Young, eds. *The Thinking Muse: Feminism and Modern French Philosophy.* Bloomington: Indiana University Press, 1989.

Andersen, H. C. *Eventyr og Historier.* Copenhagen: Gyldendal, 1965.

Andersen, Vilhelm. *Tider og Typer af dansk Aands Historie: Goethe.* 2 vols. Copenhagen: Gyldendal, 1915–16.

Andreasen, Uffe. *Poul Møller og Romantismen.* Copenhagen: Gyldendal, 1973.

Aristotle. *The Complete Works of Aristotle.* 2 vols. Edited by Jonathan Barnes. Princeton: Princeton University Press, 1984.

Bardwick, Judith M. *In Transition: How Feminism, Sexual Liberation, and the Search for Self-Fulfillment Have Altered Our Lives.* New York: Holt, Rinehart & Winston, 1979.

Barfoed, Niels. *Don Juan: En Studie i dansk Litteratur.* Copenhagen: Gyldendal, 1978.

Barrett, Lee. "The Uses and Misuses of the Comic: Reflections on the Corsair Affair." In *International Kierkegaard Commentary: The Corsair Affair,* edited by Robert L. Perkins, 123–39.

Baumgarten, Alexander. *Reflections on Poetry.* Translated and edited by Karl Aschenbrenner and William B. Holther. Berkeley and Los Angeles: University of California Press, 1964.

Beardsley, Monroe C. *Aesthetics from Classical Greece to the Present: A Short History.* New York: Macmillan, 1966.

———. "Aesthetics, History of." In *The Encyclopedia of Philosophy,* edited by Paul Edwards, 1: 18–35. New York: Macmillan, 1967.

Beauvoir, Simone de. *The Second Sex.* New York: Random House Vintage Books, 1989.

Behler, Ernst. *Irony and the Discourse of Modernity.* Seattle: University of Washington Press, 1990.

———. "The Theory of Irony in German Romanticism." In *Romantic Irony,* edited by Frederick Garber, 43–81. Budapest: Akadémiai Kiaidó, 1988.

Bem, S. L. "The Measurement of Psychological Androgyny." *Journal of Consulting and Clinical Psychology* 42 (1974): 155–62.

Bennett, E. K. *A History of the German "Novelle."* 2d ed. Revised by H. M. Waidson. Cambridge: Cambridge University Press, 1961.

Berg, Maggie. "Luce Irigaray's 'Contradictions': Poststructuralism and Feminism." *Signs: Journal of Women in Culture and Society* 17, no. 1 (1991): 50–70.

Berman, Art. *From the New Criticism to Deconstruction: The Reception of Structuralism and Post-Structuralism.* Urbana: University of Illinois Press, 1988.

Bertung, Birgit. *Om Kierkegaard Kvinder og Kærlighed—en Studie i Søren Kierkegaards Kvindesyn.* Copenhagen: C. A. Reitzels Forlag, 1987.

———, ed. *Kierkegaard—Poet of Existence.* Copenhagen: C. A. Reitzel, 1989.

Best, Steven, and Douglas Kellner. "Modernity, Mass Society, and the Media." In *International Kierkegaard Commentary: The Corsair Affair,* edited by Robert L. Perkins, 23–61.

Bigelow, Pat. *Kierkegaard and the Problem of Writing.* Tallahassee: Florida State University Press, 1987.

Billeskov Jansen, F. J. *Danmarks Digtekunst: Romantik og Romantisme.* 2d ed. Copenhagen: Munksgaard, 1964.

———. *Studier i Søren Kierkegaards litteraere Kunst.* Copenhagen: Rosenkilde & Bagger, 1951.

Billeskov Jansen, F. J., and Gustav Albeck. *Dansk Litteratur Historie.* Vol. 2, *Fra Ludvig Holberg til Carsten Hauch.* Copenhagen: Politikens Forlag, 1976.

Billeskov Jansen, F. J., and P. M. Mitchell. *Anthology of Danish Literature.* Carbondale: Southern Illinois University Press, 1964.

Blackall, Eric A. *Goethe and the Novel.* Ithaca, N.Y.: Cornell University Press, 1976.

———. *The Novels of the German Romantics.* Ithaca, N.Y.: Cornell University Press, 1983.

Block, J. H. "Conceptions of Sex Roles: Some Cross-Cultural and Longitudinal Perspectives." *American Psychologist* 28 (1973): 512–26.

Borup, Morten. *Johan Ludvig Heiberg.* 3 vols. Copenhagen: Gyldendal, 1947–49.

Bosanquet, Bernard. *A History of Aesthetic.* London: Allen & Unwin, 1949.

Braidotti, Rosi. "Embodiment, Sexual Difference, and the Nomadic Subject." *Hypatia* 8, no. 1 (1993): 1–13.

———. *Patterns of Dissonance: A Study of Women in Contemporary Philosophy.* Translated by Elizabeth Guild. New York: Routledge, 1991.

Brandes, Georg. *Samlede Skrifter.* 2 vols. Copenhagen: Gyldendalske Boghandels Forlag, 1899.

Brandt, Frithiof. *Den unge Søren Kierkegaard.* Copenhagen: Levin & Munksgaard Forlag, 1929.

———. *Syv Kierkegaard-Studier.* Copenhagen: Munksgaard, 1962.

Brown, Frank Burch. *Religious Aesthetics: A Theological Study of Making and Meaning.* Princeton: Princeton University Press, 1989.

Brown, Marshall. *The Shape of German Romanticism.* Ithaca, N.Y.: Cornell University Press, 1979.

Bullock, Marcus Paul. *Romanticism and Marxism: The Philosophical Development of Literary Theory and Literary History in Walter Benjamin and Friedrich Schlegel.* New York: Peter Lang, 1987.

Burgess, Andrew J. "A Word-Experiment on the Category of the Comic." In *International Kierkegaard Commentary: The Corsair Affair,* edited by Robert L. Perkins, 85–121.

Butler, Judith P. *Subjects of Desire: Hegelian Reflections in Twentieth-Century France.* New York: Columbia University Press, 1987.

Cain, David. "Notes on a Coach Horn: 'Going Further,' 'Revocation,' and Repetition." In *International Kierkegaard Commentary: Fear and Trembling and Repetition,* edited by Robert L. Perkins, 335–58.

———. "Reckoning with Kierkegaard: Christian Faith and Dramatic Literature." Ph.D. diss., Princeton University, 1975.

Caputo, John D. *Radical Hermeneutics: Repetition, Deconstruction, and the Hermeneutic Project.* Bloomington: Indiana University Press, 1987.

Carignan, Maurice. "The Eternal as a Synthesizing Third Term in Kierkegaard's Work." In *Kierkegaard Resources and Results,* edited by Alastair McKinnon, 74–87.

Carpenter, Peter. "Comment on Carignan." In *Kierkegaard Resources and Results,* edited by Alastair McKinnon, 88–91.

Cavell, Stanley. "Kierkegaard's *On Authority and Revelation.*" In *Kierkegaard: A Collection of Critical Essays,* edited by Josiah Thompson, 373–93.

Cixous, Hélène. "Castration and Decapitation." Translated by Annette Kuhn. *Signs: Journal of Women in Culture and Society* 7, no. 1 (1981): 41–55.

———. "The Laugh of the Medusa." Translated by Keith Cohen and Paula Cohen. *Signs: Journal of Women in Culture and Society* 1, no. 4 (1976): 875–93. Reprinted in *New French Feminisms: An Anthology,* edited by Elaine Marks and Isabelle de Courtivron, 245–64.

Cixous, Hélène, and Catharine Clément. *The Newly Born Woman.* Translated by Betsy Wing. Minneapolis: University of Minnesota Press, 1986.

Clair, André. "Médiation et répétition: Le lieu de la dialectique kierkegaardienne." *Revue des sciences philosophiques et théologiques* 59 (1975): 38–78.

Colette, J. "Musique et sensualité: Kierkegaard et le Don Juan de Mozart." *La vie spirituelle* 76 (1972): 33–45.

Connell, George. *To Be One Thing: Personal Unity in Kierkegaard's Thought.* Macon, Ga.: Mercer University Press, 1985.

Connell, George B., and C. Stephen Evans, eds. *Foundations of Kierkegaard's Vision of Community.* Atlantic Highlands, N.J.: Humanities Press, 1992.

Crites, Stephen. "Pseudonymous Authorship as Art and as Act." In *Kierkegaard: A Collection of Critical Essays,* edited by Josiah Thompson, 183–229.

Culler, Jonathan. *On Deconstruction: Theory and Criticism After Structuralism.* Ithaca, N.Y.: Cornell University Press, 1982.

Daly, Mary. *Gyn/Ecology: The Metaethics of Radical Feminism.* Boston: Beacon Press, 1978.

de Man, Paul. *Blindness and Insight: Essays in the Rhetoric of Contemporary Criticism.* 2d ed., rev. Minneapolis: University of Minnesota Press, 1983.

Dewey, Bradley R. "The Erotic-Demonic in Kierkegaard's 'Diary of the Seducer.'" *Scandinavica* 10 (1971): 1–24.

———. *The New Obedience: Kierkegaard on Imitating Christ.* Washington, D.C.: Corpus Books, 1968.

———. "Seven Seducers: A Typology of Interpretations of the Aesthetic Stage in Kierkegaard's 'The Seducer's Diary.'" Forthcoming in *International Kierkegaard Commentary: Either/Or I,* edited by Robert L. Perkins.

Dierkes, Hans. "Friedrich Schlegels Lucinde, Schleiermacher und Kierkegaard." *Deutsche Viertelsjahrschrift für Literatur und Geistesgeschichte* 57 (1983): 431–49.

Dilthey, Wilhelm. *Selected Works.* Vol. 5, *Poetry and Experience,* edited by Rudolf A. Makkreel and Firthjof Rodi. Princeton: Princeton University Press, 1985.

Dunning, Stephen N. *Kierkegaard's Dialectic of Inwardness.* Princeton: Princeton University Press, 1985.

Eagleton, Terry. *The Ideology of the Aesthetic.* Oxford: Basil Blackwell, 1990.

Eichner, Hans. *Friedrich Schlegel.* New York: Twayne, 1970.

———, ed. *"Romantic" and Its Cognates: The European History of a Word.* Toronto: University of Toronto Press, 1972.

Elias, Julius A. *Plato's Defence of Poetry.* Albany: State University of New York Press, 1984.

Elrod, John. *Kierkegaard and Christendom.* Princeton: Princeton University Press, 1981.

Engebretsen, Rune. "Kierkegaard and Poet-Existence with Special Reference to Germany and Rilke." Ph.D. diss., Stanford University, 1980.

Evans, C. Stephen. "Does Kierkegaard Think Beliefs Can Be Directly Willed?" *International Journal for Philosophy of Religion* 26, no. 3 (1989): 173–84.

———. *Kierkegaard's "Fragments" and "Postscript": The Religious Philosophy of Johannes Climacus.* Atlantic Highlands, N.J.: Humanities Press, 1983.

———. "Kierkegaard's View of the Unconscious." In *Kierkegaard—Poet of Existence,* edited by Birgit Bertung, 31–48.

———. *Passionate Reason: Making Sense of Kierkegaard's "Philosophical Fragments."* Bloomington: Indiana University Press, 1992.

Fabro, Cornelio. "Faith and Reason in Kierkegaard's Dialectic." In *A Kierkegaard Critique,* edited by Howard A. Johnson and Niels Thulstrup, 156–206.

Fallico, Arturo. *Art and Existentialism.* Englewood Cliffs, N.J.: Prentice-Hall, 1962.

Fausto-Sterling, Anne. *Myths of Gender: Biological Theories About Women and Men.* New York: Basic, 1986.

Fendt, Gene. *Works of Love? Reflections on "Works of Love."* Potomac, Md.: Scripta Humanistica, n.d.

Fenger, Henning. *Kierkegaard, the Myths and Their Origins: Studies in the Kierkegaardian Papers and Letters.* Translated by George C. Schoolfield. New Haven: Yale University Press, 1980.

Fenger, Henning, and Frederick J. Marker. *The Heibergs.* New York: Twayne, 1971.

Ferreira, M. Jamie. "Kierkegaardian Faith: 'The Condition' and the Response." *International Journal for Philosophy of Religion* 28, no. 2 (1990): 63–79.

———. "Repetition, Concreteness, and Imagination." *International Journal for Philosophy of Religion* 25, no. 1 (1989): 3–34.

———. *Transforming Vision: Imagination and Will in Kierkegaardian Faith.* Oxford: Clarendon Press, 1991.

Flax, Jane. *Thinking Fragments: Psychoanalysis, Feminism, and Postmodernism in the Contemporary West.* Berkeley and Los Angeles: University of California Press, 1990.

Forisha, Barbara Lusk. *Sex Roles and Personal Awareness.* Morristown, N.J.: General Learning Press, 1978.

Friis, Oluf, and Uffe Andreasen. *Dansk Litteratur Historie.* Vol. 3, *Fra Poul Møller til Søren Kierkegaard.* Copenhagen: Politikens Forlag, 1976.

Fuss, Diana J. " 'Essentially Speaking': Luce Irigaray's Language of Essence." *Hypatia* 3, no. 3 (1989): 94–112.

Gallop, Jane. *Thinking Through the Body.* New York: Columbia University Press, 1988.

Garff, Joakim. "The Eyes of Argus: The Point of View and Points of View with Respect to Kierkegaard's 'Activity as an Author.' " *Kierkegaardiana* 15 (1991): 29–54.

Garside, Christine. "Can a Woman Be Good in the Same Way As a Man?" *Dialogue* 10 (1971): 534–44.

Gasché, Rodolphe. *The Tain of the Mirror: Derrida and the Philosophy of Reflection.* Cambridge: Harvard University Press, 1986.

Gilbert, Katharine Everett, and Helmut Kuhn. *A History of Esthetics.* New York: Macmillan, 1939.

Gilligan, Carol. *In a Different Voice: Psychological Theory and Women's Development.* Cambridge: Harvard University Press, 1982.

———. "Remapping the Moral Domain: New Images of Self in Relationship." In *Mapping the Moral Domain: A Contribution of Women's Thinking to Psychological Theory and Education,* edited by Carol Gilligan, Janie Victoria Ward, and Jill McLean Taylor, with Betty Bardige, 3–19. Cambridge: Harvard University Press, 1988.

Giroux, Henry A., ed. *Postmodernism, Feminism, and Cultural Politics: Redrawing Educational Boundaries.* Albany: State University of New York Press, 1991.

Glenn, John D., Jr. "Kierkegaard on the Unity of Comedy and Tragedy." *Tulane Studies in Philosophy* 19 (1970): 41–53.

Gouwens, David. *Kierkegaard's Dialectic of the Imagination.* New York: Peter Lang, 1989.

Green, Ronald M. "Deciphering *Fear and Trembling*'s Secret Message." *Religious Studies* 22 (1986): 95–111.

Grimsley, Ronald. *Søren Kierkegaard and French Literature.* Cardiff: University of Wales Press, 1966.

Grosz, Elizabeth. *Sexual Subversions: Three French Feminists.* Sydney: Allen & Unwin, 1989.

Grunnet, Sanne Elisa. *Ironi og Subjektivitet: En Studie over S. Kierkegaards Disputats "Om Begrebet Ironi."* Copenhagen: C. A. Reitzels Forlag, 1987.

Hall, Ronald L. "Language and Freedom: Kierkegaard's Analysis of the Demonic in *The Concept of Anxiety.*" In *International Kierkegaard Commentary: The Concept of Anxiety,* Robert L. Perkins, 153–66.

———. *Word and Spirit: A Kierkegaardian Critique of the Modern Age.* Bloomington: Indiana University Press, 1993.

Handwerk, Gary J. *Irony and Ethics in Narrative: From Schlegel to Lacan.* New Haven: Yale University Press, 1985.

Hannay, Alastair. *Kierkegaard.* London: Routledge & Kegan Paul, 1982.

Hansen, Knud. *Søren Kierkegaard: Ideens Digter.* Copenhagen: Gyldendalske Boghandel, 1954.

Hansen, Søren Gorm. *H. C. Andersen og Søren Kierkegaard i Dannelseskulturen.* Copenhagen: Medusa, 1976.

Harries, Karsten. "Hegel on the Future of Art." *Review of Metaphysics* 27, no. 4 (1974): 677–96.

Hartshorne, M. Holmes. *Kierkegaard, Godly Deceiver: The Nature and Meaning of His Pseudonymous Writings.* New York: Columbia University Press, 1990.

Hegel, G.W.F. *Aesthetics: Lectures on Fine Art.* 2 vols. Translated by T. M. Knox. Oxford: Clarendon, 1975.

———. *Hegel's Introduction to the Lectures on the History of Philosophy.* Translated by T. M. Knox and A. V. Miller. Oxford: Clarendon, 1985.

———. *Hegel's Science of Logic.* Translated by A. V. Miller. London: Allen & Unwin, 1969.

———. *Phenomenology of Spirit.* Translated by A. V. Miller. Oxford: Clarendon, 1977.

———. *Philosophy of Right.* Translated by T. M. Knox. Oxford: Clarendon, 1958.

Heiberg, J. L. *Johan Ludvig Heibergs Prosaiske Skrifter.* 11 vols. Copenhagen: C. A. Reitzels Forlag, 1861–62.

Heidegger, Martin. *Poetry, Language, Thought.* Translated by Albert Hofstadter. New York: Harper & Row, 1971.

Henrich, Dieter. *Hegel im Kontext.* Frankfurt: Suhrkamp, 1971.

Henriksen, Aage. *Kierkegaards Romaner.* Copenhagen: Gyldendal, 1954.

Himmelstrup, J. *Sibbern.* Copenhagen: J. H. Schultz Forlag, 1934.

———. *Søren Kierkegaards Opfattelse af Sokrates.* Copenhagen: Arnold Busck, 1924.

Hofe, Gerhard vom. *Die Romantikkritik Sören Kierkegaards.* Frankfurt: Athenäum Verlag, 1972.

Hölderlin, Friedrich. *Hymns and Fragments.* Translated by Richard Sieburth. Princeton: Princeton University Press, 1984.

Holler, Clyde C., III. "Kierkegaard's Concept of Tragedy in the Context of His Pseudonymous Works." Ph.D. diss., Boston University, 1981.

Holm, Kjeld; Malthe Jacobsen; and Bjarne Troelsen. *Søren Kierkegaard og romantikerne.* Copenhagen: Berlingske Forlag, 1974.

Holmlund, Christine. "The Lesbian, the Mother, the Heterosexual Lover: Irigaray's Recodings of Difference." *Feminist Studies* 17, no. 2 (1991): 283–308.

Hong, Howard V. "The Comic, Satire, Irony, and Humor: Kierkegaardian Reflections." *Midwest Studies in Philosophy* 1 (1976): 98–105.

———. "*Tanke-Experiment* in Kierkegaard." In *Kierkegaard Resources and Results,* edited by Alastair McKinnon, 39–51.

Horn, Robert L. "Positivity and Dialectic: A Study of the Theological Method of Hans Lassen Martensen." Th.D. diss., Union Theological Seminary, 1969.

Inglis, Laura Lyn. "The Dialogue of Action: Søren Kierkegaard's Dialectical Conception of Ethics." Ph.D. diss., Princeton Theological Seminary, 1981.

Irigaray, Luce. "And the One Doesn't Stir Without the Other." Translated by Hélène Vivienne Wenzel. *Signs: Journal of Women in Culture and Society* 7, no. 1 (1981): 56–67.

———. *Marine Lover of Friedrich Nietzsche.* Translated by Gillian C. Gill. New York: Columbia University Press, 1991.

———. *Speculum of the Other Woman.* Translated by Gillian C. Gill. Ithaca, N.Y.: Cornell University Press, 1985.

———. *This Sex Which Is Not One.* Translated by Catherine Porter with Carolyn Burke. Ithaca, N.Y.: Cornell University Press, 1985.

Jardine, Alice A. *Gynesis: Configurations of Woman and Modernity.* Ithaca, N.Y.: Cornell University Press, 1985.

Johansen, Karsten Friis. "Kierkegaard on 'the Tragic.'" *Danish Yearbook of Philosophy* 13 (1976): 105–46.

Johnson, Howard A., and Thulstrup, Niels, eds. *A Kierkegaard Critique.* New York: Harper & Brothers, 1962.

Jones, Ann Rosalind. "Writing the Body: Toward an Understanding of *l'Écriture féminine.*" In *The New Feminist Criticism,* edited by Elaine Showalter, 361–77. New York: Pantheon Books, 1985.

Jones, W. Glyn. "Søren Kierkegaard and Poul Martin Møller." *Modern Language Review* 60 (1965): 73–82.

Jørgensen, Merete. *Kierkegaard som Kritiker.* Copenhagen: Gyldendal, 1978.

Kainz, Howard P. "The Relationship of Dread to Spirit in Man and Woman, According to Kierkegaard." *Modern Schoolman* 47 (1969): 1–13.

Kant, Immanuel. *Critique of Judgment.* Translated by J. H. Bernard. New York: Hafner, 1951.

———. *Critique of Reason.* Translated by Norman Kemp Smith. London: Macmillan, 1956.

Kearney, Richard. *The Wake of Imagination.* Minneapolis: University of Minnesota Press, 1988.

Keeley, Louise Carroll. "The Parables of Problem III in Kierkegaard's *Fear and Trembling.*" In *International Kierkegaard Commentary: Fear and Trembling and Repetition,* edited by Robert L. Perkins, 127–54.

Kern, Edith. *Existential Thought and Fictional Technique: Kierkegaard, Sartre, Beckett.* New Haven: Yale University Press, 1970.

Kierkegaard, Søren. *The Concept of Irony with Constant Reference to Socrates.* Translated by Lee Capel. London: Collins, 1966.

———. *Concluding Unscientific Postscript.* Translated by David F. Swenson and Walter Lowrie. Princeton: Princeton University Press, 1941.

———. *Either/Or.* 2 vols. Vol. 1 translated by David F. Swenson and Lillian Marvin Swenson, with revisions and a foreword by Howard A. Johnson. Princeton: Princeton University Press, 1959. Vol. 2 translated by Walter Lowrie, with revisions and a foreword by Howard A. Johnson. Princeton: Princeton University Press, 1972.

———. *For Self-Examination and Judge for Yourselves! and Three Discourses 1851.* Translated by Walter Lowrie. Princeton: Princeton University Press, 1968.

———. *Kierkegaard: Letters and Documents.* Translated by Henrik Rosenmeier, with introduction and notes. Princeton: Princeton University Press, 1978.

———. *Philosophical Fragments.* 2d ed. Translated by David Swenson and revised by Howard V. Hong, with a new introduction and commentary by Niels Thulstrup. Princeton: Princeton University Press, 1962.

———. *The Sickness unto Death.* Translated by Walter Lowrie. Princeton: Princeton University Press, 1968.

———. *Søren Kierkegaards Samlede Værker.* 3d ed. 20 vols. Edited by A. B. Drachmann, J. L. Heiberg, and H. O. Lange. Copenhagen: Gyldendal, 1962–64.

———. *Stages on Life's Way.* Translated by Walter Lowrie. New York: Schocken Books, 1967.

———. *Training in Christianity and the Edifying Discourse Which "Accompanied" It.* Translated by Walter Lowrie. Princeton: Princeton University Press, 1957.

Kirmmse, Bruce H. *Kierkegaard in Golden Age Denmark.* Bloomington: Indiana University Press, 1990.

Kostelanetz, Richard, ed. *Esthetics Contemporary.* New York: Prometheus, 1978.

Kristeva, Julia. *Powers of Horror: An Essay on Abjection.* New York: Columbia University Press, 1982.

———. *Tales of Love.* Translated by Leon S. Roudiez. New York: Columbia University Press, 1987.

———. "Woman Can Never Be Defined." Translated by Marilyn A. August. In *New French Feminisms: An Anthology,* edited by Elaine Marks and Isabelle de Courtivron, 137–41.

———. "Women's Time." Translated by Alice Jardine and Harry Blake. *Signs: Journal of Women in Culture and Society* 7, no. 1 (1981): 13–35.

Kundera, Milan. *The Unbearable Lightness of Being.* Translated by Michael Henry Heim. New York: Harper & Row, 1984.

Kupfer, Joseph H. *Experience as Art: Aesthetics in Everyday Life.* Albany: State University of New York Press, 1983.

Lacoue-Labarthe, Philippe, and Jean-Luc Nancy. *The Literary Absolute: The Theory of Literature in German Romanticism.* Translated by Philip Barnard and Cheryl Lester. Albany: State University of New York Press, 1988.

Langston, Douglas. "The Comical Kierkegaard." *Journal of Religious Studies* 12, no. 1 (1985): 35–45.

Lebowitz, Naomi. *Kierkegaard: A Life of Allegory.* Baton Rouge: Louisiana State University Press, 1985.

le Huray, Peter, and James Day, eds. *Music and Aesthetics in the Eighteenth and Early Nineteenth Centuries.* Cambridge: Cambridge University Press, 1988.

Lowrie, Walter. *Kierkegaard.* 2 vols. New York: Harper & Brothers, 1962.

Lowther, Leo M. "Don Juan and Comparative Literary Criticism: Four Approaches." Ph.D. diss., University of Utah, 1971.

Lyotard, Jean-François. *The Postmodern Condition: A Report on Knowledge.* Translated by Geoff Bennington and Brian Massumi. Minneapolis: University of Minnesota Press, 1984.

Maccoby, Eleanor Emmons, and Carol Nagy Jacklin. *The Psychology of Sex Differences.* Stanford: Stanford University Press, 1974.

Mackey, Louis. *Kierkegaard: A Kind of Poet.* Philadelphia: University of Pennsylvania Press, 1971.

———. "The Poetry of Inwardness." In *Kierkegaard: A Collection of Critical Essays,* edited by Josiah Thompson, 1–102.

———. *Points of View: Readings of Kierkegaard.* Tallahassee: Florida State University Press, 1986.

Magel, Charles. "An Analysis of Kierkegaard's Philosophic Categories." Ph.D. diss., University of Minnesota, 1960.

Malantschuk, Gregor. *The Controversial Kierkegaard.* Translated by Howard V. Hong and Edna H. Hong. Waterloo: Wilfrid Laurier University Press, 1980.

———. "Digter eller Praest." *Kierkegaardiana* 6 (1966): 75–96.

———. *Fribedens Problem i Kierkegaards Begrebet Angest.* Copenhagen: Rosenkilde & Bagger, 1971.

———. *Kierkegaard's Thought.* Edited and translated by Howard V. Hong and Edna H. Hong. Princeton: Princeton University Press, 1971.

Marker, F. J. *Hans Christian Andersen and the Romantic Theatre.* Toronto: University of Toronto Press, 1971.

Marks, Elaine, and Isabelle de Courtivron, eds. *New French Feminisms: An Anthology.* Amherst: University of Massachusetts Press, 1980.

McCarthy, Vincent. *The Phenomenology of Moods in Kierkegaard.* The Hague: Martinus Nijhoff, 1978.

McGowan, John. *Postmodernism and Its Critics.* Ithaca, N.Y.: Cornell University Press, 1991.

McKinnon, Alastair, ed. *Kierkegaard Resources and Results.* Montreal: Wilfred Laurier University Press, 1982.

Megill, Alan. *Prophets of Extremity: Nietzsche, Heidegger, Foucault, Derrida.* Berkeley and Los Angeles: University of California Press, 1985.

Merchant, Paul. *The Epic.* London: Methuen, 1971.

Mesnard, Pierre. "Is the Category of the 'Tragic' Absent from the Life and Thought of Kierkegaard?" In *A Kierkegaard Critique,* edited by Howard A. Johnson and Niels Thulstrup, 102–15.

Mitchell, P. M. *A History of Danish Literature.* Copenhagen: Gyldendal, 1957.

Moi, Toril, ed. *French Feminist Thought: A Reader.* Oxford: Basil Blackwell, 1987.

———. *The Kristeva Reader.* Oxford: Basil Blackwell, 1986.

Møller, Per Stig. *Erotismen: Den romantiske bevaegelse i Vesteuropa, 1790–1860.* Copenhagen: Munksgaard, 1973.

Møller Kristensen, Sven. *Den dobbelte Eros: Studier i den danske Romantik.* Copenhagen: Gyldendal, 1966.

———. *Digteren og Samfundet i Danmark i det 19. Aarhundrede.* Copenhagen: Athenaeum, 1942.

Mooney, Edward F. *Knights of Faith and Resignation: Reading Kierkegaard's "Fear and Trembling."* Albany: State University of New York Press, 1991.

Mullen, John D. "The German Romantic Background of Kierkegaard's Psychology." *Southern Journal of Philosophy* 16 (1978): 649–60.

Müller, Paul, "The God's Poem—the God's History." In *Kierkegaard—Poet of Existence,* edited by Birgit Bertung, 83–88.

Nehamas, Alexander. *Nietzsche: Life as Literature.* Cambridge: Harvard University Press, 1985.

Nicholson, Linda J., ed. *Feminism/Postmodernism.* New York: Routledge, 1990.

Nielsen, H. A. *Where the Passion Is: A Reading of Kierkegaard's "Philosophical Fragments."* Tallahassee: University Presses of Florida, 1983.

Nietzsche, Friedrich. *Thus Spake Zarathustra.* Translated by Walter Kaufmann. New York: Viking, 1966.

Nisbet, H. B., ed. *German Aesthetic and Literary Criticism: Winckelmann, Lessing, Hamann, Schiller, Goethe.* Cambridge: Cambridge University Press, 1985.

Nordentoft, Kresten. *Kierkegaard's Psychology.* Translated by Bruce H. Kirmmse. Pittsburgh, Pa.: Duquesne University Press, 1978.

Norris, Christopher. *The Deconstructive Turn: Essays in the Rhetoric of Philosophy.* London: Methuen, 1983.

———. *Derrida.* Cambridge: Harvard University Press, 1987.

———. *Paul de Man: Deconstruction and the Critique of Aesthetic Ideology.* New York: Routledge, 1988.

Ortner, Sherrie, and Harriet Whitehead, eds. *Sexual Meanings: The Cultural Construction of Gender and Sexuality.* New York: Cambridge University Press, 1981.

Otani, Masaru. "The Comical." In *Bibliotheca Kierkegaardiana,* vol. 3, *Concepts and Alternatives in Kierkegaard,* edited by Niels Thulstrup and Marie Mikulová Thulstrup, 229–35.

Parrill, Lloyd Ellison. "The Concept of Humor in the Pseudonymous Works of Søren Kierkegaard." Ph.D. diss., Drew University, 1975.

Pattison, George. *Art, Modernity, and Faith: Towards a Theology of Art.* New York: St. Martin's Press, 1991.

———. *Kierkegaard: The Aesthetic and the Religious.* London: Macmillan, 1992.

———. "Kierkegaard's Theory and Critique of Art: Its Theological Significance." Ph.D. diss., University of Durham, Great Britain, 1983.

———. "Nihilism and the Novel: Kierkegaard's Literary Reviews." *British Journal of Aesthetics* 26, no. 2 (1986): 161–71.

———, ed. *Kierkegaard on Art and Communication.* New York: St. Martin's Press, 1992.

Perkins, Robert L. "Abraham's Silence Aesthetically Considered." In *Kierkegaard on Art and Communication,* edited by George Pattison, 100–13.

———. "Beginning the System: Kierkegaard and Hegel." In *Akten des XIV. Internationalen Kongresses für Philosophie,* 478–85. Vienna: Herder, 1968.

———. "The Categories of Humor and Philosophy." *Midwest Studies in Philosophy* 1 (1976): 105–8.

———. "Comment on Hong." In *Kierkegaard Resources and Results,* edited by Alastair McKinnon, 52–55.

———. "Hegel and Kierkegaard: Two Critics of Romantic Irony." *Review of National Literatures* 1 (1970): 232–54.

———. "Kierkegaard: A Kind of Epistemologist." *History of European Ideas* 12, no. 1 (1990): 7–18.

———. "Kierkegaard's Critique of the Bourgeois State." *Inquiry* 27 (1984): 207–18.

———. "Kierkegaard's First Brush with the Press." Paper presented to the Søren Kierkegaard Society at the American Philosophical Association, December 1992.

———. Review of *Kierkegaard: Construction of the Aesthetic,* by Theodor Adorno. *Journal of Aesthetics and Art Criticism* 43 (1990): 262–63.

———, ed. *International Kierkegaard Commentary: The Concept of Anxiety.* Macon, Ga.: Mercer University Press, 1985.

———. *International Kierkegaard Commentary: The Corsair Affair.* Macon, Ga.: Mercer University Press, 1990.

———. *International Kierkegaard Commentary: Either/Or I.* Macon, Ga.: Mercer University Press. Expected 1995.

———. *International Kierkegaard Commentary: Fear and Trembling and Repetition.* Macon, Ga.: Mercer University Press, 1993.

———. *International Kierkegaard Commentary: Philosophical Fragments.* Macon, Ga.: Mercer University Press, 1994.

———. *International Kierkegaard Commentary: The Sickness unto Death.* Macon, Ga.: Mercer University Press, 1987.

———. *International Kierkegaard Commentary: Two Ages: The Present Age and the Age of Revolution: A Literary Review.* Macon, Ga.: Mercer University Press, 1984.

———. *Kierkegaard's "Fear and Trembling": Critical Appraisals.* University: University of Alabama Press, 1981.

Petersen, Carl, and Vilhelm Andersen. *Illustreret dansk Litteraturhistorie.* Vol. 3, *Den danske Litteratur i den Aarhundredes første Halvdel.* Copenhagen: Gyldendal, 1924.

———. *Illustreret dansk Litteraturhistorie.* Vol. 4, *Den danske Litteratur i den nittende Aarhundredes anden Halvdel.* Copenhagen: Gyldendal, 1925.

Petersen, Teddy. *Kierkegaards polemiske debut: Artikler 1834–36 i historisk Sammenhæng.* Odense: Odense Universitetsforlag, 1977.

Plato. *Symposium.* Translated, with introduction and notes, by Alexander Nehamas and Paul Woodruff. Indianapolis: Hackett, 1989.

Plekon, Michael. "Towards Apocalypse: Kierkegaard's *Two Ages* in Golden Age Denmark." In *International Kierkegaard Commentary: Two Ages,* edited by Robert L. Perkins, 19–52.

Pojman, Louis. "Kierkegaard on Faith and Freedom." *International Journal for Philosophy of Religion* 27, nos. 1–2 (1990): 41–61.

———. *The Logic of Subjectivity.* University: University of Alabama Press, 1984.

Polheim, Karl Konrad. *Die Arabeske: Ansichten und Ideen ans Friedrich Schlegels Poetik.* Munich: Schöningh, 1966.

Prawer, Siegbert, ed. *The Romantic Period in Germany.* New York: Schocken Books, 1970.

Roberts, Robert C. *Rethinking Kierkegaard's "Philosophical Fragments."* Macon, Ga.: Mercer University Press, 1986.

Rohde, H. P. *Gaadefulde Stadier paa Kierkegaards Vej.* Copenhagen: Rosenkilde & Bagger, 1974.

Roos, Carl. *Kierkegaard og Goethe.* Copenhagen: G.E.C. Gads Forlag, 1955.

Rorty, Richard. *Contingency, Irony, and Solidarity.* Cambridge: Cambridge University Press, 1989.

Rubow, Paul. *Dansk litteraer Kritik i det 19. Ärhundrede indtil 1870.* Copenhagen: Munksgaard, 1970.

———. *Heiberg og hans Skole i Kritiken.* Copenhagen: Gyldendal, 1953.

Sandok, Theresa H. "Kierkegaard on Irony and Humor." Ph.D. diss., University of Notre Dame, 1975.

Sawicki, Jane, and Iris Young. "Issues of Difference in Feminist Philosophy." *Feminism and Philosophy Newsletter* (April 1988): 13–17.

Schelling, Friedrich Wilhelm Joseph von. *Werke.* 6 vols. Edited by Manfred Schröter. Munich: Beck, 1956–60.

Schiller, Friedrich. *On the Aesthetic Education of Man in a Series of Letters.* Edited and translated by Elizabeth M. Wilkinson and L. A. Willoughby. Oxford: Clarendon, 1967.

Schjorring, J. H. "Martensen." In *Bibliotheca Kierkegaardiana,* vol. 10, *Kierkegaard's Teachers,* edited by Niels Thulstrup and Marie Mikulová Thulstrup, 177–207.

Schlegel, Friedrich. *Dialogue on Poetry and Literary Aphorisms.* Translated by Ernst Behler and Roman Struc. University Park: Pennsylvania State University Press, 1968.

———. *Friedrich Schlegel's Lucinde and the Fragments.* Translated by Peter Firchow. Minneapolis: University of Minnesota Press, 1971.

———. *Über das Studium der Griechischen Poesie, 1795–97.* Edited by Ernst Behler. Paderborn: Schöningh, 1982.

Schleifer, Ronald, and Robert Markley, eds. *Kierkegaard and Literature: Irony, Repetition, and Criticism.* Norman: University of Oklahoma Press, 1984.

Schousboe, Julius. *Om Begrebet Humor hos Søren Kierkegaard.* Copenhagen: Arnold Busck, 1925.

Schultz, Jørgen. "Om 'Poesi' og 'Virkelighed' hos Kierkegaard." *Kierkegaardiana* 6 (1966): 7–29.

Sechi, Vanina. "Art, Language, Creativity, and Kierkegaard." *Humanitas* 5 (1969–70): 81–97.

———. "The Poet." *Kierkegaardiana* 10 (1977): 166–81.

Sibbern, F. C. *Om Poesie og Konst.* 3 vols. Copenhagen: Forfatterens Forlag, vol. 1, 1855 (originally 1834); vol. 2, 1853; vol. 3, 1869.

Silz, Walter. *Realism and Reality: Studies in the German Novelle of Poetic Realism.* Chapel Hill: University of North Carolina Press, 1954.

Singer, Armand E. *A Bibliography of the Don Juan Theme.* Morgantown: West Virginia University Bulletin, 1954.

Singer, June. *Androgyny: Toward a New Theory of Sexuality.* Garden City, N.Y.: Anchor Books, Doubleday, 1977.

Sjursen, Harold P. "The Comic Apprehension." *Midwest Studies in Philosophy* 1 (1976): 108–13.

Smith, Ronald Gregor. *J. G. Hamann: A Study in Christian Existence with Selections from His Writings.* London: Collins, 1960.

Smyth, John Vignaux. *A Question of Eros: Irony in Sterne, Kierkegaard, and Barthes.* Tallahassee: Florida State University Press, 1986.

Sørensen, Villy. *Digtere og dæmoner: Fortolkninger og vurderinger.* Copenhagen: Gyldendal, 1973.

Spence, Janet T., and Robert L. Helmreich. *Masculinity and Femininity: Their Psychological Dimensions, Correlates, and Antecedents.* Austin: University of Texas Press, 1978.

Strawser, Michael. Review of *Kierkegaard, Godly Deceiver: The Nature and Meaning of His Pseudonymous Writings,* by M. Holmes Hartshorne. *Søren Kierkegaard Newsletter* 26 (November 1992): 10–14.

Summers, Richard. "A Study of Kierkegaard's Philosophical Development up to *Om Begrebet Ironi.*" Ph.D. diss., University of London, 1980.

Svendsen, Hans Jørgen. "Dæmon og menneske: Don Juan og Æstetiker A. i Søren Kierkegaards Enten-Eller." In *Indfaldsvinkler: 16 Fortolkninger af nordisk Digtning tilegnet Oluf Friis,* 40–57. Copenhagen: Gyldendal, 1964.

Swales, Martin. *The German Bildungsroman from Wieland to Hesse.* Princeton: Princeton University Press, 1978.

———. *The German "Novelle."* Princeton: Princeton University Press, 1977.

Tatarkiewicz, Wladyslaw. *History of Aesthetics.* 2 vols. The Hague: Mouton, 1970.

Taylor, Mark C. *Altarity.* Chicago: University of Chicago Press, 1987.

———. *Disfiguring: Art, Architecture, Religion.* Chicago: University of Chicago Press, 1992.

———. *Erring: A Postmodern A/theology.* Chicago: University of Chicago Press, 1984.

———. "Humor and Humorist." In *Bibliotheca Kierkegaardiana,* vol. 3, *Concepts and Alternatives in Kierkegaard,* edited by Niels Thulstrup and Marie Mikulová Thulstrup, 220–28.

———. *Journeys to Selfhood: Hegel and Kierkegaard.* Berkeley and Los Angeles: University of California Press, 1980.

———. *Kierkegaard's Pseudonymous Authorship.* Princeton: Princeton University Press, 1975.

Taylor, Mark Lloyd. "Ordeal and Repetition in Kierkegaard's Treatment of Abraham and Job." In *Foundations of Kierkegaard's Vision of Community,* edited by George B. Connell and C. Stephen Evans, 33–53.

Thompson, Josiah. *The Lonely Labyrinth: Kierkegaard's Pseudonymous Works.* Carbondale: Southern Illinois University Press, 1967.

———, ed. *Kierkegaard: A Collection of Critical Essays.* Garden City, N.Y.: Anchor Books, Doubleday, 1972.

Thulstrup, Marie Mikulová. "Efterfølgelsens dialektik hos Søren Kierkegaard." *Dansk teologisk Tidskrift* 21 (1958): 193–209.

Thulstrup, Niels. *Kierkegaard's Relation to Hegel.* Translated by George L. Stengren. Princeton: Princeton University Press, 1980.

Thulstrup, Niels, and Marie Mikulová Thulstrup, eds. *Bibliotheca Kierkegaardiana.*

Vol. 3, *Concepts and Alternatives in Kierkegaard.* Copenhagen: C. A. Reitzels Boghandel, 1980.
———. *Bibliotheca Kierkegaardiana.* Vol. 10, *Kierkegaard's Teachers.* Copenhagen: C. A. Reitzels Forlag, 1982.
Toftdahl, Hellmut. "Kierkegaard og digtningen." *Exil* 4 (1970): 25–44.
Tong, Rosemarie. *Feminist Thought: A Comprehensive Introduction.* Boulder: Westview Press, 1989.
Utterback, Sylvia Walsh. "Don Juan and the Representation of Spiritual Sensuousness." *Journal of the American Academy of Religion* 47, no. 4 (1979): 627–44.
———. "Kierkegaard's Dialectic of Christian Existence." Ph.D. diss., Emory University, 1975.
———. "Kierkegaard's Inverse Dialectic." *Kierkegaardiana* 11 (1980): 34–54.
Vedel, Valdemar. *Studier over Guldalderen i dansk Digtning.* 2d ed. Copenhagen: Gyldendal, 1967 (reprint of 1948 edition).
Vergote, Henri-Bernard. *Sens et répétition: Essai sur l'ironie kierkegaardienne.* Orante: Éditions du Cerf, 1982.
Viallaneix, Nelly. *Écoute, Kierkegaard: Essai sur la communication de la parole.* 2 vols. Paris: Éditions du Cerf, 1979.
———. "Kierkegaard romantique." *Romantisme* 8 (1974): 64–85.
Vogelweith, G. "Le poète et le religieux selon Kierkegaard." *Revue d'histoire et de philosophie religieuses* 61 (1981): 37–42.
Wahl, Jean. "Kierkegaard et le romantisme." *Orbis Litterarum* 10 (1955): 297–302.
Walsh, Sylvia. "Echoes of Absurdity: The Offended Consciousness and the Absolute Paradox in Kierkegaard's *Philosophical Fragments.*" In *International Kierkegaard Commentary: Philosophical Fragments,* edited by Robert L. Perkins.
———. "Forming the Heart: The Role of Love in Kierkegaard's Thought." In *The Grammar of the Heart,* edited by Richard Bell, 234–56. New York: Harper & Row, 1988.
———. "Kierkegaard: Poet of the Religious." In *Kierkegaard on Art and Communication,* edited by George Pattison, 1–22.
———. "Kierkegaard and Postmodernism." *International Journal for Philosophy of Religion* 29, no. 2 (1991): 113–22.
———. "Living Poetically: Kierkegaard and German Romanticism," *History of European Ideas* 20, nos. 1–3, in press.
———. "On 'Feminine' and 'Masculine' Despair." In *International Kierkegaard Commentary: The Sickness unto Death,* edited by Robert L. Perkins, 121–34.
———. "The Philosophical Affirmation of Gender Difference: Kierkegaard Versus Postmodern Neo-Feminism." *Journal of Psychology and Christianity* 7, no. 4 (1988): 18–26.
———. Review of *Kierkegaard: A Life of Allegory,* by Naomi Lebowitz. *International Journal for Philosophy of Religion* 26, no. 1 (1989): 57–58.
———. Review of *Om Kierkegaard Kvinder og Kærlighed—en Studie i Søren Kierkegaards Kvindesyn,* by Birgit Bertung. *Kierkegaardiana* 15 (1991): 153–57.
———. Review of *Transforming Vision: Imagination and Will in Kierkegaardian Faith,* by M. Jamie Ferreira. *Søren Kierkegaard Newsletter* 25 (1992): 5–8.
———. Review of *Works of Love? Reflections on "Works of Love,"* by Gene Fendt. *Søren Kierkegaard Newsletter* 22 (1990): 9–10.
———. "The Subjective Thinker as Artist." *History of European Ideas* 12, no. 1 (1990): 19–29.
———. "Women in Love." *Soundings* 65 (1982): 352–68.

Wellek, René. *A History of Modern Criticism: 1750–1950: The Romantic Age.* New Haven: Yale University Press, 1955.

Wernaer, Robert M. *Romanticism and the Romantic School in Germany.* New York: Haskell House, 1966.

Westphal, Merold. *Kierkegaard's Critique of Reason and Society.* Macon, Ga.: Mercer University Press, 1987.

Wheeler, Kathleen, ed. *German Aesthetic and Literary Criticism: The Romantic Ironists and Goethe.* Cambridge: Cambridge University Press, 1984.

Whitford, Margaret. *Luce Irigaray: Philosophy in the Feminine.* London: Routledge, 1991.

Widenmann, Robert. "Sibbern." In *Bibliotheca Kierkegaardiana,* vol. 10, *Kierkegaard's Teachers,* edited by Niels Thulstrup and Marie Mikulová Thulstrup, 70–88.

Wilde, Alan. *Horizons of Assent: Modernism, Postmodernism, and the Ironic Imagination.* Philadelphia: University of Pennsylvania Press, 1987.

Williams, Bernard. "Don Giovanni as an Idea." In *W. A. Mozart: "Don Giovanni,"* edited by Julian Rushton, 81–91. Cambridge: Cambridge University Press, 1981.

Wisdo, David. "Kierkegaard on Belief, Faith, and Explanation." *International Journal for Philosophy of Religion* 21, no. 2 (1987): 95–114.

Wolterstorff, Nicholas. *Art in Action: Toward a Christian Aesthetic.* Grand Rapids, Mich.: Eerdmans, 1980.

Index